THE TEACH LIKE
A CHAMPION
GUIDE TO THE SCIENCE OF READING

THE TEACH LIKE A CHAMPION
GUIDE TO THE SCIENCE OF READING

Translating Research to Reignite Joy
and Meaning in the Classroom

DOUG LEMOV
COLLEEN DRIGGS
ERICA WOOLWAY

JB JOSSEY-BASS™
A Wiley Brand

Published by John Wiley & Sons, Inc., Hoboken, New Jersey.
Published simultaneously in Canada.

ISBNs: 9781394305995 (paperback), 9781394306008 (ePDF), 9781394306015 (ePub)

For general information on our other products and services, please contact our Customer Care Department within the United States at (800) 762-2974, outside the United States at (317) 572-3993. For product technical support, you can find answers to frequently asked questions or reach us via live chat at https://support.wiley.com/s/.

If you believe you've found a mistake in this book, please bring it to our attention by emailing our reader support team at wileysupport@wiley.com with the subject line "Possible Book Errata Submission."

Wiley also publishes its books in a variety of electronic formats. Some content that appears in print may not be available in electronic formats. For more information about Wiley products, visit our web site at www.wiley.com.

Library of Congress Control Number is Available.

Cover Design: Wiley
Cover Images: © weedezign/stock.adobe.com, © Kara/stock.adobe.com
Author Photos: © Maia Lemov, © Stephanie McCauley, © Rob Richard

SKY10112956_060925

Contents

About the Authors

Doug Lemov is the founder and chief knowledge officer of Teach Like a Champion. His books on teaching and learning are among the best known in the education sector. He has taught English and history at the university, high school, and middle school levels. He holds a BA from Hamilton College, an MA from Indiana University, and an MBA from the Harvard Business School.

Colleen Driggs is a managing director of curriculum and school support of Teach Like a Champion. Colleen leads the *Reading Reconsidered* curriculum team and their work in content development and training and implementation support in schools. Before joining the Teach Like a Champion team, she taught middle school science in New York City; middle school science and literacy in New Haven, Connecticut; and middle school literacy in Rochester, New York. In Rochester, she served as the chair of the reading department, coaching literacy teachers and developing curriculum and assessments, at Rochester Prep Middle School. Colleen received her BA in psychology and education from Hamilton College and a master of education degree from Pace University.

Erica Woolway is the president and chief academic officer (CAO) for the Teach Like a Champion team. In this role, she works with the team to train thousands of high-performing teachers and school leaders across the country each year—reaching over one million students. Prior to becoming CAO, she served as both dean of students and director of staff development at Uncommon Schools and as an adjunct literacy instructor at Relay Graduate School of Education. Erica began her career in education as a kindergarten teacher and then worked as a school counselor. She received her BA in psychology and Spanish from Duke University, an

MA and master of education degree from Teachers College in school counseling, and an MA in school leadership from National Lewis University. She is a coauthor of *Practice Perfect* with Doug Lemov and Katie Yezzi and *Teach Like Champion Field Guide 3.0* with Doug Lemov, Hannah Solomon, and Sadie McCleary. She currently lives in New York City with her husband and their three boys.

Acknowledgments

We get up every day happy to go to work in large part because we have such an amazing group of colleagues on the Teach Like a Champion team. Truly they are the best, and much of what we have written here—the good parts!—is based on insights gleaned from daily conversations about instruction and lesson design with our colleagues on the Teach Like a Champion reading team, in particular, and they deserve special mention for their brilliance in writing many of the curriculum examples you see included in this book. They include Emily Badillo, Jaimie Brillante, Sarah Engstrom, Alonte Johnson-James, Patrick Pastore, Jen Rugani, and Beth Verrilli.

Perhaps the best single decision we made in writing this book was to enlist the support of Tracey Marin. As a developmental editor she did just about everything—revised our clunky prose, organized our ideas, helped us clarify our thinking, suggested additional lines of argument—and did all of those things exceptionally well. Without her this book would not likely have come to fruition. If it had, it would have been a lot less clear on what it was saying and why.

Once we got the book into plausible form Susan Geraghty, Pete Gaughan, and Amy Fandrei at John Wiley & Sons turned the manuscript into a book with skill and speed. Our agent, Rafe Sagalyn, provided critical guidance throughout as we sought to define and design this book.

The videos were edited and organized by John Costello and Rob Richard, mostly behind-the-scenes work that they do better than anyone.

In addition to the important work they have made available to teachers, several researchers were extremely generous with their time. David Paige, Tim Shanahan, and Daniel Willingham generously responded to our questions about their research. Emily Hanford was similarly generous in discussing her *Sold a Story* podcast.

Most of all we are grateful for the love and support of our families and our children in particular with whom we will always love reading.

How to Use This Book

This book is written to help teachers and leaders consider research on the science of reading and what the immediate practical applications are for literacy instruction. The two key components of this book are its videos and the aforementioned research, and we want to provide guidance on how to leverage them both.

We are immensely grateful to the teachers whose videos are captured within these pages. As with all the books that our team has had the privilege of getting to work on, without these teachers and their expert implementation of research-based practices, we would not be able to share such robust guidance.

We share these videos both to honor the teachers we have learned from and to provide critical mental models of implementation. Research tells us that a mental model—a picture in your mind that describes a cohesive picture of what the ideal solution or solutions should look like—is critical to decision-making in complex environments. A mental model is flexible, mind you. It doesn't tell you one right way and, of course, you won't do everything that you see these teachers do in their clips. You will make the techniques your own through infusing your own artistry and insights based on what you know of your students. But knowing what the end goal looks like will help you adapt and problem-solve, even if you see it slightly differently than we or the teachers in the videos do.

Please let us say one more thing about the videos:

> They are a gift, given to us by the teachers we've filmed. Were they nervous when we asked to roll up with our cameras? Were they unsure? Almost certainly. They were and are overwhelmingly humble and self-deprecating practitioners. The most common response when we asked to film was, "Why do you want to tape me?"

Answer: "Because we think you are very good at what you do and because we want people to see what it looks like with real kids and real books in a real classroom with real sneezes and nosebleeds—and a hundred other emergencies and non-emergencies—interrupting the lesson."

Will there be imperfections and flaws in videos shot under those terms? Of course! As we hope is obvious, all of the videos in this book were shot without guidance or interruption from us. There were no retakes or instructions to the students to behave differently. The videos reflect teachers doing their work as a normal day unfolds, with all its realities and challenges.

We say this because a common hobby on education social media appears to be attacking or demeaning a teacher whose video you've seen posted. Why? Because some teacher has had the temerity to demonstrate something that a viewer somewhere thinks is "obvious." Or because the teacher in the video makes some relatively small mistake while doing fifteen other things brilliantly. Or because they are "neglecting" to do some completely different thing that is more important to one viewer than what the teacher is modeling.

So please know that if anyone is bragging, it's us and only us. We think the work of the teachers whose video we share is pretty incredible, but we mostly had to convince them of that. They didn't ask to have their work shared far and wide, and we think it's far more productive in using this book—far more useful to you as the viewer—to talk about what you *can* use than to pick on some flaw in their work. And so, like we ask our participants in our workshops, we ask that you honor the teachers whose classrooms we've shared by looking at what you might borrow and adapt.

Our second topic is the research. This book is intentionally recursive. Within and across chapters, we will revisit the research and how it applies to approaches and techniques we can use with our students in the hope that they will become lifelong readers.

There are several reasons for this book's intentional recursiveness and one is based on the research itself. In *The Hidden Lives of Learners,* education researcher Graham Nuthall describes the three exposures rule: "We discovered that a student needed to encounter on at least three different occasions, the complete set of the information . . . to understand the concept . . . . We found we could predict what students would learn—and what they would not—with an accuracy rate of 80–85%." In each chapter you will encounter both new ideas and new research, as well as research that we have referenced in previous chapters in slightly different ways.

There is also a practical reason for this, as we know that schools will use different chapters, perhaps in isolation, to inform professional development and professional learning communities. While we of course hope that you'll read the entire book, we also know the life of busy school leaders and teachers, and we want each chapter to be able to stand on its own to inform a particular topic—whether that be about the best way to use different ways of reading in order to boost fluency or how to support students in tackling complex text.

Its recursiveness also speaks to the complexity of reading. Some of the research and principles apply to more than one idea or topic because so much of what we do as readers is inextricably intertwined. For example, you will likely see research on working memory cited multiple times across chapters—its impact on our attention and why reading actual books matters.

Our kids tell us that we tend to retell stories multiple times and we realize that we do this in our book too, though in this case it's intentional. We are so grateful that you have chosen to read this book, and we look forward to learning back from the different ways you implement the guidance from these pages.

Introduction: "The Science of Reading": Shockwaves from a Podcast

In October 2022, education reporter Emily Hanford released a podcast called *Sold a Story*. Hanford's topic, the flawed science behind the nation's leading primary grade reading programs, might not at first seem the stuff of blockbuster media.

But it spent weeks on Apple's top ten list and became the second most shared podcast in the country in 2023. *Time* Magazine ranked it as the third best podcast in the United States that same year and by then it had more than five million downloads.

Perhaps more important than the listener statistics and accolades, it became the topic of school board and curriculum committee meetings across the country. States put the topic on the legislative docket. More than fifteen states passed laws in response, some explicitly outlawing unscientific teaching practices in early reading, others requiring districts to choose reading programs supported by science.[1]

Sold a Story turned out to be the most influential piece of education journalism in years.

One unfortunate reason for the podcast's success was that it was about reading failure, and the failure of a child to learn to read—well, easily, or in some cases at all—is far from a niche issue in American schools. There were tens of thousands of parents listening to the podcast not because the story was a true-crime thriller for PTA types or a cautionary tale about school-gone-wrong. It was the story of their child. They were parents who had lived with the reality that their child couldn't read or wasn't progressing. They had wondered: had they done something wrong? had they read to their children enough? had they failed to spot a learning disability?

The first episode began by introducing one of them: Corinne Adams. During the pandemic, she had sat in on her son Charlie's kindergarten, which was being held via Zoom. Watching over Charlie's shoulder as his teacher tried to get twenty-five kindergarteners to follow along, Corinne quickly recognized that if she helped Charlie manage the mute button and stay focused, she would also be helping his teacher. And so she found herself sitting daily at a window into her child's previously hidden world.

At first what she saw gave her only a vague sense of dissonance. She had expected to see a lot of sounding out of words, but Charlie wasn't taught to do that. He was encouraged to use context, the first letter, or what was shown in the pictures that often accompanied the text to guess at what a word was. Initially, this just seemed like "new math": schools had a way of doing things now that wasn't intuitive to parents who'd grown up in a different era.

She was told she shouldn't encourage Charlie to sound out words deliberately when reading with him at home. She began to notice that he wanted to read aloud only from books she'd already read to him. He especially liked books with predictable patterns ("Good night, room; good night, moon," etc.). But those concerns were balanced by the school's upbeat reassurances: Charlie got good grades and earned notes praising his progress in reading.

"I'd be like, 'Oh, you're doing so great!'" Corinne recalled.

Until she was asked to give Charlie an at-home reading assessment. "I wasn't allowed to read it to him first. And I couldn't help him in any way. I could point to the words for him and that was it. He had to read it," Corinne tells Hanford.

Corinne taped the session, and on the podcast, you can hear the recording of Charlie trying to read the sentence: "This toy moves when you push it."

"You . . . . It . . . . You . . ." he guesses. He has no idea how to start. He guesses at whole words. He doesn't think to go letter-by-letter or sound-by-sound.

He has probably been taught that sounding out is a last resort, but *sounding out is all but impossible if you aren't instantly familiar with the great majority of the sounds letters and letter combinations make.*

Charlie is lost because he has not been taught how to read correctly.

And there's anxiety and desperation in his voice. He wants to do well and doesn't know how.

Corinne suddenly realizes: Charlie isn't "on his way" or "making progress," he is lost—*in danger already* of becoming a student for whom school is frustrating and nearly hopeless. Of becoming an adult who can't read a loan application, a contract, a book, or the laws that govern him.

It's every parent's nightmare. Corinne's dreams for him are suddenly weighed down with dread.

And the normalcy of it all is doubly scary. The ship of school goes sailing on, placidly sending home reassuring notes.

Has no one even noticed??

Charlie's school is on the leafy side of the education gap, mind you, with kindness assemblies and SMART Boards in every room. And still there is the disconcerting sense that this is just the way things are. As Hanford notes, 65 percent of students—two-thirds of the nation's fourth graders—were below proficient on the 2019 National Assessment of Educational Progress, even before the disruptions of the pandemic. No wonder no one blinked as a bright and able child became a struggling reader. It's the majority case, you could argue.

Perhaps that's why the podcast was often gut-wrenching for the tens of thousands of teachers who also listened to it. Many had worked for years helping children learn to read, often using the programs described in the podcast—programs that eschewed systematic phonics instruction in favor of the ineffective cueing methods Charlie tried hopelessly to use. They heard how disinterest in and dismissiveness of reading science among the designers of those programs had caused teachers like themselves to give their all and still serve students poorly.

Stunningly, the flawed reading programs Hanford described in the podcast, and which Charlie's school was using, *were among the most widely used in the country*. Many teachers who used them were unaware of the problems; others had concerns but deferred to the experts. After all, they had been told to use them by their schools or by their professors. Besides, what to do in the face of such misgivings when you are just one teacher is far from clear.

The makers of those faulty early reading programs and their advocates were not just wrong about how to teach reading, though. They were wrong *in the face of clear evidence to the contrary*. Not even cutting-edge evidence: evidence that had been available for decades; evidence they were aware of. That's the kicker.

At first, their response to indications that they had the science wrong was relatively subtle. As early advocates for cognitive science made the case for the critical importance of phonics— the process of intentionally and sequentially teaching letter-sound correspondences— defenders of the dominant programs, which had been known as *whole language* for their belief that students could learn to read naturally without breaking words down into sounds, coined the term *balanced literacy* to describe their programs instead. A rebranding never hurts. After all, the programs did—or could, if a teacher chose—contain *some* phonics alongside their cueing methods and whole language approach,[2] and the new term suggested that they were a compromise, a *resolution* to the increasingly vociferous arguments about how to teach reading that were sometimes dubbed the "reading wars."

"Balanced literacy was . . . a way to defuse the controversy and put the criticisms of whole language aside because everyone was just going to use the best of both worlds," University of Wisconsin cognitive psychologist and reading expert Mark Seidenberg said in a 2018 podcast.[3] "It didn't solve any of the underlying issues . . . [because] *Teachers already thought they were using the best of both worlds* and so they didn't . . . change anything at all."

Teachers will decide what's best: that was, and is, a critical argument of many approaches to teaching and learning, including balanced literacy. *We can resolve this by deploying the wisdom of teachers to determine what works and reconcile the disputes via their learned experience in classrooms.*

That's a powerful argument. In fact, teacher autonomy is something we too believe in, deeply. Teachers' capacity to solve problems and adapt ideas in the classroom is one of their most important and under-recognized skills. School doesn't work well without it.

But to be effective in technical and complex fields, autonomy requires decision-makers to have the knowledge required to solve problems effectively.

"Generations of teachers have been trained and remain stubbornly attached to ideas about how to teach reading that are unsupported by research and basic science," the education writer Robert Pondiscio wrote in 2023,[4] and this trend is exacerbated by the fact that "education tolerates and even encourages teachers' view of themselves as free agents, who . . . listen to the latest diktats from the district and then return to their classrooms, close the door, and do what feels right."

If we really want to give teachers the right to decide—and we think we should—we have to empower them by ensuring their access to and understanding of critical knowledge and research. Knowing those things should be a professional expectation; learning them should be the foundation of teacher training. And the culture in the sector must value, share, and prioritize the knowledge of research-backed principles.

This is especially true of reading. Learning to read involves cognitive processes that do not reveal themselves easily. They are often technical, counterintuitive, and all but impossible to infer via mere observation.

"Most of what goes into reading is subconscious," Seidenberg writes in his 2017 book, *Language at the Speed of Sight*, "We are aware of having read something—that we understood it, that we found it funny, that it conveyed a fact, idea or feeling—not the mental and neural operations that produced the outcome. People are unreliable narrators of their own cognitive lives. . . . Being an expert reader doesn't make you an expert about reading. That is why there is a science of reading: to understand this complex skill at levels that intuition cannot easily penetrate."[5]

And while observation gleaned through experience is useful in adapting scientific principles, what we notice is largely determined by what we know. Experts observe and see underlying principles at work but observers without technical knowledge are more likely to see superficial detail or to attribute causation wrongly.

"The special role of science [is] to find out to the best of our ability what is true, letting the implications fall where they may," Seidenberg writes. But "ensuring basic scientific literacy and familiarity with modern research" is "not a priority in educating teachers."[6] Professionalism requires technical knowledge and this is too often at odds with norms in the profession.

Doctors enjoy significant autonomy but constantly update their knowledge of the latest research and treatments. They accept that human health is complex and that what appears to be the cause of an illness or the likely route to a cure is not easily judged from mere observation. The resulting culture ensures there are mechanisms to share research and gives priority to its insights. Doctors would express immediate concern over a colleague who attempted to treat viral pneumonia with antibiotics, or who used antibiotics to treat a bacterial infection but failed to ensure patients administered the entire cycle of medication. Announcing "That's not how I do it" or "I don't really believe in giving the whole cycle" would only deepen their concerns.

So while teachers are not researchers and many will not have the time or inclination to read the science directly, being familiar with its findings, engaging in discussions of its tenets, and prioritizing its discoveries should be part of professional norms in education.

In many ways that broader issue—that the profession has been willing to allow and normalize a disconnection from research—is the "story" in Hanford's podcast. Even if far greater attention is now being paid to the science of early literacy, the larger conditions endure, the disconnect remains—at least in the United States.

We are often struck when we work with teachers in England how different these things are on the other side of the Atlantic. Knowledge of learning science is far more widespread among teachers in England and far more likely to be perceived as something all teachers have a responsibility to understand.

Schools in England almost universally teach systematic phonics, for example. In large part this is due to the fact that schools there have administered a universal phonics screening to all year 1 students since 2012. As a result, England's recent data on the Progress in International Reading Literacy Study, an international assessment of fourth-grade reading achievement, places them fourth among forty-three participating countries. We should all tip our caps to former Minister of State for Schools Nick Gibb, who championed the intervention. And in the United States, we should copy it.

Moreover, a much higher proportion of teachers in England are familiar with concepts like working memory, Retrieval Practice, and the role of existing background knowledge in acquiring new knowledge. In trainings there, we can reliably refer to such concepts and know that the majority of teachers will understand those references. We can simply discuss how they apply in a given situation.

Of course, there are plenty of teachers (and professors of education) in England who are exceptions. But the trend is clear: professional norms for what a teacher should know about cognitive science research are noticeably higher there than in the United States.

"You can't do a teacher training course in this country, and not come out of it without an understanding of Retrieval Practice, working memory, and the role of knowledge in reading," a head teacher recently told us.

We doubt any school leaders would say that about US teacher preparation programs. "In America prospective teachers aren't trained to teach; they are socialized into a view of the teacher's role," Seidenberg writes.[7]

A key point: This is mostly *not* teachers' "fault." Teachers in the United States endeavor to serve their students in a field where the value placed on research is low, where teacher preparation programs emphasize ideological issues over technical ones, and where many of the most widely used reading curricula (and almost every state reading assessment) are organized on flawed, unscientific ideas.

This means ideas that question the assumptions we hold are far less likely to gain traction. It means that education, for all its love of the word *innovative*, actually resists the most useful innovations—those that align practices to how learning works.[8]

And sometimes education's resistance to science can be right out in the open. That's what happened in one of the most devastating sequences Hanford describes in her podcast.

In 2001, the George W. Bush administration prioritized improving early reading outcomes and proposed to ground the initiative in science. The administration convened a national reading panel to establish as clearly as possible what research supported so they could fund it and advocate for it.

The panel quickly identified that the single most important factor in primary-level reading was diligent and sequential instruction in phonics. With intentional phonics, almost every student was likely to learn to read. Without it, it was a lottery. Some kids got it and some kids—equally bright and capable, like Charlie—didn't.

But in the classroom systematic synthetic phonics required repetition, often of simple rote-seeming activities. It was important to get things just right when describing letter sounds and blends and the exact order of lesson topics really mattered, so lessons were often scripted.

That wasn't popular. Many teachers didn't like the idea of lessons someone else wrote for them. They were skeptical of direct instruction despite research indicating that it is usually the most effective way to transmit knowledge and foster learning.[9]

And just as important, phonics didn't jibe with many educators' intuitive sense of what made for enjoyable teaching and enriched classrooms. Teaching phonics felt faintly mechanical and prescriptive. It required repetition. *Mechanical, prescriptive*, and *repetitive* weren't words that described what most teachers imagined doing when they took the job.

There was a dissonance, in other words, between what worked and what many people enjoyed doing.[10] In such an environment it was easy for curriculum designers, literacy experts, and education professors vested in existing practices to argue that what was compelling and intuition confirming yet at odds with science was preferable to what was unfamiliar, challenging, and clearly backed by research.

And then they went a step further. Advocates for the dominant reading programs didn't just try to ignore and downplay the research. Many tried to discredit it.

When the Bush administration allocated $5 billion to fund early reading programs that aligned to research through Reading First grants, advocates for whole-language and balanced literacy programs, which would not have qualified for the funding, called the research "political" and implied that the panel was an attack on teachers by ignorant and corrupt outsiders.

Sadly, the ensuing years have confirmed that the panel and the research it cited were correct, but the pushback was as successful as it was cynical. Programs using faulty methods continued to thrive. Some became more popular. And in the end, millions of children continued failing to learn to read—with all the cascading misfortunes and difficulties that implies—for two more decades.

Twenty years later, in 2022, they remained among the most popular reading programs in the country. They continued socializing teachers to coach students to guess at words rather than systematically teaching them letter-sound correspondences so they could sound them out.

WHAT'S THE LESSON?

This is not a book about phonics; it's about reading in the years after students have learned to decode. Why start by sharing the tale of *Sold a Story,* then?

We think it's an important first step to ask why. Why were ideas unequivocally supported by research so easily dismissed? If not, those same factors could prevent us from teaching reading better today.

We should be aware, for example, that important research was probably rejected because change is difficult and scary and requires us to start over at the bottom of the learning curve, for example. It's human nature when you have invested time and effort to master something to become more wedded to it. People don't like to change their minds and almost never do it easily.

But even very good ideas also need translation to work in the real world of the classroom. A lone teacher with misgivings can't very easily write her own curriculum. And even knowing that a concept helps determine whether pupils will learn is a long way from knowing how to embed it into a lesson for thirty students. Changing outcomes means providing tangible examples of how to use research successfully and enough tools to make it viable in teachers' already busy lives.

And, of course, there was the broader cultural problem within the education sector: the general undervaluing of science, the broad lack of familiarity with research, and the greater interest in what Seidenberg calls ideologies instead. Perhaps the response to *Sold a Story* will cause a realignment in the field, but there's a long way to go.

It's also important to recognize, in what today is an even more politicized era than the one in which the Reading First initiative was successfully waylaid, that we were all too ready to assign political motives to teaching ideas. It is important to ask ourselves: was critical research easy to bury because it was the Bush administration that championed it, allowing it to be tagged as "right wing" when so much of the teaching world leans left? Politics on both sides of the aisle almost assuredly continue to cloud our judgment now.

We raise these issues because we are going to share how the research as we understand it applies to the lives of developing readers after they have learned to decode. But research itself is not enough. A culture that is receptive to change is also necessary. Medicine is full of stories of cures that went unheeded well after they were understood. Ignaz Semmelweis's efforts to reduce the spread of infection in hospitals, especially in maternal wards, by requiring surgeons to wash their hands—simple, decisive, cost-effective, transformative—ended in failure. He died in an asylum, mocked for his ideas and knowing thousands of women were dying unnecessarily in childbirth every year.

The story told in Hanford's podcast was unconscionable for children and families, but horrible too for teachers.[11] The podcast shares their voices—wracked with guilt at the knowledge they had worked so earnestly yet served many of the students they loved and cared about poorly. We would never want that for ourselves, and we would never want that for you.

THE END OF AN ERA (IS A COMPLICATED THING)

Things have begun changing since *Sold a Story* hit the airwaves. Among other things, the phrase the *science of reading* is *practically everywhere now*.[12]

While beneficial, the changes contain risks of their own, as Hanford and others have pointed out. There is the risk of overcorrection, for example, when a single and previously neglected factor risks becoming, in some people's minds, the only relevant factor in reading instruction. And legislation is at best a suboptimal way to shape curricular and instructional decisions in schools. It's a blunt tool, prone to perverse incentives, and often as likely to create new problems as fix old ones.

But while legislation is an unfortunate way to address pedagogy, we should also acknowledge that it reflects, at least in part, a belief among the wider public that it is necessary—that subtler methods, perhaps even better information by itself, will not be enough to cause the required changes. The neglect of phonics helped give rise to that perception. Having squandered trust, schools and educators will have to earn it back. Nothing erodes faith in institutions faster than the realization that expertise has been misused, but nothing earns trust better than institutional effectiveness, progress, and visible change—especially when it results in greater success for everybody's children.

We are at a point of transition. The long era in which teaching was shaped primarily by ideologies is ending. We must bring it swiftly to a close. In *Why Don't Students Like School?* Daniel Willingham reminds us that we have "learned more about how the mind works in the last 25 years than we did in the previous 2,500."[13] Our knowledge is now extensive enough that we can reliably use it to shape daily practice. A new era based on empirical research must begin.

In 2017, in *Language at the Speed of Sight*, Seidenberg wrote these words about our schools:

> There is a profound disconnection between the science of reading and educational practice. Very little of what we've learned about reading as scientists has had any impact on what happens in schools because the cultures of science and education are so . . . difficult to bridge. The methods used to teach children to read are inconsistent with facts about human cognition and development. . . . They inadvertently place many children at risk of reading failure. They discriminate against poor children.[14]

Those are damning words to read. We should endeavor every day to ensure that they can never be said again of our profession. The barriers at this point are human. We should not expect the change to be easy. But there's no reason to think we can't turn the tables.

THE SCIENCE OF READING "BEYOND PHONICS"

Our book, we have noted, is *not* about systematic synthetic phonics, though we believe that in the primary grades (and for any student at any grade level who can't reliably decode) that's job one.

Our starting point is that phonics are a *starting* point—that once we have ensured that every child has mastered the code of written language, reliably and thoroughly, we are not done attending to the science. There is plenty more it can tell us—much of it overlooked and misunderstood—that is equally deserving of attention. So you might say that this book is about "the science of reading *beyond phonics*."

We've tried to show what we mean by that phrase in the following figure. At the base, you can see the rough estimate of grade levels corresponding to an individual student's journey through school.

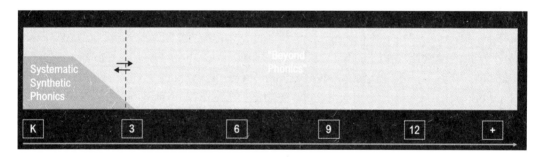

The dark gray area of the graph represents the portion of the time spent teaching and reading in each grade that should be allocated to teaching "decoding" in a scientifically supported manner. This is the primary task during the primary years.[15]

Our goal is to describe what literacy teaching should look like in the light gray area of the graph, which is by far the greatest portion of a student's journey through school.

There are two parts to the light gray portion of the graph. First, there is the part that typically happens in kindergarten, first, and second grade while students are learning to decode. The second occurs beyond roughly second or third grade and represents reading instruction after students are fluent decoders and have begun to build strong orthographic maps of familiar words.[16] This portion is what we are mainly concerned with. The primary purpose of this book is to discuss what the science says reading teachers should do after students have mastered decoding and how they can translate those ideas into practice.

But a lot of the research we describe can also be helpful in determining what else should be happening during the primary grades while teachers are focused on helping students crack the code of letter-sound correspondence, and so a secondary purpose of this book is to help with the light gray portion of the graph above the dark area in grades K–2.

Should we be building vocabulary as well during the primary years when cracking the letter-sound code is job one? Yes! Should we be reading aloud to students to build their understanding of complex language and syntax and cause them to fall in love with stories far richer than the simple texts designed specifically for decoding? Absolutely.

In early years, those things matter, too. We should be aware that reactions to the historical neglect of phonics might lead to the most important thing becoming the only thing.

The grade level along the bottom of the graph is only an estimate, we note, because systematic synthetic phonics, represented by the dark gray area, should be the primary focus of instruction until students can reliably decode with automaticity, which happens at different points for different students. While it should ideally happen by first or second grade, it doesn't always.[17]

And yet the lion's share of a student's education occurs in the area after explicit phonics instruction has been successfully completed and students have "cracked the code." That is, in grades 3–12, typically.

In this area, too, we think there is an immensely important and surprising body of research that will require us to adapt our practices in sometimes unexpected ways to ensure the success of our students. Given the size of this area on the graph, that's a big deal. If students have not mastered letter-sound correspondence in the primary years they will be sorely hampered throughout their school lives, but even if and when they have, a case could be made that we are still serving them poorly because too many teachers are not aware of the science that should shape lessons throughout the rest of their school years—the bulk of their schooling. Progress in reading scores often goes flat after the fourth grade in the United States, exactly the time that the "beyond phonics" research becomes more relevant.

As with primary level reading, some of this important research has emerged recently, but a lot of it has been known for some time—some of it hidden in plain sight. Ideas that research has demonstrated are worthy are easy to disparage when they do not jibe with what people have done in the past or think the answer should be based on other beliefs. We reiterate that this is a primary lesson of *Sold a Story*.

WHAT'S INSIDE THIS BOOK?

We began this journey long before we heard *Sold a Story*. We had our own conversion experience when we were forced to accept that much of what we had thought (and taught!) was in fact wrong. Our introduction to much of the research we will describe here began in 2014 when we were asked to rethink reading for the network of schools we then worked for. Student progress was not what it could have been. It lagged the results we saw in other disciplines. Why?

It took failure for us to begin seeking out the science, and in that sense our starting point is typical of the way change happens. The key is to acknowledge the failure.

Our previous book, *Reading Reconsidered*, describes our initial findings. They align to many of the ideas we discuss here, but there's a lot more we (the education community and we, the three of us) now know better. And we think it's doubly important to make the connections to and applications of the science more explicit than they were before.

In *Reading Reconsidered* we talked about the importance of background knowledge, for example. This was one of our first and most important discoveries from reading the research. As we discuss in Chapter One, what appeared to us in the early years of our teaching careers to be "skill" problems were in fact "knowledge" problems. We had failed to perceive this fact. It didn't help that state assessments encouraged teachers to think this way—they were literally organized on skills. But once we'd read Daniel Willingham's *Why Don't Students Like School*, for example, and learned about research like Recht and Leslie's "Baseball Study," we started to study how to use knowledge in daily lessons. We wrote a chapter about embedding nonfiction passages in the reading of books.

We have learned a lot more about creating knowledge-rich reading classrooms since—both because we have worked with teachers in scores of schools to apply it and because we have spent six years designing a curriculum that draws on the research. Chapter Four on knowledge in this book discusses a lot more than just Embedded Nonfiction. And it will show you both video examples and examples from lesson materials. If you've read *Reading Reconsidered*, we think you'll find this book almost entirely new even if the topics are similar.[18]

An important caution, though: we've visited hundreds of schools along the way to talk about and observe reading instruction. Many of them are schools that agree about the profound importance of background knowledge in reading comprehension. And yet we see, in many of those same schools, the persistence of lessons that are not especially knowledge-driven that spend forty-five minutes on the four or five or seven steps to finding the main idea, for example. In fact, we've come to coin the term *skills-y* to refer to lessons where the reading of the text is crowded out by meta-conversations about finding the main idea and making inferences or in which a single short passage is subjected to a litany of skill-based questions.

So we're forced to ask: if instruction in well-intentioned schools with smart teachers looks the same after people have become aware of the research, what is causing the disconnect? Why is it so hard to make change even when you believe in an idea?

One reason is that change implies so many different things—different "different things" for different people. Some teachers write their own lesson plans and curriculum. For those teachers, understanding how to design lessons plans is critical. You can't teach reading better if the curriculum isn't better. Some teachers use a curriculum written and designed by someone else. For them, making adaptations or additions to the plans will be critical, as will be knowing what to emphasize and how.

So in this book we will discuss not only lesson delivery—the pedagogy that we think can best emphasize what the science tells us—but lesson design as well: examples of how to write or adapt tasks and lessons to maximize learning.

We note that we are not scientists. We are translators. A field in which busy people are asked to apply a massive body of knowledge requires that. And, of course, research once established does not come embedded in lesson plans. It requires a separate skill to determine how to use it on Tuesday morning with a diverse group of sixth graders reading *Number the Stars*. Doubly so when there are multiple things the research tells us we should be doing: building background knowledge, reinforcing fluency, including writing, say. The process of turning all of that into a lesson plan is not something researchers are generally best positioned to advise on.

And so we offer ourselves, having read as much of the research as we could, having thought about and talked to hundreds of teachers about applying it, having observed what the data on their efforts to use it can tell us, and having videotaped and studied them doing so and studied the written work students produce as a result.

The changes we describe might mean adding more oral reading to build fluency or shifting the structure of vocabulary instruction to spend less time guessing at definitions and more time using words. It might mean asking students to write less but with greater intentionality to the syntax they use. It might mean adapting nonfiction articles from external sources and asking students to read them alongside a novel to help them understand more of the time and place they are reading about.

Making such changes requires two things (at least!) beyond knowledge of the research. First it requires a mental model of what the final outcome could or should look like. Nothing illustrates that better than video, of course, so this book includes videos of a wide variety of classroom teachers applying the ideas we discuss in their own classrooms. We've thanked them elsewhere and we thank them here. And we thank you, too. Because the last thing you need to make changes is a bit of bravery, honestly. We're not trying to sound patronizing when we say that. We have lived this ourselves. Changing what you do will never go perfectly and we know what it means to crash and burn in public. (Someday we'll tell you some stories!) But we know that if you take the arguments of this book to heart, there will be success and learning and a sense of accomplishment. There will also be struggle and failure, hopefully brief and transient failure on your way to glory, but failure just the same. So we wish you fearlessness and humility and wisdom. We think you're going to crush it.

THE SEVEN ARGUMENTS

This book is built on seven core arguments. Each of these is supported by research we summarize in Chapter One.

The seven arguments are as follows:

- Attention is central to every learning activity, especially reading, and building attention is a necessary step in effective reading instruction.

- Fluency is a prerequisite to reading comprehension at all grade levels.

- Once students are fluent, background knowledge is the most important driver of understanding and comprehension.

- Vocabulary is the single most important form of knowledge (but is often taught as if it were a skill).

- Intentional writing development can play a critical and synergistic role in developing better readers.

- Books are the optimal text format through which to build understanding and comprehension.

- The ability to read complex text is the gatekeeper to long-term success.

Chapters Two through Eight take each argument in turn and expand on how it can be addressed through teaching, lesson design, and text selection.

We hope a deep study of these seven arguments will be useful to teachers but also to school leaders, curriculum designers, policymakers, and parents. We think it's important for everyone involved to be aligned: for state assessments to measure useful things so teachers have the fullest incentives to teach them, for schools to share with parents how and why they choose the programs they do. The right ideas need to be shared across the spectrum of stakeholders to best serve children.

Consider the observations of a teacher at a recent workshop we ran. The discussion was about how doing more actual reading in class was beneficial, a topic we address in Chapter Three.

"Every time I read with my class," the teacher told us, "I live in fear that an administrator will walk in the room and ask me why we're reading when I should be teaching. My principal doesn't think reading counts as teaching."

One person, a teacher say, in possession of knowledge but isolated in a complex system, is not yet in a position to achieve substantive change.

Notes

1. Hanford herself had concerns about the benefits, risks, and unintended consequences of legislative responses to the issues raised in the podcast, as she discusses in episode 8 and episode 10 of *Sold a Story*.

2. A key problem is that for phonics to work it should be systematic and synthetic— carefully sequenced and technically focused on critical letter-sound formations in order. If you're doing it sporadically, you're not really doing it.

3. https://www.youtube.com/watch?v=CheEVPkhdjw.

4. https://www.commentary.org/articles/robert-pondiscio/teaching-reading-right/.

5. Mark Seidenberg, *Language at the Speed of Sight* (Basic Books, 2017), 304.

6. *Language at the Speed of Sight*, 261.

7. *Language at the Speed of Sight*, 250.

8. Most innovation fails. Evolutionarily, most adaptations result in a weaker organism and die out. For this reason it is important to value successful outcomes and then allow and test innovations, rather than valorizing innovation as being inherently good. *Innovative* is at best a neutral adjective.

9. In a nutshell, direct instruction is preferable for novices while open-ended learning processes like "discovery learning" are often better for experts. But of course very few children in the K–12 educations system are experts, no matter how much we value and respect their insights and intelligence. For more on this see Clark, Kirschner, and Sweller, "Putting Students on the Path to Learning: The Case for Fully Guided Instruction" (https://www.aft.org/sites/default/files/Clark.pdf).

10. We should note that many teachers who think they won't enjoy teaching phonics, in fact do. For one thing the children often love it because they feel accomplished and capable. Children, it turns out, like knowing things, and this makes them happy.

11. We don't imply that the plight of angst-ridden teachers is anywhere near as significant as the plight of students who cannot read, but as this is a book for teachers we think it's relevant.

12. Not surprisingly it is also broadly misused and coopted to support all sorts of mostly unscientific ideas. Buyer beware.

13. Daniel Willingham, *Why Don't Students Like School? A Cognitive Scientist Answers Questions About How the Mind Works and What It Means for the Classroom,* 2nd ed. (Jossey-Bass, 2021), xvii.

14. *Language at the Speed of Sight,* 9.

15. "Decoding" is an oversimplification. Not all phonics is systematic and synthetic, we note. In the systematic study of phonics, students learn letter-sound correspondences in an intentional and logical sequence. In synthetic phonics, students are taught individual sounds first in isolation—just a component sound or blend, detached from a word—to ensure reliable mastery. But even calling that area of the graphic *systematic synthetic phonics* is a bit of an oversimplification. Research-based early reading is not just phonics in that it includes phonemic awareness, for example, and it leads to "word reading" (i.e., less synthetic phonics) to ensure orthographic mapping.

16. *Orthographic map* refers to the process that happens after decoding and is facilitated by it in which specific words are glued to their letter combinations—our process of committing a large number of words to memory so we recognize them at a glance and no longer have to decode them.

17. Notice also that the dark gray area slopes down. As Christopher Such, one of the foremost translators of reading science for teachers, has pointed out (thread on the social media platform X, July 6, 2024), "phonics" is often interpreted as referring solely to the explicit teaching of letter-sound correspondences, but while explicit teaching is the necessary and often overlooked first step in learning the alphabetic code, isolated

mastery is not the purpose. The skills implicit in foundational reading must also be applied and practiced extensively in the context of reading actual text, and this is a long process in which decoding gradually intertwines with other reading tasks.

18. We should note that the curriculum we wrote is called *Reading Reconsidered*, too, so you'll see us use the term a lot. Please know that the book and the curriculum are different things. And you don't need to have read that book to read this one.

THE TEACH LIKE A CHAMPION
GUIDE TO THE SCIENCE OF READING

Chapter 1

The Science of Reading in Seven Key Arguments

Imagine a world in which systematic, synthetic phonics in early reading are a non-negotiable in the primary grades. This world seems increasingly possible as parents, educators, administrators, and even lawmakers become more attuned to their critical importance.

But if we changed the game for reading acquisition in the primary years, and then failed to make informed decisions about what to teach, and how, in grades 3, 5, 8, and 10, our victory would be largely pyrrhic. So it is important to ask: After we've nailed phonics in the early grades, what does the science tell us should happen in reading classes from then on?

In this area "beyond phonics," what is now common practice is often misinformed. In this area, too, change can cause anxiety and resistance. We hope to make embracing the science easy and, just maybe, to help teachers use and adapt it well to ensure success in reading—and, just maybe, joy, for students and for you, their teacher.

We'll use this chapter to describe important research that we think should inform three critical areas of literacy instruction: teaching decisions, lesson design, and text selection, because teachers can't determine what they should be doing on Monday morning until they understand how people think, read, remember, and make sense of the language they experience in a text.

But teachers also need guidance on how to translate that research into practice.

For example, let's say you're aware that there's strong research behind the power of intentional writing activities in literacy instruction. They can help increase students' mastery of complex syntax, something that also helps them when they are reading. Okay, great. Now you need some tools to figure out what it looks like to have students write more, and more intentionally, in a real classroom with thirty-two students and the clock ticking. It would be helpful to see examples of the writing exercises other teachers have used and what they've learned about them. It would be helpful to see video showing how teachers use those exercises, and how students react, in real classrooms.

To use the research, you'd want to know how to adapt those writing exercises for third graders or ninth graders. Or how they might be designed differently at the beginning of a book unit versus at the end.

You'd need to know what to do when students struggle: when you'd asked them to write, say, but they didn't actually write much of value, and you didn't know if they *wouldn't* write or *couldn't write in the way you wanted them to because no one had ever asked them to.*

You'd need some guidance on how to get them writing, and once that happened, how to combine the writing with the other things that also work? What's the dosage of each? What are the potential pitfalls? How do you adapt to different students?

Just because you know what the research says does not mean that developing and implementing better lessons is going to be automatic- or easy.

Happily, we are translators of the research, as we noted in the introduction, and this is the thing that interests us most.

We have spent a lot of time studying how the research shows up in real classrooms and, in particular, studying the moves of teachers whose results suggest they know a thing or two about what, when, and how. You'll see a lot of videos of those classrooms as you read the chapters to come.

We've also written a reading curriculum to try to help make it easier for teachers to use the research effectively. Our curriculum is for grades 5–8 but we're also developing one for high school, and we have spent a fair amount of time helping teachers in grades 3 and 4 adapt the ideas, too. We'll share lots of examples of how we tried to design lessons to leverage the science. As we hope is implicit, we don't offer them as models of perfection. You'll want to adapt and change things. You'll like some suggestions more than others. They're a starting point, surely an imperfect one, but also one that reflects a fair amount of experience and reflection.[1]

All of which is to say that we believe in research, but we think understanding it is only the beginning. Translating it requires diligent study. Like everyone else, teachers are more likely to give up on a useful idea because some foreseeable challenge caused their first efforts to go poorly. A teacher who says, "I asked them to write but they didn't" or "I asked them to write but what they wrote wasn't good" is a teacher who is at risk of becoming skeptical of or giving up on research that could make her and her students more successful. Good ideas get thrown out because they are challenging to implement. And, frankly, in a classroom of thirty students in this day and age, very few things are easy to implement.

So we spend Chapters Two through Eight getting very practical to help you bridge the gap between "get it" and "do it." But the first step is to be explicit about what we think the relevant science says about reading classrooms "beyond phonics." We'll do that in this chapter. We think knowing this research is part of being a successful teacher. And, honestly, we think you'll find it as fascinating and as we do.

A BROAD BASE OF RESEARCH

In discussing the research, we will draw on sources that examine a wide range of topics. We'll discuss the profound importance of background knowledge and vocabulary, for example, and the under-acknowledged degree to which fluency is a primary barrier to comprehension.

We'll also range a bit wider and discuss the importance of selective attention to the development of reading especially in the age of attention-fracturing smartphones. We'll look at research on writing and how it suggests teachers can accelerate the development of reading proficiency. And we'll look at research that suggests that when we encounter information in stories, especially in "long form" (i.e., books) the result is especially effective for learning. As we indicated in the Introduction, we will discuss only in small part the overwhelming importance of phonemic awareness and a systematic, synthetic approach to phonics in early reading acquisition. In primary grades they are a non-negotiable and we presume their application here.

We hope to make the research we present here easy to use well and flexibly to ensure students' success. And just maybe to create more joyful reading classrooms. For students and for you, their teacher.

Let us linger on the topic of joyful classrooms for a moment. One common argument we hear is that students won't like instruction that is better aligned to science. Perhaps some of this is projection—teachers worry that *they* won't enjoy a different approach to teaching but justify it on the grounds that students won't—but some of it is sincere worry. Won't using science be formulaic and joyless for students? We've met teachers who are aware that reading problems are mostly knowledge-based but think instilling that knowledge will be boring.

Happily, we don't think this is true and we think we can prove it to you by showing you classrooms where it is emphatically not the case. In fact, we think teaching that applies the science of reading and learning is very likely to be *more* engaging for students. After all, as education researcher Carl Hendrick points out, "Motivation doesn't always lead to achievement, but achievement often leads to motivation."[2] Or, put another way, "the actual effect of achievement on self-perception is stronger than the other way round."[3] Perhaps the biggest motivation to a learner is the knowledge that they are succeeding and making progress.

So let us start this book by sharing the key arguments that we think should shape reading instruction "beyond phonics."

SEVEN KEY RESEARCH-BACKED ARGUMENTS ABOUT "POST-PHONICS" READING

In the remainder of this chapter we describe each of the book's seven key arguments and the basis for our belief in them. We will expand on each argument and dig deeper into how to apply the research in each area in the subsequent chapters.

Attention Is Central to Every Learning Activity, Especially Reading, and Building Attention Is a Necessary Step in Effective Reading Instruction

> *Attention is the currency of learning in almost any task. But reading, especially, relies on and requires states of sustained focus and concentration. If the smartphone has taught us one thing it's that people's attention is malleable, but this also means we can intentionally build students' capacity to attend to what they read.*

Attention is "central . . . for every function we perform," writes reading researcher Maryanne Wolf.[4] It is the cognitive function that allows us to select what sensory inputs we pay attention to and sustain our focus there for a period of time, locking in on the task at hand and locking out potential distractions.

We know that the quality of attention paid by learners shapes the outcome of most learning endeavors. You can only learn about what you are paying attention to. Attention is always a prerequisite to learning.

But reading poses particular challenges to attentional skills. Staying focused on a long and challenging text for an extended period of time requires an especially high level of focus and self-regulation, for example, and all aspects of reading, from letter recognition to the most advanced forms of comprehension, are highly responsive a student's ability to focus attention on the task at hand (or lack thereof). Perhaps not surprisingly, then, Courtney Stevens and Daphne Bavelier describe attention as having "reverberating effects" on language and literacy.[5]

"Readers' attention had significant effects on reading speed, prosody, word recognition and comprehension," Mustafa Yildiz and Ezgi Çetinkaya conclude in a study of fourth graders. "To improve good readers' prosodic reading skills and increase their reading speeds, attention-enhancing activities are needed."[6]

And in fact it turns out that the ability to sustain and manage one's own attention is not fixed. "Selective attention is also highly malleable," Stevens and Bavelier write. "Data indicate that attention skills can be enhanced, and distractor suppression may be especially modifiable. In a classroom context, there may be large benefits to incorporating attention-training activities into the school context . . . with evidence for improvements in children's selective attention."[7] Attentional capacity is affected by our habits and is subject to change.

One reason for this has to do with the idea that reading is relatively new, biologically speaking. As a species, we've been reading for perhaps five thousand years (and for most of that time only a comparative minority of the species could read). Compare that to speaking, which we have been doing some form of somewhere between half a million and a million years.[8] The result is that our brains have had time to evolve for speech but not for reading. There are portions of the brain dedicated to speech and so this capacity develops naturally. A baby left untaught will begin to babble. It will copy its parent(s) and most likely learn to speak without intervention or support. Speech is "natural," this is to say. Reading is not. There is no reading portion of the brain; a baby left to its own devices will not learn to read. In fact, when we learn to read we are repurposing portions of our brain designed for other activities and rewiring them in service of deciphering text, Wolf notes in *Reader Come Home*.[9]

The idea that the brain wires and rewires based on what we use it for is called *neuroplasticity*. One important implication of this is that our neurons "wire how they fire," that is, students are rewiring every time they read shapes how they will and can read going forward. This is relevant in a variety of ways but in particular in preparing students to sustain attention in an age of persistent technological distraction. When we read on screens, we toggle to new sources of information constantly and so risk wiring our brains first to expect distraction and then to seek it out, to be hoping to be distracted by some cognitively easier task while we read. The more we read in a state of distracted half-attention, the more we come to hunger for new stimulus, the more distracted we are as readers, and the more we degrade our capacity to read with focus for a sustained period of time. This has always been a challenge but it is exponentially more so now. It's not just that smartphones make us read less; it's that they cause us to read differently.

"The process of learning to read changes our brain, but so does what we read, how we read, and on what we read (print, e-reader, phone, laptop)," writes Wolf. "This is especially important in our new reality, when many people are tethered to multiple screens at any given moment."[10]

Imagine a certain teenager. Perhaps he is one of your authors' very own children. Imagine him lying on the living room couch reading a book with his cellphone resting on his chest. Every few seconds, it vibrates with a new notification. He ignores some of them but they still break his concentration. And every so often he picks up his phone to check. His attention is broken. He returns to the book after a while but his experience of it is different. He's only partially in the world of Jonas in *The Giver* or the Youngers in *A Raisin in the Sun*. The experience is not as all-encompassing and immersive: he reads not just less but less deeply and, as Wolf puts it, "Deep reading is our species' bridge to insight and novel thought."[11]

At first it is the cellphone itself that distracts him but after a time it's as if the cellphone were inside of him. His brain has rewired to seek out distractions, even when the phone is not providing them.

Fortunately attentional skills can also be increased. Making a habit of concentrating for sustained periods of time makes us better at concentrating for sustained periods of time. *Sustained focus and deep immersion in the text are habits we have to instill in students if we want them to have them.* It just takes intentional action by teachers.

One of the simplest ways to do this is to go "low tech/high text" in the classroom. That is, to reduce the number of screens—given that the mere presence of screens tends to increase distractibility—and the amount of screen time, and to increase the amount of time spent in sustained reading of text. A great reading classroom, we argue, should feature text in hard copy with students annotating to shape and focus their attention as they read. So while many teachers are encouraged to think they are not teaching when they are reading with their students, we disagree. We are all in favor of class time spent reading—a topic we take up in Chapters Two, Seven, and Nine.

Fluency Is a Prerequisite to Reading Comprehension at All Grade Levels

Fluency is the ability to read words quickly and easily as soon as they are encountered. Quickly and easily are important: they imply the lack of reliance on working memory. If the reading itself requires conscious thought, that process will crowd out other more advanced cognitive activities that are required to make meaning of text.

The simplest definition of reading fluency is "the ability to read *at the speed of sight.*" We take this from Mark Seidenberg's book of that title. It refers to the ability to absorb the meaning of written text as soon as you look at it—to decode not only individual sounds but words and phrases as soon as you perceive them.

Fluent readers rarely have to hesitate to think about what the words they are reading say or how they link together. Of course, there are times—with an especially complex text or when attention has drifted—when even fluent readers may have to reread a passage to make sense of it, but for the most part meaning accrues as words are glimpsed. There is no discernable delay and little conscious effort.

When you can read effortlessly, without having to think about it, your working memory, that critical part of your brain for encoding memory and building understanding, is free to do other things, like think about the meaning of the text or perceive details within it. When the first parts of reading are automatic, conscious thought and attention are freed and can be used elsewhere. If you cannot read at the speed of sight, your ability to understand, think about, and remember what you have read will be limited. Period. For this reason, *fluency is a prerequisite to comprehension.*

In fact in most cases a fluent reader can't *not* read a piece of text in their native language. You see a road sign and have processed that it says "No Parking" as soon as you've perceived the words. The reading happens so quickly, effortlessly, and automatically[12] that you do not have time to decide not to read it. Making a conscious decision takes about half a second and by then you would have read the words. Only if you were highly distracted could you look at the sign and *not* read it.

If you are a fan of Duolingo, say, or have experience trying to learn a foreign language, particularly as an adult, you have probably experienced the sort of effortful reading that is common for dysfluent readers. You must pause to consciously recall word meanings or decipher phrases. You can often figure these out within a few seconds, but only through conscious effort. By the time you've done that you have to circle back to put the ideas together meaningfully. Read the first part of the sentence again, to put the ideas together. When listening or reading, you can keep up for a sentence or two but your working memory is soon overloaded and you lose the ability to sustain meaning making. It's intense cognitive work and you tire quickly. As long as you have to extend effort to decipher the words, you are not yet able to read in the fullest sense of the word.

In fact, fluency requires three distinct things at once. First, it requires accuracy. You must reliably read the sounds and the words correctly. While decoding is the name of this process for speech sounds, orthographic mapping is the name for the process by which each unique sequence of letters becomes "glued" in your mind as a word. You see it, recognize the word nearly simultaneously, and no longer need to fully decode it.

But fluency also requires automaticity, which is accuracy at speed. Reading rate is an important precursor to reading comprehension. Faster isn't always better but a certain base level of rapidity is almost always required. Many researchers posit 110 words per minute as a baseline rate. For example, in a 2003 study, 91% of students who had oral reading fluency scores at or above 110 words per minute also scored proficient (level 3 or above) on the Florida Comprehensive Assessment Test.[13] Students who did not score 80 words per minute correct were almost assured to do poorly on the FCAT.[14] Students who cannot read accurately *and quickly* are at high levels of risk for reading failure.

Finally, fluency requires prosody, which is "appropriate expression or intonation coupled with phrasing that allows for maintenance of meaning."[15] Prosody enables us to invest the words we are reading with meaningful expression so they sound like they might if they were spoken aloud. It allows us to emphasize a certain word in a sentence or to link the words in a phrase together. It is *meaning made audible.*

Accuracy plus automaticity plus prosody is the fluency formula, and multiple studies have demonstrated its deep connection to comprehension as well as the fact that far fewer students have mastered it than you might expect.

Studies find that about half of demonstrated reading comprehension is predicted by reading fluency. David Paige and his colleagues at the Northern Illinois University found, in a study of sixth- and seventh-grade students, that oral reading fluency explained between 50 percent and 62 percent of differences in reading comprehension.[16] J. Sabatini, Z. Wang, and T. O'Reilly[17] studied the connection between fluency and overall scores on the 2002 NAEP reading assessment and found that "the strongest predictor of NAEP comprehension scores was reading rate." Christy Bloomquist (2017) found that 45 percent of the variation in reading comprehension levels among fourth- and fifth-grade students in Colorado[18] was attributable to oral reading fluency.[19] It's likely that the predictiveness of fluency declines slightly as students age but Chris Schatschneider and colleagues[20] found that reading fluency accounted for about a third (32 percent) of reading comprehension scores among tenth graders. Even that late in a student's career, the connection remains strong.[21]

"Slow, capacity-draining word recognition processes require cognitive resources that should be allocated to comprehension. Thus reading for meaning is hindered," Keith Stanovich and Anne Cunningham summarized in their 1998 analysis *What Reading Does for the Mind*. They also outlined a secondary effect of dysfluency: "Unrewarding reading experiences multiply." Struggling to understand and reading without understanding much makes reading appear to have less value. Place this alongside the greater cost in terms of effort required for dysfluent readers and the value calculus tips away from reading. "Practice is avoided or merely tolerated," Stanovich and Cunningham note, and it is done "without real cognitive involvement."[22] Dysfluent readers stop wanting to read or experience reading to be not especially meaningful. The gaps between them and their classmates widen.

Though research into the scale of dysfluency is limited, studies suggest that it is a widespread problem. Analyzing the data from John Sabatini's study of more than seventeen hundred fourth graders, for example, Paige notes that "41.7% of 4th grade students—almost half—appear to have reading fluency issues," and that such issues are "strongly associated with poor performance on the NAEP."[23] A 1995 report by the National Center for Education Statistics found similarly that just "55 percent of fourth graders were considered to be fluent," and that after reading a passage twice silently, only about 13 percent of the fourth graders in a NAEP study "could read with expressive interpretation and consistent preservation of the author's syntax."[24]

Moreover, fluency remains a pervasive issue among older students. Paige found gaps in fluency and a strong correlation to comprehension among sixth- and seventh-grade students, well beyond the years where most schools remain attentive to fluency, and in Schatschneider's study of Florida students, more than half of tested tenth graders demonstrated fluency rates below proficient.

And the effects are of course not limited to testing. A study of Italian[25] students found that "reading fluency predicted all school marks in all literacy-based subjects, with reading rapidity being the most important predictor." The authors added, "School level did not moderate the relationship between reading fluency and school outcomes, confirming the importance of effortless and automatized reading even in higher school levels."[26]

Two findings jump out from that statement—first the simple importance of rapid reading specifically and second that fluency matters at all grade levels—though it is least likely to be assessed and therefore recognized among older students. (The students in this study were in grades 4–9.)

Despite this data, "fluency has been relatively neglected beyond the elementary grades," Paige observes. There is, he writes, "little instruction occurring . . . to improve reading fluency" beyond the mid-elementary years and by middle and high school, teachers are more likely to "employ work-arounds so students don't have to read text" during class.[27]

Research suggests that fluency poses a hindrance to comprehension for close to half of students even into high school in other words. "At the end of the day, my hunch is that 40 percent to 50 percent of middle school students do not have proper reading fluency," Paige told us. "In schools where students generally struggle with academic attainment, this percentage is likely closer to 80 percent."[28]

Given that the texts students are expected to read become more complex and therefore demanding from a fluency standpoint, there is little reason to suspect there are not large numbers of students in high school and even college for whom reading fluency is a massive and hidden barrier to reading comprehension. And when that is the case, we are less and less likely to know about it. When was the last time the average ninth grader's oral reading fluency was assessed?

A colleague of ours observed that, as a teacher, she rarely asked older students to read aloud and so knew little about their fluency. The same was true with her own children, who were in middle school. "I suddenly realized that it has been years since I even thought about their fluency."

She's right to be worried, especially given that almost all of the existing research data was conducted before the precipitous rise of the smartphone and social media, which have dramatically reduced independent reading outside of school among American teenagers to a fraction of what it once was (see Chapter Two). The problem is almost assuredly worse now.

Once Students Are Fluent, Background Knowledge Is the Most Important Driver of Understanding and Comprehension

A common misunderstanding about reading comprehension is that it involves transferable skills like making inferences that once learned can be applied to other texts. Unfortunately there is little evidence that these skills translate, but significant evidence that they happen naturally when readers have sufficient background knowledge to disambiguate texts.

One of the themes of *Middlemarch*, George Eliott's classic nineteenth-century novel, is Mr. Casaubon's fruitless pursuit of a concept he refers to as "the key to all mythologies." A scholar, he imagines a single understanding that will illuminate the true meaning of every tale. He spends his life toiling at the task of finding this universal key.

It's hopeless, of course. The novel reveals his delusions. When he dies, his once-admiring wife, Dorothea, at last reads his papers and can see that the project was absurd from the start, but the reality proved all but impossible to acknowledge *because the dream was so beautiful.* It was a "chimera," something so alluring the believer desperately wants it to exist even when the facts are saying it cannot be so.

The belief in transferable skills is perhaps the most common chimera among teachers of reading. Imagine a handful of universal tools we could teach students and in so doing enable them to understand every text they read. Who wouldn't seek out "the key to all inferences," for example, knowing that once mastered this skill would allow our students to unlock what was unspoken in every story? Or the "key to main ideas," which would enable them after a bit of diligent study to grasp the gist of any passage we put in front of them for the rest of their lives. Who among us would not dream such a beautiful dream?

The problem is that for all the beauty of the dream, the evidence is squarely against it. Beyond a bare minimum amount, "Practice brings no benefit to reading-comprehension strategy use," Daniel Willingham writes.[29] Summarizing the finding of recent studies, he writes that beyond a very small amount of brief explanation, "There was no evidence that increasing instructional time for comprehension strategies—even by 400 percent!—brought any benefit."[30]

Take inferences, for example. While we make inferences constantly while reading, and while doing so clearly assists with comprehension, *practicing* strategies like making inferences doesn't help much and there's no evidence that the ability to make inferences well transfers from one book to another. "People don't decide that they're going to make these inferences, the mind just makes them happen," Willingham says.[31] The reason for this is that our ability to inference is a function of our prior knowledge.

Here's an example from a third-grade classroom we recently visited. The class was reading *Charlotte's Web* when they came across this scene:

> *"But Charlotte," said Wilbur, "I'm not terrific."*
> *"That doesn't make a particle of difference," replied Charlotte. "Not a particle. People believe almost anything they see in print. Does anybody know how to spell terrific?"*

"I think," said the gander, "It's tee double ee double rr double rr double eye double see see see see see."

"What kind of acrobat do you think I am?" said Charlotte in disgust.

The teacher paused and asked why Charlotte was disgusted. Two students responded. The first said because the gander always talked too much. The second because the gander always said everything three times. Both of which are true and both of which are wrong if the goal is to explain why Charlotte was disgusted.

Perhaps students didn't understand how to infer a character's point of view from her words. This would be the assumption in a lot of classrooms, and the result would be a lesson (or a series of lessons) on the "skill" of inferencing.

But the source of the problem was revealed when the teacher asked, "Who knows what an acrobat is?"

There was a smattering of two or three hesitant hands. A boy who'd raised his responded, "It's a little bit like a magician, I think."

Charlotte, for those who haven't read *Charlotte's Web*, is disgusted because she intends to write the word in a spider web and the gander's very long spelling of the word implies lots of work hanging precariously from a web for her. But if you don't know what an acrobat is, you cannot know that. The problem was not a skill problem. Knowledge cues an inference and without it, no further explanation of how to make an inference or what an inference is will help much.

The knowledge enables the inference. This is an inconvenient fact. It means we can't just explain and practice and have students get better at inferencing. There is no Casaubon-like short cut. We instead have to go the long way around and make sure students have the background knowledge they need to make better sense of what they read.

As Dylan Wiliam writes in *Creating the Schools Our Children Need,* "The big mistake we have made in the United States is to assume that if we want students to be able to think, then our curriculum should give our students lots of practice thinking. This is a mistake because what our students need is more to think with." [32]

A classic study by Donna Recht and Lauren Leslie, known as "The Baseball Study," [33] demonstrates this. The authors divided sixty-four seventh- and eighth-grade students into two groups based on their reading levels: weak readers and strong readers. But they also divided those groups again, based on whether the students knew a lot about baseball. Now they had four groups: good readers who knew a lot about baseball and good readers who knew very little about baseball; weak readers who knew a lot about baseball and weak readers who knew very little about baseball.

They gave them a passage about baseball to read. Here are the first few lines:

Churniak swings and hits a slow bouncing ball toward the shortstop. Haley comes in, fields it, and throws to first, but too late. Churniak is on first with a single . . .

After students read the passage, the researchers tested the four groups of students to see how much of the passage they understood. Some of the results were exactly what you'd expect:

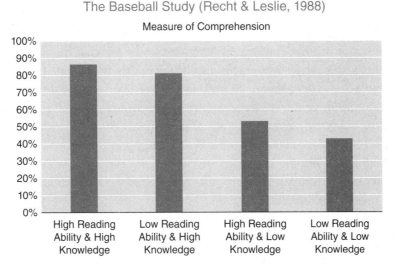

The Baseball Study (Recht & Leslie, 1988)

The students with high reading ability and strong knowledge of baseball had no trouble with the passage. They got almost all of the answers correct. By contrast, the weak readers with weak knowledge of baseball really struggled. They got less than half the questions right, scoring little above the level you'd expect them to get if they were merely guessing.

The surprise was in the two middle groups. The students with low reading ability but strong knowledge of baseball did better than the high-ability readers with little knowledge of baseball. Quite a lot better in fact—they were a few points behind the top group and scored almost 30 percent better than the students who were "better" readers but knew less about the topic of the passage.

It's a study that has been repeated many times with students reading about different topics, and it demonstrates quite elegantly that you read well and successfully when and because you have background knowledge of what you are reading about. To return to Dylan Wiliam's point: if we want students to understand and think more deeply about what they read we should focus on knowledge and not waste time trying to teach them abstract skills like making inferences or finding the main idea.

The reason why this is the case has to do with what you might call the inherent ambiguity of every text. As Daniel Willingham recently pointed out,[34] every sentence is to some degree ambiguous. An author never tells you everything. If he or she did, reading would be incredibly tedious and meaning making would become nearly impossible.

As an example, we've rewritten the previous two sentences to eliminate ambiguity and ensure your accurate comprehension of our exact point regardless of background knowledge:

> *An author of a book, article, poem, treatise or other example of a written text in English or any other language never tells you—in this case the reader but also people like the reader who might also be reading or be imagined to be reading said text—everything that he or she intends to communicate in that text because if he or she did, reading would become incredibly tedious due to the overwhelming load of marginally relevant information jammed into the sentence in order to clarify every possible misunderstanding or gap in perception, and meaning making would become nearly impossible because every text would read like a dense contract between two corporate entities seeking to eliminate any possible gray area to a transaction.*

Authors by necessity always make assumptions about what readers know and assume they will fill in gaps. This is always true, even when they aren't deliberately leaving blanks and ambiguities for stylistic or artistic reasons. Understanding any text always involves "disambiguating" it.

Here's a very short text, the ambiguities of which make an interesting case study:

> *The wooden box was massive. She placed her bear on the ground. It was going to be hard to carry.*

The ambiguities are probably not even apparent to you at first because you resolved them simply and easily with inferences you didn't know you made. One ambiguity is that her "bear" is not a real bear but a teddy bear. There's no way she'd be carrying a real bear. As a result you probably inferred that "she" was a child. Another ambiguity involves resolving what noun the pronoun "it" refers in the second sentence. Grammatically it's just as plausible for it to refer to the teddy bear as the box. But you knew that it referred to the box. It doesn't make sense for a teddy bear to be hard to carry but a massive wooden box, yes. Especially for a child. You disambiguated because you had knowledge—the weights of common things, that someone with a teddy bear is probably a child—that the author assumed you would have.

But what if the author assumes you know something you don't. Like in this sentence:

For pudding she allowed herself some cake.

If you're a reader in England, where "pudding" means roughly the same thing as "dessert" does to an American, the sentence is easily disambiguated. She ordered cake after dinner. It was a small indulgence. This is implied by the phrase "she allowed herself."

But if you lack that background knowledge, the sentence is nonsensical, even if you are a very good reader.

Your working memory is busy wrestling with what seems like a riddle—for pudding she had cake? How could she have cake for pudding? Does the author mean "instead of pudding" maybe? (If you are English imagine the sentence "For custard she had cake" to get the general sense for how an American might experience the text.) You not only failed to understand the first part, you might not have even noticed or perceived the subtle implications of the word *allowed*, which tells you quite a bit about the "she" in the sentence and the small indulgence of permitting herself a piece of cake that perhaps she wouldn't ordinarily consider: perhaps she is conscious of her weight, perhaps she is conscious of money. When your working memory is overloaded wrestling with something you don't immediately understand, your perceptiveness of other details is also degraded. Meaning is interrupted everywhere. There is no "story" in the sentence for readers who don't have background knowledge about what "pudding" means.

Comprehension, this is to say, is knowledge-based. We make better inferences, we perceive more, we have working memory to think more deeply, when we know more about what the author assumes we know enough about. We can't do those things when we don't have this knowledge.

In a 2020 review of the literature, Reid Smith and colleagues "consistently found that higher levels of background knowledge enable children to better comprehend a text. Readers who have a strong knowledge of a particular topic, both in terms of quantity and quality of knowledge, are more able to comprehend a text than a similarly cohesive text for which they lack background knowledge. This was evident for both skilled and low skilled readers."[35]

"Controlling for other factors, knowledge plays the largest role in comprehension. The more a reader knows about a topic, the more likely they are to successfully comprehend a text about it," literacy specialist Jennifer Walker of Youngstown State writes,[36] summarizing the broader literature on the topic.

In fact, the connection between knowledge and all types of high-order thinking is clear, if often overlooked. "Data from the last 30 years lead to a conclusion that is not scientifically challengeable: thinking well requires knowing facts. . . . The very processes that teachers care about most—critical thinking processes like reasoning and problem solving—are intimately intertwined with factual knowledge that is in long-term memory," Daniel Willingham writes. "Most people believe that thinking processes are akin to those of a calculator. A calculator has a set of procedures available (addition, multiplication, and so on). . . . If you learn a new a new thinking operation "for example how to make inferences, 'it seems like that operation should be applicable to all' such settings. But the human mind does not work that way. . . Critical thinking processes are tied to background knowledge."[37]

Somehow this fact does not seem to be getting through to schools. Perhaps it's the chimerical nature of skills-based instruction. We just can't let go of how beautiful it would be if we could just give students a super skill, a universal key, and the hours we spend chasing that dream is time taken from far more productive tasks.

Again, we don't blame teachers for this. Even at the highest levels of policy, even in schools of education, the misconception prevails.

In his book *Why Knowledge Matters*, E. D. Hirsch tells the story of France, which had among the best and most equitable school systems in Europe before the French replaced their knowledge-rich curriculum with a skills-intensive approach. Results declined steeply overall and gaps between rich and poor students expanded. Scotland followed suit a few years later. It "downgraded the status of knowledge and adopted a competence-based approach, emphasizing the development of transferable skills and interdisciplinary learning," Sonia Sodha wrote in *The Guardian*.[38] The results? Scottish students lost an average of about six months progress in reading on the 2022 Programme for International Student Assessment, which is used to evaluate country's school systems, while inequality increased. The lowest-status group fell twice as fast (a drop of twenty points) as in the highest-status group,[39] Lindsay Paterson, a professor of Education Policy at the University of Edinburgh observed.

You can find a thousand voices on the internet telling us to choose less knowledge and more skills, but even asking what the right balance is between skills and knowledge is the wrong question, education researcher and author Daisy Christodoulou has observed. It is like asking what the right balance is between ingredients and cake. The ingredients become the cake; the knowledge becomes the skill. If you want deeper thinking, if you want better reading, start by building students' knowledge. You can do quite a bit of that if you don't spend hours explaining what an inference is.

Vocabulary Is the Single Most Important Form of Knowledge (But Is Often Taught As If It Were a Skill)

Knowledge of words—both deep and broad—is a particularly important form of background knowledge but it is often taught in ways that do not reflect how it is acquired and used.

Of all the forms of background knowledge, the most important from a reading perspective is vocabulary, and there is a consistent and strong connection between an individual's vocabulary and reading comprehension.[40] Studies typically find strong correlations between the two—between 0.55 and 0.85 according to Anne Cunningham and Keith Stanovich, for example.[41] That is, about half to three-quarters of a student's reading comprehension is explained by knowing the extent of their word knowledge.

Assessing a wide range of causal factors of reading comprehension among ninth graders, Jennifer Cromley and Roger Azevedo found that, "vocabulary and background knowledge made the largest contributions to comprehension."[42] "For any encounter with a given text it is a reader's word knowledge (for as well as meaning) . . . that is crucial to comprehension," write Charles Perfetti and Suzanne Adlof.[43] Some researchers note a tendency toward larger correlations among students with more reading skill and experience,[44] that is, vocabulary may play a growing role in reading comprehension over time and with expertise.

It's worth noting that there's a lot we don't know about the connection between vocabulary and reading and there simply aren't enough good studies (the 2000 National Reading Panel emphasized this point). One common flaw is that studies often successfully establish correlation, but causation is harder to unpack, and it seems likely that what causation exists runs both ways: that better vocabulary leads to better reading comprehension and that better reading comprehension (and certainly doing more reading) leads to stronger vocabulary. Both things are almost assuredly true. This is in many ways a key rationale for the two-part approach to vocabulary (Implicit and Explicit Instruction) that we share in Chapter Five.

Still, studies that look explicitly for causation do appear to show that vocabulary instruction can lead to better comprehension[45] and that students with reading difficulties benefit the most from such instruction (three times as much according to one study)[46].

Another issue is that "vocabulary" is actually a tricky thing to measure. Understanding occurs on a continuum. You can know a little about a word or a lot. A student might have a strong vocabulary as measured by breadth of word knowledge (the number of words they know) or depth of word knowledge (how well they know the words they know). The net seems to be that breadth and depth both matter deeply (and are surely correlated).

The very simple and basic idea that we started with—that vocabulary is a form of knowledge—is important to return to. In fact, we could probably have simply included vocabulary in our broader discussion of background knowledge. After all, our example of the classroom where students reading *Charlotte's Web* didn't understand what Charlotte meant because they didn't know the word *acrobat* was an example of vocabulary creating a barrier to comprehension. But vocabulary is so important and its role so distinctive in reading that we have chosen to discuss it separately, primarily because teachers often think about and teach vocabulary separately from other things they do to build background knowledge in the classroom.

When they do teach vocabulary, we are often struck by how frequently teachers teach it as if it were a skill, assuming, for example, that inferring word meanings from context is something students can master and apply universally. Another chimera! In fact almost every state assessment in the United States tests vocabulary this way—via Context Clues, that is—so teachers are tacitly encouraged to teach that way as well. In contrast to methods in which the purpose of vocabulary instruction is to arrive (and usually guess at) the definition, we argue that a good, student-friendly definition is the starting point, not the end point, of effective vocabulary instruction.

In Chapter Five we discuss the ramifications of this more extensively: starting vocabulary instruction with a definition and then asking students to engage in what Isabel Beck and colleagues call "thought-provoking interactive playful follow up."[47]

We've also broken out vocabulary as its own topic because where and when challenging words are likely to occur is also important. The short answer is: in print. Almost exclusively.

Stanovich and Cunningham analyzed the number of rare words that appeared in various formats of print and speech. When college graduates speak to other adults, they use about seventeen rare words per thousand, for example, and the median word they use—measured for how common or unusual it is—is the 496th most common word in the English language. Prime time television, which we might use as a proxy for broadcast media more broadly, is similar in its characteristics: there are about twenty-three rare words per thousand and the median word is the 490th most common in the English language.

To get a sense for what these numbers mean and why they are important, compare that data to the same measures of the language used in a typical children's book. Though produced for children rather than an adult audience, a children's book is far more sophisticated in its vocabulary, featuring thirty-one rare words per thousand on average with the median word checking in as the 627th most common.

"Children's books have 50% more rare words in them than educated adults use when speaking aloud," Stanovich and Cunningham note.[48] In fact, *even preschool books have a higher median word rank than adult conversation.*

Now consider the data for books written for adults. There readers encounter fifty-three rare words per thousand and the median word is the 1058th most common. In newspapers there are sixty-eight rare words per thousand and the average word is the 1690th most common. For abstracts of scientific articles there are 128 rare words per thousand and the median word is the 4,389th most common in the English language.

Prevalence of Rare Words in Various Spoken & Written Language Sources (adapted from Cunningham & Stanovich 1998)		
	Rank of Median Word	Rare Words per 1000
Printed text: Abstracts of Scientific Articles	4389	128
Printed text: Newspapers	1690	68.3
Printed text: Popular Magazines	1399	65.7
Printed text: Adult books	1058	52.7
Printed text: Children's books	627	30.9
Printed text: Preschool books	578	16.3
Primetime adult television	490	22.7
Adult speech (College graduates to friends/spouses)	496	17.3

A 2022 study by Oxford psychologist Kate Nation and colleagues stuck a similar theme. "Exposure to book language provides opportunities for learning words and syntactic constructions that are only rarely encountered in speech and . . . in turn, this rich experience drives further developments in language and literacy."[49]

What does this tell us? First that exposure to spoken language, even fairly advanced adult conversation, is inadequate to develop students' vocabulary. "Conversation," Stanovich and Cunnigham say, "is not a substitute for reading."

You're probably familiar with the feeling of knowing what a word means but not being confident in your ability to pronounce it correctly in conversation. This is evidence of words you've learned exclusively through reading. For example we are still not 100 percent sure whether *forte* is pronounced "fort" or "fortay" and whether ancillary is "AN-sill-ary" or "an-SILL-ary." But we're not embarrassed by this. The fact that we aren't sure means that we learned those words from reading!

Second, while Explicit Vocabulary Instruction—choosing and teaching words deliberately—is immensely valuable, *most of the words a student learns in their lifetime will be learned via encountering them in their reading.* This means that if we want students to learn new words, it is important that we have them spend a lot of time reading. As they do that, we can help them to learn more words if we use intentional strategies to cause them to notice and learn more from the words they encounter as they read.[50]

This is not to say that spoken language is irrelevant. A 2023 study by Jeanne Wanzek and colleagues showed that when teachers intentionally use advanced vocabulary while teaching, it makes a big difference. "The proportion of academic words used by teachers during the school day significantly predicted students' end-of-year vocabulary. Teachers who used more academic words had students with higher vocabulary achievement at the end of the school year," they note.[51] So how we talk to students also matters. Again, the research suggests to us that we need vocabulary *methods*, not a single method—learning words is something we need to attend to in a variety of settings. But we also need to be thinking about exposure and how to make more attentive exposure to a wider range of words a regular part of our teaching.

Knowing a word, we noted, is multileveled thing, and knowledge of specific words is "learned incrementally and refined over time," as Gene Oulette and Emma Shaw point out.[52] This is important for teachers to recognize because the nuances are what matter in reading.

Imagine you're reading a scene about two students walking home from school and find this sentence:

> On the way home Shauna mimicked Ms. Groves, saying, "I'm really proud of you, Kayla."

Perhaps you know that the word *mimic* means something similar to imitate. In that case, you would get the general gist of the sentence. But if you know that the word *mimic* also suggests imitating in order to ridicule and entertain, then you understand the sentence much better. Shauna *imitating* Ms. Groves could mean a lot of things. Perhaps she is rehashing some happy moment of success that Kayla achieved. But Shauna *mimicking* Ms. Groves is much more charged. A story of resentment and sarcasm starts to take shape. Your depth of reading the passage hinges on your understanding the depth of the word. You cannot inter-pret something you don't notice.

We find examples such as this one especially interesting because one common approach to teaching vocabulary is to introduce a word such as *mimic* and provide a simple synonym for it: *imitate*. And indeed, the two words' meanings overlap to a large degree. If my purpose is a very general understanding of the word *mimic*, providing a synonym may be helpful. But if my goal is to help you use the word *mimic* as a reader, then the differences are just as important. If two words meanings overlap by 80 percent, it is the 20 percent that is different that matters most when I encounter one of them in a text.[53]

Teaching a simple synonym-based definition is unlikely to lead to perceptive reading. As Isabel Beck, Margaret McKeown, and Linda Kucan point out in *Bringing Words to Life*, depth of word knowledge correlates almost as strongly to reading as breadth of knowledge. "Studies have demonstrated that people with more extensive vocabularies not only know more words but also know more about the words they know, and that people with high and lower vocabularies differ as to their depth of knowledge about even fairly common words,"[54] they write. So when we teach words we need to think about both quality and quantity of understanding.

Teaching words is often given short shrift, we think. It's a nice to have in many classrooms rather than a bedrock of learning. And while we think the research tells a clear story, we'll let W. H. Auden have the last word. "Language," he wrote, "is the mother, not the handmaiden of thought."[55] What words you have available to you do not merely reflect what you think, they shape it. You see what you know, and you know what you can name. In many ways it is difficult even to conceptualize something you don't have a word for.

Intentional Writing Development Can Play a Critical and Synergistic Role in Developing Better Readers

Done carefully, writing in response to reading can assist in memory formation and help students develop mastery of the written code that reading relies on. Short exercises that can be easily and quickly revised and that intentionally develop students' control of syntactic forms are especially useful.

Reading and writing are in many ways two sides of the same coin. To write is to produce ideas via the same system of language we use when reading. As students get better at creating and producing with writing—and especially syntax—they also get better at understanding and perceiving the nuances of language and syntax when others use them. You can improve your knowledge of the code by studying it from productive and receptive angles.

But writing might help improve reading even if we used different systems for it and for reading—if we read in Japanese and wrote in English, say—because it fosters memory formation and can slow and deepen thinking.

There are multiple connections between reading and writing, this is to say, so it's not surprising that research indicates that between 50 percent and 70 percent of the variation in reading and writing abilities are shared.[56] That is, if we understand how well a student writes, we can predict half to three-quarters of their reading skill level. And while this connection describes a correlation, not a causation, perhaps the most comprehensive summary of research on writing in literacy classrooms, the Carnegie Corporation of New York's 2010 report *Writing to Read*, provides evidence that whether students write (and more importantly how they write) can directly affect reading outcomes. "The evidence shows that having students write about the material they read does enhance their reading abilities," the study noted, with fifty-seven out of sixty-one studies reviewed yielding positive effects. "Writing about a text proved to be better than just reading it, reading and rereading it, reading and studying it, [or] reading and discussing it," the study added. Further, "the impact of writing about reading applied broadly across different levels of schooling. These positive effects were evident when students wrote about text in science and social studies as well as in English."[57]

Writing summaries of texts was one especially valuable form of writing, the report found. "Transforming a mental summary of text into writing requires additional thought about the essence of the material, and the permanence of writing creates an external record of this synopsis that can be readily critiqued and reworked. For students in grades 3–12, writing summaries about text showed a consistently positive impact on reading comprehension."[58] So writing in response to text and especially summarizing it, can help build memory and understanding. This is particularly true for lower-achieving students: "In twelve studies involving such students, the average weighted effect size for writing about a text was 0.63," the study reports.[59]

Students annotating as they read also demonstrated consistently positive effects across studies. The average weighted effect size of note-taking was 0.47 across twenty-three studies, the report reveals, though it also notes that what "note-taking" meant varied widely across the studies. We share further thoughts on annotation in Chapter Two.

But the strongest findings from the Carnegie report dealt with explicitly teaching students to use syntactic forms to express ideas via an expanding range of structures. The best writing exercises for developing students' reading abilities were often those where students were explicitly instructed in how to use specific writing forms effectively. This is a note Judith Hochman and Natalie Wexler sound repeatedly in their book, *The Writing Revolution*. American teachers assign writing a lot, but they don't teach it, deliberately and intentionally, nearly as much. It's this piece that often delivers the value.

This is because the prior knowledge students need to read successfully includes not only *background knowledge* about the text and its subject matter, not only robust *word knowledge* (that is to say, vocabulary), but also *syntactic knowledge*: an understanding of arrangements and constructions of phrases, clause, and sentences. This form of knowledge is often overlooked and is a frequent barrier to understanding. Students who struggle to read are often undone by complex or unfamiliar syntax—by a compound subject, by a subject a long way from its object, by the subordination of one idea to another.

For example, a student may have experienced only the comparatively narrow range of sentence constructions familiar to contemporary writing, especially that which tends to appear in youth fiction. To such a student the opening line of a book like Jane Austen's *Pride and Prejudice,* which describes not a "universally acknowledged truth" but a "truth universally acknowledged" that a single man "in possession of a good fortune" must "be in want of" (that is, need) a wife, is likely to be as problematic for its advanced syntax as much as or more so than for its advanced vocabulary.

Being able to create increasingly complex sentences with precision and accuracy helps student to master syntax: to have enough knowledge of it to support their reading and enough control of it to empower their writing. These work in synergy. Students who write repetitive and wooden subject-verb-object sentences are the same students who are likely to struggle when asked to read a sentence that, like the one you are reading, uses a variety of unfamiliar and unusual forms such as compound subjects to express the relationship between and among ideas.

Indeed, the Carnegie report gave particular notice to the benefits of writing instruction that involved intentional tools such as sentence combining for developing syntactic control[60] (the ability to use forms of grammar and syntax to create sentences that capture a wide range of complex ideas).

The report found significant evidence—with an average effect size of 0.79, albeit across only four studies—for the benefits of intentional instruction in sentence construction skills. It notes, for example, that "the practice of putting smaller units of writing together to create more complex ones should result in greater skill in understanding such units in reading" and that "teaching patterns for constructing sentences or larger units of text should improve reading skills."[61]

This also jibes with the science of deliberate practice. Just assigning lots of writing won't cause students to expand their ability to use complex forms to capture complex ideas. To be effective, writing instruction has to show students how to use syntax and give them extensive opportunities to employ those tools in a controlled setting, with attention directed to the forms of language teachers want them to master.

A last benefit to writing is worth touching on here. Teachers should always be aware of loads on working memory. When working memory is overloaded people forget what they are thinking about and perceive less in their environment. One way this often shows up in class-rooms is during discussions about books. If students are trying to hold their own thoughts about a story in their minds while their peers are talking, their working memory will likely be overloaded if they also try to listen intently. They will have to choose between listening fully and trying to remember what they were thinking. If we give them the opportunity to jot down their thoughts before a discussion, however, we help them to unburden their working memory and put their thoughts in a place where they can simply and easily review them later as needed.

Books Are the Optimal Text Format Through Which to Build Understanding and Comprehension

Books package information and ideas in a unique form to which our brains are especially receptive. They create arguments of depth and nuance in ways that are critically important to read in a digital society that reinforces "hot takes" and facile opinions arrived at quickly. Moreover books provide the best opportunity to create for students the sort of shared social experience that is critical to their sense of belonging in schools.

We are "unapologetic about the book," by which we mean that we think a good reading program should be built around students reading the best books we can find for them, in their entirety, and most often together as a group.

What's the big deal about books? Why do they matter and what is the science that supports reading them over, say, passages or stories or even YouTube videos (which, as of 2023, the National Council of Teachers of English was shamefully advocating for more of in reading and English classes)?

A phrase from the social theorist Marshall McLuhan's 1975 book *Understanding Media* has proven one of the most enduring and important observations about human communication.

The medium, McLuhan observed, is the message; every means of communication shapes the way we see the world. It is, in the words of Johann Hari, "guiding us to see the world according to a new set of codes."[62]

Part of the implicit message of social media platforms is that, as Hari puts it, "the world can be understood in short simple statements of 280 characters," and "can be interpreted and confidently understood very quickly." [63] All around us we see evidence of this message taking root. A cacophony of hasty and simplistic world views are shouted back and forth.

By contrast, Hari writes, "the medium of the book tells us, that . . . the world is complex and requires steady focus to understand; it needs to be thought about and comprehended slowly."[64] First impressions turn out to be wrong. The truth is complex and nuanced. Nothing instills an idea of the world as a complex place demanding deep understanding like a book does because a book is almost always an extended narration on this idea. A book always involves a change in thinking about the world. If there is a hope for our increasingly fractious society, it lies in part in students learning that lesson.

We also learn especially well from stories. Cognitive psychologists often describe them as "psychologically" or "cognitively privileged." Researchers find that people remember ideas and insights better when they encounter them in a story. We remember the facts because they are connected to a story and the more memorable and compelling the story—the deeper our relationship to it—and the more context we have to understand it, the better. This is one unique power of books.

Stories also improve people's capacity for empathy, their ability and desire to understand what other people think and feel, and the longer and deeper the story the greater the benefits. When you build a relationship with a narrator and care about him or her, you are primed to build memory and understanding.

This is the power of historical fiction in particular. We remember the facts because we are connected to the story. If background knowledge is critical to comprehension, books are a powerful place to get it, and to get it in the sustained, connected webs of understanding (called *schema*) that most aid us in comprehension.

Finally, books are the format in which the important ideas of society have been transmitted for centuries. The world is full of allusions and references to ideas contained in books, so it is a gift to students whom we want to be full participants in society to let them be party to the shared knowledge they contain.

But books can be hard. They are often old, written in the parlance of a bygone era. They are often complex, occasionally even resisting the efforts of readers to make easy meaning of them.

This is beneficial. Students should learn to be comfortable struggling. The only way to sustain access to the ideas encoded in the history of books is to struggle with archaic syntax, say, and to read it two and three times until its style becomes more accessible. If students never read text that is more than, say, fifty or a one hundred years old, the writing of the past will increasingly slip further and further away from them. Do we want a society where students lack the familiarity with outdated writing and the mindset to persist at the challenges it presents? Our next and final principle of reading instruction will discuss how complex text is the gatekeeper to future success and books are the best source of many of the forms of complexity students require exposure to and experience with. Decisions in society are especially likely to be entrusted to those who can access its most complex texts. We can't imagine it will be a good thing when only a small number of experts can read directly from *Origin of Species* or the Constitution of the United States.

How does this pro-book vision contrast to what English and reading classes are based on today? What are schools doing if not reading books? Why does one even need to make the case for the book?

There are several alternative models to book-based literacy instruction prevalent in K–12 classrooms today. One is what we might call "passage-based" reading instruction. In this model, which often goes hand in hand with the belief that reading is made up of transferrable skills, reading consists of a series of short passages, a different one every few days, with the passages chosen and organized based on the "skills" they enable teachers to instill. So, if we're working on being able to explain the main idea, we'll read an "interesting" passage about cooking empanadas and tomorrow we might read one about the American Revolution. The unifying theme is that the teacher is asking students to find the main idea in each of these passages.

In some versions of this model, the class might read a novel like Lois Lowry's *The Giver*, but mostly as a device to present main idea questions to students, rather than to reflect on humanity, free will, and society. The book is passage-ized. And nothing kills a book faster than making it a tool for strategies practice, and nothing is less likely to help students become effective readers.

Another alternative is the "choice-based" model. In these classrooms students do read books but each student chooses and reads their own book on the premise that students will be more motivated if they choose what they like. Beyond the fact that this presumption is questionable (a student who has read a handful of books is unlikely to choose something great, something that changes her world view, something that causes her to see the world differently, whereas an well-read adult is well positioned to do so), a key part of the experience of a book is lost when it isn't shared. We benefit from discussions in which we hear different interpretations and reactions and come to change our point of view, and we benefit from being connected through sharing the experiences and emotions a book provides and elicits.

We want to be clear in expressing these reservations about "choice" as a tool to promote reading. We are not talking about limiting students' choice in their independent reading. We are all for encouraging and assigning independent reading beyond what happens in class, and we're all for students choosing what interests them. But in class, in the reading that makes up the core of our curriculum, we think the benefits, in terms of shared experience and motivation to read, are strongly on the side of shared books chosen and curated carefully by teachers. In part this is because, in an era when social media disconnects and isolates young people, books can connect them through a shared experience of reading together, and in part because we think experiencing the best books through the eyes of a teacher who can bring them to life most likely will help students to develop as readers, most likely will expand their conception of what books can be, and most likely will motivate students to become more consistent readers.

Given that precious few kids are reading books at all—on their own and in the classrooms—it is ironic that there's so much *sturm und drang* about book choice and book restriction. Even college professors report difficulty in getting students to read books when they are assigned. What if this sad state of affairs is not the cause, but the result, of how much a love of reading has been driven out of our K–12 classrooms, where we've failed to light students' minds on fire and maximize their learning by giving them interesting and important books to read?

For these reasons we are "unapologetic about the book": we believe that even—perhaps especially—in a digital age, books create a critical experience that can be created through no other means. Ensuring that students read books—excellent books, whole books, together in groups, often aloud to maximize the sense of connection they create—will maximize the chances that they become better readers, more knowledgeable students, and that they come to love and value reading.

The Ability to Read Complex Text Is the Gatekeeper to Long-Term Success

Asking students to read only texts that are readily accessible to them can seem sensible and supportive in the short run, but in the long run students must learn to read challenging texts and become comfortable struggling to make meaning.

A 2006 study by the makers of the ACT, one of the two major college admissions tests in the United States, provided a series of crucial insights into the skills and experience of students who'd taken the test. The report revealed that only about half of ACT test takers were prepared for college based on their reading skills. Worse, they found that the number of students who were on track to be "college ready" appeared to diminish between the eighth and twelfth grades. Something was happening—or NOT happening—in high school that caused thousands of students to slide out of the zone of likely success.

The analysis studied the results of more than a million ACT test takers. Researchers first determined what ACT score predicted college success. A 21 on the Reading portion of the ACT indicated "the level of achievement required for students to have a high probability of success . . . in such college courses as Psychology and U.S. History," with probable success defined as "a 75 percent chance or better of earning a course grade of C or better [and] a 50 percent chance of earning a B or better."[65]

Researchers called this the "college-ready benchmark." Achieve a score of 21 and your chances of persisting and succeeding in college were strong. Fail to meet that score and the chances that you would struggle to stay in school or in the major you chose were higher. "Poor readers struggle to learn in text-heavy courses and are frequently blocked from taking . . . more challenging courses," the study's authors reported. They meant extra, remedial courses that did not provide graduation credits. Poor reading skills were a financial tax on marginal students, extending their time in college and increasing the amount of fees and loans required.

So what was the key to scoring a 21? The test makers ran a series of analyses. First they tried to discern whether the ability to get beyond literal questions and to think inferentially was the problem. Here's the difference in the number of literal and inferential questions test takers typically got correct for each score on the ACT:

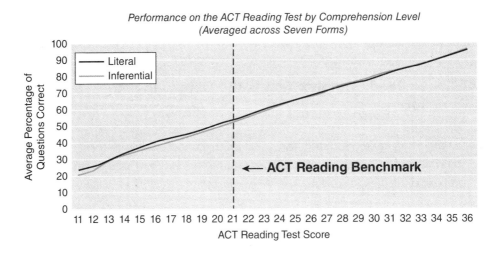

Performance on the ACT Reading Test by Comprehension Level
(Averaged across Seven Forms)

As you can see, there is almost no difference between how test takers of any level perform on literal versus inferential questions. If you were a strong reader or a poor reader you essentially did exactly the same on both types of question. Inferential questions were no more of a challenge to weak readers than literal questions.

When the test makers disaggregated scores by question type—that is by the "skill" they were assessing—they again found little differentiation. There's not much difference in how a typical test taker, strong or weak, does on a main idea question as compared to a question about supporting details.

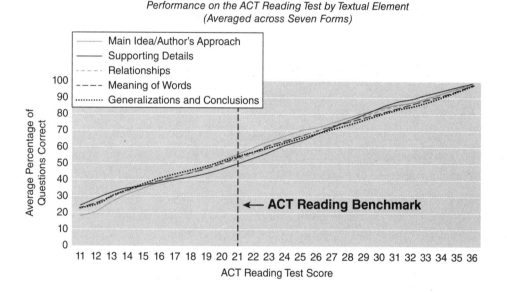

Performance on the ACT Reading Test by Textual Element
(Averaged across Seven Forms)

"Given these steadily increasing linear relationships between ACT Reading Test score and reading proficiency, there is no clear differentiator here between those students who are ready for college-level reading and those who are not," the study observes.

We take particular interest in this analysis since it provides additional support for the idea that these sorts of transferable skills are in fact discrete competencies. If these five different types of questions really represented different "skills" everyone would not likely be equally competent at all of them. But we don't see any differentiation in how students scored on them at any different level of proficiency, suggesting that perhaps they aren't discrete skills after all.

The next analysis the test makers ran, in which they disaggregated performance by the difficulty of the text in the passage, was far more revealing, however. Here's the data:

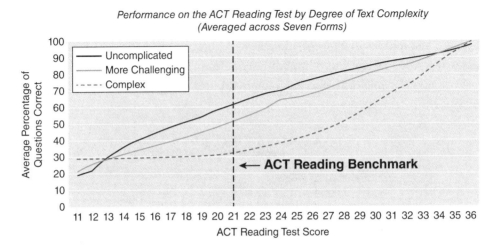

As you can see, when questions were assessed by the difficulty of the text in the passage, dramatic differences in test-taker performance emerged. Students who were at risk of not reaching the benchmark were especially likely to struggle when asked to read complex text. In fact, with an average of 30 percent correct, these students tended to perform little better than if they had been guessing, given that the test is multiple choice. They were stumped when passages did not yield meaning easily. Weaker students could not read fluently, perhaps. Or they could not unlock the syntax. Or maybe they weren't familiar with the experience of struggle with resistant text.

In the words of the test makers, "performance on complex texts is the clearest differentiator in reading between students who are likely to be ready for college and those who are not." The ability to read difficult text, out of your comfort zone, was the gatekeeper. What's more, the test makers noted, "This is true for both genders, all racial/ethnic groups, and all annual family income levels."[66]

This might offer one explanation why students were dropping out of the "prepared for college" zone as they went through high school. They were not exposed to difficult text, did not learn to grapple with text that resisted easy meaning-making, and were not able to track complex syntax and vocabulary. It is very, very hard to be prepared for college and advance knowledge work unless you can do those things.

That said, the idea of textual complexity lacks a consistent definition. Sentence length could be a factor (longer sentences might place more demands on attention and working memory), complex or unusual syntax might be a factor, so might vocabulary. But no one knows for sure. As Tim Shanahan notes, "while shorter sentences tend to be easier to comprehend than long sentences, there are many exceptions to this correlation. If sentences are shortened to omit explicitly stated causal connections, for instance, the brevity tends to reduce understanding more than it facilitates it."[67]

Commonly used measures of complexity are also unreliable. You might expect a measure like Lexiles to be helpful in identifying difficult text but there are also quite evident gaps in using it—or any algorithm—as the primary arbiter of complexity. William Golding's *Lord of the Flies* and S. E. Hinton's young adult novel *The Outsiders* both score about the same in difficulty according to the Lexile framework, but as we discussed in *Reading Reconsidered*, there is no comparison between the texts in terms of difficulty. *Lord of the Flies*, full of complex archaic syntax, complex symbolism, and allusions to mid-twentieth-century British culture is incomparably more difficult. We have never met a teacher who knows both books and did not agree with this assessment.

That said, despite the difficulties of measuring complex text, we think research suggests it is a critical factor for teachers to be alert to.

"The type of text to which students are exposed . . . has a significant impact on their readiness for college-level reading. Specifically, students need to be able to read complex texts if they are to be ready for college," the authors of the ACT study write. "In a nation where 13- and 17-year-olds have increasingly less exposure to or interaction with books outside of the classroom . . . schools must still play the primary role in providing students with the kinds of complex reading materials and experiences they need in order to be college and work ready." [68]

Interestingly, the importance of text complexity also emphasizes the critical role of background knowledge in teaching reading. Researchers use the term *coherence* to describe "the extent to which the text provides information and clues to help the reader relate information across different parts of the text." A low-coherence text tends to be more complex because, as Reid Smith and colleagues note in their literature review, "a reader facing a low-coherence text needs to rely more heavily upon their background knowledge to help fill the coherence gaps by making inferences."[69] The most challenging texts, the gatekeepers to the next steps in a student's journey, are the most reliant on background knowledge. In Chapter 8, we discuss how close reading can help students master complexity with confidence.

"THE SINGLE MOST IMPORTANT THING FOR TEACHERS TO KNOW"

The seven arguments we've described in this chapter each align to a chapter in the book. In Chapter Two we discuss attention and how to rebuild it. In Chapter Three we discuss the ways to read in the classroom—aloud by the teacher, aloud by students, silently by students—and how to use the different ways of reading to build fluency among other goals. In Chapter Four we discuss how to organize lessons around knowledge instead of transferrable skills. Chapter Five takes on the topic of vocabulary—a critical topic for teachers in every discipline, we note. Chapter Six discusses writing, including the ways writing can be used to increase reading comprehension for students. Chapter Seven is a deeper discussion of books, including more about why, which ones, and how to choose them. Chapter Eight is about Close Reading, which is the strategic use of rereading and other techniques we describe in this book to help students confidently unlock complex text.

But there is one more body of research that is critical for teachers to understand and that is referenced in almost every chapter—including this one. That topic is cognitive load theory: the science of how working memory, long-term memory, and perception interact in the mind of the learner. Dylan Wiliam has called it "the single most important thing for teachers to know."[70] Its implications are far-reaching and help teachers understand almost every aspect of what students do when they learn generally and learn to read specifically. So while cognitive load theory doesn't get its own chapter, that's only because its relevance is everywhere. And because that everywhere includes the chapters of this book, we propose to summarize it with the other research we've discussed.

Understanding cognitive load theory starts with understanding the idea of working memory. "Working memory is . . . the mental space where we place information we are thinking about, whether it comes from the environment, our memories and knowledge or both at the same time," writes Héctor Ruiz Martín.[71] When we are intentionally trying to remember something that we have just heard, like a phone number, say, we must hold it in our working memory to be able to then use it to dial someone. But we don't just hold information in working memory. We think about it, and our working memory gives us the capacity to manipulate and analyze ideas we hold there to develop understandings about them to a degree that has no comparison in any species the planet. High-order thinking, logical analysis, all of the key cognitive abilities that make humans unique are in large part products of working memory.[72]

A decent synonym for working memory is *conscious thinking*: if you are aware that you are thinking, you are almost assuredly using working memory.

Working memory is powerful in helping us to understand complex phenomena but the understanding it helps us achieve is not learning. Only when ideas are transferred from our working memory into long-term memory can we be said to have learned, Paul Kirschner, John Sweller, and Richard Clark point out. They define learning as "a change in long-term memory" and add that "The aim of all instruction is to alter long-term memory. If nothing has changed in long term memory, nothing has been learned."[73]

This is a profoundly important observation with important implications. First, it means that when we see understanding and insight among students in the classroom, what we see is not yet learning. It may be forgotten. In fact most of what we think about in our working memory is forgotten and therefore not learned.[74] If the phone number you are trying to remember is really important, you will probably start repeating it to yourself. This is because you recognize a key flaw in your own working memory: it is fragile. It's so easy to forget what you're holding there if you don't concentrate on it. Maybe some friends are talking in the background as you try to remember that phone number and this makes the prospect of remembering it doubly tenuous. You can feel their incessant talking disrupting your ability to remember the number. Another challenge: working memory is tiny. Phone numbers around the world are seven digits maximum because people cannot generally hold more than that much information in working memory. If you begin to pay attention to what your friends are saying—a difficult thing not to do—your working memory, already at the limits of what it can hold in trying to remember the digits be overloaded. You will forget the number. Possibly you will start to get anxious. Maybe you will bark at your friends: *stop talking I need to remember this number*. Hopefully they understand that working memory overloads are stressful and will forgive you.

You might think, given all the things we try to remember, that we'd have evolved over time to remember more of what's in our working memory but in many ways its fragility is a design feature not a glitch. You use your working memory for thousands of things every day that you don't wish to remember: you are reading the menu at a restaurant and have to hold in your working memory the descriptions of two things you might wish to order. As you hold on to the descriptions of them you must compare them—which sounds better? Healthier? Which are you less likely to spill on your shirt and cause your dining companion to be unimpressed? You have no wish to remember your deliberation and decision about the pasta puttanesca in the future. For this reason, your brain is designed to dump most of what you hold in your working memory.

So far cognitive load theory has told us some really useful things. The part of your brain that thinks consciously about ideas and generates understandings is powerful but small. When what you're trying to use it for is more complex than strings of numbers, you can really think about one or two things at a time. If you overload it and try to do more than that, you will almost assuredly forget, which is to say, fail to learn because learning is a change in long-term memory. And the process of overloading your working memory will likely be unpleasant.

But working memory has more functions than just conscious thinking. It is also the primary means by which we encode things in long-term memory. This might sound like a contradiction. We forget most of what we use working memory to think about but working memory is the tool of remembering? Strangely, yes.

One of the saddest things about being a human being is that we cannot control our own memories. We cannot simply decide to learn something, no matter how important. A study by T. S. Hyde and J. J. Jenkins established this in 1973. Participants' intention to remember information had very little effect on their ability to do so.[75]

We cannot simply decide to remember something, but interestingly, the way we use our working memory to think about it can change the odds of remembering it. The basic rule is that desirable difficulty causes learning. The term *desirable difficulty* comes from UCLA cognitive psychologist Robert Bjork.[76] Working hard to think about a learning object causes us to remember it better, Bjork proposed.

Summarizing this idea, Daniel Willingham writes, "Memory is the residue of thought."[77] If we can get students to think hard about an idea[78] we maximize their odds of encoding it in memory, with encoding being the first of two steps necessary to remembering something. (We'll come to the other, retrieval, in a moment.) Let's say a teacher asks students to make a poster about a book they've read in class. Is this a good learning activity? Willingham suggests asking about the task: "Does it demand deep understanding or is it possible to complete it with just a surface knowledge of the material?" The important question will be: how much does the assignment cause students to spend time thinking hard about the book—its meaning, its language, the historical context—and how much does it cause them to think about the construction of a poster: cutting out images to paste to the poster, writing headlines in large letters, and so on. Making a poster may be engaging—that is, students may enjoy doing it—but it does not necessarily cause students to think hard about the book. Some parts of the task will allocate time to things that don't result in learning.

Héctor Ruiz Martín summarizes this idea: "The more deeply we process information in terms of meaning, the more firmly it is [likely to be] rooted in our memory." But, crucially, he adds, "Thinking about something in terms of its meaning involves associating new information to our prior knowledge … . The more relationships we establish with our prior knowledge while reflecting on the learning object, the more solid its assimilation will be." In other words, a key part of desirable difficulty is building connections between the learning object and what the learner already knows. The more such connections are built, the better.

Learning, Ruiz Martín says, requires "a connection between prior knowledge and new information fostered by the effort to make it meaningful."[79] This also provides an explanation for much of the research we have cited on the importance of background knowledge to reading. Without relevant concepts to connect new information to, learning is difficult.

Learning is likely to happen when we focus students' attention on the learning task—getting something into working memory requires attending to it, then thinking about its meaning and connecting it to other knowledge that we have previously learned.

Let us add one more concept to this understanding of how learning happens: the *generation effect* is the principle that there is a "memory benefit for self-generated compared with read or experimenter-provided information."[80] There is a significant advantage in terms of memory when students "generate" some version of the content they are learning.[81] When students describe a phenomenon or idea in writing or when they explain it briefly to a peer it helps them to remember it. Students who sit silently in class, are not as likely to remember and learn as are students who are caused by teacher's actions to actively engage in the content they are learning—by summarizing it or rephrasing it or explaining it or making a connection to it—either verbally or in writing. This is true regardless of their motivation. "High internal behavioral engagement did not guarantee student achievement if the engagement was not accompanied by talk," K. Sedova and M. Sedlacek concluded in a recent study of Czech students.[82] Very few people have the self-discipline to self-generate a version of what they are learning without an environment that causes it to happen. Further, by beginning the process of encoding, self-generation also probably unburdens working memory, which makes students more receptive to more new information.

This process of self-generation should be guided and directed by the teacher, by the way. In the majority of cases, the expert should shape the question that students use to reflect. "The best results are obtained when the teacher guides . . . the experiences and directs the reasoning and reflection of the students," writes Ruiz Martín.[83]

One other note about working memory is important to address here: its role in perception. We process the world around us first with our senses and then usually with our working memory. This means that if working memory is overloaded, perception will likely be degraded. New York State, where the three of us live, has a law restricting drivers from holding cellphones to make calls while driving. On some levels this is a very good law. When you are talking on the phone you are far more likely to have an accident because when you are using your working memory to hold a conversation, your perception is degraded. You are less likely to notice a vehicle in your blind spot or the sharpness of a curve in the road.

But a hands-free cellphone law is only partially effective. Holding your phone isn't the biggest problem. You can drive perfectly well with a cup of coffee in your hand. What you need to be a safe driver is free working memory. Having a conversation hands-free is still a risk.

As we discussed previously, this explains why dysfluency is so problematic. When you can't read at the speed of sight, the process places a heavy load on working memory. Making sense of what is written becomes more difficult and students fail to perceive things about the text that might otherwise be obvious to them. Reading, this reminds us, is fundamentally an act of perception.

This is also why we will refer multiple times in this book to the transient information effect. "The transient information effect occurs when explanatory information disappears before it can be adequately processed and leads to inferior learning than more permanent sources of information," write Singh and colleagues.[84] If we can't look at what we are trying to think about, we have to use a great deal of our scarce working memory capacity simply trying to remember it and hold that recollection in our heads. If, however, the subject of our analysis is placed where we can see it and constantly review it, thereby refreshing it in our working memory, we don't have to spend scarce cognitive resources trying to remember the thing we're talking about. We have more working memory to analyze, perceive, and learn. When we are talking about especially demanding tasks like Close Reading sections of complex text, whether the passage under study remains easily in view of learners is a big deal.

Previously we noted that encoding—transferring ideas from working memory to long-term memory—was the first of the two-step process of learning something. Let us conclude our discussion of cognitive load theory with a brief discussion of the second step: retrieval.

Once something is encoded in our long-term memory we can potentially recall it with no load on working memory. This is an incredibly important observation because it means we can instantly connect something we perceive to a great deal of information and make sense of it quickly. We can read a line by a narrator and recognize that it alludes to the fence-painting scene in Tom Sawyer, that it sounds like Toni Morrison's writing, or that its tone is ironic. If a student said those things in our classroom we might perceive them to be examples of outstanding critical thinking but in fact they are really linkages between perception and knowledge in long-term memory. "Much of the time, when we see someone apparently engaged in logical thinking," Willingham writes, "they are actually engaged in memory retrieval."[85]

This also tells us that using concepts or information we have learned requires both encoding in and retrieval from long-term memory, and these are separate processes. Students are best able to use knowledge when both encoding and retrieval strength are strong. We've talked a bit about what causes strong encoding—the more connections to other knowledge in long-term memory the better—but not about what causes strong retrieval. The answer there is Retrieval Practice: the process of recalling previously encoded information back into working memory after a period of forgetting.

There is vast research on the science of retrieval so we will give it only the briefest gloss here. To be able to use information to assist in thinking, research suggests that students need to encounter it multiple times with the retrieval spaced over intervals of increasing duration.[86] As we discuss in Chapter Four, designing knowledge-rich reading environments involves planning for and implementing Retrieval Practice: with vocabulary, with story elements—reading a book is a lot to remember—and, via knowledge organizers, with key background knowledge.

The speed with which we can use knowledge once it is deeply encoded in our long-term memory is nothing short of remarkable. In a flash an expert—someone with broad knowledge of a topic deeply encoded—can see a stimulus and understand its meaning with something like prescience. A quarterback in the NFL is a good example. In the blink of an eye a successful quarterback can glance at the defense and—under intense pressure—predict their actions and the decisions that will yield success. If he can't do this, he's not going to be a quarterback for long.

One of our favorite examples of this was provided by Dallas Cowboys quarterback turned television analyst Tony Romo. During the 2019 AFC Championship game between the New England Patriots and the Kansas City Chiefs, Romo was describing the action on a critical fourth and one for the Patriots. As the Patriots were settling into their formation Romo breathlessly announced, "They're killing it! This [the formation the Patriots were in] usually means 'motion' and run outside to the right!" Seconds later the Patriots sent a player in motion and ran right for a touchdown.

But there is a downside to this remarkable capacity for insight. The curse of knowledge (sometimes called the curse of expertise) is the idea that once you are an expert, what you understand comes so quickly and seems so effortless that it can be very difficult to recognize the degree to which a novice won't understand or perceive all—or any—of the things that seem quite plainly intuitive to you.

A teacher of course is an expert—or at least far more expert than her students. Which means that it will be difficult for her to recognize what they won't understand. She will read a passage in the book and it will be "obviously" ironic to her. Not only is there a good chance that that irony will not register with her students, but the recognition may come so Tony-Romo-fast to her that it will be difficult for her even to be aware of their confusion. She may assume they see what she sees. She may assume they understand when they don't. For obvious reasons then a teacher must always strive to be aware of the curse of knowledge.

BUT WILL STUDENTS DISLIKE IT?

We promised previously to respond to the concern that teaching in accordance with the research we've described here will be less engaging and joyful, and that building lessons using background knowledge and complex texts, say, will create stultifying Gradgrindian classrooms and demotivated students.

Ironically, we think the opposite is true. We're confident of it in fact. And we think the research supports us.

Curiosity, for example, is helpful for both motivation and memory. Héctor Ruiz Martín notes that in one study, students recalled 30 percent more information when their curiosity was engaged during the initial learning process. But, Ruiz Martín notes, curiosity is also connected to knowledge. "The more prior knowledge we have about something, the easier it is to learn about related things," he writes. "Learning occurs by making connections between prior knowledge and new information. Hence, the more knowledge we have about something, the more connections we can make."[87] In the aggregate you are more likely to feel curiosity when you know more about a topic because you see more interesting connections. Of course, you probably can think of times when something new sparked your interest, but more often something you can connect to other things you know about is most likely to engage your interest.

This is fascinating because somehow thousands of educators have been convinced that the opposite is true: that studying facts will dampen curiosity and cause students to find a topic boring. We're not sure how so many came to believe that knowing more about something would diminish our interest in it but the argument is unscientific.

Carl Hendrick and Paul Kirschner remind us that one of the most reliable sources of motivation is success. "What we know from research is this: there's neither a causal relationship nor a reciprocal relationship between motivation and learning. It is learning that leads to motivation. Achievement is far more likely to result in motivation than motivation is likely to lead to achievement. We have the causation backwards."[88]

In part this is because, Héctor Ruiz Martín writes, "when a student faces a learning task, they immediately make judgments about their own ability to complete it successfully. If their perception is that they will not be able to do it, their motivation will plummet."[89] In other words, teaching students in a way that causes them to succeed causes them to be more likely to want to persist in learning. This is why ensuring *successful struggle* (not always but often) is important to creating desirable difficulty.

Video game makers understand this. In fact they call it the *Nintendo effect*. They design games so that players are constantly leveling up, forever seeing clear evidence of their own progress. This ensures their continued motivation to play.

Being taught in a way that causes you to learn more successfully, that causes you to be aware that you are making progress, and increases the intrinsic reward you derive from learning things creates the motivation to learn. Being taught well and seeing the results are the best motivators.

With that in mind we present Christine Torres, fifth-grade English teacher at Springfield Prep Charter School in Springfield, Massachusetts.

The video, *Christine Torres: Brave*, was shot during a lesson on Lois Lowry's novel, *Number the Stars* and shows segments from several elements within the lesson vocabulary, a bit of shared reading, and then a short discussion.

To watch the video *Christine Torres: Brave*, use this QR code or find the video at the URL https://vimeo.com/1058239056/f834f3b677.

Let's start with the vocabulary portion. You don't have to watch much to find yourself struck by the profound level of engagement and enthusiasm of the students in Christine's class. At every question their hands shoot into the air. When there are Turn and Talks to discuss applications of the word *implore* the room explodes to life. Perhaps you suspect we did something to manipulate the setting—promised them all ice cream if they behaved like model students. But honestly, we just rolled up, stood in the back with a camera, and pressed record.

Which is ironic because many teachers dread teaching vocabulary, finding it to be a low-energy activity. They think students don't like it. The evidence certainly appears to point that way. Does anyone know what the word *implore* means, a typical teacher might ask? Can you guess from the context? But when we teach vocabulary that way we make the kind of response we're seeing from Christine's students all but impossible. Half the class has never heard the word *implore* so they have no grounds to guess. It's the same three or four students over and over and often their guesses aren't that good. So the teacher is presented with the choice of accepting a B− definition or, after a period of desultory guessing, telling students what she wished they'd said. Now they might be wondering why they bothered.

Which is why what Christine does is so fascinating. She starts by giving students the definition of the word. Once they've repeated the word and reread the definition and an example, she asks them a series of interesting and playful questions in which they are not guessing at knowledge they don't have but applying knowledge she's given them. And as they do so successfully, their motivation and curiosity build. We discuss Christine's approach to vocabulary more in Chapter Five, but for now be aware that the explosion of student interest in vocabulary is a response to teaching in alignment with cognitive science. Knowledge, when put to use, is not so boring after all.

The success of the discussion in the second section of the video is also striking. Students' comments are heartfelt and serious. They are all-in for their analysis of Kirsti's bravery. They do not want the conversation to end when Christine cuts it off. It legitimately looks like she'll have takers when she says they can discuss it later with her during down time—maybe recess!? When she tells them at the end of the clip that those who are done early can steal a few minutes to read ahead, one student in the back, pictured here, actually dabs.

In part this engagement is influenced by vocabulary. A few days prior Christine taught students the word *naive*. Can you tell? Of course you can. It's central to their discussion of Kirsti's actions. So is their definition of *bravery*, which comes from a short nonfiction text they read as a Do Now, and which discussed at length what bravery is and how people had thought about it historically. Knowledge again increases engagement and curiosity.

But their motivation to discuss Kirsti is about more than knowledge. It's about connection and relationship—to the book—and empathy. You can't have a discussion like this if students don't care deeply about the characters. In part this is a result of reading books instead of short text passages and excerpts. When you read a book, you build a relationship to its ideas and characters. Some of the moments students reference in their enthusiastic and heartfelt discussion are scenes they read aloud together. Christine and her class brought them to life through shared oral reading—another thing we are told students don't like.

Those scenes are vivid and real to them in part because they experienced them together and in part because, as we discuss in Chapter Seven, stories themselves are psychologically or cognitively privileged. We have evolved to learn well from them and develop empathy for characters in them.

You will see this level of engagement and enthusiasm in many of the clips that we share with you in this book. Like Christine's, we think they will often inspire you and sometimes surprise you. And we think they will help us to describe practical ways to bring the research to life in classrooms that are both joyful and rigorous. We think this will result in students who are not just better readers but wiser, more engaged, and more motivated, both in classrooms and in their lives beyond it.

Notes

1. Not just our own, either. We have a team of curriculum developers who are all experienced teachers and who we think are brilliant, and we've worked with hundreds of teachers in schools in several countries developing and designing our materials.
2. https://carlhendrick.com/2017/05/06/five-things-i-wish-i-knew-when-i-started-teaching/comment-page-1/.
3. Quotation is from Carl Hendrick (https://carlhendrick.com/2017/05/06/five-things-i-wish-i-knew-when-i-started-teaching/comment-page-1/) glossing Fréréric Guay, Herbert Marsh, and Michel Bolvin's 2003 paper on the bidirectionality of academic self-concept and achievement, https://psycnet.apa.org/record/2003-01605-011.
4. Maryanne Wolf, *Reader Come Home: The Reading Brain in a Digital World* (Harper Collins, 2018), 23.
5. Courtney Stevens and Daphne Bavelier, "The Role of Selective Attention on Academic Foundations: A Cognitive Neuroscience Perspective," *Developmental Cognitive Neuroscience* 2 (2011): S30–S48.
6. https://files.eric.ed.gov/fulltext/EJ1134476.pdf.
7. Stevens and Bavelier, "The Role of Selective Attention on Academic Foundations."
8. This is a hotly debated topic among evolutionary biologists! Much of the answer probably depends on how you define speaking, but even if it were half the range we cite, the point—that we have had time to evolve our brains to speaking—would still hold. If

you're interested in the evolution of speech, Steven Mithen is a good place to start, and his appearance on the podcast *History Unplugged* on June 27, 2024 is engaging listening.

9. *Reader Come Home*, 18.

10. https://www.theguardian.com/commentisfree/2020/aug/24/deep-literacy-technology-child-development-reading-skills.

11. Ibid.

12. Héctor Ruiz Martín notes that the physical act of "reading is procedural knowledge, and as such, it is impossible to avoid doing it when we see words" (*How Do We Learn? A Scientific Approach to Learning and Teaching* [Jossey-Bass, 2024], 32).

13. J. Buck and J. Torgesen, *The Relationship Between Performance on a Measure of Oral Reading Fluency and Performance on the Florida Comprehensive Assessment Test* (FCRR Technical Report 1) (Florida Center for Reading Research, 2003).

14. https://eric.ed.gov/?id=ED587807.

15. R. Kuhn, P. J. Schwanenflugel, E. B. Meisinger, B. A. Levy, and T. V. Rasinski, eds., "Aligning Theory and Assessment of Reading Fluency: Automaticity, Prosody, and Definitions of Fluency," *Reading Research Quarterly* 45, no. 2 (2010): 230–51. https://doi.org/10.1598/RRQ.45.2.4.

16. David D. Paige, "Engaging Struggling Adolescent Readers Through Situational Interest: A Model Proposing the Relationships Among Extrinsic Motivation, Oral Reading Fluency, Comprehension, and Academic Achievement," *Reading Psychology* 32, no. 5 (2011): 395–425.

17. https://psycnet.apa.org/record/2018-39179-001.

18. https://digitalcommons.usu.edu/cgi/viewcontent.cgi?article=6744&context=etd.

19. Fifty-three percent was attributable to the different but less frequently assessed skill of silent reading fluency.

20. https://files.eric.ed.gov/fulltext/ED495465.pdf.

21. Elsewhere, Paige and colleagues write: "We argue that fluency be made an integral part of reading instruction for secondary students struggling in reading." See David D. Paige, Timothy V. Rasinski, and Theresa Magpuri-Lavell, "Is Fluent, Expressive Reading Important for High School Readers?" *Reading Psychology* 32, no. 5 (2011): 395–425.

22. https://eric.ed.gov/?id=EJ571299.

23. Interview with David Paige by the authors, December 11, 2023.

24. https://nces.ed.gov/pubs95/web/95762.asp.

25. We'd argue that all subjects are literacy-based! We also note here that English is more orthographically complex than Italian. This is to say it's less predictable and consistent

in spellings and sounds. It's harder to read fluently and so we might conjecture that the study's findings would be even more strongly manifested among subjects reading in English (L. Bigozzi, C. Tarchi, L. Vagnoli, E. Valente, and G. Pinto, "Reading Fluency as a Predictor of School Outcomes Across Grades 4–9," *Frontiers in Psychology* 8 [2017]: Article 200).

26. https://pubmed.ncbi.nlm.nih.gov/28261134/.

27. https://www.scirp.org/journal/paperinformation?paperid=60253.

28. Interview with the authors, December 11, 2023.

29. https://www.ascd.org/el/articles/beyond-comprehension.

30. Increasing instructional time to more than a bare minimum of a few minutes, this is to say. In other words, everything you need to know about what an inference is can be taught in less than a single lesson. Beyond that, you are wasting your time.

31. https://ascd.org/el/articles/beyond-comprehension.

32. https://fordhaminstitute.org/national/commentary/dylan-wiliams-guide-clear-education-thinking.

33. https://psycnet.apa.org/record/1988-24805-001. Also described here: https://www.coreknowledge.org/blog/baseball-experiment-two-wisconsin-researchers-discovered-comprehension-gap-knowledge-gap/.

34. Discussed on the *Melissa and Lori Love Literacy* podcast, episode 139, January 13, 2023, and partially transcribed on Doug's blog here: https://teachlikeachampion.org/blog/a-slightly-annotated-willingham-on-science-of-reading/.

35. https://www.tandfonline.com/doi/full/10.1080/02702711.2021.1888348.

36. https://education.ohio.gov/getattachment/Topics/Learning-in-Ohio/Literacy/Literacy-Academy/2023-Literacy-Academy/Language-Comprehension-Components-Necessary-for-Reading-Comprehension.pdf.aspx?lang=en-US. Walker refers to J. G. Cromley and R. Azevedo, "Testing and Refining the Direct and Inferential Mediation Model of Reading Comprehension," *Journal of Educational Psychology* 99, no. 2 (2007): 311–325. https://doi.org/10.1037/0022-0663.99.2.311; Y. Ozuru, K. Dempsey, and D. S. McNamara, "Prior Knowledge, Reading Skill, and Text Cohesion in the Comprehension of Science Texts," *Learning and Instruction* 19, no. 3 (2009): 228–242. https://doi.org/10.1016/j.learninstruc.2008.04.003; among other studies.

37. Daniel T. Willingham, *Why Don't Students Like School?: A Cognitive Scientist Answers Questions About How the Mind Works and What It Means for the Classroom*, 2nd ed. (Jossey-Bass, 2021), 28–29.

38. https://www.theguardian.com/commentisfree/2023/dec/10/scottish-schools-have-tumbled-from-top-of-the-class-this-is-what-went-wrong.

39. https://reformscotland.com/2023/12/pisa-2022-in-scotland-declining-attainment-and-growing-social-inequality-lindsay-paterson/.

40. Not a huge surprise given that it is a form of background knowledge.

41. https://www.tandfonline.com/doi/abs/10.1207/s1532799xssr1004_3 and https://www.ncbi.nlm.nih.gov/pmc/articles/PMC4331220/.

42. https://www.researchgate.net/publication/216458681_Testing_and_refining_the_direct_and_inferential_model_of_reading_comprehension.

43. https://www.researchgate.net/publication/294687164_Reading_comprehension_A_conceptual_framework_from_word_meaning_to_text_meaning.

44. https://www.tandfonline.com/doi/abs/10.1207/s1532799xssr0102_4 and https://www.ncbi.nlm.nih.gov/pmc/articles/PMC4331220/.

45. https://www.researchgate.net/publication/254316536_The_State_of_Vocabulary_Research.

46. https://www.tandfonline.com/doi/full/10.1080/19345740802539200.

47. I. L. Beck, M. G. McKeown, and L. Kucan, *Bringing Words to Life: Robust Vocabulary Instruction* (Guildford, 2013), 3.

48. A. E. Cunningham and K. E. Stanovich, "What Reading Does for the Mind?," *American Educator* 22 (1998): 8–15.

49. https://journals.sagepub.com/doi/full/10.1177/09637214221103264.

50. One very simple and often overlooked way to develop students' vocabulary is to read aloud to them from text that is more advanced (and therefore contains more advanced words and syntax) than what they could read simply on their own.

51. https://pubmed.ncbi.nlm.nih.gov/37541302/#:~:text=Results%3A%20Findings%20reveal%20second%20grade,words%20in%20the%20English%20language.

52. https://www.cairn.info/revue-l-annee-psychologique1-2014-4-page-623.htm.

53. Isabel L. Beck, Margaret G. McKeown, and Linda Kucan, *Bringing Words to Life: Robust Vocabulary Instruction* (Guilford Press, 2002).

54. *Bringing Words to Life*, 179. They reference M. E. Curtis and R. Glaser's 1983 study of depth of vocabulary knowledge (https://psycnet.apa.org/record/1984-05278-001) and M. M. Van Daalen-Kapteijns and M. Elshout-Mohr's 1981 study (https://psycnet.apa.org/record/1982-04924-001).

55. Maria Konnikov, *The Biggest Bluff: How I Learned to Pay Attention, Master Myself, and Win* (Penguin, 2020), 133.

56. T. Shanahan, "Nature of the Reading–Writing Relation: An Exploratory Multivariate Analysis," *Journal of Educational Psychology* 76, no. 3 (1984): 466–477. https://doi.org/10.1037/0022-0663.76.3.466.

57. Steve Graham and Michael Hebert, *Writing to Read: Evidence for How Writing Can Improve Reading. A Carnegie Corporation Time to Act Report* (Alliance for Excellent Education, 2010), 13.

58. Ibid., 14.

59. Ibid., 13.

60. The term *syntactic control* term is originally Bruce Saddler's. His 2012 book, *The Teacher's Guide to Effective Sentence Writing*, is excellent.

61. Ibid., 17.

62. Johann Hari, *Stolen Focus: Why You Can't Pay Attention* (Bloomsbury, 2023), 83.

63. Ibid.

64. Ibid., 84.

65. ACT, "Reading Between the Lines: What the ACT Reveals About College Readiness in Reading" (2006).

66. Ibid., 16–17.

67. https://www.readingrockets.org/blogs/shanahan-on-literacy/more-bad-ideas-about-why-we-should-avoid-complex-text-reading.

68. "Reading Between the Lines," 24.

69. https://www.tandfonline.com/doi/full/10.1080/02702711.2021.1888348.

70. Wiliam posted on the social media platform X (then Twitter), "I've come to the conclusion Sweller's Cognitive Load Theory is the single most important thing for teachers to know," on January 26, 2017.

71. *How Do We Learn?*, 26–27.

72. We are forever referring to working memory as a part of our brains, but this is a misnomer in many ways. Working memory does not have a specific location—it is a state of consciousness supported by disparate functions from around the brain. Probably for that reason, Héctor Ruiz Martín is careful to call it a *mental space*.

73. P. A. Kirschner, J. Sweller, and R. E. Clark, "Why Minimal Guidance During Instruction Does Not Work: An Analysis of the Failure of Constructivist, Discovery, Problem-Based, Experiential, and Inquiry-Based Teaching," *Educational Psychologist* 41, no. 2 (2006): 75–86, https://doi.org/10.1207/s15326985ep4102_1.

74. Sean Achor writes, "Scientists estimate that we remember only one out of every 100 pieces of information we receive" in *The Happiness Advantage: How a Positive Brain Fuels Success in Work and Life* (Crown, 2010), 94.

75. https://psycnet.apa.org/record/1974-08440-001.

76. https://augmentingcognition.com/assets/Bjork1994.pdf.

77. This phrase appears repeatedly throughout *Why Don't Students Like School?*

78. Important note: if we make it too hard learners tend to shut down; they need to think hard but generally successfully about a learning object.

79. *How Do We Learn?*, 41.

80. https://link.springer.com/article/10.3758/s13423-020-01762-3?utm_source= snacks.pepsmccrea.com&utm_medium=newsletter&utm_campaign=externalising-thinking&_bhlid=6a1631ab86343e9a12fa5b769670a8f5bed83a41.

81. https://psycnet.apa.org/doiLanding?doi=10.1037%2F0278-7393.15.4.669.

82. K. Sedova, and M. Sedlacek, "How Vocal and Silent Forms of Participation in Combination Relate to Student Achievement," *Instructional Science* (2023). https://psycnet.apa.org/record/2023-41662-001, https://psycnet.apa.org/record/2023-41662-001.

83. *How Do We Learn?*, 40.

84. A.-M. Singh, N. Marcus, and P. Ayres, "The Transient Information Effect: Investigating the Impact of Segmentation on Spoken and Written Text," *Applied Cognitive Psychology* 26 no. 6 (2012): 848–53.

85. *Why Don't Students Like School?*, 37.

86. See Graham Nutall, *The Hidden Lives of Learners*. "We discovered that a student needed to encounter, on at least three different occasions, the complete set of the information she or he needed to understand a concept" (2007, 63). For a good and through treatment of Retrieval Practice see Peter C. Brown, Henry L. Roediger, and Mark A. McDaniel, *Make It Stick: The Science of Successful Learning* (Belknap, 2014).

87. *How Do We Learn?*, 118.

88. Paul A. Kirschner and Carl Hendrick, *How Learning Happens: Seminal Works in Educational Psychology and What They Mean in Practice* (Routledge, 2020), 101.

89. *How Do We Learn?*, 128.

Chapter 2

Attending to Attention

The universal adoption of smartphones and other digital devices has changed the life of every young person we teach. The changes wrought have been at times beneficial and at times foreboding—at times both things at once. Sometimes, given the pace and complexity of the changes, it's hard to even say what they mean and what their consequences will be.

And, of course, we experience a version of those changes alongside our students. As we write this, for example, we note that we are shortening our sentences. We are told that readers will be far less likely to persist in reading this if the sentences are too long and complex.

The decline of attentional skills associated with time spent in a digital world characterized by constant distraction means that we and our students find tasks that require sustained concentration—like making sense of this longish sentence—a little harder. And when it comes to harder things, we are a little less likely to persist than we once were.

Poor Charles Dickens. The mark of his craft was the intertwining of multiple ideas and perspectives within a single, complex sentence. The resulting sentences could be thirty or forty words in length. With writing like that, he'd struggle to find readers in the twenty-first century. In fact, in most classrooms he does struggle—and for exactly that reason.

The fact that his books are long was, once upon a time, a positive attribute. He was the nineteenth century's most popular English-language writer, not so much despite his lengthy writing but because of it. Picking up *David Copperfield* (1,024 pages) was, to a nineteenth-century audience armed with the stamina to read without interruption for hours at a time, more or less like binge-watching a Netflix series today.[1] You built your evenings around it. Jane Austen is often said to have been ahead of her time, but her observation that "If a book is well-written, I always find it too short"[2] is now an anachronism.

Today, long, like complex, is not a virtue. There is internet slang for this: tl;dr (too long; didn't read), which the Cambridge dictionary glosses as "used to comment on something that someone has written: If a commenter responds to a post with 'tl;dr,' it expresses an expectation to be entertained without needing to pay attention or to think."

Even in university settings, tl;dr is in the zeitgeist. "Students are intimidated by anything over 10 pages and seem to walk away from reading of as little as 20 pages with no real understanding," one professor recently wrote.[3]

"Fewer and fewer are reading the materials I assign. On a good day, maybe 30 percent of any given class has done the reading," wrote another.[4]

Yet another professor notes "I've come to the conclusion that assigning students to read more than one five-page academic-journal article for a particular class session is, in sum, too much."[5]

In *Stolen Focus*, Johann Hari chats with a Harvard professor who struggles to get students "to read even quite short books" and so now offers them "podcasts and YouTube clips . . . instead."[6]

And in an *Atlantic* piece on "The Elite College Students Who Can't Read Books," a first-year student at Columbia University told her professor that his assignments of novels to be read over the course of a week or two were too challenging because "at her public high school, she had never been required to read an entire book. She had been assigned excerpts, poetry, and news articles, but not a single book cover to cover."[7]

Reading, increasingly, is too hard, too long, and too tedious to minds attuned to the arrival of novel stimulus every few seconds—or at least it is if we make no effort to build young people's capacity to focus and sustain concentration.

Then again, we could ask, is this just moral panic—the judgment of every generation that the subsequent one is lacking? It's an important question to ask, but the answer is, probably not. There's a lot of science to suggest exposure to screens changes attention in measurable ways.

Research tells us that your nearby cellphone, even turned off and face down on a table, distracts you. A 2023 study by Jeanette Skowronek and colleagues assessed how students performed on a test of "concentration and attention" under two conditions: when a phone was visible nearby but turned off or when it had been left in another room. They found that "participants under the smartphone presence condition show significantly lower performance . . . compared to participants who complete the attention test in the absence of the smartphone." In other words, "the mere presence of a smartphone results in lower cognitive performance."[8]

Similarly, University of Texas professor Adrian Ward and colleagues found that even unused, "smartphones can adversely affect . . . available working memory capacity and functional fluid intelligence."[9] Part of the reason for this is that it takes cognitive resources to inhibit the impulse to look at it as soon as you are aware of its presence.

You see a device and it triggers a desire to find out what's become new in the past fraction of a minute. While it doesn't even need to be turned on to have this effect, it usually is, of course. And turned on—almost always on and constantly attended to—means an attractive distraction from a difficult task is pushed into your consciousness every few seconds.

In time, you don't even need your phone to be present to become wired for distractibility. Researchers at Temple University found that "heavier investment in mobile devices is correlated with a relatively weaker tendency to delay gratification . . . and a greater inclination toward impulsive behavior."[10]

"If kids' brains become accustomed to constant changes, the brain finds it difficult to adapt to a nondigital activity where things don't move quite as fast," Michael Manos, clinical director of the Center for Attention and Learning at Cleveland Clinic, recently told the *Wall Street Journal*.[11]

For teens who are constantly exposed to screens—and for the rest of us too, in all probability—this has rewired not only the way they think when their phones are in-hand but the way they think, period.

While this surely demands greater reflection among schools, most relevant to this book are the particular implications those changes have for reading and reading teachers.

THE BOOK IS DYING

Consider the fact that far fewer students read for pleasure compared with just a few years ago. For time immemorial, we teachers have cajoled, encouraged, and prodded students to read on their own. But even multiplying our efforts tenfold now won't get us back to baseline reading rates of, say, 2005. The numbers of students who read outside of school and the amount of reading they do have fallen through the floor.

Take data gathered by San Diego State professor Jean Twenge. She and her colleagues have studied responses by about fifty thousand nationally representative teens to a survey that has been administered since 1975, enabling broadscale changes over time to be easily observed and tracked.[12]

In 2016, Twenge found that only 16 percent of twelfth-grade students read a book, magazine, or newspaper on their own regularly.[13] That's about half of the 35 percent of students who reported doing so as recently as 2005.

The survey also found that the percentage of twelfth graders who reported reading no books on their own at all in the last year nearly *tripled* since 1976, reaching one out of three by 2016. This is dispiriting in its own right, but doubly so because 2016 was a long time ago, technology-wise—the salad days practically, *before* the precipitous rise in social media use post-2020 and the advent of the most recent wave of especially addictive social media platforms like TikTok.

And, of course, any type or amount of reading shows up just the same in the survey, whether it's one hundred pages of Dickens or a short article on Taylor Swift's latest outfit. In other words, even a yes on the survey still belies changes.

"This is not just a decline in reading on paper—it's a decline in reading long-form text," Twenge noted.

Other studies of young people's reading behavior are consistent with Twenge's findings. The 2023 American Time Use Survey found that teens aged fifteen to nineteen spent eight minutes a day reading for personal interest. Compare that to the "up to 9 hours per day" the American teenager spends on screen time.[14] If that number seems absurdly high, consolation can perhaps be found in the 2023 Gallup Familial and Adolescent Health Survey. Teens in that study reported spending on average "only" about five hours per day on screens.

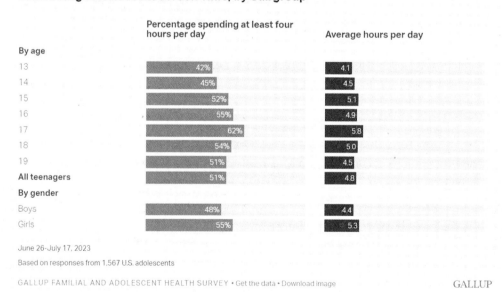

U.S. Average Adolescent Screen Time, by Subgroup

	Percentage spending at least four hours per day	Average hours per day
By age		
13	42%	4.1
14	45%	4.5
15	52%	5.1
16	55%	4.9
17	62%	5.8
18	54%	5.0
19	51%	4.5
All teenagers	51%	4.8
By gender		
Boys	48%	4.4
Girls	55%	5.3

June 26-July 17, 2023

Based on responses from 1,567 U.S. adolescents

GALLUP FAMILIAL AND ADOLESCENT HEALTH SURVEY • Get the data • Download image   GALLUP

Data from the 2022 National Assessment of Educational Progress show that the percentage of thirteen-year-old students who "never or hardly ever" read has increased fourfold since 1984, to 31 percent, while the number of students who read "almost every day" has dropped from 35 percent to 14 percent, a 60 percentage point decrease.[15]

This means that while as recently as 2000, classrooms were composed of three to four times as many daily readers as nonreaders, those numbers are now reversed. We can expect there to be less than half as many students who read regularly outside of class as there are students who never do so.

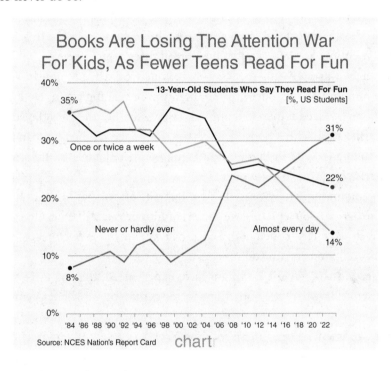

Books Are Losing The Attention War For Kids, As Fewer Teens Read For Fun

Let's hope that they are reading books cover to cover inside our classrooms, then, because they almost certainly are not outside it.

What does it mean for teachers if students are increasingly likely to be attentionally challenged, yet sustained reading is among the most attentionally demanding activities in which we can engage?

What are the implications for text selection in a world where the only books many students read will be the ones we assign?

What are the implications for the development of fluency and vocabulary when students are less and less likely to read beyond the classroom walls?

What does it mean to assign nightly reading when we cannot assume that students will go home and read, when doing so requires them to resist the pull of a bright and shiny device far more compelling in the short run and always within reach?

What does it mean that even those students who go home and pull out the book as assigned read in a different cognitive state than we might hope or imagine, again with a phone likely competing for their attention?

Consider: one of us—we won't say which—has a teenager whom we require to read regularly. We wish this teenager chose to read every day, but he doesn't, and we love him and know that whether he reads is too important to leave to chance—especially when "chance" pits a sixteen-year-old against tech giants spending billions of dollars to fragment and commercialize his attention. So, we've mandated he read three hours a week.

He read when he was twelve, by the way—voraciously. Sometimes now he remembers the feeling it gave him and he sets out with the intention of reading again. He knows it's good for him. He knows he loved it then and might love it again. But then, on the way to his room or the couch or the patio with a book in one hand, he glances at the phone in the other. The snapchats are rolling in. The Instagram notifications. There's a feed of tailored videos—his favorite comedian, his favorite point guard.

Suddenly twenty minutes have passed. Then forty. The book has lost again.

But let us further develop a picture we shared of him in Chapter One. On one of his reading days he is reclined on the couch with a copy of *The Boys in the Boat* held aloft—briefly!—but also with his cellphone resting on his chest.

Every few seconds the reverie he might have experienced, the cognitive state he might have been immersed in where the book transported him to the world of Olympic athletes, is interrupted.

Perhaps for a moment he imagines himself in a scull on a lake at dawn as he . . .

Bzzzz. Dude! Sup?

Is interrupted by every manner of trivial and alluring distraction . . .

Bzzzzz. U coming over? We at B's.

. . . which results on net in a different type of engagement with the book. There is no getting lost in . . .

Bzzzz. That new point guard. Peep this vid. Filth, bro!

. . . a different world or context. The level of empathetic connection to the protagonist . . .

Bzzzz. When U gonna text Kiley from math class. Think she digs you!

. . . is just not the same.

The experience of reading a book with fractured concentration is qualitatively different.

Bzzzz.

So there is both a "less reading" problem and a "shallow reading" problem. And, as we will see, reduced *application* of focused attention over time can become reduced *ability* to pay attention.[16]

We have written about the broader effects of smartphones and the ubiquitous digital world elsewhere. So have others—often far more insightfully. Here, we will skip over profoundly important issues of welfare and mental health: anxiety, depression, and the inexorable dismantling of community and institutions of connection and belonging. Instead, we will focus on what the research can tell us about the consequences of technology for those of us who teach reading.

We remind you that these forces affect practically every student and adult, regardless of whether they have a phone, and often regardless of their individual behavior in terms of their phone. Reading is a social behavior, something we do as we do in part, at least, because we learn it from others around us and see it reinforced by them. In this way, even students below the (steadily lowering) "age of first device" are affected. Are their older siblings shaping their behaviors by curling up with a book like they once might have? Are their parents?

Plus, while the phone is the primary tool technology companies use to fracture attention, the digital world is always encroaching. Think, for example, of when a five-year-old is handed an iPad in response to a bit of restiveness in the ten slow minutes before food arrives at a café, when they might otherwise have been handed a beloved book or been engaged in conversation with their family.

In the classroom—especially the reading classroom—these changes present us with a choice. We can, on the one hand, accede to them, accept that they are inevitable, and try to reduce the attentional and cognitive demands in the classroom in response. We can present text in shorter, simpler formats, and we can use more video and graphic formats, too, as the National Council of Teachers of English has proposed,[17] and as the Harvard professor Hari interviewed had done, replacing written texts as a source of learning and knowledge.

It's certainly easier in many ways to choose this approach. We could tell ourselves to do the best we can with the students we get—it's not our responsibility to try to change them. It would be reasonable simply to decide to adapt ourselves to a brave new world.

We are not yet ready to concede, however. There is too much at stake, we think, in accepting a reduction for our young people—and soon enough adults—in the ability to sustain focus and attention in text. We think the idea that only specialists might be able to read, say, the founding documents of our governments, or the journal articles that describe scientific discovery, to be problematic. We don't think that an impulsive body politic that requires instant gratification or is not adept at sustaining attention is a good thing.

New York Times columnist Ross Douthat has written that "the humanities need to be proudly reactionary in some way, to push consciously against the digital order in some fashion, to self-consciously separate and make a virtue of the separation."[18] English or literature classrooms are best positioned to build the conscious alternative to digital society precisely because of the great books they can offer and that we think ought to form the bulk of our classroom reading material. Our cultures have spent several hundred years stocking the war chest, so to speak, with great things to read—books that, once engaged, give students something more rewarding than the "hot takes" of "influencers" of the digital world. We think young people will get plenty of those things on their own.

What attracts us in the short run—the constant roll of new information and novel stimulation—is not actually what gives us pleasure in the long run. Far more people—yes, even teens—look back at an evening of scrolling or idle swiping with more regret than pleasure. You are drawn to it in the moment but waylaid by your own attention: you later wish you'd gone to the gym, practiced the guitar, read a book. You wish you'd accomplished something, and that you had been doing something that felt meaningful afterwards.

Books, we argue, are a medium that holds a unique key to strengthening attentional skills—one of the gifts that schooling should give to young people. Reading—deeply and with focus—offers not only a privileged form of access to knowledge but a profound form of enjoyment that is unique and, in many ways, more lasting than instantly accessed forms of gratification.

In fact, one of the most pleasurable states a human can experience is something called the "flow" state, extensively studied by the psychologist Mihaly Csikszentmihalyi. Flow state is the mindset you enter into when you lose yourself in a task that interests you. You become less self-conscious, less aware of almost everything else, even the passage of time. It is essentially a state of deep and unbroken attention.

Perhaps you have felt this playing a sport you love or, as Csikszentmihalyi first studied, while engaging in a form of creative expression like playing a musical instrument or drawing.

Flow is gratifying even if it requires effort—perhaps *because* it requires it. "The more flow you experience the better you feel," notes Hari. And, he adds, "one of the simplest and most common forms of flow that people experience in their lives is reading a book."[19]

If phones have ruptured our students' attention spans by rewarding them with brief flashes of shallow pleasure, books can provide an antidote: helping our students retrain their attention spans, and offering them the reward of deeper, longer-lasting pleasure. The trick, of course, is getting students to pick up and engage with a book for long enough to actually experience this.

This chapter, then, provides a road map for those of us who choose not to accept, for our students and for ourselves, lives of reduced attention, and to seek to create in our classrooms an environment where we enrich students through reading.

We begin by presenting a key principle that can guide us in how to improve attention and other capacities that are critical to developing young people who can engage in sustained and meaningful thought; then we share three ways to enact that principle in the classroom.

WE WIRE HOW WE FIRE

Our brains are rewired by the act of reading, so how we read affects our capacity for future reading. We can shape students' reading experiences in our classrooms carefully, intentionally, developing them into more attentive and deeper readers—and ones who enjoy it more.

We begin with the most important phrase in this chapter: *We wire how we fire*.

The brain is plastic. As we noted in Chapter One, the act of reading is a rewiring of portions of the cortex originally intended for other functions. *We are already rewiring when we read*, and *how* we read shapes how that wiring happens: how we can, and probably will, read.

If we read in a state of constant half-attention, indulging and anticipating distractions, and therefore always standing slightly outside the world a text offers us, our brains learn that is what reading is—it wires for a liminal, fractured state in which we only partially think about the protagonist and his dilemma or the meaning embedded in the syntax of a passage of constitutional law.

But thankfully that key phrase, *we wire how we fire*, cuts both ways. If we build a habit in which reading is done with focus and concentration and even, to go a step further, with empathy and connectedness, and if we do that regularly for a sustained period of time, our brains will get better at reading that way—more familiar with and attuned to such attentional states. We are likely to do less searching for distraction and novel stimulus as we read. We're also less likely to drift on the surface of a text, but instead to read deeply and to comprehend more fully. And because we are understanding better and are less distracted, we are more likely to persist.

In other words, we can rebuild attention and empathy in part by causing students to engage in stretches of sustained and fully engaged reading. This implies more actual reading in the classroom with more attention paid by teachers to *how* that reading unfolds. Attending to how we read—thinking of the reading we do in the classroom as "wiring"—gives us an opportunity to shape the reading experience intentionally for students. Those who read better, more meaningfully, with more empathy, more socially, more gratifyingly will read more and get more out of what they read.

A colleague of ours advised—a few years ago and with the best of intentions—that there should be very little actual reading in English classrooms. "The reading happens at home and the classroom is about discussion," he opined. We love discussion and see plenty of room for it in the classroom, but we think text-centered reading classrooms are strong ones. This argument is doubly urgent now. We are for making the text itself and the act of reading central to the daily life of the classroom. Even if we weren't at a time when it's clear that without classroom reading, very little reading would be done at all, we would still advocate for this practice. We think the science supports us.

Surprise: Attention Is Contagious

We have been reflecting on the power of people reading together since we visited a brilliant school—Rivers Primary Academy in Walsall, England. On visiting, we were struck by the consistently high quality of teaching. In room after room teachers were excellent and intentional. Each had his or her own style, but the foundational principles were shared.

We asked head teacher Becky Anderson how she had done it, and she noted that reading was one of the key parts of her school's professional development. Teachers would arrive for professional development sessions and she would give them a passage from a book on pedagogy, say. They would read it together in silence before discussing, planning, and practicing.

"Reading communicates depth, that the ideas are not superficial," Becky noted. She had initially tried assigning the reading as "homework," but people were busy. Not everyone did the reading. Not everyone who did the reading read well and with full attention and focus. People skimmed. They were giving their kids dinner. They were reading it on a screen and so were less attentive. They meant to read and didn't. Or they did, but the conditions were suboptimal for maximum focus.

So she tried shared reading. The teachers arrived and were given ten or fifteen minutes to read, all of them together in the room and at once. The teachers didn't mind. They found it pleasant, calming even. They were more focused. The ideas, still fresh in their working memory when they began to engage in discussion, were quickly translated into learning and action. And, the exercise gave them the opportunity to once again experience what it's like to be a student, however briefly.

We loved that, so we tried it ourselves. First with about one hundred teachers, then with three hundred, and finally with seven hundred teachers during a training, to whom we gave five or so pages of reading and twelve or so minutes in which to read it.

For the full twelve minutes the hall was pin-drop silent despite there being seven hundred people present. In fact, it was probably silent *because* of the seven hundred people. Social norms affect us powerfully even when they shape activities that feel passive and where they are less overt. The hum of others reading deeply around you focuses your own concentration. If your attention wanders you soon refocus it because, well, there were seven hundred people around you implicitly reminding you that you can and should.

Reading silently and independently in a group can be surprisingly productive for sustaining focus and attention.

Research by Noah Forrin and colleagues demonstrates the ways that attention is, in their words, "contagious." Students who were subjects of Forrin's study watched lectures with another student in the room. Unbeknownst to them, the second student was a confederate of the experimenters. Sometimes that second student leaned forward and took eager notes on the lecture. Sometimes that student slouched and did not bother to write anything down. Sometimes the student who was the subject of the experiment could see the confederate. Sometimes the confederate was behind the subject and could not be seen directly. The subjects reliably sensed and reacted to the actions of the other student in the room. Whether or not they could see them directly, students paired with an attentive classmate reported higher levels of attention, behaved more attentively (e.g., took more notes), and had better memory of the lecture content (i.e., learned more). Students paired with an inattentive confederate were far less attentive themselves. They remembered less.[20]

We are always noticing and reacting to norms. Attention is shaped by the environment in which it is deployed. Over time, it becomes habit and then capacity. This applies more broadly but also specifically to the task of reading.[21]

In part, it's what Becky Anderson was doing with her staff. We are not suggesting that this is an action you borrow with a few hundred students tomorrow necessarily—you need a strong culture and systems in place for the social norm to be mutually communicated in a productive way.[22] But the principle abides: attention and attentional habits are shaped by environment.

Moreover, though we rarely think about it this way, reading is a social act, and norms are always communicated, whether we read aloud or silently. We can use this fact to emphasize the attributes we desire. The environment in which you are asked to read shapes the way you learn to read. If we bring reading back into the classroom, we can curate the forms in which it fires and thus wires.

So: read in the classroom, regularly, in an environment you shape and control!

Reading Socially Leads to Reading Better

A few months ago, watching a movie with his family, Doug found himself looking around at his wife and children in the dark. When he laughed, he found himself peering across at his children on the couch to see if they were also laughing. Why did he want to know that, he wondered?

Answer: because laughing was more gratifying if they were laughing, too. Shared laughter—or tears, or surprise, or relief—connects people. This is why it's somehow more enjoyable to watch a movie with friends and family, even if just sitting in a dark room staring at a screen together. Part of the pleasure lies in the fact we have experienced it *together*.

The same is true of books. Part of the pleasure of reading is in sharing the experiences within the text with others. (Perhaps this makes it easier to understand why, while rates of reading are declining among adults these days, book clubs have never been more popular.)

"The brain, it seems, does not make much of a distinction between reading about an experience and encountering it in real life; in each case, the same neurological regions are stimulated," writes Annie Murphy Paul.[23] In the same way going on a hilarious or challenging road trip would cause a group of students to connect, so too can the shared experience of reading something meaningful together—perhaps not to the exact same degree, but not inconsequentially. Discussing a text can connect us, but so can experiencing it, especially when it is read aloud so the signals of shared connection are made more evident and our reactions happen in sync as the story unfolds. We've already seen that being among other readers shapes how individuals experience reading in terms of their attention. This is true of other aspects of their reading experience as well. We can socialize students to read in a manner where they wire for deeper, more thoughtful reading. Or more empathetic reading. It's more or less the flip side of the experience of our teenager for whom constant push notifications disrupt the depth and meaningfulness of his experience with books. When a student receives "notifications" from peers that they are all-in, engaged, and connected with their reading, it can positively influence his manner of reading.

Hearing the majority of his peers laugh at an amusing passage, for example, encourages him to enjoy the humor he perceives more deeply and openly. He is more receptive to his own enjoyment in part because he experiences it in the company of peers whose enjoyment is made evident, much as Doug experienced when watching a movie with his family.

As Peps McCrea discusses in his book *Motivated Teaching*, the individual's perception of peer norms is the greatest influence on his behavior and motivation. When teachers magnify the norm and make it more evident and more forceful, they shape culture.[24]

Being together with peers who are caught up in a book—experiencing a flow-like state, eagerly showing interest at moments of surprise or suspense (and sharing a mutual connection)—shapes our teen's perception of the experience a book can deliver. The norm—we're all all-in—magnifies the shared experience of reading the book together.

People take on the values of groups they feel more connected to more strongly. If the majority of the student's class is clearly eager to find out if Jonas and Gabe will survive at the end of *The Giver*, he is reminded that his peers share feelings of empathy and concern. He is connected to his own incipient feelings by witnessing theirs.

If he makes a comment about the book in discussion afterward and his peers nod and respond, he sees a world where people care about the ideas in books and value him when he reflects on them. You could see that in the video of Christine Torres's classroom that we shared in Chapter One. Students are all-in for a discussion about whether Kirsti in *Number the Stars* is brave because they have come to care about Kirsti but also because they can see that their peers do as well.

We should strive to build a shared experience where reading comes alive for students, because when we do so, we shape their experience of what reading is and how books can be meaningful. Over time and with consistency, that experience is wired into the cortex.

You can see some examples of what this might look like in several of the other videos that accompany this book. For example, watch the video *Maggie Johnson: Grew Serious*. Maggie is reading *To Kill a Mockingbird* with her eighth graders. After Maggie models a bit of expressive reading herself, Arshé picks up. He reads well but, prompted to "give me a little more than that" by Maggie, he reads with even more expression. Notice the students laughing along with his portrayal of Scout as he reads a second time. His classmates are signaling: *we appreciate the story; we appreciate you when you read like that*. It's a social reward. This causes him to put even

To watch the video *Maggie Johnson: Grew Serious*, use this QR code or find the video at the URL https://vimeo.com/1058243769/07650fdcc8.

a bit more into it. Brianna reads next. She stumbles at first but works her way into the story. Then Maggie "bridges," reading a passage herself to carry the momentum and ensure a sense of "flow." Notice the young man in the foreground (pictured).

and what it's meant to Macomb County through the years

He's spontaneously annotating the text. That is, he is underlining it and marking it up because what is happening in the book has become important to him. He wants to remember it. To talk about it later. *No one has told him to do this.* He is motivated to do it because of the carefully constructed experience of shared reading and of the reading habits that have been established; he is connected in a psychological and emotional sense. All of the students are, and in a public and visible way. They laugh at the same moments because they "get" that the scene is both funny and that its humor is well portrayed by Arshé, Ronnie, and others. They share a collective appreciation of the humor, the sadness, and the richness of a great novel. The book is coming to life.

To watch the video *Gabby Woolf: The Carew Murder Case*, use this QR code or find the video at the URL https:// vimeo.com/1058244332/0047f02419.

Or, in the video *Gabby Woolf: The Carew Murder Case*, consider how the students in Gabby's class engage in a partner reading of *Dr. Jekyll and Mr. Hyde* with enthusiasm and expression. You can hear them competing to bring the text to life, to capture the full extent of its Victorian sensationalism.

What we see in these videos is the nature of the reading experience shaping how students' neurons fire—how attentive they are, but also how connected to the text they are on a psychological level. If students fire this way, they have the best chance of wiring this way—of learning to read in a deeply engaged way, and of learning that reading is this sort of experience.

If the book has a chance to win in its struggle against the phone, its best hope is in the social—in the connections a book, read together, can engender, and the shared experiences it can create.

To that end, the next three sections will share specific ideas to create classrooms that intentionally wire students so that they fire as better, more sustained readers. They are: employing intentional ways of reading to maximize attention and connection; ensuring a high text, low tech classroom; and using book-driven objectives.

INTENTIONAL WAYS OF READING FOR ATTENTION AND CONNECTION

Shape the reading experience to help students find pleasure and value in persistence and focus.

We thought extensively about how to shape reading in the classroom when we developed our *Reading Reconsidered* curriculum, embedding what we call *Reading Cycles*, or blocks of time for sustained, attentive reading that occur multiple times per lesson.

These cycles rely on three ways of reading: Teacher Read Aloud, teachers and students reading together (FASE Reading), and shared silent reading (AIR). Once these ways of reading are instilled in a classroom, an effective balance between them is crucial to building habits of attention and a culture of reading that brings books alive for students. (Chapter Three on fluency will delve into the ways to implement these ways of reading; in this chapter, we'll preview them and focus on how they can support attention and culture building.)

One key benefit of teachers and students reading aloud is that oral reading can build momentum and create a feeling of flow; it can cause a story to come dynamically to life as teachers and students share in the experience of reading. Flow states, as we have mentioned, are powerful—among the most pleasurable and productive states a human can experience. Though they are harder to enter into than the superficial world of instant gratification, they are far more enduring in the fulfilment they create.

Johann Hari describes the core components of the flow state: three things that are required for people to lose themselves in a task and become attentionally hyper-focused.

The first thing you need is a clear single task. "Flow can only come when you are monotasking," Hari writes.

The second thing you need is "to be doing something that is meaningful to you," says Hari. "This is part of a basic truth about attention: we evolved to pay attention to things that are meaningful to us." He quotes the eminent social psychologist Roy Baumeister: A frog will look at a fly it can eat much longer than a stone it can't eat.

"To a frog," Hari observes, "a fly is meaningful and a stone is not."[25]

The third thing you need is for the task to be at the right level of difficulty. You don't feel flow doing things that are too easy. You get bored. However, it's also hard to lose yourself in something you don't know how to do. Flow requires challenge, but not so much difficulty that learners feel stuck.

To watch the video *Julia Pearlman: Chains Reading Cycles*, use this QR code or find the video at the URL https://vimeo.com/1058251087/703e9ae489.

There's an excellent illustration of how these factors combine in an effective, sustained reading cycle in the clip, *Julia Pearlman: Chains Reading Cycle*. You can see its effect on attention and student engagement in meaningful reading.

The clip is long, we warn you. Fourteen minutes! Even after we tried to trim out every extraneous moment we could. We know that makes it harder to study,[26] but it's also part of the point. It shows a cycle of sustained, attentionally focused reading that builds a flow state for students.

The clip starts with Julia briefly reviewing the previous days' reading. "Before we dig in," she says, "I want to do a quick review." The review surely helps lock in insights from Chapter One by offering students the chance to do a bit of Retrieval Practice but, just as importantly, it brings the memory of the narrative back into students' working memory. "Looking at page 61, what did Isabel overhear and how did she respond?" Julia asks. Responding to Julia's question will help students connect to—and make meaning from—today's pages. It will be easier for students to lose themselves in the sort of flow state we have described.

At about 1:45 of the video, Julia asks her students to read aloud using the FASE technique you will read more about in Chapter Three. Darielle is called on to read. The rest of the class is reading along silently, and you can see many of them already annotating their texts, unprompted by Julia, to make note of important observations and details from the text. After Darielle reads, Julia bridges briefly. That is, she inserts a bit of Teacher Read Aloud within the FASE Reading. Note that Julia slows the pace of her reading while modeling expression,[27] socializing her students to read for expression rather than speed.

Then she hands off to Maya and then to Salamah, both of whom, like Darielle, read beautifully and expressively. They are bring the story to life. The class is focused and attentive.

There's a brief pause in the reading at 3:12 when Julia prompts students to make a margin note about the protagonists' feelings. After they take a few seconds to do so, Julia asks some students to share their observations, then says, "Keep that in your brains as we continue reading." She wants to socialize annotation as a habit since it supports engagement, comprehension, and metacognition ("What's important here? Why?"), but she is quick about it. She wants to keep the text alive and students' working memory focused. The process mirrors that of an attentive independent reader who occasionally stops to make note of brief insights without losing focus.

Next, it's Hamid's turn to read. There's another brief pause for a margin note after that. We love that Julia doesn't ask students to talk about their notes here, just to show them to her so she knows they are building the annotation habit. Then, back into the book while its heart is still beating, but now Julia is reading.

She pauses to ask a few brief questions—about the word *freezing* and what the italics show—to make sure students understand. It's worth noting how deeply engaged in the story these students are, their minds in the eighteenth-century dilemma of Isabel. You can see the evidence in their eagerness to engage. Here they are when Julia asks what the italics designate. It's a sea of raised hands.

Julia's reading is lovely and effective throughout, but it's especially good starting at about 8:00. She reads slowly but expressively. She models how the book should sound, bringing it to life, engaging students in the text. But something else is happening. When she pauses for one last summary margin note, students have been reading almost nonstop in one format or another for more than ten minutes, sustaining deep attention on the text.

Students in Julia's class are rewiring their brains for reading during reading cycles like this one. The way they read—the way Julia shapes the experience of reading—causes their brains to be attentive, thoughtful, persistent, and focused. She is building her students' capacity to pay attention, to focus on a single task, to eschew distraction, and to enjoy and value the experience.

It's possible, this is to say. And it's valuable. And students tend to enjoy it.

Following, we present some further thoughts on how you can help your own students experience this by adapting the three ways of reading in service of attention and flow.

Teacher Read Aloud

The first of the three "ways of reading" is a straightforward concept, simply understood but requiring nuance in the execution. It's also one that is typically thought of as being useful mostly in the lower grades, though it is just as vital in the upper grades. When a teacher reads aloud, the text is suddenly full of the meaning she infuses it with, as well as the expression she embeds in it, modeling prosody. To be fair, the other ways of reading can also infuse the text with meaning. For example, it's especially powerful to see your peers read aloud expressively and with meaning. But a Teacher Read Aloud is also efficient. Speed is not irrelevant: it lets you get through (and gain the benefits of) more text. The teacher can also fluently read more complex passages that remain ahead of all or some students' ability to read fluently themselves, but which are full of rich and diverse forms of syntax and vocabulary.

For example, when one of Doug's daughters was small, he read aloud to her Scott O'Dell's young adult novel *Island of the Blue Dolphins*. It's a beautiful story and she was transfixed. But she was in third grade at the time, encountering many passages beyond what she could read on her own. This one for example: "As I crouched there in the toyon bushes, trying not to fall over the cliff, trying to keep myself hidden and yet to see and hear what went on below me, a boat left the ship. Six men with long oars were rowing."

In the first sentence there are, among other challenges, two embedded parallel participial phrases. Each starts with the word *trying* and they suggest two tasks happening at the same time and potentially in conflict. These are also in conflict with the desire described in the clause after "and yet," which uses a compound predicate, "to see and hear" what was going on below.

The level of syntactic complexity in that sentence was perhaps beyond what Doug's daughter could read on her own. But *hearing* it read with inflection and prosody by a knowledgeable reader who could create meaning in it enabled her not only to follow the syntax *in the moment* but to build up deep knowledge of complex forms of syntax through this and a thousand other successful interactions with complex sentences in the course of reading the book.

Syntax is a form of knowledge, one that's often overlooked. Like vocabulary, it responds to experience; like vocabulary, its complex forms occur overwhelmingly in printed rather than spoken language. Mastery and control of advanced forms of syntax—the ability to make meaning of them and create them—comes from thousands of trial-and-error experiments that lead us to understand the patterns in what Mark Seidenberg calls the "quasi-regular" system of "statistical tendencies but not inviolable rules."[28] Having encountered a few thousand complex and ornate passages made legible and accessible in reading *Island of the Blue Dolphins*, Doug's daughter was more likely to be ready when she came across such passages when reading on her own, even years later.

The book also contains rich vocabulary in doses and densities above what she could read on her own, but hearing *glisten*, *befall*, and *pelt* read aloud with context and inflection— and the occasional definition provided—accelerated the accretion of knowledge about those words far more than if she had been them silently on the page, alone, with her working memory heavily loaded and little additional context provided.

Interestingly, Doug's son, who was older, was also listening in. Could he have read *Island of the Blue Dolphins* on his own? Probably yes—but more slowly. Going faster *accelerated* the rate of his exposure to, among other things, new terms and phrases. Sometimes it's good to walk. And sometimes it's good to take the bus.

Reading aloud feeds knowledge to students at an accelerated rate. And in addition to maximizing exposure to some elements of text—advanced vocabulary and syntax, background knowledge—speed also can create momentum.

As a teacher, we can *read a class into a chapter*. That is, we start reading aloud, the suspense rising, the story moving along at pace and with a bit of drama—and then release students to finish it on their own, the story brought to life, the voice of the narrator in their heads. Being read to aloud creates a model of prosody—what the book should sound like echoes in students' heads as they read independently.

Hearing text read aloud also helps students to hear what Steven Mithen, who studies the evolution of language and music, calls *expressive phrasing*, or "how the acoustic properties of both spoken and musical phrasing can be modulated to convey emphasis and emotion."[29] This is probably why, as Tim Shanahan has pointed out, better prosody in oral reading often translates to improved silent reading for students.[30]

You can see Gabby Woolf do this in the video *Gabby Woolf: Gory Details*. She starts by building a bit of background knowledge (as we mentioned in Chapter One and will take up again in Chapter Four). Students have read a bit of Embedded Nonfiction about Victorian middle-class expectations, which they discuss briefly at the outset of the lesson, mostly to summarize the information and bring it to the forefront of students' attention. Then they see a few Embellishments—sample sensationalist headlines from nineteenth-century newspapers—for greater context. Per Johann Hari's rules, the more students understand, the more meaningful the experience is and the more likely they'll be able to sustain their focus.

To watch the video *Gabby Woolf: Gory Details*, use this QR code or find the video at the URL https://vimeo.com/1058259972/cf8bb97f43.

Then Gabby starts to read. She tells students they are going to "focus on the gory details. In the spirit of being sensationalist we want to read it as . . . Stevenson would want his readers to imagine it." Her reading is beautiful and richly expressive and brings the story to life in a way that students reading to themselves would be unlikely to do. The class is primed to be attentive. And, of course, as they listen, they are likely learning and comprehending more. Listen to how she reads the phrase "and fell into a dream of musing . . ." at about 5:45, for example. Notice the expressive phrasing of the word *musing* and how much information about the word is communicated for students in the room—probably most of them—who are unfamiliar with it. Her tone alone conveys that there is something tranquil and reflective about it. They also understand the text—who was this maid? what did she think?—due to Gabby's dramatization of the story. The experience will help them to mirror her expressiveness in their own reading—both orally, as we hear later in the clip, and silently.

It's important to note just how complex the syntax is in *Dr. Jekyll and Mr. Hyde*. Here are a few sentences from the passage Gabby reads, for example:

> *It seems she was romantically given, for she sat down upon her box, which stood immediately under the window, and fell into a dream of musing. Never (she used to say, with streaming tears, when she narrated that experience) never had she felt more at peace with all men or thought more kindly of the world. And as she*

so sat she became aware of an aged and beautiful gentleman with white hair, drawing near along the lane; and advancing to meet him, another and very small gentleman, to whom at first she paid less attention.

Though Gabby's students are just a few years away from university they are in this moment much like Doug's daughter. They are absorbing how complex syntax works and the pieces can fit together. They are hearing quite rare and challenging forms of syntax—"as she so sat"; "another and very small gentleman." This will prepare them for when they are required to read such challenging text on their own. You can hear this preparedness even in the video. Imram's sentence—"It did not seem as if the subject of his address were of great importance; indeed, from his pointing, it sometimes appeared as if he were only inquiring his way"—is a doozy. But he is more than up to it.

FASE Reading

The second way of reading is FASE Reading. (FASE is an acronym for fluent, accountable, social, and expressive—the characteristics of productive student oral reading.) It is a structured method of having students read aloud in an unpredictable pattern—often in combination with occasional Teacher Read Aloud sprinkled in. We discuss it more extensively in Chapter Three, but for now it will be helpful to note that when students read in the classrooms of Maggie Johnson, Gabby Woolf, and Julia Pearlman they are using FASE and not coincidentally, they are all-in.

As students read together as a group, they internalize positive norm signals. They laugh or feel tension; they see the willingness of their peers to read expressively. The book and the act of reading it are made social. The story becomes a means through which they connect. We are taken back to the root of storytelling, back to the campfires where we evolved to privilege the information in stories because it gave us a dual survival advantage—accumulated information about the world and connection to our peers that enabled us to form the groups that were necessary to our survival.

In *The Singing Neanderthals*, which charts the interrelated development of both music and language, Steven Mithen writes that music is "first and foremost a shared activity . . . throughout human cultures and history" and that communal music-making actively creates, rather than merely reflects, a "pleasing sense of unity." This sense of unity leads to "boundary loss," the "blurring of self-awareness," and a "heightening of fellow feeling with all," he continues.

The shared creation of music "creates for us a social rather than a merely individual identity," he concludes. The qualities that accomplish this—coordination, expression, shared emotion, turn-taking—are also present in shared oral reading which, Mithen points out has musical qualities in its prosody and expressive phrasing.[31]

The social connection established through shared reading is evident throughout the videos we share of students reading together. Look at the student who turns around as Imran is reading at about 6:06 of the video of Gabby's lesson, for example, and the warmth and approval in her smile.

Accountable Independent Reading (AIR)

The third way of reading is silently and independently, ideally for sustained periods of time. But silent independent reading has some risks. Are students actually reading? Carefully? Are they understanding? Are they skipping words and barely paying attention? It is important to be able to test for the productivity of independent reading, especially because it is variable. Readers, Recht and Leslie taught us with their "Baseball Study," might read successfully from one text and struggle mightily with another because of differences in knowledge. Or vocabulary. Or syntax. So good independent reading should be made accountable—with tools to manage and assess what students are doing and thinking and attending to as they read independently.

We should release students for small batches of independent reading at first and ask them to annotate or underline specific things so we can see if they understand. For example, with *Dr. Jekyll and Mr. Hyde*, Gabby might say, "Read to the bottom of page 62 and jot in the margin where the maid was sitting when she witnessed the crime." Now she can walk around the room, glancing over students' shoulders and quickly tell whether they were able to follow along with Stevenson's ornate Victorian prose.

It's often beneficial to use a segment of AIR right after a segment of FASE Reading or Teacher Read Aloud so the students' internal reading voice is influenced by and becomes as expressive as the voices they hear reading aloud. A student who brings expression and engagement to her internal reading voice during silent reading is a student who is one step closer to finding the flow state that makes reading so powerful.

Preparation: The Key to Synergistic Reading Cycles

In our reading cycles, we seek to unlock synergies among the three ways of reading. For example, the cycle starts with the teacher reading aloud for a few paragraphs. The book comes to life for students. Next they join in, being called on to read aloud using FASE. They are now participating in building the culture of reading and their attention is more or less unbroken. They are next released to read silently for a few minutes, the teacher checking to make sure they've understood. Perhaps she rereads a scene briefly that they have read on their own to study it further. Then, they finish the chapter on their own, reading for ten more minutes independently.

We should note that, in our curriculum, we always make recommendations, not requirements, for which of the three ways of reading to use or to combine. We want teachers to read the room, then respond to the level of difficulty of the text and the knowledge and skills of their students. The right balance of the three ways might change with a new book or within a book. It might even change with the same passage but a different group of students—for instance, when you are working with a smaller intervention group as opposed to a larger classroom of mostly proficient readers.

Here's an example class agenda from our *Reading Reconsidered* curriculum that is included in the teacher-facing lesson plan for our fifth-grade unit on *Number the Stars*. Note that within one lesson, students have an opportunity to engage in each of the three ways of reading.

Agenda:
- Do Now (10 minutes)
- Language Practice (15 minutes)
- Cycle 1 – Read Aloud or FASE Reading: Pages 11-13 and "Fairy Tales" (20 minutes)
- Cycle 2 – AIR: Novel Pages 13-14 (10 minutes)
- Cycle 3 – Read Aloud or FASE Reading: Pages 14-16 (10 minutes)
- Cycle 4 – Read Aloud or FASE Reading: Pages 16-17 (15 minutes)
- Exit Ticket (10 minutes)

One key element we discuss further in Chapter Three is how important it is to prepare for reading in the classroom. You can't get attention and flow and optimal states of psychological connection if you open the book on the spur of the moment and hope for the best.

Here, for example, is a page from Lois Lowry's *The Giver* that one of our colleagues prepared in anticipation of reading the book in class. She's chosen specific sections for bridging— she'll read aloud there, bringing the book to life and building momentum. She may change plans in the moment but for now she's thought through the sections where she thinks it's most important for it to be her voice because they are tricky, or subtle, or where she thinks that pacing might lag.

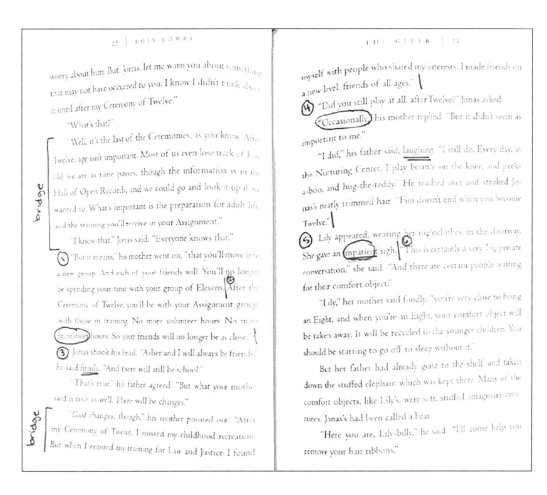

You can also see that she's chosen places to select a new reader. That's what the numbers and slashes refer to. She probably has a specific student or a type of student (weaker or stronger reader, or an especially expressive one) for each. In many cases, she might put initials in the margin.

And, she's underlined key dialogue tags and descriptors that guide expressive phrasing during read aloud: "he said firmly"; "his father said laughing"; "She gave an impatient sigh." She's circled words that might be tricky for her students (*recreation*, *occasionally*, *impatient*) so she can quickly drop in a pronunciation or definition and maintain the thread of the narrative.

Though the format of reading changes, students are in the text the whole time, for significant stretches of time, without distraction. They are wiring to sustain focus. And the book is coming to life. The experience is social. They are also wiring to engage and connect.

Needless to say, there is no set formula to accomplish this. It's different for every book, every passage, every group of students. Over time, the balance of the ways of reading might change as might the duration of the reading cycles as students learn to sustain focus for longer stretches of time. There are only tools and the judgment of the teacher informed by awareness of the goal.

HIGH TEXT, LOW TECH

Read books in hard copy to lessen digital distraction and focus attention. Annotate as you go.

The format of reading, is not the only factor to consider in seeking to wire meaningful and attentive reading. Another critical tool for shaping attention during reading is considering the medium in which we read, as this affects our ability to annotate—which itself has great benefits for reading.

There is extensive research that students remember more when they read in hard copy.[32] In their meta-analysis on the effects of reading media on reading comprehension, for example, Delgado and colleagues found "a clear picture" of "inferior" comprehension when students read on screens. The lower reading comprehension outcomes for digital texts compared to printed texts "represent approximately 2/3 of the yearly growth in comprehension in elementary school, and 1/2 of the effect of remedial interventions," they wrote.[33]

Delgado and colleagues also found a greater benefit to reading on paper under time constraints, and when reading nonfiction—in more challenging settings you might say. Interestingly they also found that "the advantage of print reading significantly increased from 2000 to 2017."[34] One interpretation of this finding is that as screens become more pervasive the benefits of reading on paper increase. Another explanation might be a generational effect: students who did more of their early reading in hard copy might have better attentional skills and be more resistant to the distracting effects of reading on screens.

A 2019 meta-analysis by Virginia Clinton found similar effects. "Reading from screens had a negative effect on reading performance relative to paper," Clinton noted, with the effect about a quarter of a standard deviation. Again, the difference was greater with expository texts. But, interestingly, her research adds the finding that "readers had better calibrated (more accurate) judgement of their performance from paper compared to screens."[35] That is, from a metacognitive perspective they were more aware of whether they understood or not when they read in hard copy.

Hard copy isn't just better for reading: there's further extensive research to suggest that we learn and remember more when we take notes by hand.[36]

Handwritten notes appear to be superior because they are more deliberate. While typewritten notes tend to be a running record, handwritten notes involve more selection and processing. The act of discriminating between what's important and what's not, for example, is the first step toward assigning meaning to an idea and beginning to remember it better. And handwritten notes allow for diagrams and images and other non-letter forms of processing—a double underline, a word circled, a diagram to compare ideas.

More broadly, as we discuss in Chapter One, writing assists in memory formation because it is effortful. Want to remember? Write it down.

But there's a specific subcategory of writing that has particular benefits for the reader, benefits that are maximized when using a hard copy of a text: annotation. Annotation is the process by which a reader marks up a text. At a foundational level it is critical to helping students understand a text. When students annotate, they make decisions and decide which things are important as they read. They note what they wish to remember, what matters to them. This requires reading actively, discriminating and prioritizing their attention more narrowly. They engage with the text more actively and intentionally, and the process of doing so sustains their focus. We saw the student in Maggie Johnson's English class doing that previously in the chapter.

In our *Reading Reconsidered* curriculum, we almost always give students an annotation task during their reading cycles. For example, Lesson 6 of our unit on Lorraine Hansberry's play *A Raisin in the Sun* includes four different cycles of reading: three from the play and a shorter one from a nonfiction passage about Hansberry's reflections on her own father.

We give students a different annotation task for each of these cycles:

Pages 46-48

Annotation Task: Recall that in the stage directions introducing Beneatha on p. 35, her speech is described as "different from the rest of the family's." As we read this scene, annotate any moments in which Beneatha seems "different from the rest of the [family]."

Pages 48-50: On Your Own

Annotation Task: As you read, annotate any moments in which Ruth seems younger (like Beneatha's peer) and any moments in which she seems older or more aligned with Mama.

Annotation Task: As we read this article about Lorraine Hansberry and her father, Carl, annotate any lines that remind you of characters or situations in *A Raisin in the Sun*.

Pages 50-53

Annotation Task: As we read, annotate evidence of strong emotions and conflict between Mama and Beneatha.

Notes

Notice the consistency of annotation. Each time we read we are attending to something (usually just one). Each time we read we do so with a pencil in our hand. Notice how each annotation prompt shapes student attention in a specific and useful way—and also how readily they lend themselves to a teacher circulating as students read and quickly being able to discern whether students appear to be noticing the right things.

There are other passages where we might assign annotation but not with a specific task, however, simply saying, "As you read, be sure to annotate."

You might call these two different approaches: directive and nondirective annotation. Directive annotation asks students to pay attention to and make notes about something specific that we think is worthy of their attention. Nondirective annotation asks students to build the habit of prioritizing and thinking about what is important but allows them to decide for themselves what that is. Both of these approaches are worthy means of focusing attention, and it is probably better when students are able to practice them both. That is, if a teacher consistently directs students to make note of worthy things as they read, the student learns to look for those types of things. They get better at looking for what's important. They learn the skill with more direction. But we also want them to use the skill on their own when we don't prompt them, so it's important to give them opportunities to do that and see the value.

The variation of these annotation tasks, even within a single lesson, suggests something important. There are two purposes to annotation. One is to cause students to actively engage as they read—to discriminate and prioritize and thus to pay better and more active attention generally. The second is to cause them to attend to certain things that are especially useful or important. Direct someone's attention to something that is important to perceive, and they are more likely to see it.

In other words, annotation *shapes attention* among readers and supports comprehension. To direct students to a particularly important theme, image, idea, or relationship helps focus their attention on an idea that we know as teachers will support their comprehension. As we've pointed out, attention is the foundation of learning. We must first attend to something for it to then enter our working memory and potentially be encoded in long-term memory. Student annotation can also support us as teachers. When we are circulating around the room as students read independently, their annotations make their comprehension visible, which allows us to better gather data on reading comprehension during silent reading.

Shaping attention, focusing it in productive directions, is critical to learning. Doing so before students read makes them more likely to notice important details and to think about them.

But, of course, what's useful in any given moment changes. Knowing where you direct your attention is one of the hallmarks of expertise. In Doug's book *The Coach's Guide to Teaching*, he discusses how professional athletes' ability to know where to direct their eyes to find the right information is central to their successful decision-making. What makes great athletes great is often their knowledge about where to direct their attention.

It's better, we think, when a generalized, uniform approach to annotation is not taught.[37] For example, we studied the classroom of a teacher whose work we loved on several levels. At the beginning of the year, she rolled out an annotation system that her students always used. They boxed figurative language, circled vocabulary words, underlined important plot moments and double underlined important characterizations. The plan was to use that same system of mark-up all year.

Such a generalized approach—always annotate for the same things—we realized, is driven more by skills than meaning. We spend a lot of time installing a system where we circle *x* and underline *y* and box *z*, but that pulls student attention away from what's happening here and what's important right now in the text, specific details that will support comprehension as they read. Instead, it puts the focus on what you might call extraneous cognitive load—what's the process and how does it work?—rather than intrinsic cognitive load—what am I trying to pay attention to in the text? In time, it becomes reflexive: we look for what we always look for, whether it's relevant to what we're reading now.

The optimum state for memory formation while reading would be making handwritten notes in text students are reading in hard copy: high text, low tech.

A hard copy vibe in the classroom enables you to limit the attention-fracturing influence of screens. Remember that, even if the screens are disconnected from the internet, students are habituated to see them and desire distraction—a habit that's embedded deeply enough that it probably shapes behavior regardless of whether actual task-switching occurs.

As we've argued elsewhere, we think it's especially important that students read books whenever possible because of the privileged way in which books sustain concentration and attention. Well, we also think those books should be in hard copy.

One argument against books in hard copy that we often hear is the cost. It's $10 a book if we want to let students write in them and keep them. True enough, we acknowledge. We're not saying the expense isn't real in a time of tightening budgets. But schools routinely find money for SMART Boards for every room and Chromebooks for every student. So we'd ask the district and school leaders reading this to explore whether perhaps there's enough around the margin for books themselves, especially when we consider how important it is to read in hard copy. Like everything else in a school's budget, it's a question of priorities. It may be that we can't have every book that students read in hard copy. Or that students can have them in hard copy but can't write in them. Or that students get one book a year in hard copy in which they can annotate. But we urge schools to make decisions at least knowing what the optimal case is if the mastery of reading and writing matter. A book in students' hands, where they can flip back to page 47 and a margin note they made there, is a beautiful and powerful thing from a learning point of view.

Teachers who want to employ hard copies in their classrooms but lack the necessary resources should know that there are workarounds—imperfect, but better than nothing if you can't get students working in hard copy. One colleague described having students keep a journal of notes as they read. They made fewer annotations than they could if they under-lined and made margin notes, but perhaps reflected on them deeply. If you aren't able to buy students books, you could selectively choose to copy the day's reading—perhaps once a week, or perhaps when you know you will be reading especially deeply—to allow students to make annotations on printed copies of the text at least occasionally.

BOOK-DRIVEN OBJECTIVES

Let the book and its value to readers inform the purpose of your lesson.

Another key element of attentionally focused reading classrooms might seem surprising: the nature of lesson objectives.

Objectives in reading and English classes are often "skill-driven," such as, *Students will be able to make inferences about a character in the text.*[38]

Compare that to a "book-driven" (or "text-driven," if you are reading a poem or story) objective. Here's one from the unit on *Catherine, Called Birdy* in our *Reading Reconsidered* curriculum: *Students will analyze Catherine's reflections and realizations about marriage.*

Skill-driven objectives like the first one are organized around and presume the importance of transferrable "skills" that research indicates are not really skills in that they don't respond to practice and almost assuredly are not transferable, as we discuss in Chapter One. They socialize teachers to engage in reading instruction in which the class sets out to make inferences because the purpose of the day's lesson is to make inferences. The purpose for reading is not to make *meaning from this particular text* but to make *inferences*. It's a significant issue if the purpose of a lesson is distant and disconnected from the story itself—if the story is there to conveniently serve some other goal, rather than to be understood.[39]

Further, skill-driven objectives are organized in units. A class using them might be working for a few weeks on the "skill" of making character inferences and so that objective or some version of it reoccurs for six or seven or ten days in a row. This *massing* of practice, doing it all at once and then moving on to some other type of question, further reduces the value in making inferences. Almost any skill or form of knowledge is learned and remembered better when application and retrieval are spaced.[40]

Massing practice is a recipe for forgetting; spacing practice is a recipe for remembering.

The following illustration demonstrates a simplified example. At the top we see the questions students answer in an English class when using skill-based objectives. For three days in a row, they answer four questions about "character perspective," represented by the medium gray blocks. Each block is a question. Students repeat the skill multiple times for those lessons, causing those questions to be the focal point of any discussion. Then they move on to three days of main idea questions, represented by the darker boxes. Again, it's three intense days of focused practice on a new type of question. Then it's on to a few days of questions about how evidence is used to support conclusions (lighter boxes). At this point, the teacher is no longer asking character inference questions. That was last week's thing.

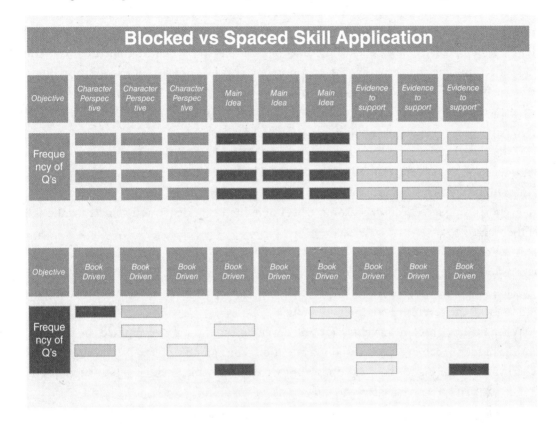

In the second model, "book-driven" objectives ask students to answer the questions required to make meaning of the text or to attend to some key issue or theme (Catherine's perceptions of marriage, say). In so doing, they respond to questions that require a mix of skills. Over the weeks, the application of the skills is interleaved. This causes greater learning. Even if you believe that these skills can be practiced—or even if you are accountable for results on a state test that requires students to answer them over and over and so you'd like to hedge your bets—you're likely to get better mastery if you use the second model. You make better inferences if you are attentive to practicing them every so often over the course of the year as suggested by the story rather than all at once for a few intense days or weeks and then stop using them.

But at a deeper level, the organizational structure of skill-based objectives is the cart before the horse. It proposes applying a skill without a reason.

A much better answer to the question "Why are we making an inference?" than "Because it is today's objective" is "Because something in the text prompts it." When students make an inference in response to something in the text, they are learning to respond to what the book demands of a reader. They are learning to let perceptions from the text guide their thinking and reflection. They perceive that a description or a phrase is unusual or revealing or alludes to some prior event and so proceed to think more deeply about it. That is more or less what it means to read.[41] And even if our goals include mastery of skills, part of that mastery—the hard part—is recognizing when its application makes sense.

If the book becomes a vehicle for determining the main idea of various passages because a sequence of objectives requires it, one result will be that students pay less attention to other things in the text. This can ultimately lead to taking a worthy book, perhaps even a great one, and repurposing its reflection on some aspect of human experience as a vehicle for the skill of the week.

Imagine the effect on a group of students reading *The Giver* and encountering to the passage where Jonas learns what "release" means, and that his father is the one who does the releasing of babies, only to have their teacher say, "Let us pause to ask about the main idea and to recall the seven steps of main idea-ing."

When the book becomes a vehicle for skill development, the story becomes less meaningful. Flow is harder to achieve. So is sustained attention. You can never quite be all-in on reading when you are waiting for the next opportunity to look at which evidence best supports the conclusion. There is no faster way to kill a book.

A book-based objective like *Students will understand what is entailed in a "release" and analyze how this knowledge affects Jonas's perception of his family and the Community* attempts to focus students' attention on something that is important to think about to make the story meaningful.

Book-based objectives are also more interesting because they are never quite the same. In a skill-driven unit you might have a very similar objective for weeks at a time while you "learned how to identify the main idea of a passage" and then "practiced finding the main idea" in passages from *A Raisin in the Sun*.

In our unit on *A Raisin in the Sun*, the objective of Lesson 6 is to *Analyze the dynamics of the relationships among the play's three central women*. For Lesson 7 it's *Examine how Hansberry intensifies conflict and raises the stakes in Scene Two*. For Lesson 8 it's *Consider influences on Beneatha's exploration of her identity*. For Lesson 9 it's *Analyze the confrontation at the end of Act I.* And for Lesson 10 it's *Write a paragraph response analyzing Walter and Lena's perspectives.*

Each day's objective is different because it focuses on something especially important to the development of the play's story and ideas—usually they are linked to one of three or four *essential understandings* of the book, which are outlined in the unit plan. Linking objectives to essential understandings ensures a throughline through the lessons, helping the reading of the entire book feel cohesive for the students. By keeping the overall goals that you want students to arrive at in mind, you are better able to discern book-driven lesson objectives that meet those goals.

Interestingly, the objective for Lesson 10, above, does involve a "skill" that might look familiar to teachers who use skill-based objectives: Analyze two different characters' perspectives. But here, it's used because the play makes the topic relevant. It's the right time to ask this. Similarly, students should still discuss the inferences they can draw from a text; they should just do that as part of making meaning out of an important work. In so doing, the text becomes more cohesive and meaningful to them, and attention is focused and sustained—building them into better readers.

Another reason teachers might hesitate to use book-driven objectives instead of skills-driven ones is the need to align lessons with standards, which tend to be skills-focused rather than text-focused. However, it's possible to write a book-driven objective that aligns with standards—and, as we've discussed, the book-driven lesson will better help students actually master the skills enumerated in the standards, but in an authentic way. If necessary, consider writing a hybrid objective that mentions a skill to be employed in service of the book-driven objective to help show how you are meeting the standards. For example, "Students will be able to consider influences on Beneatha's exploration of her identity using evidence to support their claims" combines the book-driven objective with a skill that will be used.

Ultimately, students should still do things like discuss the inferences they can draw from a text; they should just do that as part of making meaning out of an important work. In so doing, the text becomes more cohesive and meaningful to them, and attention is focused and sustained—building them into better readers.

PRINCIPLES OF READING IN ACTION

Now that we've shared three ways to help students fire so that they wire as better readers, we'll pause to share some examples of what all of these look like in action together. The following examples are both from book units in our own curriculum and can be found in their entirety in Appendix A.

Example 1: Lesson from Kate Cushman's Novel *Catherine, Called Birdy*[42]

The first cycle in this lesson requires students to read four pages (87–91), essentially without interruption, for ten or fifteen minutes. The lesson plan leaves it to the teacher to decide on the proper balance of teacher oral reading, FASE, and AIR but recommends FASE and Teacher Read Aloud in particular.

- **Read: Read Aloud** or use **FASE Reading** to read pp. 87-91, from the 27th Day of February through the 7th Day of March ("only been a seven-night"). While reading, ask students to **annotate** details about how Catherine and her family observe Lent.
  - ○ **Establish Meaning Questions During Reading**
    - (p. 87, after "have done the others") *Who is Catherine referring to as "the bearded pig"? Why does Catherine think her father says, "Learn to like it"?*
    - (p. 90, after "laughing and spring rain") *What is Catherine imagining? What's surprising about her daydreams? What's not surprising?*
  - ○ *Note: Students will use their annotations to respond to **Q1**, so there is no need for a separate debrief.*
  - ○ **Annotation Task: As we read pp. 87-91, annotate details about how Catherine and her family observe Lent.**
    - *First day of Lent. We are but dust and to dust shall return. I tried to be thoughtful and morbid on this day but spoiled it by skipping in the yard after dinner from pure joy. I am not dust yet! (p. 88)*
    - *We heard mass this morning (p. 90)*
    - *The church seems strange, undressed as it is for Lent. Father Hew wears plain robes with no silver gilt threads. The cross and statues are covered with veils. There are no flowers and no music. It is meant to make us feel sad, but mostly just makes me bored. (p. 90)*
    - *Edward has sent to us three holy books from which he says we must read each night during Lent to put us in the proper morose and holy mood. (pp. 90-91)*

The annotation task pushes students to pay attention to discussions of Lent. Note that students have already read a nonfiction article about Lent to build their background knowledge, so now they are ready to bring deeper understanding and greater insight to its role in the story. Consider throughout this lesson how critical it is for students to be high text, low tech—the annotation tasks would be considerably harder were students unable to mark up a physical copy of the text or were they distracted by their devices (even trying to track page numbers on a digital copy of a book can be a pain that slows down learning!).

Notice that the lesson plan also includes Establish Meaning questions. These are questions designed to ensure that students grasp the events clearly before analyzing them. They are critical because students are so often asked to analyze before we know they've understood. These questions are also critical because they socialize students to read attentively to make sure they are understanding, to lock in and not skim, leading to a familiarity with attentive reading and a better metacognitive awareness that they may be reading but not understanding. This is important: lack of understanding disrupts concentration and focus.

The second reading cycle is similar. This time, students read pages 91–93—slightly shorter but still with sustained and singular focus. Again, the lesson recommends more oral reading to help students hear the text and to build connection. Again, there is a single specific annotation task that is particular to this portion of the text. Again, there are Establish Meaning questions.

The next two reading cycles (pages 93–96 and 96–100) are different. Here we specifically recommend independent reading: ten or more steady uninterrupted minutes' worth for each. (You can see the reading cycles in the lesson plan in Appendix A.)

There's a brief Embellishment included in the student facing materials to make sure students understand what leprosy is when there are references to it and a new annotation task to shape students' attention in a useful direction:

Pages 93-96: On Your Own

Annotation Task: As you read, annotate details that help answer the following question

- Why is Catherine punished?
- Who is Geoffrey? What is Catherine's perspective on him?

Leprosy is a devastating disease that causes skin lesions and nerve damage. Because the condition is so contagious, lepers were shunned and not considered a part of society anymore. In medieval England, lepers had to ring a bell like the one in this image to signal their presence in public places.

Notes

The objective of this lesson is to consider Catherine's experiences during the season of Lent, and the questions gradually draw out observations. Students not only read deeply but discuss efficiently and engagingly with peers, often in the same groups of three or four, using Turn and Talk, Stop and Jot, or via brief discussion. As students' brains fire in this way, they become wired for these now-familiar routines, which enables them to engage more fully in the text. Their working memory is hacked[43] because they don't have to think about the how, just the what.

The second example is from Lorraine Hansberry's *A Raisin in the Sun*.[44] The same principles as the previous lesson are at play in this lesson from *A Raisin in the Sun*, which you can find in Appendix B. One major difference is that this lesson involves a fair amount of rereading. With each reread, students are given a different annotation task or focus to activate a different lens for discussion.

CHAPTER RECAP

The digital world, and particularly the ubiquitous smartphone, has rewired our brains so that we do not have a sustained capacity for attention. Reading books is on the decline, yet books, with their reward of deeper, longer-lasting pleasure, offer an important antidote to repair our ruptured attention spans, especially when we read socially.

Because our brains wire how we fire, how we read consistently affects our neurological capacity for attention and for future reading. In other words, if we fire a certain way consistently, we can rewire our brains to be more attentive and better, deeper readers.

Employ the following practices to take advantage of this fact for students:

- Use intentional ways of reading—Teacher Read Aloud, FASE Reading, and AIR reading—to shape the reading experience and help students find pleasure and value in persistence and focus.

- Keep classrooms high text, low tech. Read books in hard copy and annotate them to lessen digital distractions and shape attention.

- Shape lessons around book-driven objectives rather than skills-driven objectives. Let the book and its value to readers inform the purpose of your lesson.

Notes

1. In fact they were serialized, meaning that they were—like many Netflix series—released in installments that occasionally dragged out the plot and caused readers to yearn for the next part to arrive.
2. Claire Tomalin. *Jane Austen: A Life* (Knopf Doubleday, 2007), 71.
3. Theologian Adam Kotsko. https://slate.com/human-interest/2024/02/literacy-crisis-reading-comprehension-college.html.
4. Theresa MacPhail, "Are You Assigning Too Much Reading?," *Chronicle of Higher Education* (January 27, 2019), https://www.chronicle.com/article/are-you-assigning-too-much-reading-or-just-too-much-boring-reading/.
5. Ibid.
6. Johann Hari, *Stolen Focus: Why You Can't Pay Attention—and How to Think Deeply Again* (Crown, 2022).

7. https://www.theatlantic.com/magazine/archive/2024/11/the-elite-college-students-who-cant-read-books/679945/

8. https://www.nature.com/articles/s41598-023-36256-4.

9. The presence of smartphones—even unused—may "impair cognitive performance by affecting the allocation of attentional resources, even when consumers successfully resist the urge to multitask, mind-wander, or otherwise (consciously) attend to their phones—that is, when their phones are merely present. Despite the frequency with which individuals use their smartphones, we note that these devices are quite often present but *not* in use—and that the attractiveness of these high-priority stimuli should predict not just their ability to capture the orientation of attention, but also the cognitive costs associated with inhibiting this automatic attention response." https://www.journals.uchicago.edu/doi/full/10.1086/691462.

10. H. H. Wilmer and J. M. Chein, "Mobile Technology Habits: Patterns of Association Among Device Usage, Intertemporal Preference, Impulse Control, and Reward Sensitivity," *Psychonomic Bulletin & Review* 23, no. 5 (2016): 1607–1614.

11. https://www.wsj.com/articles/tiktok-brain-explained-why-some-kids-seem-hooked-on-social-video-feeds-11648866192

12. Another attribute of Twenge's survey instrument is that she and her colleagues ask students about behaviors and attitudes across a wide spectrum of topics so questions about reading are embedded among questions about a dozen other topics. Most studies of reading behaviors rely on self-report—necessarily—and so if students, who mostly know they "should read more" know they are primarily being surveyed about their reading behaviors, specifically, they're perhaps more likely to round up a bit—they know they really should be doing more of it.

13. Jean M. Twenge, *iGen: Why Today's Super-Connected Kids Are Growing Up Less Rebellious, More Tolerant, Less Happy–and Completely Unprepared for Adulthood–and What That Means for the Rest of Us* (Atria Books, 2017).

14. https://www.aacap.org/AACAP/Families_and_Youth/Facts_for_Families/FFF-Guide/Children-And-Watching-TV-054.aspx. If you're wondering, the data on reading for adults over fifteen was 15.6 minutes a day (in 2018). That number was down 28 percent in just fifteen years. It was almost twenty-two minutes per day in 2003.

15. https://www.nationsreportcard.gov/ltt/reading/student-experiences/?age=13.

16. Someone somewhere is wondering about their child's capacity to sustain a state of obsessive attention while playing video games. Isn't this driving him (he is statistically highly likely to be male) to build his attentional capacity? It is not—at least not to low-stimulus events. He is learning to lose himself in a world that constantly offers maximum immediate stimulation and gratification. If you wish for him to sustain attention while reading a medical chart, a novel of historical importance, or the Constitution of the United States, you will be disappointed.

17. They have come out in favor of something called "decentering the text," which sounds a lot like a word salad for lowering expectations to us. "The time has come to decenter book reading and essay writing as the pinnacles of English language arts education," they wrote in a recent position statement. "It behooves our profession, as stewards of the communication arts, to confront and challenge the tacit and implicit ways in which print media is valorized." Call us crazy. We think it's actually the job of English teachers to *reinforce* the value of reading and writing.

18. https://www.nytimes.com/2023/03/08/opinion/humanities-internet-novels.html.

19. *Stolen Focus*, 57.

20. N. D. Forrin, A. C. Huynh, A. C. Smith, E. N. Cyr, D. B. McLean, J. Siklos-Whillans, E. F. Risko, D. Smilek, and C. M. MacLeod, "Attention Spreads Between Students in a Learning Environment," *Journal of Experimental Psychology Applications* 27, no. 2 (2021): 276–9, doi: https://doi.org/10.1037/xap0000341; N. D. Forrin, N. Kudsi, E. N. Cyr, F. Sana, I. Davidesco, and J. A. Kim, "Investigating Attention Contagion Between Students in a Lecture Hall," *Scholarship of Teaching and Learning in Psychology* (2024). Advance online publication, https://doi.org/10.1037/stl0000419.

21. Jan Bietenbeck found, for example, that having visibly motivated classmates in the room increased learning for other students, who observed and adapted to the observed norm: "exposure to motivated classmates causally affects achievement, an effect that operates over and above spillovers of classmates' past achievement and socio-demographic composition." https://academic.oup.com/ej/advance-article-abstract/doi/10.1093/ej/ueae060/7700695?redirectedFrom=fulltext&login=false.

22. In Chapter Three, we help you build some of those systems and norms.

23. https://www.nytimes.com/2012/03/18/opinion/sunday/the-neuroscience-of-your-brain-on-fiction.html.

24. Peps McCrea, *Motivated Teaching: Harnessing the Science of Motivation to Boost Attention and Effort in the Classroom* (CreateSpace Independent Publishing Platform, 2020).

25. Johann Hari, *Stolen Focus: Why You Can't Pay Attention—and How to Think Deeply Again* (Crown, 2022), 56.

26. Our working theory is that video clips of teaching should be about three minutes in length or less because video is dense and working memory is small. It's difficult even for adults to sustain deep focus on video and remember the details of what they've seen for much longer, in contrast to a book with a single compelling narrative.

27. In trainings we often advise teachers to read aloud at 90 percent of their natural pace and 110 percent of their natural expression.

28. *Language at the Speed of Sight* (Basic Books, 2017), 23.

29. Steven J. Mithen, *The Singing Neanderthals: The Origins of Music, Language, Mind, and Body* (Harvard University Press, 2006), 24.

30. https://www.shanahanonliteracy.com/blog/wake-up-reading-wars-combatants-fluency-instruction-is-part-of-the-science-of-reading.

31. Steven J. Mithen, *The Singing Neanderthals: The Origins of Music, Language, Mind, and Body* (Harvard University Press, 2006) 205–15.

32. https://onlinelibrary.wiley.com/doi/abs/10.1111/1467-9817.12269; https://journals.sagepub.com/doi/abs/10.3102/0034654317722961; https://www.sciencedirect.com/science/article/pii/S1747938X18300101.

33. Pablo Delgado, Cristina Vargas, Rakefet Ackerman, and Ladislao Salmerón, "Don't Throw Away Your Printed Books: A Meta-Analysis on the Effects of Reading Media on Reading Comprehension," *Educational Research Review* 25 (2018): 23–38,

34. Ibid.

35. https://onlinelibrary.wiley.com/doi/abs/10.1111/1467-9817.12269.

36. https://www.learningscientists.org/blog/2024/7/18-1; https://link.springer.com/article/10.1007/s10648-024-09914-w.

37. We should note that we've recommended a standard system of annotation ourselves, *interactive reading*, in our previous book on reading, *Reading Reconsidered*. We've since evolved away from such systems for the reasons discussed in this book.

38. There's also a growing movement advocating for "strategy-driven" instruction, which, while slightly different than "skills," overfocuses on strategies and leads to similar unproductive outcomes.

39. Student Achievement Partners, a nonprofit that studies research to inform teaching, expresses it this way: "The standards themselves are not the goal of daily instruction; understanding the texts encountered and being able to express that understanding is." Text-at-the-Center-Report-V5.pdf, 4.

40. This is one of the most established findings in cognitive psychology. Peter C. Brown, Henry L. Roediger, and Mark A. McDaniel, *Make It Stick: The Science of Successful Learning* (Belknap, 2014) provides an accessible summary of this research.

41. Some readers might worry that the teacher-provided prompts we recommend, such as the annotation tasks we mentioned in the last section, might be liable to the same criticism we level at skills-based objectives here. But the answer to "Why are we making this annotation?" should not be "Because the teacher told us to," but "Because something in the text prompts it (and the teacher's prompting helps us realize that)." These guided prompts that support perception while students read will habituate them over time to making these sorts of perceptions on their own when reading independently.

42. Lesson 13.

43. We use *hack* with a positive connotation here to mean—"finds a short-cut for that makes it more efficient."

44. Lesson 7.

Chapter **3**

Fluency and Ways of Reading

In Chapter One we make the case for the critical importance of fluency, which we define as "reading at the speed of sight." But imagine stepping into a fourth-, sixth-, or eighth-grade classroom and hearing the teacher announce the start of fluency practice.

They're still doing fluency? you might ask. In fact you might assume you were observing a remedial classroom. Or perhaps you'd wonder, *Fluency? How do you teach that?*

After second grade, we have noted, most teachers rarely think about the importance of fluency.[1] Among those who do, it's even rarer to see them devote class time specifically to practicing it.

Yet this is what many of the teachers you'll see in this chapter do. And it's exactly how Scott Wells, Goldsmith Primary Academy in England's year five teacher (the US equivalent of fourth grade), began a recent lesson on Phillip Pullman's novel, *The Firework-Maker's Daughter*. You can watch that lesson in the video *Scott Wells: Fluency Part 1*. It turns out that these fifteen minutes of fluency instruction might be the most important moments of Scott's students' day.

To watch the video *Scott Wells: Fluency Part 1*, use this QR code or find the video at the URL https://vimeo.com/1058356671/b89bbff795.

As you'll recall from Chapter One, there are three key elements of fluency: accuracy—the ability to decode the words in a text as they are written; automaticity—the ability to decode at the speed of sight and thus with no load on working memory; and prosody—the ability to read a text with the cadence and expression of speech. The best way by far to improve fluency is to provide students opportunities to hear, read, and reread text aloud. Scott's students have an opportunity to do all three as part of their lesson.

Scott begins his fluency practice by modeling prosodic reading for students. Hearing the book read well, with depth and meaning, will help them to read the text well on their own. It will help students to recreate prosodic reading like Scott's and so be able to voice their own expressive version of the text. And it will also help them read the text more meaningfully, more responsively, and with greater comprehension. Expressive oral reading leads to expressive silent reading, which in turn is characteristic of better readers. Presumably that's one reason why reading researcher Tim Shanahan notes that oral reading fluency translates to improved silent reading ability.[2]

Since the model is an important part of fluency practice, Scott is sure to direct students' attention before he begins. He "calls his shot," telling students what to pay attention to as he reads so they are more likely to notice it.

"When I'm reading the text today, I would like you please to be looking out for how I am conveying the emotion of the characters," Scott tells his class. "In this next passage . . . I want you to think about how my voice changes when I am reading that particular passage."

It's worth noting that there are lots of ways Scott might have shaped students' attention before a model. He could have said, "Notice the pace at which I read. I don't rush. Good reading is expressive, not fast. Try to notice when I pause." Or he could have noted—as a professor of Doug's once did before reading aloud to undergraduates—"Notice that I am going to try to emphasize any contrasting words I see in each line, to make the tension between them clearer."

There are a thousand ways we could direct attention. And we may not need to direct attention every time we model prosody. But it is worth noting that models are powerful tools for learning—we learn much of what we learn by copying others, often without fully realizing it[3]—so taking a moment to steer what students attend to can be a useful step.

Scott is thinking of student attention again in the next moments of the lesson. "We're beginning from the start of Chapter Six, page 81. Can everyone point to the first word for me, please?"

This might be our favorite moment in the clip because, at Scott's prompting, students take out their books—in hard copy—and put their screens away. It's an attentionally ideal setting now: high text, low tech.

He asks for a brief choral response—"The first word is??" "How!!!!"—so he knows that every student is reading along with him. Seeing the words as he reads them will assist students with orthographic mapping, focus their attention, and, as we will see later, prepare them to be ready to read themselves.

And then he is off and running, reading about two full pages to students, engaging them deeply in the text. You can see evidence of this when he asks them to Turn and Talk briefly to discuss what they've noticed, just after 1:30 of the video. His students are so eager to talk about what they've heard that the roof nearly blows off the room. A story, brought to life is a beautiful thing, not just from a teacher's perspective but from a student's.

A student named Nathan briefly describes some of the things he's noticed Scott doing to create expression in his reading. We like that Scott only takes one answer from his class here. Observations are useful and Scott wants to make sure they listened carefully for the things he asked them to, but the goal was to get them to attend carefully to the model so they would be prepared and motivated to try to replicate it. Talking about the things he's done with his expressive reading may be less valuable than hearing them and trying them.

Which is exactly what students do next. Scott has planned a few minutes of paired reading in which students reread the passage Scott modeled to one another. This means that there are several minutes of sustained fluency practice in which every student in the class will get the opportunity to read and during which Scott will have the opportunity to gather data on their fluency.

It's important to note that Scott is asking students to *reread* a section of the book that he has already read to them. Not all fluency practice has to do this, but there is very strong support in the research for the benefits of repeated reading: having students read a passage more than once, seeking to read it more fluently and expressively each time. One recent review of research on repeated reading by researcher and author Nathaniel Hansford[4] found "strong evidence of efficacy (regardless of assessment conditions, or student age)." And while rereading appears to benefit students without an initial prosodic teacher model, the review also found "a very significant impact for [a teacher] reading the text to students first."[5]

Studies on repeated reading are mostly done in small-group remedial settings, it's important to note. (If that's a topic of interest we highly recommend Christopher Such's *The Art and Science of Teaching Primary Reading* [Corwin, 2021], which we have found immensely practical and insightful on the topic.) But given that Hansford found that "Repeated Reading is clearly the most evidence-based fluency intervention," and given the likely extent of unacknowledged dysfluency, we think there's good reason to try it occasionally in the general classroom as well. Before we leave the topic of repeated reading we'll offer this last observation of Hansford's: "It is interesting to note that while Repeated Reading worked better in elementary school, [there] was still a high impact in secondary school."

A few seconds later, Scott's students are off reading. Notice that he "manages turns," a term we use in our discussion of Turn and Talks in *Teach Like a Champion* for the idea that a teacher can designate one student in each discussion pair (e.g., "window side" or "wall side") to start the conversation, thus causing the students who most like to talk to more often have to listen, and the students who are inclined to be more passive to speak more. Ensuring equity and balance by sometimes choosing which partner starts in a partner read is also immensely valuable.

As students read, Scott circulates. He listens carefully to each student—some of them are lovely readers!—and gives occasional feedback. We've kept a few examples of that in the video for you to see.

To watch the video *Scott Wells: Fluency Part 2*, use this QR code or find the video at the URL https://vimeo.com/1058356806/3fb28ca07a.

After praising his students' oral reading, Scott shifts his approach to fluent reading. Now it's the whole class reading together. You can watch the second part of Scott's fluency lesson in *Scott Wells: Fluency Part 2*.

There are some instantly noticeable similarities between the second part of Scott's fluency lesson and the first. Again, Scott starts by making sure all students have found the right spot in the book. And, again, he starts by modeling the type of prosody students should strive for. There's a lovely moment of emphasis on the vocabulary word *grovel* at about 36 seconds.

When Scott finishes his reading, he asks Harlow, then Ruby, and then Toby to read. Each student reader is comfortable and confident when they're called on to read, and Toby's reading is especially expressive and meaning-laden.

The technique that Scott is using here is FASE Reading, a system to foster productive student oral reading in the classroom, which we discuss in Chapter Two. We'll study it in more depth later in this chapter, but for now, we note that the goal of FASE is to optimize several benefits of shared oral reading—making it fluent, attentive, social, and expressive, with fluency foremost among them. In this case FASE means the text is read aloud by both students (selected by the teacher to ensure a wide variety of readers) and by the teacher (Scott reads two passages).

Before we delve into what makes teaching fluency effective, let's revisit that initial reaction some teachers may have had: "Why is he teaching fluency at this stage in school?" In Chapter

One, we refer to a body of research that illustrates the critical link between fluency and reading comprehension. Frighteningly, we note, far more students are probably dysfluent than most educators realize. It's even more shocking that as far as we know, no one knows for sure how high the rate of dysfluency is in the upper grades because it doesn't get measured. What percentage of middle or high school students do studies suggest are dysfluent? We couldn't find any data so we asked David Paige, one of the foremost researchers on reading fluency. Even he had to try to back his way into numbers from the data tables in the appendix of one study, and even then what he gave us was his best guess. Given the critical importance of fluency, our lack of data—what's the status of American high school students—or assessment infrastructure beyond the primary grades is shocking.

As we discuss further in Chapter Four, reading is complex and relies on multiple processes happening simultaneously in the brain. Christopher Such explains that this complexity makes it difficult to diagnose reading issues because "apparent difficulties in one area of comprehension might be the result of difficulties in another."[6] A student who can't successfully make a character inference from a text might not be able to do so because she doesn't understand the character, but she also might not be able to read the passage with fluency.

In fact dysfluency is almost assured of causing comprehension challenges because when a student's working memory is heavily loaded by navigating the words and syntax of a passage, they no longer have capacity to perceive and remember the meaning of the text. Unbeknownst to many teachers and parents, dysfluency is often at the root of comprehension issues. If you have experience trying to learn a foreign language, particularly as an adult, you have probably experienced the sort of effortful reading that is common for dysfluent readers. You read and must pause to consciously remember words and decipher phrases. You can often figure them out within a few seconds, but only through conscious effort, and by the time you've done that, you then have to circle back and read the sentence again, possibly several times, to figure out what it actually means. When listening or reading, you can keep up for a sentence or two, but your working memory is soon overloaded and you lose the ability to sustain meaning making. As long as you have to extend effort to decipher the words, you are not yet able to read in the fullest sense of the word. Comprehension is a struggle.

So in many classrooms, fluency gaps are almost assuredly misdiagnosed as comprehension problems and students do not receive the support that would improve their fluent reading. So when we don't get regular data on student fluency, we're likely to miss both the cause of and the solution to many reading issues.

ORTHOGRAPHIC MAPPING

Strong fluency relies on orthographic mapping, a process by which individual words we have seen repeatedly become stored in our long-term memory, ideally connected to meaning. When words are orthographically mapped, we can read them "at the speed of sight" without effortful decoding. "Fluent reading is acquired only through repeated decoding; it is this that allows . . . words to become 'glued' to the pronunciations stored in the reader's memory," Christopher Such writes. "This process is called orthographic mapping."[7]

This process, and others implicit in fluency, relies on an immense quantity of practice in which correct mapping is reinforced and incorrect mapping revealed and corrected.

Orthographic mapping is critical for students in the primary grades as they learn to read, but it continues to affect meaning making even into adulthood in part because of the increasing linguistic and syntactic complexity of the texts that older readers encounter. The words that readers must recognize at a glance are always changing and increasing. As students read harder texts, they are likely to encounter new and more complex vocabulary, which they may not have mapped. When students read texts with a high number of words that they have not yet had sufficient exposure to map, fluency breaks down. Thus it is likely that a measure of a student's fluency would change based on the text he or she is reading.

A side note that syntax also becomes more complex over time, and, like words, also demands close to speed-of-sight recognition. The primary challenge of the first year of law school is largely syntactical for many students. They are learning to read case law. Even if they understand the arcane vocabulary, the convoluted syntax is laborious to untangle. Until this process is automatized (that is, can be done without engaging working memory) many high achievers are barely able to make sense of what they read. Similarly, students who appear fluent in grade six, say, might find fluency an unexpected barrier to comprehension as they read increasingly complex texts.

The extent of a developing reader's orthographic mapping affects all three aspects of fluent reading. Much of accuracy is mere recognition of mapped words. Automaticity relies on instant recognition, so a large portion of reading rate is determined by the depth of a student's orthographic map. And though it may be less intuitive, orthographic mapping also contributes to prosody. When we see a word that we know, we immediately and automatically start to draw on our knowledge of and affective associations with the word, using them to make meaning, which is necessary to expressive, prosodic reading. It is *possible* to map a word independent of its meaning, but most words that we map as units of symbols we also map as units of meaning.

Orthographic mapping is foundational to all aspects of fluency, in other words. We've tried to capture that in this chart.

Most of accuracy is the result of orthographic mapping. There are a small number of cases where unfamiliar words and forms of wordshave to be decoded (e.g., names, new vocab).

Orthographic mapping is also probably the dominant element within automaticity. To be automatic is to recognize words at the speed of sight, though also to link words and chunk them and attend to punctuation, infer syntax, etc.

Orthographic also probably contributes to prosody. Having more fluid recognition frees working memory to think about expression and familiar words are likely to be mapped with associations in terms of affect and knowledge that can assist in expressive reading.

Given its importance, then, we should try to reinforce orthographic map building as often as possible as students read at all grade levels.

- One of the simplest things we can do to reinforce orthographic mapping is to cause students to repeat a word when they have read it aloud and don't know it. ("That word is *pejorative*. Try that: *pejorative*.") Orthographic mapping is a sight-sound connection. It's hard to map a word you can't say.

- Another effective move is to provide a very quick definition. ("That word is *pejorative*. Try that: *pejorative*. Good. *Pejorative* means expressing disapproval.") This is because when we map words connected to meaning, it makes our memory of them more durable.

- A final move is to engage the student very briefly in thinking about the word, again to imprint the memory of it more strongly. ("That word is *pejorative*. Try that: *pejorative*. Good. *Pejorative* means expressing disapproval. Who's being pejorative toward whom in this scene?")

We discuss these moves more in Chapter Five on vocabulary. Part of what we recommend there is that teachers use a set of tools that look very much like the three just described to reinforce vocabulary implicitly—as students read. Much of what we are doing in those cases is in fact seeking to cause students to attend to the correct reading of the word more carefully so it is more likely to be encoded in their orthographic map. Not coincidentally, the moves we describe mostly rely on students to be reading aloud. One more reason why reading aloud is so valuable.

To watch the video *Patrick Pastore: Bedevil*, use this QR code or find the video at the URL https://vimeo.com/1058357022/65c768e90b.

In the video *Patrick Pastore: Bedevil*, you can clearly see the relationship between orthographic mapping and fluency. A student in Patrick's sixth-grade class struggles to decode the word *bedevil*, but Patrick assists him in decoding it and there is a sudden moment of recognition. "Oh, bedevil," the student says. Turns out it's a familiar word. He now has a stronger map for it.

So, orthographic mapping is a hidden driver of fluent reading. It is constantly developing but is also constantly challenged by exposure to increasingly difficult texts. And reading aloud gives us ideal opportunities to reinforce it. This means lots of reading is critical for students of all ages. "This might seem obvious, but many schools seem to pay little attention to [the] quantitative aspect of reading instruction in their classrooms," argues Christopher Such.[8]

It doesn't seem revelatory to suggest that we should offer more opportunities for reading in our literacy classes, but given the decline of reading outside of school, the time students spend immersed in text within our classroom walls is more critical than ever. In many cases, much of the time spent in discussions of interpretations of text or study of the illusory "skills" implicit in meaning making would be better spent just reading, as we discuss in Chapter One.

Running is a decent analogy. If you want to be a distance runner, you have to put in the miles. Sure, you can improve your results by refining your strategy and studying up on the best training plans. In the end, though, there is no way around the fact that success requires a lot of road miles. In the case of reading, we sometimes refer to this as "miles on the page." Quantity of reading matters. But more reading doesn't automatically lead to better fluency. To ensure the time we invest in reading is more productive, we should be intentional about *how* we use it so that we maximize the potential benefits in terms of fluency and comprehension.

Scott Wells's lesson is effective in part because of the amount of time students spend reading, but it's even more effective because of his intentional modeling and careful design of different types of fluent reading activities. As teachers of literacy (and other disciplines!), we are faced with a great opportunity to support our students in reading widely and extensively, to spend more time immersed in great texts building fluency and comprehension, and to inspire students to read more when outside of our classroom walls.

In this chapter, we will discuss ways to build and reinforce fluency, especially through the shared reading of a whole-class text. We'll focus on different actions teachers can take while using the three ways of reading we discussed in another of our books, *Reading Reconsidered*, and that we refer to throughout much of this book: Teacher Read Aloud, shared oral reading (FASE Reading), and independent reading (Accountable Independent Reading: AIR). We'll reflect on how we can implement and adapt each of these tools to help students read more fluently, enjoy reading, and accrue the benefits of extensive reading. We'll start with a look at how these three approaches to reading work in synergy to support student fluency.

BALANCING THREE WAYS OF READING

We want students to read a lot but we want to think about how they read in order to ensure student success. The way Teacher Read Aloud, FASE Reading, and AIR are implemented—and the balance among them—can have a dramatic impact not just on the amount of reading miles students cover but also on their fluency and the quality of their reading—even their love and passion for reading.

There are clear benefits to giving students robust opportunities to interact with text in each of the three ways, but each also has limitations. In *Reading Reconsidered*, we outline the benefits and limitations of each way of reading and describe ways to maximize the benefits and minimize the limitations of each.

A teacher reading aloud can model prosody that students can copy, for example. But students will need opportunities to practice oral reading if we want them to turn that model into their own expressive reading. If they do that, they're more likely to have strong prosody in their silent reading.

It's not a competition, in other words. The strengths of one address the limitations of another. The three ways of reading work in synergy and require balance: there is no formula for which one, when, and how much. The goal is to achieve the right combination in light of the students you have in the room and the specific demands of the text they're reading. If we do that, we can reliably create for students meaningful, productive, and joyful interactions with text.

One of the core principles of learning that cognitive science has established is the power of "gradual release" (of responsibility). Instruction often works best when learners first see a model, then practice completing a version of the model as a group, attending to different component parts. Then they complete increasingly complex versions of the model independently. As the following figure illustrates, the three ways of reading can be used similarly. Teacher Read Aloud models strong fluent reading. FASE Reading and Read Aloud together model independent reading. AIR provides students opportunities to apply what they have learned. It's a deliberate effort to harness the transfer of oral reading fluency instruction and turn it into silent reading ability.

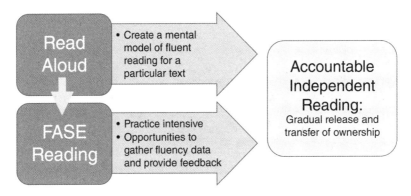

Again, we don't recommend that these are used sequentially or for a set amount of time in every lesson. As with so many of our recommendations in this book, it's important to choose which way of reading is best given your knowledge of the text and its complexity, and your knowledge of your students and their reading abilities. The more complex or critical the section of text, the more it might benefit from Teacher Read Aloud. Beginnings of texts are also useful, important sections to consider reading aloud or practicing together using FASE Reading, as students are exposed for the first time to an author's style and voice as well as new context. As the following figure illustrates, teachers can move between ways of reading throughout a text based on their readers and the demands of the text.

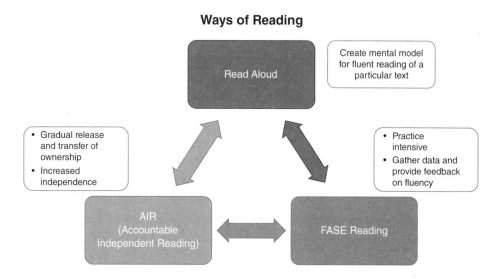

Ways of Reading

Read Aloud

Create mental model for fluent reading of a particular text

- Gradual release and transfer of ownership
- Increased independence

- Practice intensive
- Gather data and provide feedback on fluency

AIR (Accountable Independent Reading)

FASE Reading

The deep dive into each of the ways of reading that follows will help you consider other times when it might be appropriate to use each type of reading, as well as discuss further ways that the three work collectively.

TEACHER READ ALOUD

Teacher Read Aloud is a critical tool for modeling fluent reading of challenging texts, so it's important to plan and practice for it with intentionality. Students will apply what they learn through Read Aloud models in their own oral and silent reading.

You may be surprised that we've decided to start with Read Aloud in a book intended to address literacy instruction beyond the primary grades. In *Reading Reconsidered*, we saved it for last. Maybe we were feeling a little sheepish about advocating for it at first. We aren't now.

Read Aloud is the simple act of teachers (or parents) reading aloud *to* students. It can and should be an opportunity to share in, relish, and savor the beauty of books—one of the most joyful parts of the students' and teachers' day. It is also more critical to building fluency and preparing students to comprehend rich, complex texts than we originally understood.

You might be familiar with Scarborough's rope, an iconic diagram first published by Dr. Hollis Scarborough in 2001. It separates into "strands" the skills and knowledge that ultimately combine in successful reading and shows how they develop independently of each other. While students are learning to decode, they are learning vocabulary and syntax through oral language. They will later apply this knowledge in deciphering written language.

Read Aloud enables teachers to focus on the language comprehension strands and build students' understanding of the language forms and features they'll begin to encounter as they read increasingly complex texts. A good Read Aloud allows students to access a text well beyond what they can read on their own, enabling them to familiarize themselves with more complex vocabulary, rhythm, and patterns of syntax. Not only does hearing text read aloud provide them access to more complex and sophisticated texts, this exposure to new knowledge, vocabulary, and syntax prepares them to independently make meaning as they encounter increasingly challenging texts. (We'll go deeper on the importance of knowledge and vocabulary in Chapters Four and Five.)

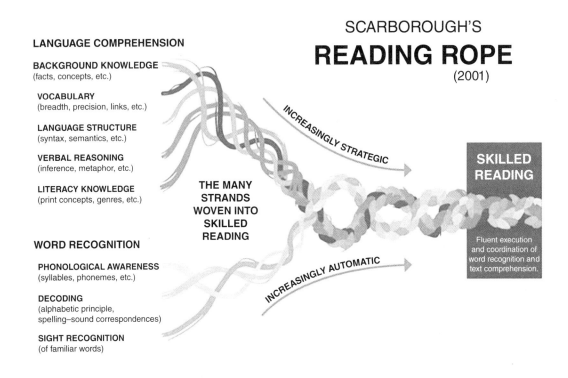

SCARBOROUGH'S
READING ROPE
(2001)

LANGUAGE COMPREHENSION

BACKGROUND KNOWLEDGE
(facts, concepts, etc.)

VOCABULARY
(breadth, precision, links, etc.)

LANGUAGE STRUCTURE
(syntax, semantics, etc.)

VERBAL REASONING
(inference, metaphor, etc.)

LITERACY KNOWLEDGE
(print concepts, genres, etc.)

WORD RECOGNITION

PHONOLOGICAL AWARENESS
(syllables, phonemes, etc.)

DECODING
(alphabetic principle, spelling–sound correspondences)

SIGHT RECOGNITION
(of familiar words)

INCREASINGLY STRATEGIC

THE MANY STRANDS WOVEN INTO SKILLED READING

INCREASINGLY AUTOMATIC

SKILLED READING

Fluent execution and coordination of word recognition and text comprehension.

In her book *The Knowledge Gap*, Natalie Wexler describes the importance of reading aloud:

> Teachers need to read those [complex] texts *aloud* to the whole class and lead discussions focused on the content. It's been found that children can take in more complex concepts and vocabulary through listening than through their own reading until about age 13, on average. Once they've acquired knowledge about a topic through listening and discussion, it can fuel their ability to read and write about *that topic*. And eventually, through learning about a series of specific topics, they'll acquire the critical mass of academic vocabulary that will boost their general reading comprehension.[9]

Read Aloud also has the benefit of speed. This statement might seem ironic because we often remark on how the best oral reading is not only not fast but a little bit slow. But even so—even read at 90 percent of the oral rate—a teacher reading a book aloud to students can often cover more ground, more quickly, than the students themselves could if they were reading on their own, especially if the text is more complex and challenging than students could ably and reliably decode on their own. When the text is hard and the teacher reads it aloud faster than students can, the rate of exposure to key ideas, background knowledge, rare words, and technical vocabulary is accelerated. If quantity of experience is necessary to master reading the quasi-regular system that we know as the English language, Read Aloud can do more than just bring the text to life: it can accelerate the absorption of knowledge.

We believe that every classroom—all grades and across subjects—will benefit from a healthy dose of Read Aloud. It should be an integral part of any successful reading program in order to do the following:

- Model fluent reading for students.
- Expose students to texts (and ideas!) above their reading level.
- Instill a love of reading and a love a literature in our students.
- Build shared and collective experiences through reading.

We see this as a particularly important topic because the older a child gets, the less that child is read aloud to—both at home and in the classroom. This means that even in families where students were read aloud to as toddlers and young children, when they reach middle school, they are likely being read aloud to significantly less, if at all, both at home and at school. It is therefore even more critical that Read Aloud becomes an important part of reading instruction across grade levels. In the following sections, we'll describe how to use Read Aloud in a way that intentionally builds student fluency.

Model Fluent and Expressive Reading

As we saw in Scott's class, Read Aloud provides a model of fluent expressive reading for students. Having a mental model, or a conception of what high-level execution of the end goal looks (and sounds!) like, is critical for execution and adaptation of any complex task. This includes helping students hear what language sounds like when read aloud with mastery. Our mental models are critical for helping kids develop an ear for the diverse texts we read: Frederick Douglass sounds different read aloud than Roald Dahl; scientific or historical texts have a different sound when read aloud with strong prosody, as well.

Here is a passage on basic cell structure from a National Cancer Institute training module:[10]

> *The cell membrane separates the material outside the cell, extracellular, from the material inside the cell, intracellular. It maintains the integrity of a cell and controls passage of materials into and out of the cell. All materials within a cell must have access to the cell membrane (the cell's boundary) for the needed exchange.*
>
> *The cell membrane is a double layer of phospholipid molecules. Proteins in the cell membrane provide structural support, form channels for passage of materials, act as receptor sites, function as carrier molecules, and provide identification markers.*

To read this passage correctly requires a mental model of what scientific text sounds like. The words *extracellular* and *intracellular* in the first sentence are appositives that give the technical name for what's just been described. In reading them aloud (or silently), one would probably pause briefly before them and emphasize them to express their importance. They are key terms to remember with definitions provided at their first appearance. The parenthetical "the cell's boundary" would probably be read in a lower voice and deemphasized slightly to express the idea that this a reminder of a common synonym for the term "cell membrane," which is preferred. The last sentence is constructed of a series of phrases describing the functions of proteins in the cell membrane. If you (or your students) were new to this content, you would read it slowly, pausing briefly between each point and perhaps annotating or underlining if the material was new and less familiar. An expert, by contrast, would gallop through them as a brief reminder.

Developing such a mental model, research suggests, will not only inform how students themselves read aloud but also how they read silently. The model shapes what you perceive and expect to perceive. "Mental construction of daily activities, more than the activity itself, defines our reality," the social scientist researcher Shawn Achor points out. In his study of the psychological benefits of gratitude, he refers to a "cognitive afterimage," the idea that you get better at seeing what you practice looking for and attending to.[11] Achor calls this the *Tetris effect*: gamers who play Tetris frequently start to see its component shapes everywhere. Your perception is influenced by what you pay attention to.

One of the core outcomes we seek as reading teachers is a sort of cognitive afterimage in our students when they read silently. We want their internal reading voice to be characterized by expression and prosody that bring the book to life during independent reading, thus enhancing meaning and perhaps pleasure. Remember the fluent and confident reading of Scott Wells's students? Scott had provided them with a mental model of how to convey character emotions in the way Philip Pullman intended. When practicing their own reading aloud, Scott's students were able to perceive the text better, leading to a stronger, more prosodic reading of the text.

Read Aloud is important for letting students hear fluent readers so that they have a mental model of what expressive reading sounds like and can work to emulate it. It is important to model expression and linger over words with pleasure, both to convey our passion for reading and to enable students to access and engage with the text. You need only to compare two classrooms in which one teacher reads expressively and the other reads dryly, and you immediately see the differences in both student engagement and comprehension. Modeling expressive and dramatic reading may involve some risk-taking— especially if you're not the dramatic type. But the risk is

To watch the video *The Read Aloud Montage*, use this QR code or find the video at the URL https://vimeo. com/1058357159/2c507deb0b.

worth it: you will not only show kids how to unlock the expressive parts of language but also make it safe for them to take the risk of reading with spirit and enthusiasm when they engage in their own opportunities to read aloud. *The Read Aloud Montage* presents five examples of teachers whose Read Alouds model what we are speaking about here.

Don't fall into the trap of thinking Read Aloud should only be saved for the most dramatic moments in a book, or even just for fiction. As you prepare to read aloud, it's important to be intentional about modeling prosodic reading, which involves appropriate phrasing and intonation (or rise and fall in tone); appropriate stress or emphasis given to particular words, syllables, or phrases; and the rhythm with which you read. Each of these elements is important to model for kids—in lots of different types of texts. It can be tempting to choose to read aloud only the most dramatic sections of text filled with emotional or suspenseful dialogue. However, students are more likely to read these sections of text with lots of expression on their own anyway, but struggle more when trying to read a biology textbook in a way that the author probably intended.

Reading is like making music. The notes and rests have different lengths, implicit in both how they are written and how they are interpreted. In the first sentence of this paragraph, for example, the words *making* and *music* run together slightly more than the other words for most readers. Most strong readers would group those words for emphasis and rhythm, thereby emphasizing and making clearer the sentence's meaning. As with music, some of the meaning is made visible by punctuation, while other aspects are less obvious.

When you read, help students recognize how the text should sound by conscious grouping. Seek to model stringing words together in logical groups that students will ultimately replicate in their own reading. Look, for example, for words in prepositional phrases to stick together, for a drop in the voice and a slight acceleration for a parenthetical (which occur more frequently in nonnarrative nonfiction texts). Also consider emphasizing especially important words in a passage and letting your intonation fall when reading less critical words or phrases. Important words are often identified by italics, capitals, and underlines, but you might also consider other textual aspects to highlight based on either plot or genre.

Remember that as an expert reader, the speed of your natural reading may make it difficult for students to follow along in the text, hindering their ability to derive meaning from the text and making it less likely they'll be able to replicate your model. Christopher Such recommends reading slightly slower than your typical reading pace to allow students to absorb more from your model.[12] Of course, reading too slowly can also impede prosody, so it's best to aim for a slower-than-typical speed that's not so slow it significantly hampers prosody. When we, as adult readers, read a bit more slowly, students can keep up with our pace of reading, attend carefully to the words and process them with a bit more time, allowing them to linger over particular scenes or more carefully attend tone words or phrases.

To watch the video *Gabby Woolf: The Carew Murder Case*, use this QR code or find the video at the URL https://vimeo.com/1058357578/78ce4d0219.

We'd love you to rewatch *Gabby Woolf: The Carew Murder Case* (originally shared in Chapter Two) as she reads aloud from *Dr. Jekyll and Mr. Hyde* to her year 10 (ninth grade) students, this time with a focus on fluency. As she reads aloud, she connects her model to an idea that will be critical to students' larger understanding—Victorian sensationalism. She's clearly prepared to make sure she's able not just to read the book with expression but also to make the sensationalist theme more legible. Notice how she lingers on the bones being "audibly shattered"—she *must* have practiced that! Notice also that she is at about a 90 percent pace. We often suggest a rule of thumb in workshops of 90 percent pace, 10 percent expression as the ideal to support students prosodic reading and enable them to perceive rich concepts like the use of sensationalism that Gabby emphasizes.

Expressive models are equally important whether you are reading *Dr. Jekyll and Mr. Hyde, Frog and Toad,* "A Summary of the Oxygen Cycle," or the directions to a word problem. In fact, students may have the least developed ear for the latter two examples and may therefore get the most out of hearing those read aloud fluently.

A particularly important time for expressive models is at the start of a longer section of oral reading or when starting up again after a break for discussion. Reading the first few sentences yourself models and normalizes expressiveness and helps engage and sustain interest in the text by getting it off to an exciting start. The energy, expressiveness, and intonation you bring to oral reading will be reflected in your students' oral (and silent) reading through increased fluency and, ultimately, pleasure in reading.

Watch Jill Murray in *Jill Murray: The Quartering Act* as she reads aloud in her third grade class in the Bronx, New York from a nonfiction text about the Quartering Act. Many teachers fear that nonfiction will be dry or boring for kids, but Jill's reading brings to life the drama between the colonists and the British. As a result, kids are riveted as they listen, on the edge of their seats wanting to know more, and are more fluent when they themselves read the nonfiction text aloud.

To watch the video *Jill Murray: The Quartering Act,* use this QR code or find the video at the URL https://vimeo.com/1058357792/ a68a546b26.

In order to help your students perceive better and attend to what you're trying to model, it's helpful to be explicit about what they're listening for as you read. We saw this earlier when Scott Wells called his shot at the start of the chapter on *The Firework-Maker's Daughter.* We saw him do something similar in a recent lesson focused on the novel *Wonder* by R. J. Palacio. Scott explained to his students that the mood of the chapter they were about to read was "quite sad and unhappy." Then, just before he began his read aloud, he said, "I'm going to read this next chapter in a really moody tone, a really unhappy tone. Make sure you're listening for that." This explicit description of his model supports students in their comprehension and makes them more attentive to what "moody" narration sounds like, something they'll now be more likely be able to copy in their own reading. We also watched a teacher recently call her shot by asking students to attend to a grammatical feature. "Listen to me pause at commas," she said, causing her students to be more attentive to the presence of punctuation marks—surely a common barrier to fluent reading for many students.

Inspiring a Love of Reading

If a teacher shows love for (or interest in, or fascination with) the text that she is reading, it is likely that her students will, too. For most of us, it is not hard to rave about a favorite book, and this passion comes through in our reading. In cases when our scope and sequence or curriculum map includes a text that doesn't light us up, it's important to work to do some research to consider what makes it a great text worth reading, and to take a small risk of showing some passion in our reading of it.

Becoming passionate about books and recognizing that reading can bring pleasure are especially vital for our most struggling readers who haven't experienced success in literacy classes. For many students, reading may have been a consistent point of frustration. Helping them see what joy and pleasure reading can bring will unlock a barrier to achievement. Read Aloud, with its model for what effective reading looks like, can open students' eyes to the enjoyable side of reading that they might not otherwise be able to access, helping to instill a passion for literature so that students want it for themselves.

You can see an example of this as you watch Eric Snider in *Eric Snider: Epic Voyage* read an excerpt from *Endurance: Shackleton's Epic Voyage* by Alfred Lansing with his sixth-grade students. He conveys his appreciation of the author's words not just explicitly ("Oooh! I just really like his writing style!") but also through his dramatic reading of the story of Shackleton's adventures. Listen carefully, and you can hear Kyle, the student Eric calls on to read aloud, try to copy Eric's expressive model, even in this complex text.

To watch the video *Eric Snider: Epic Voyage*, use this QR code or find the video at the URL https://vimeo.com/1058358047/51838a3168.

Advanced Preparation and Practice

In order to effectively model fluent and expressive reading, it's important to preview the text in advance to determine which words to emphasize and where to add emotion. Reading the text in advance of teaching it also will enable you to convey more meaning when reading aloud in front of students because you yourself know where the story is headed.

Consider the following example that one of our colleagues prepared for a Read Aloud from the opening of Lois Lowry's *The Giver*. Her goal in reading aloud was to convey the ominous tone and mood Lowry creates in her opening, as well as to help students orient themselves in a passage that deliberately creates a bit of mystery and uncertainty. You'll note the stage directions she's jotted to herself at the top ("ominous tone and mood") as well as reminders at key moments about how she wants to read—"slow and low" for the first paragraph and "through a speaker" on page 2. Additionally, she's provided an annotation task for kids and noted annotations to herself. This will remind her to read those sections with intentionality to support students' meaning making as they follow along.

You'll also notice that she plans to pause to model her own confusion about the curious behavior of Jonas's community members when they see the jet fly overhead, which normalizes the idea that sometimes it takes a bit of reading (and rereading) to figure out the author's intended meaning. In this case, it's a moment critical to our later understanding of this dystopian community, but sometimes it's something as simple as an unclear pronoun referent ("*It* is used three times. I want to go back and double check to make sure I know what *it* refers to.").

Read aloud: (pgs. 1-3)
- ominous tone and mood

Annotation task:
- What is Jonas remembering?
- Details that seem frightening

ONE

IT WAS ALMOST December, and Jonas was beginning to be frightened. No. Wrong word, Jonas thought. Frightened meant that deep, sickening feeling of something terrible about to happen. Frightened was the way he had felt a year ago when an unidentified aircraft had overflown the community twice. He had seen it both times. Squinting toward the sky, he had seen the sleek jet, almost a blur at its high speed, go past, and a second later heard the blast of sound that followed. Then one more time, a moment later, from the opposite direction, the same plane.

slow + low

At first, he had been only fascinated. He had never seen aircraft so close, for it was against the rules for Pilots to fly over the community. Occasionally, when supplies were deliv-

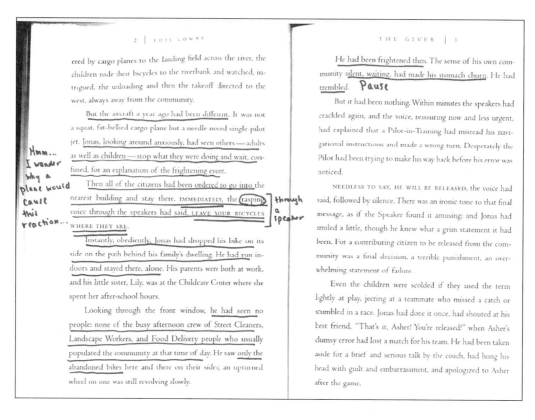

ered by cargo planes to the landing field across the river, the children rode their bicycles to the riverbank and watched, intrigued, the unloading and then the takeoff directed to the west, always away from the community.

But the aircraft a year ago had been different. It was not a squat, fat-bellied cargo plane but a needle-nosed single-pilot jet. Jonas, looking around anxiously, had seen others — adults as well as children — stop what they were doing and wait, confused, for an explanation of the frightening event.

Hmm... I wonder why a plane would cause this reaction...

Then all of the citizens had been ordered to go into the nearest building and stay there. IMMEDIATELY, the rasping voice through the speakers had said, LEAVE YOUR BICYCLES WHERE THEY ARE.

through a speaker

Instantly, obediently, Jonas had dropped his bike on its side on the path behind his family's dwelling. He had run indoors and stayed there, alone. His parents were both at work, and his little sister, Lily, was at the Childcare Center where she spent her after-school hours.

Looking through the front window, he had seen no people: none of the busy afternoon crew of Street Cleaners, Landscape Workers, and Food Delivery people who usually populated the community at that time of day. He saw only the abandoned bikes here and there on their sides; an upturned wheel on one was still revolving slowly.

He had been frightened then. The sense of his own community silent, waiting, had made his stomach churn. He had trembled. *Pause*

But it had been nothing. Within minutes the speakers had crackled again, and the voice, reassuring now and less urgent, had explained that a Pilot-in-Training had misread his navigational instructions and made a wrong turn. Desperately the Pilot had been trying to make his way back before his error was noticed.

NEEDLESS TO SAY, HE WILL BE RELEASED, the voice had said, followed by silence. There was an ironic tone to that final message, as if the Speaker found it amusing; and Jonas had smiled a little, though he knew what a grim statement it had been. For a contributing citizen to be released from the community was a final decision, a terrible punishment, an overwhelming statement of failure.

Even the children were scolded if they used the term lightly at play, jeering at a teammate who missed a catch or stumbled in a race. Jonas had done it once, had shouted at his best friend, "That's it, Asher! You're released!" when Asher's clumsy error had lost a match for his team. He had been taken aside for a brief and serious talk by the coach, had hung his head with guilt and embarrassment, and apologized to Asher after the game.

Here are some other text features you might attend to carefully in planning a strong Read Aloud:

- **Complex sentence structure.** Identify sentences that have multiple clauses or more sophisticated syntactical structures that might be hard for kids to untangle. Read them more slowly, or consider reading them twice to support comprehension. These are the sentences that can cause even expert readers (when reading aloud) to stumble, so a bit of advanced preparation will ensure a smoother read aloud.

- **Dialogue.** Knowing in advance when characters are speaking and how an author uses dialogue to convey character emotion is critical in bringing the text and all its drama to life for students.

- **Punctuation.** Developing readers tend to read through punctuation because their working memories are focused on accurately decoding words. Model for them pausing at commas and periods and slightly raising your intonation at question marks.

- **Difficult vocabulary.** As we discuss in Chapter Five, Read Aloud is a prime time to expose kids to complex vocabulary. Identify challenging words in advance and prepare a brief definition to share as you're reading in order to remove barriers to comprehension.

A common mistake that teachers make in reading aloud to students is neglecting to practice. Simply picking the passage that you want to read for your students is not enough. Pick it and pre-read it to ensure that your model is intentional and instructive. While it's completely fine to make mistakes and correct ourselves when reading (in fact, we'd argue it's important for building a culture where error is acceptable), we do want to be sufficiently prepared for an instructive model that our students learn from as we read. We can inadvertently disrupt accurate orthographic mapping for students with our own mispronunciation of words.

Make Read Aloud an Active Experience for Students

One challenge of Read Aloud is ensuring that it is a productive learning activity during which students are actively listening and making meaning of the text. In addition to bringing the text to life for students with fluent and expressive reading, you can support their attentiveness and comprehension by asking kids to annotate while they read (see more in Chapter Two) and pausing periodically to check for understanding to ensure they are effectively establishing meaning. Basic questions like, "Where does Anne Marie find herself now?" "Which character is speaking?" or "What just happened?" can prevent students from zoning out and support them in following along with the text.

In addition to asking questions about the text, it's also important to drop in key pieces of background knowledge or vocabulary that might be barriers to comprehension for students. While reading the opening pages of *The Outsiders*, when Ponyboy refers to Paul Newman, you might pause briefly from your reading to say, "Paul Newman was a famous movie star in the 1960s," before immediately picking up with your reading. This technique, Knowledge Feeding, which we describe more fully in Chapter Four, can support students in fully engaging with the text and following the narrative, argument, or exposition. Chapter Five on vocabulary instruction goes into more depth on how to teach vocabulary words as you read aloud.

Here's the opening of another Lois Lowry novel, *Number the Stars*, that a teacher prepared to do a Read Aloud for his class. You'll notice that he's included an annotation task as well as the ideal annotations so that he can reinforce and support students in their own annotations while reading. In this example, we can see how the teacher has thought intentionally about how to support engagement and meaning making. He's identified and jotted definitions for key vocabulary, and just after he reads the first page to his students, he's planned a question to Establish Meaning (EM) or confirm understanding ("What are the girls doing? Why?") before moving to the second page.

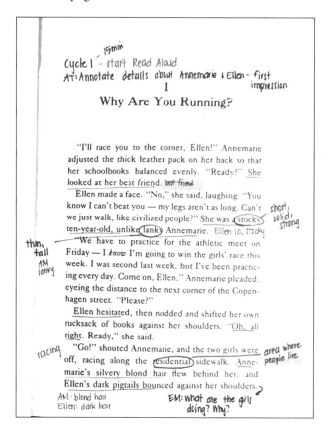

(Sometimes) Incorporate Audiobook Readings

Teachers often ask us if they can use an audiobook rather than read the text aloud themselves. We love the idea of exposing students to the reading of a professional reader, or even better, hearing the story read by the author themselves. That said, audiobooks shouldn't replace Read Aloud entirely because they don't allow you to model with intentionality based on the reading needs of your students. If (and when, and we hope you do!) you use an audiobook, be sure to plan pause points to feed critical knowledge or ask questions to Establish Meaning and confirm understanding. Similarly, when students use audiobooks to support their independent reading, it's important for them also to follow along in the book to support their fluency and orthographic mapping.

FASE READING

FASE Reading is a system for shared oral reading designed to be productive and engaging. It provides opportunities for students to practice their fluency and get immediate feedback from the expert reader in the room, their teacher. When carefully and systematically implemented, FASE contributes to a culture where students love reading and read a lot.

The acronym FASE stands for the type of reading the system is designed to reinforce: fluent, attentive, social, and expressive. It's a consistent approach to having students read aloud so that they follow along and are always ready to read themselves, and it's a critical tool to reinforce correct orthographic mapping and reveal and correct incorrect mapping.

The practice of healthy doses of shared oral reading dissents from widely used literacy practices in the last several decades. We are often struck by the number of veteran teachers for whom the idea of the shared reading of a whole-class text feels inconceivable or even taboo. They have come to believe that writing about and discussing texts are more valuable classroom activities for students than the act of actually reading (and enjoying) those texts. However, as Christopher Such explains, "This [children writing after reading] is a good way for the teacher to assess whether something has been understood, but it is the reading itself and the related discussion that best advances children's ability to read." He goes on to advise, "If in doubt, aim for roughly two-thirds of the lesson to comprise reading and one-third of the lesson to compromise discussion."[13]

Since fluent reading develops mostly through students hearing and practicing it, FASE Reading is a critical tool for building fluency for students of all age levels—not just primary-level students. In addition to providing opportunities to practice and apply expressive reading, it enables a teacher to efficiently gather lots of data, not just on student fluency but on comprehension—it's hard to bring meaning to a text with strong oral reading if you don't understand it. At the same time student reading reveals fluency and decoding issues and gaps in orthographic mapping. In many cases we can address this immediately, ensuring that students are not encoding inaccurate pronunciations of words or internalizing stilted or wooden reading practices. Fluency is both an indicator and driver of reading comprehension, so shared reading supports students in comprehending text, especially complex texts that might otherwise be at the edge of their comprehension capacity.

Additionally, FASE Reading makes other aspects of reading visible and therefore part of students' mental models: pausing to take notes, clarify meaning, or rereading. Ultimately, FASE provides students with practice at this key task of reading—ideally pleasurable and meaningful practice in a setting of shared appreciation among peers—and helps expand the model that Read Aloud builds. In FASE Reading, when one student is reading aloud, everyone attentively reads along with them. This is in contrast to traditional round-robin reading, which begins with a teacher assigning every student an excerpt from the text (often a paragraph each) with students waiting to read until the class arrives at their assigned passage. As a result, students can tune out while others are reading because they know their reading assignment—what it is and when it's coming. Teachers using FASE invite students to read aloud as the text unfolds, incentivizing everyone to follow along. Another important feature of FASE is that teachers are able to intentionally assign students passages of varying length and complexity to support them in successfully reading aloud. The techniques in this section describe the intentional moves teachers can make to build a strong system for FASE Reading and ensure that all students benefit from shared reading, especially when it comes to building and reinforcing fluency, as well as feel safe, comfortable, and excited to read aloud alongside their peers.

Building Fluency and Expressiveness

One of the greatest benefits of FASE Reading is that it enables students to practice fluency and decoding and demonstrate comprehension, while enabling teachers to assess and support them. All teachers (literacy and otherwise) need to have tools to support students in continuing to accurately decode and develop fluency—especially given that teachers in the upper grades, who often aren't explicitly trained in how to teach phonics and decoding, are often teaching students who have skill gaps or who are reading difficult and challenging texts.

Without FASE Reading and an intentional focus on increasing students' opportunities to read aloud, occasions for both student practice and teacher support become few and far between.

Given the restrictions on the time we have to explicitly teach and practice fluency past second or third grade, it is vital that all teachers are adept at modeling, requiring, and reinforcing fluency at different points during instruction. In the upper grades, fluency and decoding will rarely, if ever, be the explicit objective of an entire lesson, but should be constantly practiced and implicitly taught by giving students ample opportunities to read aloud because it will be a critical factor in helping them accomplish their objective.

FASE in High School

Beth Verrilli

By eighth grade, oral reading fluency differences still explain 25 percent of the variance in reading comprehension.[14] We're sure this doesn't magically disappear once those eighth graders walk into their ninth grade classrooms, so making time for Read Aloud or FASE Reading is still critical in high school. FASE can help us identify the students who continue to struggle with reading so we can intervene. But even when faced with a whole class of fluent high school readers, we still need to read aloud and together.

High schoolers are tackling increasingly complex texts. Since we know that hearing text read aloud with fluency supports understanding, it makes sense that the more demanding the reading task, the more necessary it is for students to hear text read aloud—or to read it aloud themselves, so that they make decisions about which words or phrases should be emphasized or stressed, and therefore paid attention to. Think about how much more we understand when we hear a Shakespearean actor read Romeo's words aloud, rather than reading them silently ourselves on a page.

Also, consider the structure of most high school English classes: reading is done independently, outside of class, as a basis for class discussion. This means that reading is done at a distance—completing reading "before class," even for a conscientious student, means that soccer practice, their

(continued)

babysitting job, and a round of other classes separates their reading from the class discussion. Selecting key passages to reread aloud in class puts the text back into working memory, reactivating recall of details necessary for a discussion grounded in Close Reading and textual analysis.

Finally, sharing text together is a way to build community in our classrooms and nurture a lifelong love of reading. What English teacher doesn't want to be present as their students encounter, in real time, a major event of a gripping story? Planning to read a compelling section of text aloud and together as (spoiler alert!) Fitzgerald sends Gatsby to the swimming pool for one last dip or Morrison sends Milkman leaping toward Guitar ensures that students build memories about great stories together.

In classrooms where FASE Reading is used effectively, reading is done joyfully with expression and care. At times, the teacher will model fluent and expressive reading—what we refer to as *bridging*—then ask students to do the same. Bridging involves teachers reading a short segment of text—serving as a bridge—in between student readers. Effective bridging relies on best practices for Read Aloud (as described), but for shorter segments of text. In a typical sequence of bridging, a teacher might have Arjun read for three sentences and then read one sentence herself. Then she might have Maria read four sentences and read two sentences herself before asking Nikki to read for six sentences before passing off to Joaquin, and so on.

The benefit of this method is that it moves the story along quickly and keeps the narrative thread alive, while supporting and maximizing fluency and comprehension with interspersed models of teacher-quality expressive reading. Because students don't know who will be called on to read, all students follow along attentively in the text—increasing the amount of quality road miles they get on the page.

To watch the video *Christine Torres: Discovered*, use this QR code or find the video at the URL https://vimeo.com/1058358210/5ba3f7345f.

You can see these ideas in action in Christine Torres's fifth-grade class in *Christine Torres: Discovered*. Christine and her students are reading a suspenseful scene in *Number the Stars*. The clip starts with one of Christine's students reading. His reading is fluent and he sounds confident. It's clear that he's had lots of practice reading aloud, and his peers are following along attentively.

Christine has taught her students how to listen carefully and respectfully while a peer is reading, so each individual is maximizing their miles on the page. The second student reader struggles a bit, but Christine is there to support, asking the student to reread, echoing her model of a key (but tricky) phrase and providing accurate pronunciations of words. And then Christine herself picks up the reading. Her intentional bridging brings back the momentum of the text and emphasizes the drama of the moment. In the midst of her bridging, she pauses to briefly to provide a critical piece of knowledge (a picture of a handkerchief), and then continues her bridging for a bit before inviting her next student reader to own the voice.

Just as reading aloud expressively is good for students, so too is prompting students to read expressively by calling their attention to text features, dialogue tags, and vocabulary that can give them cues for appropriate expression. Such prompting causes them to practice looking for the meaning in words and to pay attention to syntax and punctuation. We recently led a series of trainings on fluency and FASE for a group of teachers using our curriculum. Teachers reported that after a period of intentional focus on fluency, students were more attentive to their mistakes and more likely to self-correct. To make oral reading consistently more fluent, try the following strategies:

Capture the mood. As accuracy and automaticity improve, some students still struggle to read with appropriate expressiveness. You can combat this wooden reading by identifying (or asking students to infer) the kind of expression they should impart to the passage based on the general mood or on the affect of a specific character. Then ask them to apply it. In terms of general mood, it might involve asking a student to try to capture the tension of a key scene in the way he reads it. In terms of a specific character's affect, a teacher might say, "Wilbur is upset, Diamond. Can you read that sentence in a way that shows that?" or "How is Wilbur feeling right now? What emotion is he feeling? Good . . . can you show me that in your reading?"

Asking students to capture the mood of a scene or character conveys to students that *how* they read a text matters. It also directly supports student comprehension. You can help students do this by calling their attention to dialogue tags and their role as "stage directions." "The passage says, "'I don't want any," Mr. Malone said sharply.' Read that again so his words are sharp." You can also model the applicable tone in your own reading by intentionally bridging around a dialogue tag and asking students to apply it to the sentence they are reading. In this example, you might say the word *sharply* in a sharp tone of voice that students could then imitate. We saw an example of this in the video from Chapter Two when Maggie Johnson challenges her students, "Who can give me an irritated Atticus?" before calling on a student to read a sentence in which Scout describes being "stung by her father's curtness." In doing so, Maggie not only provides a fluency prompt, she provides a bit of vocabulary support for the word *curtness*, which is a word less familiar to students than *irritated*.

Echo reading and choral reading. Literacy experts suggest echo reading—a teacher models how to read a word, phrase, or sentence, and a student echoes it back, trying to capture the same pronunciation and expression as the teacher—as a strategy to support more fluent reading. This is a practice that can be seamlessly incorporated into your FASE Reading. You might read a sentence and ask a student to begin their reading by echoing your sentence. For some students, this can build their confidence in reading aloud in front of the class. You might also use echo reading to correct dysfluency. Model with the appropriate accuracy or prosody and then ask the student to repeat in order to reinforce stronger fluency. Similarly, you can rely on choral reading for particularly challenging, complex, or dramatic sentences. Rather than ask just one student to read, invite your whole class to copy your model.

Check the mechanics. Developing readers see punctuation but often do not grasp what it is telling them to do in terms of meaning or inflection. Similarly, the importance of syntax—the relationship of the pieces of a sentence and its effect on meaning—is often lost on weak readers. The idea that the word *though* or *besides* sets the rest of the sentence in contrast to the initial phrase is a critical part of effective reading. We've all heard students who can read words accurately, but struggle to understand the syntactical arrangement of the sentences, causing them to read without attention to punctuation, sentence structure, or intentional groupings of words.

Making explicit references to punctuation and asking students to demonstrate their understanding of it in their oral reading is a useful way to build this important habit of attention. ("There's a comma there. Remember to pause." "I want you to pause and breathe whenever you see a period." "Don't forget that the quotation mark means that Pony Boy is talking.") For syntax, questions like asking students to identify which words told them that a sentence was a question or which words told them that two ideas were in contrast helps them to improve their fluency and therefore their comprehension.

Read, then read again. Not only should we have students reread frequently to support comprehension and when Close Reading but we should also consider asking them to reread for fluency once they have successfully decoded and established the meaning of words and phrases in a sentence. As we discussed previously in the chapter, there's strong evidence that repeated reading is among the most effective tools for building fluency. Even adult readers may need to read a complex passage or a sentence multiple times before it finally makes sense to them. Asking our students to do the same to improve fluency is an important way to support comprehension. By consistently enforcing your expectations and giving students multiple opportunities to read and reread a text, you can encourage students to build lifelong habits that make them fluent readers who love great (and complex) books.

For dysfluent readers, the practice of rereading is even more critical. Our colleague Jen Rugani, a former elementary school teacher and principal, explains that rereading is a nonnegotiable for dysfluent readers because it allows students to practice improving reading rate as words become more automatic. When dysfluent readers read a new text for the first time, they often go back to square one (accuracy and decoding) and can't incorporate the other aspects of fluency because they don't yet have automaticity. Rereading is actually *more* at the speed of sight than an initial read, which is why it's so important for improving fluency. Ideally this happens in slightly longer bursts than FASE Reading typically allows, which reminds us that FASE is helpful but not sufficient in supporting dysfluent readers.

Asking students to reread something they've read aloud can also be an opportunity to celebrate fluent reading and build a culture of excitement for reading. In the clip *Hannah Lofthus: Some Story,* Hannah Lofthus pauses one of her second-grade students, Cartier, in the midst of FASE Reading and asks him to reread because she "loves" the way he just read. After Cartier's second reading, Cartier is rewarded with peals of laughter from his classmates for his ability to bring a funny moment to life, and with precise praise from Hannah about what he did

To watch the video *Hannah Lofthus: Some Story*, use this QR code or find the video at the URL https://vimeo.com/1058360706/e5af3b96b5.

"that good readers do." By asking students to describe the tone with which Cartier read ("incredulous"), Hannah uses this moment to reinforce strong fluency as well as vocabulary.

Intentionally Assign Passages

Teachers who most successfully use FASE Reading intentionally plan in advance which students will read which sentences or passages, and for how long. This enables teachers to match struggling readers to shorter, less complex chunks of text and more advanced readers to longer and trickier passages, which effectively differentiates the task of reading aloud in a way that best supports all readers. Struggling readers aren't accidentally mismatched with an overly challenging chunk of text, potentially undercutting quality road miles, disrupting fluency and comprehension, or causing them undue anxiety. Gradually, as all readers get stronger and more fluent, the goal is to lengthen the chunk of text they read.

We should note that just because you've planned ahead and intentionally matched passages to students does not mean you should tell the students ahead of time who will be reading what, or how much they will be reading.

When you ask your primary reader to read, *don't* specify how long you want him to read before he begins. Simply ask him to start reading. "Start reading for me please, James" or "Pick up please, James" is a far better thing to say than "Read the next paragraph for me, James." The unpredictability of durations ensures that other students in the class don't know when a new reader will be asked to pick up, giving them a strong incentive to follow along carefully. Unpredictability encourages attentiveness from secondary readers. A teacher who announces that she'll go around the room in a predictable order (as is often done in round-robin reading) reduces incentives to follow along, which then negatively affects comprehension.

Here's an example of how a teacher prepared to use FASE for the reading of a short, Embedded Nonfiction text that they were reading to support their understanding of "Justice" by Langston Hughes:

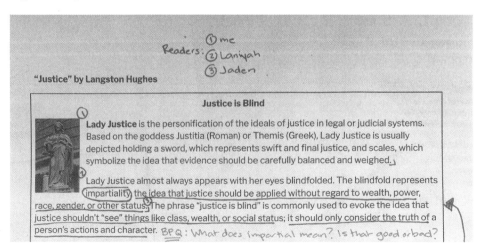

You can see that the teacher has determined in advance which students should read each part of the text. When students are less familiar with the system of FASE or are less fluent in their reading, we recommend assigning shorter durations of reading. Reading short segments maximizes the concentration of the primary and secondary readers. It enables students to invest real expressive energy in reading, focus intently, and sustain fluent and even dramatic reading.

After attending one of our workshops Steve Kuninsky, a high school chemistry teacher at the Gwinnett School of Mathematics, Science and Technology in Georgia, decided to incorporate more FASE Reading into his lessons. Watch in *Steve Kuninsky: VSEPR Theory* as he briefly explains to students what they can expect when it's their turn to read, and then immediately invites individual students to read brief excerpts from their textbook. You'll notice that students read just one or two sentences at a time to ensure they feel successful and confident.

To watch the video *Steve Kuninsky: VSEPR Theory*, use this QR code or find the video at the URL https://vimeo.com/1058361064/8bafb525d3.

Shorter durations of reading in a complex text yield higher-quality oral reading and is one step to ensuring that shared reading is an inclusive activity where all students feel comfortable and excited about their opportunity to participate. For struggling readers, shorter durations make the reading feel more manageable. We'll note that assigning some students shorter durations than others doesn't mean that they have to read aloud less than their peers. You can call on the same reader twice—each time asking him or her to read short sections of text while providing decoding support and fluency reinforcement—within a short span of your lesson to ensure these students still receive the same amount of practice time as their peers given longer durations.

As students become more fluent through the course of the year or as they become more familiar with the author's style and voice in a given book, you'll want to increase the length of text you ask students to read aloud. Extending the durations of reading validates the progress they've made with fluency and builds their stamina for longer periods of high-quality reading.

Partner Reading

One of the great benefits of FASE is that it is a system to teach students to read aloud optimally. Once they know how to do that, you can give them more ownership and autonomy (and practice!) by asking them to read with a partner. Partner reading is particularly impactful because it instantly increases the amount of oral reading practice for every student in your classroom. Just like any other system in your classroom, strong partner reading requires a clear rollout, quality models, and lots of student practice with feedback from you. As you plan your partner reading system, here are a few things to consider:

- **Deliver a rollout.** Briefly explain to your students why partner reading is important and how it will work in your classroom.

- **Provide a model.** Show students what it looks like to read with a partner. You might model with a student in your class or ask another teacher to be your partner reader.

- **Assign clear roles.** Be explicit in your expectations for both the reader and the listener. Like Scott Wells, you may also manage turns to ensure that both partners get relatively equal reading time.

- **Support struggling readers.** You may consider in advance how to support struggling readers. Christopher Such recommends pairing them with a stronger reader or an adult in the room, or giving them practice opportunities with the text before the lesson.[15]

- **Observe and provide feedback.** As your students are reading together, be an active listener. Circulate to listen in on multiple groups and provide feedback on the system (how well they're working as reader and listener) as well as the content of their reading (fluency, expressiveness).

Ensuring FASE Works for All Readers

One of the most powerful elements of FASE is the influence it has on creating a culture of reading in a classroom. As we describe in Chapter One, sharing stories is an integral part of the history of humanity, and FASE Reading offers opportunities for students and teachers to build connections through the shared experience of reading beautiful stories. It also builds a culture where kids know the value of reading aloud, and feel safe and successful in doing so, but only if we're thoughtful about how we roll out and implement the system. In order to make it a positive and inclusive experience for all students, particularly our most reluctant readers, we must shape the culture of shared reading with intentionality and plan carefully to ensure that all of our students feel safe and successful when invited to read in front of their peers.

When we first describe FASE in a workshop, teachers often express concerns about students' level of comfort with reading aloud in front of their peers, especially thinking about their most struggling readers. FASE, like so many of the tools we use in our classrooms, relies on a strong culture of error. Before they're asked to read aloud, students must know that making errors (in this case, while reading) is a normal and valuable part of the learning process. In building a culture of error, teachers must explicitly message the normalcy of error and implicitly reinforce that message by correcting reading mistakes warmly and consistently. Being consistent in providing corrections or prompts to correct inaccuracy, ignored words, or dropped endings is important for ensuring students are reading with accuracy and sends the message to students that everyone makes mistakes from time to time—it's not just struggling readers who need corrections.

These kinds of consistent, warmly applied corrections pay off. One school leader described how kids were more confident in reading aloud after several weeks of practice with FASE. As they realized it was safe to make mistakes, they were more eager and confident in their reading. Specifically, she explained, "The volume of student oral reading rose significantly. Feedback to students was normalized. Student engagement rose."

In *Jessica Bracey: Circle of Gold*, Jessica Bracey is using FASE Reading with her fifth graders as they read *Circle of Gold* by Candy Dawson Boyd. Jessica has built a strong system for FASE Reading in her classroom— students follow along attentively while the primary reader reads, Jessica incorporates bridging with intentionality, and students in her class are ready (and eager) to pick up reading when it's their turn. We're also struck by the strong culture of error in Jessica's lesson. All of Jessica's students are following along attentively with the text as one reader, who struggles a bit with the text,

To watch the video *Jessica Bracey: Circle of Gold*, use this QR code or find the video at the URL https://vimeo.com/1058361064/8bafb525d3.

reads aloud. Jessica warmly and calmly supports this struggling reader, providing the pronunciation of the word *emphatically* and giving the student multiple opportunities to try it out until she reads it with proper accuracy and intonation. Jessica then calls on several other students, each of them receiving quick decoding and fluency support as necessary, before giving the original reader a chance to read again. Like the first bit of reading this student did, it's short and manageable. She receives support from Jessica, and she finishes her section of reading with strong fluency and expressiveness. In this clip, we see the way that FASE Reading, carefully managed in a classroom with a strong culture of error like Jessica's, sets the stage for an inclusive reading experience where all students feel safe and comfortable reading, making errors, and correcting their errors.

One thing that's important to remember about Jessica's video (like most of the videos we've included in this chapter) is that it shows what happens when a strong culture of fluent expressive reading is built and sustained over time. Students come to love reading and they read better. In other words, the first time you try FASE with your class we hope students respond like Jessica's students, but they might not. They'll likely be a bit hesitant—of course, it's new and a bit risky—and their skills will still be developing.

We thought it would be worth showing you an earlier stage FASE clip then to normalize that process a bit. To be clear: we think the teaching technique in this clip is just as good as any of the teachers we've watched so far. The class is just in the earlier stages of the journey.

To watch the video *Travis Mapp: Night,* use this QR code or find the video at the URL https://vimeo.com/1058360881/17f1f0461e.

This clip, *Travis Mapp: Night,* comes from the eighth-grade class of Travis Mapp at Alma Del Mar Charter School in New Bedford, Massachusetts. Before watching the video, we want to note that because Travis and students are reading an account of the Holocaust, it can feel jarring for us viewers when we "step into" his classroom for the first time. Specifically, we will start watching right as Travis reads aloud the moment when a Nazi officer sends the narrator's mother and sister away to be killed in the gas chambers.

At the outset of the unit on *Night,* Travis thoughtfully prepared his students for studying and reading about (with an empathetic lens) the horrifying and tragic events of this historical period. While we don't see all of that in this video, it's important to consider how to create safe classroom spaces for processing the emotions evoked when reading content of this nature. With that in mind, we also wanted to give you a warning here before you watch the video.

As we watch Travis's reading, we're struck by how prepared he is and how committed to modeling fluent reading. You can see a couple of his students are still a tiny bit distracted but the majority of them are all-in—raising their hands, eager to read and to get into the game. And you can also hear the way the book is brought more fully to life. As we discuss in Chapter Seven, we can expect to build students' empathy and understanding when they experience the book both together and read aloud.

Beyond creating a classroom culture where struggling readers feel safe and supported reading aloud, there are specific measures teachers can take to ensure that FASE is positive and inclusive of readers of all levels. Some students benefit from advance practice with a text before being asked to read aloud in front of their peers. For those students, consider identifying the excerpt(s) of text they'll read in class and give them opportunities to practice reading that aloud. You may find time to do this in school—with you in class just before the reading starts or with another teacher in the building if the student receives pull-out services—or you may assign it for homework to practice with a family member or caregiver. Any of these options offers the student an opportunity to practice reading the excerpt aloud with success to build confidence and accuracy before being asked to read for their peers.

Intentional bridging before and after struggling readers is another effective practice (and another move we see in Jessica Bracey's lesson). By reading just before calling on a struggling reader, you are building momentum in the text and providing a model of fluency they can follow. Picking up the reading just after a struggling reader enables you to regain the flow of the text and any momentum that might have flagged. In a lesson at Baychester Middle School, we observed a teacher use bridging to proactively support a struggling reader's fluency by modeling a line and asking the reader to read again, following the way she'd modeled the line. Successful echo reading helped to get the reader up and running with confidence before starting to read more of the text on her own.

At Emerson Elementary School in Amarillo, Texas, we watched fourth-grade teacher Juliane Pairsh lead a productive and joyful FASE Reading. It was clear that she'd planned her readers with intentionality and all readers were ready and confident when it was their turn to read—evidence of their practice with and investment in the system. At one point, she called on a struggling reader to read, and as the student began, Juliane casually strolled over to stand next to the student to quietly support her during reading. As the student worked through her section of the reading, Juliane quietly affirmed her successes with "hmmhmms" and a gentle pat on the back. When the student struggled, Juliane was there to whisper corrections to the student that she could immediately apply in her own reading. It's not something that we'd necessarily recommend every time, but in this moment, in Ms. Pairsh's classroom, we were struck by the power of proximity—as a calming presence and as a resource to privately support a student through a text just at the edge of what she could read aloud.

We also recommend identifying the most common mistakes that kids may make ahead of time and noting them in the text so you can provide a quick decoding prompt or correction. Christopher Such points out that common errors are most likely to involve blending adjacent consonants and making sense of multisyllabic words. You might also post word lists and do choral reading practice of the more challenging words that students will encounter just before a round of FASE Reading. (See more on this in the AIR section later in this chapter.)

FASE and Decoding

Teachers who don't teach decoding as part of their curriculum (typically any teacher after third grade) often don't think about it (or perhaps wish they had the tools to better support students below grade level). It can be a blind spot for some upper elementary, middle, and high school teachers, as it appears to some to be a mundane, "lower-order" skill that should have been established in the earlier grades. However, because its mastery is a prerequisite to all reading comprehension, decoding support remains vital in the upper grades. Incomplete mastery of decoding can persist well beyond the elementary grades, which interferes with fluency and can ultimately hamper the overall academic success of older students.

There are many reasons a student might make an error while reading, and regardless of the root cause, if a student reads something different than what is printed, we should prompt and support their accuracy. When unaddressed, these errors can interfere with comprehension and unintentionally reinforce poor reading. Tools to systematically address other decoding errors to build a habit of careful reading can be found in Appendix C.

Advanced Preparation

As with Read Aloud, strong implementation of FASE Reading relies on advanced preparation and practice. Here's a model of a teacher's text preparation for FASE Reading:

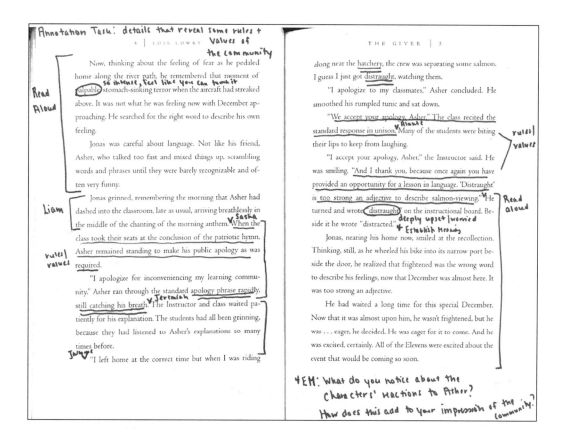

You can see how this teacher has planned in advance where she'll read aloud and which student readers she'll call on and when. In order to support fluency, she's also noted words that might present decoding challenges (*hatchery* and *distraught*) and notes to remind student readers about reading with a particular type of expression ("[Asher ran through the standard] apology phrase rapidly, still catching his breath").

You'll also notice some of the same preparation practices that we describe in the Read Aloud section—providing an annotation task, including Establish Meaning questions and noting critical vocabulary definitions—all in support of attentiveness and meaning making.

Fluency Remediation

We are often asked about how to support students with foundational skills gaps (e.g., phonics and decoding) after second grade as we ask them to read and make meaning of complex grade-level texts. It starts with teachers assessing the depth and extent of the issues they are seeing. There can be different root causes behind students who "can't read grade-level text" but in most cases the issue is likely to be a combination of students who are dysfluent and those who have significant decoding gaps. Each group is different, but teachers need to figure out where their kids fall on this spectrum. The best way to assess these students is by listening to their oral reading.

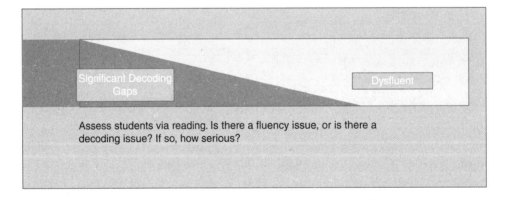

Significant Decoding Gaps

Dysfluent

Assess students via reading. Is there a fluency issue, or is there a decoding issue? If so, how serious?

In some cases, students don't reliably know their letter-sound correspondences. The issue is deep and wide-ranging. In this case, in-class remediation is insufficient. Students that are code deficient need significant time with a reading specialist using a scientifically based program of systematic synthetic phonics.

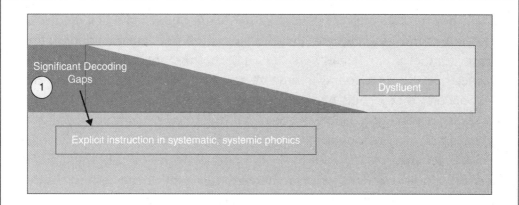

In other cases, students know the great majority of letter-sound correspondences. They're lacking automaticity, likely due to poor or labored orthographic mapping. They know how to sound out words (their accuracy is strong), but to build automaticity, they need to read and practice . . . a lot. For these students, FASE Reading alone will also be insufficient. They'll require additional fluency practice, ideally in small groups to focus on repeated readings.

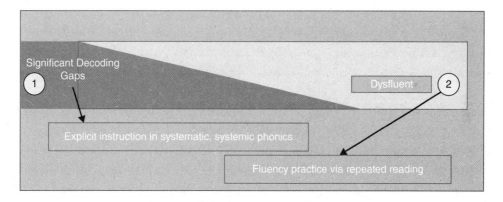

In our middle school *Reading Reconsidered* curriculum we provide companion fluency sets for each of our novel units (for example, see Appendix C for samples from a fluency intervention text set to accompany *The Giver*). In these fluency sets, students are given slightly simplified sentences from upcoming lessons that they practice reading repeatedly for fluency in small groups. As a result, they get lots of productive, focused, extra fluency practice, and when the whole group lesson arrives, they are more prepared and confident to read along with the group. It's also worth noting that the pre-reading and fluency practice helps these students internalize some of the background knowledge in advance so that, if their working memory is more focused on fluency during class, their meaning making will not suffer. If your curriculum or school does not have fluency sets for your texts, you can create your own fluency practice passages for students. Choose (or write) short passages (ideally one hundred to two hundred words) that students can read with 85 percent (or better) accuracy and give students opportunities to reread (multiple times), each time focusing on improving reading rate and prosody.

ACCOUNTABLE INDEPENDENT READING (AIR)

Supporting students in reading independently requires us to make a series of decisions based on the complexity of the text and our knowledge of our students. Consider the length of text, how you might guide students' attention while reading, and how AIR is an opportunity to independently practice the fluency building you've done through Read Aloud and FASE.

Independent reading will be the primary form of reading that our students do in their adult lives—both professionally and personally. So, it's critical that we build their capacity for it and give them opportunities to independently practice what we've modeled and reinforced through Read Aloud and FASE Reading, which are the only ways to ensure that silent reading is done with an inner voice that brings text fully to life. One of the biggest limitations of silent, independent reading is that students can practice poorly, reinforcing inaccurate decoding or weak fluency. As Mark Seidenberg explains in *Language at the Speed of Sight*, "Children who struggle when reading texts aloud do not become good readers if left to read silently; their dysfluency merely becomes inaudible."[16] The mental models from Read Aloud and opportunities to practice and get feedback during FASE are important measures to support higher-quality silent, independent reading. AIR enables teachers to ensure that their students are in fact practicing fluency, not dysfluency, when reading on their own, while still allowing increased independence and ownership over the texts.

To effectively bring AIR to your classroom, you want to encode success in reading independently, then start to increase both difficulty and length to build stamina. The key to AIR is to incorporate short bursts of independent reading with teacher support to allow for practice that is purposeful. As described, AIR provides students opportunities to apply what they hear during FASE Reading and Read Aloud to their inner reading voice as they tackle the text on their own.

In the section that follows, we'll describe actions we can take to give our students meaningful and productive opportunities to read independently, with a particular emphasis on supporting fluency.

Before Reading: Prepare Students with Advanced Supports

Text selection. AIR should begin with strategically selected text that is not overly complex and read in short intervals before gradually moving toward longer, more complex stretches and extended reading assigned for homework. It's better to start by reading smaller chunks with greater attentiveness and comprehension than to read more text at lower quality. For developing readers or for very hard texts, you might start with chunks as small as a single sentence and build up to a paragraph.

The goal is to make a habit of reading independently and reading well, even if that means starting with and confirming comprehension after just a few lines of text. Starting with limited sections of text enables you to assess comprehension more accurately and consistently at frequent intervals (we'll dive into how to do so shortly). The goal is for students to become socialized to reading *well* every time they read, at least as much as it is to increase the amount of time they read. Our colleague Emily Badillo likens AIR to bowling with bumpers. We give students independence to navigate texts but with guardrails in place to ensure their success. If students do not spend their time reading well, then increased time is wasted time and for some of our most struggling readers, reading independently can reinforce poor reading habits and possibly make them feel frustration about their inability to independently make meaning of a text.

Preview and practice challenging words and vocabulary. After you've selected a section of text that students will be reading independently, it's helpful to review the text for words that could present decoding challenges for your students. Prepare students to successfully read these words independently by previewing them in advance: provide an accurate pronunciation and ask students to repeat chorally. In a fifth-grade class reading from *Number the Stars*, you might ask students to chorally repeat a list of challenging polysyllabic words after modeling the correct pronunciation of each, as in the following example:

4

It Will Be a Long Night

Alone in the apartment while Mama was out shopping with Kirsti, Annemarie and Ellen were sprawled on the living room floor playing with paper dolls. They had cut the dolls from Mama's magazines, old ones she had saved from past years. The paper ladies had old-fashioned hair styles and clothes, and the girls had given them names from Mama's very favorite book. Mama had told Annemarie and Ellen the entire story of *Gone With the Wind*, and the girls thought it much more interesting and romantic than the king-and-queen tales that Kirsti loved.

"Come, Melanie," Annemarie said, walking her doll across the edge of the rug. "Let's dress for the ball."

"All right, Scarlett, I'm coming," Ellen replied in a sophisticated voice. She was a talented performer; she often played the leading roles in school dramatics. Games of the imagination were always fun when Ellen played.

The door opened and Kirsti stomped in, her face tear-stained and glowering. Mama followed her with

21 • NUMBER THE STARS — *Frustrated*

an exasperated look and set a package down on the table.

"I won't!" Kirsti sputtered. "I won't ever, *ever* wear them! Not if you chain me in a prison and beat me with sticks!"

Annemarie giggled and looked questioningly at her mother. Mrs. Johansen sighed. "I bought Kirsti some new shoes," she explained. "She's outgrown her old ones."

"Goodness, Kirsti," Ellen said, "I wish my mother would get *me* some new shoes. I love new things, and it's so hard to find them in the stores."

"Not if you go to a *fish* store!" Kirsti bellowed. "But most mothers wouldn't make their daughters wear ugly *fish* shoes!"

"Kirsten," Mama said soothingly, "you know it wasn't a fish store. And we were lucky to find shoes at all."

Kirsti sniffed. "Show them," she commanded. "Show Annemarie and Ellen how ugly they are."

Mama opened the package and took out a pair of little girl's shoes. She held them up, and Kirsti looked away in disgust.

Word List
sophisticated
glowering
exasperated
questioningly

You can also preview challenging vocabulary or terms that kids might not have background knowledge about, as we discuss more in Chapter Five, on vocabulary. For example, after practicing the pronunciation of *exasperated*, you might say, "*Exasperated* means frustrated. Circle that word and jot frustrated in the margin" in order to support comprehension (and fluency!) during reading. You might even include a vocabulary list in student facing materials or (post it in your classroom) like in this example:

Words to Watch For					
Page	Word or Phrase	Meaning in Context	Page	Word or Phrase	Meaning in Context
131	tweaking	making small adjustments to	132	monopoly	complete control or ownership
131	rebel	one who resists the people in charge or authority	132	arrogant	thinking you are overly important

Proximity matters. The goal of much of the student and teacher reading aloud we advocate is, ironically, successful silent, independent reading. The idea is, if we model rich expressive reading and productive habits like annotation they will transfer to the format in which students will do the lion's share of their reading. If the purpose is transfer, it's worth thinking about how we might make it easy for ideas and habits to cross over from the first two ways of reading to the third. One of the simplest ways to do that is to put them next to each other.

Let's say I am reading *The Giver* with my class, and I want my students to read in an inner voice rich in expression and full of meaning. My first step is to model that kind of expression myself in my read aloud, then to ask for it, encourage it, and coach it when I ask students to read aloud. So perhaps, I start Chapter One myself and then transition to FASE Reading for a bit. Then after eight or ten students have read aloud, maybe I take the reading back again and read aloud for another page very consciously emphasizing the uncertainty and tension of the text. Perhaps I choose a moment that feels like a real cliffhanger. Perhaps this paragraph:

> NEEDLESS TO SAY, HE WILL BE RELEASED, the voice had said, followed by silence. There was an ironic tone to that final message, as if the Speaker found it amusing; and Jonas had smiled a little, though he knew what a grim statement it had been. For a contributing citizen to be released from the community was a final decision, a terrible punishment, an overwhelming statement of failure.

I read to the end of it and at the moment of maximum drama say: "Okay, you're reading on your own from here until the end of the next page. Be sure to annotate for moments that seem especially threatening or ominous. Go!"

What I've done here is put the AIR right next to the Read Aloud. Even just a short bit of it. And at a moment when students are especially engaged. Perhaps later we go back to more Read Aloud and then more AIR. The point is that if we want transfer, we should put the AIR right next to especially rich moments of Read Aloud and FASE Reading so that the feeling of one blends into the other and so that students almost can't help reading with energy and expression.

Differentiation for struggling readers. As any teacher of thirty students can tell you, there will be a wide range of comprehension in AIR across a classroom. Some students will read quickly but not understand much. Others will read slowly and have a firm grasp on comprehension. And still others will both read slowly and have trouble comprehending the text. Given the range of possibilities found in any one classroom, you'll want to think about how best to differentiate AIR tasks to support and meet the needs of all students.

In order to prep some of your most struggling readers, consider giving them opportunities to preview the text with an adult before asking them to engage with the text in class, and support them in accessing the most challenging parts. When possible, leverage co-teacher support to read (or reread) sections you've identified for AIR with students who will struggle independently. You might also suggest that students use part of intervention time to preread sections of the text with a teacher that the class will later read using AIR. Additionally, you might annotate (or have them annotate) the text for decoding and pronunciation support of challenging words and have them practice reading it aloud or read it aloud to them. It's also helpful to provide them with additional vocabulary definitions and Knowledge Feeds (described in Chapter Five). Having an understanding of critical vocabulary and knowledge can support students' comprehension even when decoding and fluency might present challenges. To build students' initial comfort with and capacity for AIR, you might start by asking them to reread a section that you've already read as a class using Teacher Read Aloud or FASE.

During and After Reading: Observe and Respond to Support

As students read on their own, you'll want to observe their progress and support as needed. On the surface, it can be difficult to know how well students are understanding what they're reading. For older students, annotations are windows into their thinking, and monitoring annotations carefully allows you to intervene as necessary—providing prompts, questions, or suggestions for rereading—when you notice understanding is lacking or inaccurate. As you recall from Chapter Two, annotation is critical to all forms of reading (you can review that chapter for best practices in annotation tasks).

For example, you might say, "As you read this next paragraph independently, look for three details that describe the setting of our story" or "Take one minute to read the next paragraph on your own. I'm going to ask you what Theo learns about his mother in this paragraph, so make sure you underline details that help you figure this out." Tell students what they should look for before they start reading. As is true of any skill, mastery (in this case, students' comprehension and readiness to take on longer reading) can be gauged only through reliably checking for understanding. Assigning a concrete annotation task gives you a more reliable (and visible) measure.

You can watch Breonna Tindall (in *BreOnna Tindall: Check if Correct*) and Danielle Lee (in *Danielle Lee: Myths*) set their students up for AIR by launching a clear and specific annotation task. We especially appreciate how Danielle has posted her annotation task so kids have a visual anchor to support attentiveness and focus.

As you circulate to observe students' reading and annotations, you might pause periodically to ask students to read aloud to you (quietly) while the rest of the class reads independently. As David Paige explains, "Students who use appropriate prosody when reading are more likely to comprehend what they read."[17] A brief check-in when you ask a student to read to you can give you a lot of information on how well they're comprehending what they're reading. If students struggle, you might ask them to reread aloud (or whisper read) to you, or you might read the section aloud to them before asking them to reread and annotate on their own. For younger students, or students who are still solidifying letter-sound correspondence, it's important for them to be able to hear themselves read, so you should encourage them to whisper read during independent reading time.

After independently reading, you might ask students a series of questions to gather information about how well they understood what they read. Watch Dan Cosgrove (in *Dan Cosgrove: Earthworm)* as he does a series of brief check-ins interspersed with moments of silent reading, as his students independently work through *James and the Giant Peach*.

Previously in the chapter we showed an example of how a teacher prepared for a Read Aloud of the opening pages of *The Giver*. After her students experienced the text through her read aloud, they had a chance to read it again, this time on their own. Here's how she prepared her own text for this AIR part of the lesson:

To watch the video *BreOnna Tindall: Check If Correct*, use this QR code or find the video at the URL https://vimeo.com/1058361624/1aa9cc3933.

To watch the video *Danielle Lee: Myths*, use this QR code or find the video at the URL https://vimeo.com/1058361850/be726f0b3b.

To watch the video *Dan Cosgrove: Earthworm*, use this QR code or find the video at the URL https://vimeo.com/1058361471/e1ea9e45d3.

ONE

· 3 mins to read and annotate (w/ new focus)

Start.

IT WAS ALMOST December, and Jonas was beginning to be frightened. No. Wrong word, Jonas thought. Frightened meant that deep, sickening feeling of something terrible about to happen. Frightened was the way he had felt a year ago when an unidentified aircraft had overflown the community twice. He had seen it both times. Squinting toward the sky, he had seen the sleek jet, almost a blur at its high speed, go past, and a second later heard the blast of sound that followed. Then one more time, a moment later, from the opposite direction, the same plane.

At first, he had been only *fascinated*. He had never seen *(disobedient)* aircraft so close, for it was against the rules for Pilots to fly over the community. *Occasionally*, when supplies were deliv-

ered by cargo planes to the landing field across the river, the children rode their bicycles to the riverbank and watched, intrigued, the unloading and then the takeoff directed to the west, always away from the community.

But the aircraft a year ago had been different. It was not a squat, fat-bellied cargo plane but a needle-nosed single-pilot jet. Jonas, looking around anxiously, had seen others—adults as well as children—stop what they were doing and wait, confused, for an explanation of the frightening event. *obedient*

Then all of the citizens had been ordered to go into the nearest building and stay there. IMMEDIATELY, the rasping voice through the speakers had said. LEAVE YOUR BICYCLES WHERE THEY ARE.

obedient Instantly, *obediently*, Jonas had dropped his bike on its side on the path behind his family's dwelling. He had run indoors and stayed there, alone. His parents were both at work, and his little sister, Lily, was at the Childcare Center where she spent her after-school hours.

Looking through the front window, he had seen no people; none of the busy afternoon crew of Street Cleaners, Landscape Workers, and Food Delivery people who usually populated the community at that time of day. He saw only the abandoned bikes here and there on their sides; an upturned wheel on one was still revolving slowly.

He had been frightened then. The sense of his own community silent, waiting, had made his stomach churn. He had trembled. *Stop AIR*

But it had been nothing. Within minutes the speakers had crackled again, and the voice, reassuring now and less urgent, had explained that a Pilot-in-Training had misread his navigational instructions and made a wrong turn. Desperately the Pilot had been trying to make his way back before his error was noticed.

NEEDLESS TO SAY, HE WILL BE RELEASED, the voice had said, followed by silence. There was an ironic tone to that final message, as if the Speaker found it amusing; and Jonas had smiled a little, though he knew what a grim statement it had been. For a contributing citizen to be released from the community was a final decision, a terrible punishment, an overwhelming statement of failure.

Even the children were scolded if they used the term lightly at play, jeering at a teammate who missed a catch or stumbled in a race. Jonas had done it once, had shouted at his best friend, "That's it, Asher! You're released!" when Asher's clumsy error had lost a match for his team. He had been taken aside for a brief and serious talk by the coach, had hung his head with guilt and embarrassment, and apologized to Asher after the game.

A couple of things you'll notice:

- Once again, she provides a clear annotation task. It's a bit different this time ("Look for examples of obedient/disobedient behavior being described") than in the first round ("What is Jonas remembering? What details seem frightening?"). It's designed to help them better understand the story and to help reinforce one of the vocabulary words they learned at the outset of the lesson (*obedient*).

- She's made her own text annotations to be able to support students. What's not visible here is that she circulates to observe their annotations.

- Just like in the *Number the Stars* example, she's identified challenging words to decode in order to provide students some advanced practice reading them.

Building Stamina, Self-Awareness, and Ownership

To build stamina over time, increase the amount of independent reading done in class. Lengthening the amount of text for AIR does not necessarily mean you should simply look to add a paragraph or a sentence each day. This can vary text to text—in one text, students might be able to read several pages at a time independently but need shorter sections in a new text with a different layer of complexity. Gather data through questioning and observation (both written and oral) to ensure that annotations, written work, and student oral reading demonstrate that students comprehend what they read independently before you add longer or more complex chunks of text. Before assigning longer or more challenging independent portions, it's important to keep a pulse on pacing and accuracy.

As students increase their comfort and success with reading independently—later in the year or as they've become accustomed to the style and voice of a particular author as you progress through a book—consider assigning longer sections of reading. Over time, of course, you'll want to gradually release students to read longer chunks of text, for longer periods of time, with less scaffolding. As students progress, you might include questions for analysis and slowly eliminating focal points before AIR—but only after your students have reliably demonstrated their ability to Establish Meaning of key elements of the text.

We want to help students build their self-awareness by giving them feedback on their progress as readers. We should make transparent for students when something might be a little bit of a challenge or when we've noticed that they're making really good progress in their reading, with the goal of them self-monitoring whether a text feels simple and straightforward or if it feels really challenging to them. There's value in being transparent about how and why we're managing AIR time. For instance, a teacher might say, "My sense is that we're still figuring Douglass out. We're going to keep reading independently in small chunks until we're a bit more familiar with his style and voice," or "We're really starting to 'get' Douglass. I'm going to challenge you to do more on your own."

To watch the video *Kirby Jarrell: A Doubtful Freedom*, use this QR code or find the video at the URL https://vimeo.com/1058362079/e8b4b74bbd.

In *Kirby Jarrell: A Doubtful* Freedom, Kirby Jarrell's students are working diligently to independently read and annotate *A Narrative of the Life of Frederick Douglass*, written in 1851. As with *Night*, Frederick Douglass's narrative is a nonfiction text about life circumstances so horrifying that they are difficult for us to imagine. In our curriculum, we intentionally support teachers in how to negotiate that in class with students. For this context, we want to let you know that the content being read and discussed is about Douglass imagining his escape plan from enslavement so you can prepare yourself if helpful as a viewer. After launching her AIR task, Kirby immediately begins to monitor, providing feedback and individual support. You'll note that it's a basic task designed to help students Establish Meaning in this complex and rich text. After students have completed their AIR and annotations, she adapts how students process their annotations based on her observations of their annotations. She'd planned to give them time to share in a Turn and Talk, but because annotations are so strong, she decides to go straight to a whole-group discussion. At the end of the clip, Kirby takes a few seconds to acknowledge students' progress with the text. They've been working with Douglass for weeks, and can now independently unpack dense text that may have stumped them at the beginning of the unit. It's a small but powerful move that makes transparent for students the struggle and value of working independently with rigorous language.

CHAPTER RECAP

There are three key indicators of fluency:

- **Accuracy:** the ability to decode the words in a text as they are written

- **Automaticity:** the ability to decode at the speed of sight and thus with no load on working memory

- **Prosody:** the ability to read a text with the cadence and expression of speech

Fluency is critical to comprehension for students of all ages, so it is worth teaching and reinforcing beyond the primary grades. In order to support fluency and comprehension and facilitate high-quality, engaged reading (and rereading) consider incorporating three ways of reading into your lessons:

- **Teacher Read Aloud** is a critical tool for modeling fluent reading of challenging texts, so it's important to plan and practice for it with intentionality. Students will apply what they learn through Read Aloud models in their own oral and silent reading.

- **FASE Reading** is a system for shared oral reading designed to be productive and engaging. It provides opportunities for students to practice their fluency and get immediate feedback from the expert reader in the room, their teacher. When carefully and systematically implemented, FASE contributes to a culture where students love reading and read a lot.

- **Accountable Independent Reading (AIR)** is an opportunity to independently practice the fluency building you've done through Teacher Read Aloud and FASE Reading. Supporting students in reading independently requires us to make a series of decisions based on the complexity of the text and our knowledge of our students.

Notes

1. The schools they work for don't either. There's almost no systematic assessment of it after, say, third or fourth grade.
2. https://www.shanahanonliteracy.com/blog/wake-up-reading-wars-combatants-fluency-instruction-is-part-of-the-science-of-reading.
3. Evolutionary biologists describe the human tendency to over-imitate. To assume there is meaningful information in the details of a process, they observe a knowledgeable person perform and therefore to copy it. Since over the long arc of prehistory this generally proved correct, and copying conferred immense competitive advantage on copiers, we developed an inclination to copy models, often without realizing we are doing it. See, for example, studies in which human children copy clearly unnecessary steps in opening a puzzle box while chimpanzees do not: http://www.replicatedtypo.com/imitation-and-social-cognition-in-humans-and-chimpanzees-i-imitation-overimitation-and-conformity/3112.html.
4. See Nathan Hansford, *The Scientific Principles of Reading Instruction*.
5. Nathan Hansford, "Repeated Reading Is Part of the Science of Reading,"

https://www.teachingbyscience.com/repeated-reading.

6. *The Art and Science of Teaching Primary Reading*, 90.

7. *The Art and Science of Teaching Primary Reading*, 40.

8. *The Art and Science of Teaching Primary Reading*, 41.

9. Natalie Wexler, *The Knowledge Gap: The Hidden Cause of America's Broken Education System—and How to Fix It* (Avery, 2019).

10. https://training.seer.cancer.gov/anatomy/cells_tissues_membranes/cells/structure.html#:~:text=A%20cell%20consists%20of%20three,but%20distinct%20structures%20called%20organelles.

11. Shawn Achor, *The Happiness Advantage: How a Positive Brain Fuels Success in Work and Life* (Crown, 2010), 71.

12. *The Art and Science of Teaching Primary Reading*, 44–45.

13. *The Art and Science of Teaching Primary Reading*, 131.

14. https://www.shanahanonliteracy.com/blog/fluency-instruction-for-older-kids-really#:~:text=Teachers%20are%20often%20told%20to,the%20comprehension%20differences%20by%2025%25.

15. *The Art and Science of Teaching Primary Reading*, 130.

16. *Language at the Speed of Sight*, 130.

17. David D. Paige and Theresa Magpuri-Lavell, "Reading Fluency in the Middel and Secondary Grades," *International Electronic Journal of Elementary Education* 7, no. 1 (2014): 83-96. [Quote on pp. 84–85.]

Chapter 4

The Hidden Power of Background Knowledge

A teacher, Ms. Hoover, stands in front of her fifth-grade class, novel in hand. "Class, today we're going to begin reading our novel, *Bud Not Buddy*," she says. "Let's start by thinking about what we know about the time period in which the book takes place. Raise your hand if you've ever heard of the Great Depression."

A smattering of students raise their hand and share vague and partially accurate descriptions of the Great Depression. The teacher begins to write their answers on what is often called a *K-W-L chart*. It captures what students

"Know" (perhaps "People were very poor!")

"Want to know" (maybe "Why were they so poor?")

and, in a third column intended to be completed later but often neglected,

Have "learned" by the end of the unit. In this case, the Great Depression.

This activity might look knowledge-driven—after all the teacher is "activating prior knowledge"—but it's not likely to improve understanding and comprehension much.

"Activating prior knowledge" in this case means making a list of haphazard, partially informed, and often superficial facts offered by students. The information isn't selected for relevance or organized in a logical way by the teacher—what's on the list is mostly accidental, and it's probably soon forgotten since little happens to organize it or cause it to be encoded into long-term memory. The lesson is not especially equitable, either. The students who knew more about the Great Depression still know more, and the students who knew less—or nothing—still know less.

Ms. Hoover has been encouraged to use the K-W-L chart to make her classroom more "knowledge rich" but it's mostly an illusion. She's been misled.

Down the hall, though, Ms. Coolidge is familiar with the famous Recht and Leslie "Baseball Study" we discuss in Chapter One. She knows her students need background knowledge to understand the events in the novel and the experiences of the characters. So, she distributes a short passage, "The Story of the Great Depression," that she has sourced on Newsela. The class reads it and then watches a video on the same topic while taking notes. Ms. Coolidge finishes the lesson and looks forward to starting the novel with students, hopeful that they now have the knowledge they need to be able to grapple with the book and understand the protagonist Bud's experiences.

By reading an article and watching a video, Ms. Coolidge has helped students access richer and more useful information than Ms. Hoover. Both sources have been developed by experts and present accurate and important information about the Great Depression, but it's one interaction. It's never used explicitly to make sense of the novel. How well will students remember it four weeks into the novel? And with very little knowledge to connect it to, students may not be absorbing as much as Ms. Coolidge thinks they are as they read. After all, she's taken American History in high school and college. When the video mentions the New Deal, she knows just what the narrator is talking about. She picks up on details she hadn't known before as she watches video of men in the Civilian Conservation Corps (CCC) construct buildings on a farm. But her students have no context for the video. The section on the New Deal washes over them. They have no idea what the CCC is. What are those men doing and why?

The importance of background knowledge for comprehension is clear, but a key challenge we see when we visit schools is that many teachers don't know how to optimally translate that research into practice.

Ms. Hoover and Ms. Coolidge are doing their best to translate research into practice, but they may not understand the mechanisms by which knowledge can foster learning. For example, they may not understand that building knowledge is about building *networks of* connected knowledge. "The more relationships we establish with our prior knowledge while reflecting on the learning object, the more solid its assimilation will be," Héctor Ruiz Martín writes.[1] Their students will need articles and other sources of information regularly throughout the unit. And they'll need to apply that knowledge to the book they are reading.

And with the threat of the state test looming, there's a good chance these fictional teachers are hedging their bets, doing what they can to supply background knowledge to their students, but still focusing on skills like "making inferences" or "identifying the main idea" just in case. It's risky not to ask the same questions the state test will ask. And they know they are supposed to respond to data that identifies skill gaps in their students—the district has bought a software package to provide the charts and graphs. And skills are what they've always done.

There are a lot of reasons why hard-working teachers, even those who believe in knowledge-rich classrooms, could get stuck trying to make the necessary changes.

Our goal is to help teachers be successful in using background knowledge so students can become better readers. In this chapter we'll try to draw a map to explain how. We will expand our discussion on the role of knowledge in reading comprehension, outline key reasons why instructional practices have been so slow to change, and then share tools you can use to effectively build and reinforce background knowledge in support of student literacy and learning.

RESEARCH ON KNOWLEDGE

Background knowledge, particularly *when it is encoded in long-term memory*, is a key driver of reading comprehension. It allows students to draw inferences and see connections that are critical to reading. This is what Daniel Willingham means when he says that critical thinking skills are "domain specific." We can think critically about something when we know a lot about it and when we don't, we can't. Your ability to think critically about why ionization energy increases as the nuclear charge in an atom increases is probably limited, unless you are a chemistry teacher (one, apparently, with a secret fascination for books on the science of reading).

To think critically, students must be able to draw relevant knowledge, and the more they can do that without increasing the load on their working memory, the more insight they can bring. You may recall Daniel Willingham's observation which we mention in Chapter One: "Much of the time, when we see someone apparently engaged in logical thinking, they are actually engaged in memory retrieval."[2]

What looks like a sharp inference or a bold insight while reading is often a sudden connection to another idea in long-term memory and that connection is not even conscious or intentional: "People don't decide that they're going to make . . . inferences, the mind just makes them happen," Daniel Willingham also tells us in Chapter One.[3] Or at least it does that when it has rich knowledge to draw on. With critical thinking, knowledge mostly drives the insight.

In a recent position paper, the Knowledge Matters Campaign's Scientific Advisory Committee writes that "Sense-making requires knowledge that must be systematically built (not just activated!) through instructional experiences and curricula." They draw the same conclusion we do: "Knowledge matters."[4]

Building knowledge to support reading requires the regular presentation of rich, organized and connected knowledge, followed by intentional steps causing it to be used and thought about by students so that it is encoded in memory. Lastly, it should be supported by Retrieval Practice to ensure that students remember it and can recall it quickly and easily to foster connections as they read. This is one reason why a single interaction with an article on the Great Depression may not help much in making sense of the time period in *Bud, Not Buddy*.

In her book *The Knowledge Gap*, Natalie Wexler explains the science behind the importance of knowledge through an analogy, "The more knowledge a child starts with, the more likely she is to acquire yet more knowledge. She'll read more and understand and retain information better, because knowledge, like Velcro, sticks best to other related knowledge."[5]

Every time we learn something new, our brain tries to connect it to something we already know. If you know something about climate in the Rocky Mountains, it's easier for you to learn and retain information about climate in the Himalayas. And then be able to think about how the climates of the two mountain chains are similar or different. Suddenly the knowledge is forming connections. "Isolated facts" don't *stay* isolated for very long.

Wexler's research highlights the fact that our brains are wired to think analogously along interconnected networks of knowledge. "The more meaningful the knowledge we have of something, the more new information we can acquire related to it, and the more new ideas we can build," writes Héctor Ruiz Martín. "The more we know the more we can learn."[6] The more networks of connected facts that we have, the easier it is to form new networks. In classroom speak, we often refer to these networks of organized and connected facts as *schema*, and schema are something we want to build. "Organized and connected" matters. That's one of the flaws in Ms. Hoover's K-W-L chart, with a list of randomly sourced facts about the Great Depression.

So far we have tried to describe the mechanism by which learning happens, detailing how central knowledge is to almost all of the core processes. But understanding how the brain works is different from understanding whether knowledge-based instruction actually causes learning.

In a 2009 study by Margaret McKeown and colleagues, skills-based versus knowledge-based approaches to reading were compared. "Student comprehension of common texts was examined under the following approaches: strategies instruction, content instruction, and basal instruction [a control group]." The researchers found that students who received the content instruction outperformed the other groups on open-ended recall tasks and were able to give both longer and more detailed summaries of the texts that they read. Interestingly they also found that "content students [students who receive knowledge-driven instruction] outperformed strategies students [those who receives skill-based instruction], and occasionally, the basal control students outperformed strategies students."[7] According to this study, knowledge helps and interestingly, skills-based instruction can even be counterproductive, distracting students from what's important. In the McKeown and colleagues' study the strategies, group yielded weaker results than the control group. Similarly, as we note in Chapter One, among French and Scottish students, achievement in reading comprehension declined after those nations abandoned knowledge-rich curricula for a skills-based model.

E. D. Hirsch, in his pivotal book *The Knowledge Deficit,* was among the first to ring the alarm about the critical importance of knowledge to reading, asserting that "general reading comprehension ability is much more than comprehension strategies; it requires a definite range of general knowledge."[8] Pervasive neglect of this fact, he asserts, has led to what he describes as a "tragic" gap in our students' reading ability. These "well-intentioned yet mistaken views are the chief reason (more than other more frequently blamed factors, even poverty) that many children do not attain reading proficiency, thus crippling their later schooling."[9]

Hirsch's summary of the research came out almost twenty years ago, and our literacy practices have not changed much despite his warnings. Even with clear evidence in favor of the importance of knowledge to comprehension and literacy, skill-based approaches still proliferate. If you're getting *Sold a Story* vibes from hearing that, so are we.

WE KNOW KNOWLEDGE MATTERS—WHY DON'T WE ACT THAT WAY?

So why does our practice look much the same as it always has? Old habits die hard, and the habits of skills-based instruction seem to die harder than others. An understanding of the barriers to changing instruction is a precursor to knowing what specific actions we can take to rectify our practices.

One possibility for the lack of change in instruction is that the way we assess reading is problematic. We want to be clear: we believe in the importance of standardized assessments.

They are a critical tool for improving schools and ensuring accountability. But to do its job, a test must measure the right thing. And we are pretty sure that most statewide reading assessments measure the wrong thing. One of the greatest determinants of whether a student will understand a text they are reading, for example, is their relevant background knowledge as Recht and Lesley discovered in the "Baseball Study." An assessment where the passages are about random, unpredictable topics is to a significant degree a generalized measure of student background knowledge. And when you insist on measuring skills, for example, assessing vocabulary not by asking students to define and use words but to infer the meaning of obscure words and phrases from context, you are "measuring" something that is mostly irrelevant and distracting people from what actually matters.

Compare this to the guidance given the schools in England as they prepare their students for the English Literature General Certificate of Secondary Education (GCSE) exam in the United Kingdom:

"Students should study a range of high quality, intellectually challenging, and substantial whole texts in detail. These must include:

- at least one play by Shakespeare

- at least one 19th century novel

- a selection of poetry since 1789, including representative Romantic poetry

- fiction or drama from the British Isles from 1914 onwards."

On the UK standardized test, students are asked questions about texts from these broad categories. The incentive is to read deeply from important periods in literature and understand broad themes and relevant knowledge so that students will be prepared to connect that knowledge to actual texts from that era.

In the United States, reading assessments are content agnostic. This disincentivizes teachers from teaching what science tells us is important (knowledge) and to focus on a practice that is counterproductive (skills). As Natalie Wexler recently wrote, "Reading tests claim to measure general skills like making inferences or finding the main idea of a text, using passages on topics students may or may not be familiar with. But research has shown that the more you know about the topic you're reading about, the better your comprehension. Standardized tests—including those used to determine reading levels—don't take account of that. And yet these measures are routinely used to guide instruction and determine what individual students are or are not capable of doing."[10]

It's hard to create change when teachers are under intense pressure to get their students to perform well on an exam that is measuring the wrong things. Doubly so when generally effective data-driven practices can lead us astray. Good schools take their assessment results and use them to guide instruction. They disaggregate results by question type and identify places where more instruction is needed—in math this works very well. If students have done well on adding fractions but poorly on multiplying them, we know what to do: reteach multiplying fractions, monitor for progress, and reassess. Just maybe reassess our curriculum and teaching and ask, where was the gap the first time around?

This is exactly what a good school should do with data and those that do it tend to be successful,[11] causing them to be wedded to the process. The problem is that process doesn't work especially well with reading.

Dr. Hollis Scarborough's Reading Rope, which we discuss briefly in Chapter Three, can be useful in explaining why:

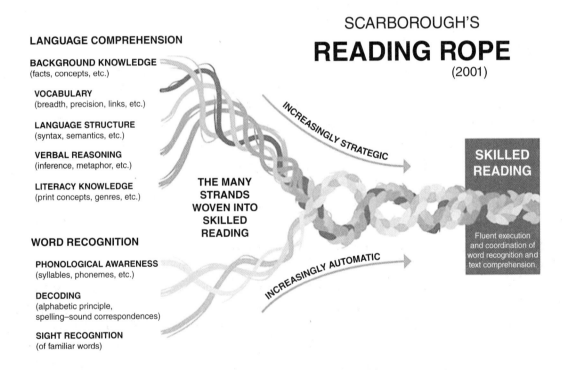

SCARBOROUGH'S
READING ROPE
(2001)

LANGUAGE COMPREHENSION

BACKGROUND KNOWLEDGE
(facts, concepts, etc.)

VOCABULARY
(breadth, precision, links, etc.)

LANGUAGE STRUCTURE
(syntax, semantics, etc.)

VERBAL REASONING
(inference, metaphor, etc.)

LITERACY KNOWLEDGE
(print concepts, genres, etc.)

WORD RECOGNITION

PHONOLOGICAL AWARENESS
(syllables, phonemes, etc.)

DECODING
(alphabetic principle,
spelling–sound correspondences)

SIGHT RECOGNITION
(of familiar words)

INCREASINGLY STRATEGIC

INCREASINGLY AUTOMATIC

THE MANY
STRANDS
WOVEN INTO
SKILLED
READING

**SKILLED
READING**

Fluent execution
and coordination of
word recognition and
text comprehension.

As students become skilled readers, they progress from left to right on Scarborough's rope. As this happens, a series of disparate strands (skills and forms of knowledge) are woven together. They are learned separately but ultimately tightly coordinated so that they appear to function as a single process. The left-hand side of the diagram emphasizes that there are two broad categories within these strands: word recognition and language comprehension. The word recognition strand is essentially the set of processes that systematic synthetic phonics instruction helps students master. The language comprehension strand involves many of the competencies and content we discuss in this book: vocabulary, syntax, and background knowledge.

As students progress in their reading ability, the language comprehension and word recognition strands combine. They look like one fluid process, but there are still many component parts.

The figure expresses how this complex process comes to look simple. This is critical because it tells us that when reading breaks down, the number of potential causes is large. And because the component parts are interwoven, it is hard to tell where the problem is.

We may learn that a student has failed to comprehend a passage because he cannot tell us the main idea. But unlike with math, the number of potential causes is large. It *might* be that he does not understand that when he is asked to describe the main idea he is being asked what the passage is *mostly about* and so it *might* be that if we explain that to him and perhaps ask him repeat a chant—main idea is *who or what the passage is about*!!—and then practice with a few unrelated passages, we might fix the problem.

But probably not.

Far more likely sources of causation exist. It might be that our student didn't understand key background knowledge that the passage assumed he would have. Perhaps the passage was about the naked mole rat and one sentence read: "Naked mole rats are the only mammals known to have a colony structure similar to that of social insects, such as honeybees and ants." Colony structure? Social insects? The symptom of his confusion would be the failure to explain the main idea. But that wouldn't be the cause.

Or the problem could be with vocabulary in the passage. Perhaps he didn't know the noun form of the words *confine* and *burrow*. The passage read "Their loose, hairless skin helps them to turn easily within the confines of their burrows," and our student was suddenly lost. Again, the signal of the problem would be a flashing red light next to main idea. But that would have little to do with the cause.

Or he might not have been able to read the passage fluently. Perhaps he is broadly dysfluent. Perhaps the passage had unusual syntax that caused him to have to engage his working memory. Again, our indication that this was the case would be his failure to describe the main idea rather than his lack of fluency.

This is one reason why reading is hard to teach. Causation is very difficult to determine. And this is also one reason why disaggregating test results by question type works so poorly in reading when it works so well in math. In reading, it not only fails to diagnose the problem, it suggests a false solution: *Patrick doesn't understand how to find the main idea!* The more data analysis based on question types serves us well in other disciplines, the more it leads us astray in reading.

A second (related) incentive in favor of a skills-based approach is that, once students have mastered the word recognition strand—a transition often described as moving from "learning to read" to "reading to learn"—teaching via knowledge is a long game. It's scary to bet on the idea that students will be far better readers if we make the correct long-run investments when this also means not pursuing the short-term promise that we can prop up scores in a few months by making students better at answering certain types of questions. We probably can achieve small gains by doing this. But getting better at answering specific questions isn't learning to comprehend deeply.

The perceived safety of skills-based instruction also tends to lead to what one New York City English teacher called "the passage-ification of English classes."[12] Instead of teaching rich canonical texts to our students, we have replaced the novel with a series of passages designed to forefront the skills that will appear on state assessments. It's one example of the ways that the pursuit of short-run gains can get in the way of long-run learning (which, we note, will also show up on assessments and much more positively, albeit on a slightly longer timeline).

A third reason why instruction hasn't become knowledge-based in many schools is that teachers are often worried that students will be bored by the methods we rely on to build knowledge: reading nonfiction, brief bursts of direct instruction, and often Retrieval Practice. We think the videos in this book, Christine Torres's lesson from Chapter One, for example, show that's not true.

Perhaps teachers think nonfiction is boring because of the skill-based way it has often been taught. If our questions are "What organizing pattern does the article use?" "What is the purpose of the caption under diagram A?" and "Can you identify the main idea of the third section?" the article becomes a vehicle for teaching students the skills of reading nonfiction (boring), rather than a tool for building knowledge (potential for excitement and intrigue!). Students tend to enjoy knowing things. Especially when they can use that knowledge to learn more and understand.

Moreover, a skills-based approach to nonfiction doesn't reflect how we read nonfiction as adult readers. We usually read nonfiction to help us understand something important to us. If we can replicate that in class—say by reading nonfiction to better understand a story we've come to care about—we make it more interesting and more realistic.

In a policy report for the Fordham Institute, teacher and education writer Daniel Buck recently noted, "Like many medicines, reading strategies can be toxic when administered too frequently or in excessive doses—in this case, because they crowd out beneficial opportunities for students to learn content from text."[13]

We saw this recently when a teacher—a very good one—paused her reading of a short piece about ants to do a Call and Response: "Informational text!" she called, and the students responded, "It's how we get our knowledge!!" While that may be true, it crowds out the opportunity to reinforce the actual content in the passage. Instruction frequently neglects to use informational texts to make a long-term investment in student knowledge—which is what can make reading nonfiction interesting for students.

The mistake is that we don't spend enough time reading for knowledge by asking things like "Let's make a summary of five important things we learned about ants" or "The article says ants can carry objects 100 times their weight. Amazing! How and why does it say they are able to do that?" or "Let's write some questions we could ask our little sisters and brothers to answer if they read this. . ."

Additionally, a skills-based approach to nonfiction results in students being unable to synthesize new and unfamiliar information because the topics are often disjointed. If our goal is to "be able to identify the organizational features of informational texts," it often means reading an article on the naked mole rat one day and on the Industrial Revolution the next. When we organize the nonfiction reading on skills rather than knowledge, students are less likely to connect ideas and see links across articles, as they would if they read a series of articles that are organized and connected through a topic or theme that would cause students to develop schema (and interest and curiosity). If they have a connection to a fictional text, all the better. Now we have Velcro: the knowledge is more likely to stick and much more interesting to learn (and teach).

A fourth reason why it's hard to make the transition from skills to knowledge is one that's often hard to admit—our own background knowledge is often lacking. In school, for example, Erica read George Orwell's *Animal Farm* as though it was a book about talking animals. Enjoyable? Yes. Informative in a way that built lasting knowledge about the Russian Revolution and Communism? No. If Erica wanted to teach *Animal Farm* now, she'd have a lot of studying up to do on Lenin and Trotsky and propaganda and the psychology of manipulation. Because we often weren't taught in a knowledge-rich way as students, we have a lot more work to do if we want to do it that way as teachers.

In professional development teachers spend so much time on lesser topics—pedagogy, true—but also how to use the SMART Board, and what the grading policy is and, this year, what the future of artificial intelligence might look like. We forget—or fail to find time—to invest in our own content knowledge for the books and subjects that we teach. One of the best ideas we've borrowed from New York City's highly successful Success Academies is knowledge-based book preparation. Before a book is taught, the grade-level team and the department chair meet explicitly to discuss the background knowledge that will help them teach the book. They mutually share facts and sources, which will be most useful to students and where to include them in lessons. This is a clear statement about the importance of teacher content knowledge. The fact that this sort of meeting is a rarity reveals the general undervaluation of "mere facts."

Consider how one of the oldest and most popular pedagogical theories is often interpreted in a way that degrades the role of knowledge. For years, teacher-prep programs, traditional and nontraditional alike, have hailed the value of Bloom's taxonomy. The taxonomy proposes six major categories of question types: knowledge, comprehension, application, analysis, synthesis, and evaluation. "The categories were presented by its designers as 'skills and abilities,' with the understanding that knowledge is the necessary precondition for putting these skills and abilities into practice."[14]

The Problem with Blooms

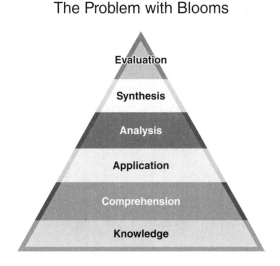

Ironically, this is the opposite of how Bloom's taxonomy is often interpreted. Perhaps because of the traditional pyramid image, which puts knowledge at the bottom, teachers often believe that knowledge-based questions, especially via recall and Retrieval Practice, are the lowest form of question, and the least important to ask. No one wants to be at the bottom of the pyramid. Because teachers are told knowledge questions are far less cognitively complex tasks than evaluation questions, they view them as less worthy of class time. In schools of education, Bloom's is often taught this way—it overlooks the overwhelming consensus of cognitive psychology that knowledge is an essential foundation to more cognitively complex tasks. Asking about the balance between knowledge and skills "is like asking what the right balance is between ingredients and cake," writes Daisy Christodoulou. "The ingredients make the cake, just as the knowledge makes the skill."[15]

Believing that knowledge questions—even mere recall of facts—are low value doesn't jibe with the overwhelming consensus of cognitive science. Daniel Willingham summarizes: "Data from the last thirty years lead to a conclusion that is not scientifically challengeable: thinking well requires knowing facts, and that's true not simply because you need something to think about." He continues, "The very processes that teachers care about most—critical thinking processes such as reasoning and problem solving—are intimately intertwined with factual knowledge that is in long-term memory (not just found in the environment)."[16] In other words, there are two parts to the equation. You not only have to teach a lot of facts to enable students to think deeply, but you must reinforce knowledge enough to install it in long-term memory or you can't do any of the activities at the top of the pyramid.

When we blogged about this idea in 2017, Barbara Davidson at StandardsWork proposed the idea of "turning the pyramid on its side." The result was a big improvement in that it erodes some of the hierarchy implicit in getting to the top:

Knowledge ··▶ Comprehension ··▶ Application ··▶ Analysis ··▶ Synthesis ··▶ Evaluation

standardswork.org

Later in this chapter, we'll talk a bit more about what this might look like in practice, in particular focusing on how Retrieval Practice is vitally important to encoding knowledge.

A final reason why reading instruction hasn't kept up with the knowledge-based research comes from the conversations and observations that we have had at some of the highest performing schools in New York City. In these conversations, we've come to realize that in seeking solutions to gaps in literacy, we might be looking in the wrong place. When you look at the results from Bronx Classical and Success Academy, which consistently score in the 80th to 90th percentile in reading on the New York State ELA Test, versus the majority of other schools in New York City, which are seemingly stuck in the 50th to 60th percentile of reading scores, the gap in these results has been a consistent head scratcher.

PERFORMANCE ON THE NEW YORK STATE ELA END-OF-YEAR STATE TEST GRADES 3–8 (2022–2023)[17]

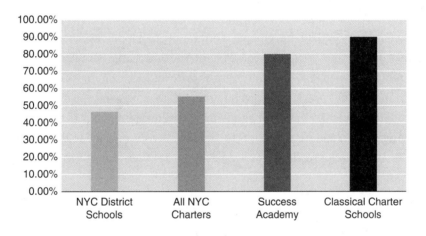

The most distinctive aspect of these schools—the thing that differentiates them most from district schools and even other charter schools that use similar operational practices—is their intentional and robust investment in knowledge—one that often occurs just as much *outside* of the literacy block as it does within the literacy block. It's what is happening in science and social studies, in their intense focus on vocabulary and knowledge development in art and music and every subject area. In these schools, from as early as kindergarten, there is a relentless, strategic, consistent, and unapologetic approach to building knowledge and rigorous vocabulary outside of the literacy block that translates to improved reading comprehension.

Research supports the assertion that knowledge development everywhere increases reading proficiency. According to a study by the Fordham Institute's Adam Tyner and Sarah Kabourek, students across a nationally representative selection of schools "who receive an additional thirty minutes of social studies instruction per day . . . outperform students with less social studies time by 15 percent of a standard deviation on the fifth-grade reading assessment."[18]

Classical and Success go farther than most in this programmatic investment in background knowledge. Bronx Classical has daily social studies and Latin beginning in third grade. Success has an intense focus on science starting early in primary school and robust and frequent "field studies." A robust investment in knowledge—both inside and outside of the literacy classroom—is a key ingredient in the secret sauce for these highest performing schools. And they suggest that while this book focuses on what happens in reading classes, the tools for developing knowledge-rich instruction can be applied to any discipline.

When we think about changing our behavior as teachers and leaders, it's useful to draw on the guidance from Chip and Dan Heath's book *Switch: How to Create Change When Change Is Hard* (Crown Currency, 2010): that change is often slow to happen because people are unclear about what actions to take. We'll aim to shed light on some of the actions teachers can take to ensure they build knowledge in the classroom shortly and we'll share video examples to help create mental models of knowledge-driven literacy classrooms and several tools you can use with your students to incorporate more knowledge building into your lessons. The four tools in the following section will help teachers to *build* lasting knowledge in their classrooms and to ensure that students can retrieve this knowledge from their long-term memory.

Self-Assessment: How to Know If Your Schools' Literacy Instruction Is Still More Skills-Based Than Knowledge-Based?

- Your early literacy instruction is strong in phonics and phonemic awareness but your students' reading results have stagnated in the upper grades.

- Your copy room is full of printouts of one- to three-page passages followed by multiple-choice questions.

- When you talk about knowledge or ask what you consider a knowledge-based question, it's actually about literary knowledge (e.g., "What diction tells you . . .?").

- Your lesson objectives consistently focus on literary skills (e.g., "Students will be able to identify figurative language.").

EMBEDDED NONFICTION

Embedded Nonfiction texts are short informational texts that build and reinforce important networks of knowledge for deep comprehension of a primary text. They enrich students' analysis and provide a more equitable reading experience by building requisite background knowledge for all students.

The first of these tools, *Embedded Nonfiction*, is perhaps the knowledge building tool that we have observed used most widely in schools. When used effectively, Embedded Nonfiction texts enrich students' analysis by creating a shared body of relevant knowledge students can use to draw connections and develop insights—a critically important way for students to be able to create deeper understanding when they read.

We would generally put the many rich examples of Embedded Nonfiction we've seen employed by teachers around the world in two categories. Some of these are examples that we would describe as being "in the bull's eye"—those that provide knowledge that is directly related to the topic and time period a primary text is about. If you are reading *Animal Farm*, an article about the Russian Revolution is in the bull's eye. These types of Embedded Nonfiction are especially helpful in ensuring that students understand the text fully. Other examples we describe as being "outside the bull's eye"—nonfiction about knowledge that perhaps isn't directly related to the topic of the central text but that can help unlock deeper meaning or pathways for analysis for students. An article about how shared singing builds loyalty and connection among groups of people is relevant and just may be fascinating if you want to understand the pigs' behavior. These types of Embedded Nonfiction can help students make connections to ideas beyond the book. Check out Appendix E for several rich examples of each type.

To watch the video *Patrick Pastore: Civil War*, use this QR code or find the video at the URL https://vimeo.com/1058362474/f5f2a14355.

In the video *Patrick Pastore: Civil War,* you can see Patrick Pastore of Rochester, New York, use an example of an Embedded Nonfiction text in the bull's eye. The article about the Civil War was carefully selected to provide his eighth graders with the context they would need to better understand "An Occurrence at Owl Creek Bridge," a nineteenth-century short nonfiction story that takes place during the Civil War.

Students read the passage independently and answer questions in writing as part of their Do Now. In reviewing the answers, Patrick briefly makes sure that students have understood the content of the nonfiction text, asking them to reread the sections to provide evidence for their assertions. He is explicit with students that some of the questions are "basic but important." He is making sure students understand references to the "South," "Confederates," the "North" and the "Union Army," and that the last of these groups is also referred to as the *Federalists.* That's a lot to keep straight if you don't already have robust background knowledge about the Civil War.[19]

And in fact, in answering his question, one student confuses "Federalists" with "Democrats." It's a perfect illustration of how a lack of background knowledge can disrupt comprehension. If a student reads a story about the "Federal Army" (as they are about to do in the short story) but don't know that Federalist are soldiers from the North and Confederates are soldiers from the South—that lack of background knowledge will have a compounding negative effect on their ability to understand the fictional text. If you don't understand those "basic but important" things, almost nothing in the story is going to make sense.

But Patrick is not done with the article. When his students read Ambrose Bierce's story, Patrick poses questions that encourage them to use what they've learned from the nonfiction text to understand events and perspective in the story. The text as you can see is dense and archaic:

The Library of America • Story of the Week
From *Ambrose Bierce: The Devil's Dictionary, Tales, & Memoirs*
(The Library of America, 2011), pages 10–19.

First published in the *San Francisco Examiner*, July 13, 1890, and first collected
in the 1892 edition of *In the Midst of Life (Tales of Soldiers and Civilians)*.

An Occurrence at Owl Creek Bridge

AMBROSE BIERCE

I

A MAN stood upon a railroad bridge in northern Alabama, looking down into the swift water twenty feet below. The man's hands were behind his back, the wrists bound with a cord. A rope closely encircled his neck. It was attached to a stout cross-timber above his head and the slack fell to the level of his knees. Some loose boards laid upon the sleepers supporting the metals of the railway supplied a footing for him and his executioners—two private soldiers of the Federal army, directed by a sergeant who in civil life may have been a deputy sheriff. At a short remove upon the same temporary platform was an officer in the uniform of his rank, armed. He was a captain. A sentinel at each end of the bridge stood with his rifle in the position known as "support," that is to say, vertical in front of the left shoulder, the hammer resting on the forearm thrown straight across the chest—a formal and unnatural position, enforcing an erect carriage of the body. It did not appear to be the duty of these two men to know what was occurring at the center of the bridge; they merely blockaded the two ends of the foot planking that traversed it.

Patrick asks questions that require students to apply knowledge from the nonfiction to the story. They come to understand that the protagonist is a Confederate soldier and that the other men are Union soldiers. They now understand the broad outlines of the conflict—knowledge that Bierce almost assuredly took for granted in his readers. Just as important, students have applied terms like *Confederate* and *Federalist* from the nonfiction reading to the story, helping them to encode this knowledge more deeply. This is because thinking about the meaning of the learning object—what is a Confederate—and connecting it to other knowledge—the Confederate soldier is being guarded by Federalists—is Héctor Ruiz Martín's definition of active learning. And, Ruiz Martín writes, "Since prior knowledge constitutes the base on which we learn new things, trying to learn something without first having learned its fundamentals proves futile."[20] It's going to be very hard to learn much from the story without understanding the basics.

It's a powerful illustration of knowledge-based instruction supporting comprehension. Without the knowledge to help them to identify who is who in the story, students wouldn't have understood even the basics and it would have resulted in incomplete and insufficient answers and no deeper knowledge of the time period, or of the short story. Asking students to make an inference about what was happening in the text would likely only have been answered correctly by a handful of students who might have brought that knowledge with them to class. In this way, building knowledge helps to level the playing field for all readers so that they can all access complex texts.

In the clip *Patrick Pastore: Histrionic Personality Disorder*, we see an example of an Embedded Nonfiction passage that is outside the bull's eye. Patrick embeds an article on histrionic personality disorder while reading his favorite book *The Westing Game* by Ellen Raskin with his sixth graders. Patrick has assigned the following article for homework to help students better understand a character from their novel:

To watch the video *Patrick Pastore: Histrionic Personality Disorder*, use this QR code or find the video at the URL https://vimeo.com/1058362844/6c375aafd8.

Histrionic Personality Disorder

What is histrionic personality disorder?
Histrionic personality disorder is one of a group of conditions called dramatic personality disorders. People with these disorders have intense, unstable emotions and distorted self-images. For people with histrionic personality disorder, their self-esteem depends on the approval of others and does not arise from a true feeling of self-worth. They have an overwhelming desire to be noticed, and often behave dramatically or inappropriately to get attention. The word *histrionic* means "dramatic or theatrical."

This disorder is more common in women than in men and usually is evident by early adulthood.

What are the symptoms of histrionic personality disorder?
In many cases, people with histrionic personality disorder have good social skills; however, they tend to use these skills to manipulate others so that they can be the center of attention.

A person with this disorder might also:

The first question that Patrick asks is to establish students' understanding of the article. "If someone has histrionic personality disorder, they constantly seek something. What is it that they seek?" He then follows up with a question about their primary text, "What heir from our book would most likely be diagnosed with this disorder?" Eager hands shoot up in the air, suggesting not only comprehension of both texts but the interest and engagement inherent in this thinking task. This type of embedding experience isn't typical of what we see in most classrooms. It's not only incredibly effective in increasing broad background knowledge, it's also very interesting to students as it helps them understand a character on a psychological level. Reading this article alongside their reading of *The Westing Game* deepens not only their comprehension of the article on histrionic personality disorder because they have something (or someone) to apply this new idea to, but also deepens their understanding of the primary text.

In Chapter One, we introduce the idea that "stories are cognitively privileged," meaning that students remember more from content that is embedded in a story. When we apply this principle to Embedded Nonfiction, it reminds us that not only does the nonfiction help us better understand the fiction because we've been exposed to important context, but also that the opposite is true—the stories we ask students to connect the knowledge to will help them to better remember facts and information from the nonfiction. Nonfiction taught in isolation may be less immediately engaging for students because there is not a story arc to follow or a protagonist to endear us. But when nonfiction is connected to a story that students are deeply invested in, it's easier to remember and care about the new information because it's more cognitively privileged than when it's read in isolation.

Embedded Nonfiction is a powerful tool for knowledge building, an ideal starting point for teachers looking to increase knowledge in their classrooms. This is particularly true for any teacher who is "on an island"—teaching in a school without a robust curriculum or a strong professional adult learning culture. Many of the requisites to knowledge building—such as a curriculum that emphasizes knowledge development in a systematic way—tend to be school- or district-level decisions and are beyond the purview of the individual teacher.

A first step for using Embedded Nonfiction is simply to brainstorm potential topics that you might want to embed alongside the novel that you are teaching, and to consider when you'll embed them. This guidance is supported by Susan Neuman, a professor of childhood and literacy education, and her colleagues at New York University who emphasize the importance of previewing a text as a teacher to consider the knowledge demands and what requisite background knowledge needs to be taught or activated in advance.[21]

Let's take a look at how Helen Howell, an English Advanced Skills Teacher and Lead Teacher for Literacy at The Radclyffe School in Oldham, Manchester, applied the idea of Embedded Nonfiction to her year 9 class (eighth grade in the United States) as they read *Macbeth*.[22] Helen has mapped out throughout the course of the text where she could add rich nonfiction articles, both to help build background knowledge (and therefore comprehension) of *Macbeth* and also to help students get more out of (and better at) reading nonfiction by making it connect directly to their experience of reading *Macbeth*.

Embedding Nonfiction "just makes sense to me," Helen says. "It enables students to understand the world in which characters live (which can be quite alien to them) and their character motives much more thoroughly as well as giving them much-needed exposure to this kind of text. In our GCSE [UK Standardized Tests], students have to tackle unseen nonfiction with often very challenging language, so it is essential we give them as much practice with this as possible."

Helen's list of embedding opportunities is incredibly rich and diverse and some of their original sources are footnoted next.

Macbeth Embedded Nonfiction Ideas

Embedded Nonfiction Topic	Purpose for Embedding
The witch mania of King James I	To understand Shakespeare's influence when creating the witches and the links to the Jacobean era
Guy Fawkes and the Gunpowder Plot	To explore themes of treason, loyalty, and the conflicts between Protestants and Catholics
Ego and ambition[23]	To explore themes of treason, loyalty and the conflicts between Protestants and Catholics Question to ask students: "Agree or disagree: 'Ambition is just another word for greed.'"
Macbeth as a tragic hero[24]	To understand the concept of a tragic hero and how Macbeth fits this description
Experiment on how power corrupts[25]	To explore the influence of power on even the most honest people
Science of psychosis and hallucinations	To understand how Lady Macbeth's guilt begins to physically manifest itself and leads to her eventual suicide
Science of sleepwalking	To understand the symptoms that affect Lady Macbeth such as stress and sleep deprivation
Misogyny in the Jacobean Era	To explore the links between contemporary perceptions of women and Shakespeare's characterization of Lady Macbeth and the witches as well as the association of cruelty with masculinity
Free will versus the influence of fate, the idea of prophecies	To explore whether Macbeth is truly in control of his own actions or if the witches are controlling him through their prophecies
Use of weather motifs in literature	To understand how Shakespeare uses weather to symbolize chaos, disorder, return to order, and menace

We don't know about you, but we can assure you that this is not how the three of us were taught how to read Shakespeare. But from a knowledge perspective, imagine if we were? Beyond having a shaky memory of Macbeth's "Tomorrow, and tomorrow, and tomorrow" speech, with the approach just described, we'd likely not only have had a deeper understanding of the play when we read it but also a more nuanced and *lasting* understanding of it—not to mention that it would have been a more robust and interesting way to read the Bard. You can imagine also how Natalie Wexler's Velcro analogy could be applied here—the knowledge from the embedded texts would help with better understanding Macbeth and also make some of the themes more relevant and therefore lasting. We call this idea *Absorption Rate*—students' ability to understand and assimilate new information increases when they have more knowledge to help make it stick or be absorbed.

Inherent in Helen's plan is the idea of when to Embed Nonfiction in a text. Teachers typically tend to embed only at the outset of a novel—to frontload knowledge at the beginning of a new novel. That's important for context setting, but it's a missed opportunity not to spiral back to it or layer additional knowledge on later in the text. In our planning guidance to teachers, we encourage them to think carefully about both *when* and *what* to embed. And like many things, we learned from our own mistakes in this area. When Colleen first taught Lois Lowry's *Number the Stars* with her fifth graders, she'd often start the unit with a week of nonfiction reading on World War II and the historical context before even starting the novel. But with that much frontloading, it was harder for students to recall and apply the knowledge when it came up later in the text.

Instead, embedding readings at critical points in which they are relevant to the text is a better way to leverage students' working memories and can take better advantage of the Velcro effect. New knowledge introduced later in the text can be better absorbed when it isn't delivered all at once.

We find that when we're strategic about embedding these ideas throughout the novel, at the moment they're most relevant, students are better able to absorb more information about both texts in smaller chunks. This gives students a clear reason to invest and engage in the information they are learning. You can imagine, if a teacher gives students an article about Swedish neutrality in week one of a *Number the Stars* unit, it would be really dry for students—they won't really understand why they're learning about it because the idea of Swedish neutrality, for example, doesn't become relevant until near the end of *Number the Stars* when the Rosens are smuggled to Sweden. But if the idea of Swedish neutrality becomes critical to the safety of this family—a family we as readers have grown to care about—suddenly the class is more invested in learning about it. Not only will students absorb more, but it also makes them more interested in the knowledge and topics they're learning about when they're introduced at the right point in the reading. Other topics that we might consider embedding throughout *Number the Stars* might include Embedded Nonfiction that provides social and historical context at the start of the novel—perhaps about the idea of occupying armies or about the Nazi worldview. In Chapter Four, we might embed articles on rationing to more thoroughly understand brief references to this idea. In Chapter Six, it could be helpful to look at resistance movements or Sweden's role in WWII. In Chapter Seven, learning more about the customs and celebrations of Rosh Hashanah will deepen students' understanding of the family's adapted traditions here during wartime. These are all topics that are directly and explicitly mentioned in the text, and if students know more about them, their analysis of the novel will be deeper. We also could embed information about literary themes like reality and childhood in Chapter Eight to better understand Kirsti's understanding of the world. Or we might also consider embedding across genres, like having students read Hans Christian Andersen's fairy tales, which Lowry alludes to several times in the novel beginning in Chapter Two.

To watch the video *Scott Wells: Craniofacial Abnormalities*, use this QR code or find the video at the URL https://vimeo.com/1058362265/d7fb8def67.

We can see effective uses of timely and topical embedding in *Scott Wells: Craniofacial Abnormalities* as year 5 (fourth-grade) teacher Scott Wells at Goldsmith Primary Academy in Birmingham, England, as he embeds an article on craniofacial differences while reading R. J. Palacio's *Wonder* (from the *Reading Reconsidered* curriculum). The idea of "craniofacial abnormalities" is a term that comes up early in the novel so the knowledge building that happens at this point (pp. 19–34 of the novel) is important. Scott's use of the Embedded Text deepens students' understanding of the primary text by grounding readers in the protagonist's medical condition and how his disability is perceived by society so that students can have a better understanding of how it affects him throughout the novel, thereby enriching both their understanding of the protagonist as well as their literary analysis.

As the clip opens, you'll notice that Scott is reading aloud to his students the nonfiction passage here. It is rich both with relevant background knowledge and with new vocabulary like *abnormality*, *cognition*, and *anomalies*. You'll notice that students use some of these words in their discussion because they have been defined for them and expanded on in the article.

Do Now

Directions: Read this article on **disability** and **craniofacial differences** and underline anything that reminds you of August's experience in the novel so far.

Disability and Difference

The term disability refers to any condition of the mind or body that makes it more difficult for a person to do certain activities or interact with the world around them. According to the Centers for Disease Control, one in four adults in the United States lives with some type of disability. While some disabilities may be hidden or not easy to see, others are immediately obvious and can <u>impact</u> the way an individual is treated by those around them.

Disabilities that affect the head and face can be particularly challenging because of their visibility and their impact on important body processes. According to the Children's Craniofacial Association, "A craniofacial difference (medically often called a disorder) refers to an **abnormality** of the face and/or the head." Eating, drinking, breathing, speaking, seeing, and hearing can all be impacted by craniofacial differences. However, these types of disabilities do not often impact **cognition** or mental development. Dr. Steven Buchman, a pediatric plastic surgeon, explains:

> Craniofacial anomalies often require surgery — sometimes many operations — and can require long-term follow-up care, but many of the conditions are, for the most part, physical conditions that do not really affect developmental growth [...] Kids with craniofacial [conditions] like to do the same things a lot of other kids like to do, play the same way other kids like to play. These kids, for all intents and purposes, are just like any other kid.

However, as humans, we are wired to notice difference, and disabilities of the head and face are likely to attract our attention. People with craniofacial differences often encounter unwanted staring, questions, or teasing about their appearance. "It's a survival instinct for something that looks different to catch your eye, but how you respond to someone that looks different is what counts." says Jacqueline Kaufman, a pediatric neuropsychologist.

abnormality: something that is not usual, expected, or normal
cognition: mental processes involved in knowledge, comprehension, and memory

---

1. Reread Dr. Steven Buchman's quote in the article. Would August be likely to agree with this **perspective**? Why or why not?

_____

_____

_____

Reading this passage aloud for students draws on several of the ideas that we introduce in Chapter Three, especially the importance of prosodic reading of nonfiction texts to support meaning making.

As he reads, Scott pauses to ask what we call an *Overlapping Question*—one that asks students to draw on both the fiction and nonfiction text in order to answer, "I'm wondering, would August agree with this perspective?" Overlapping Questions require students to activate and apply their knowledge of a secondary text in order to understand and deepen their analysis of their primary text. Scott gives students a minute to jot their thoughts and then share them with a partner. In the discussion that ensues, students draw upon the knowledge of the article and connect it to August being an "ordinary kid," a theme that comes up early in the novel. The clip ends with students responding to the following prompt in writing:

2. The article explains that while it might be natural to notice a **craniofacial difference**, "how you respond to someone that looks different is what counts." In the chart below, jot some advice you might give someone who was meeting August for the first time. What should they do? What should they avoid doing?

Do	Avoid

This final step asks students to apply their new knowledge to their own lives, making connections between the learning object and concepts already in their long-term memory.

To watch the video *Emily Di Matteo: Manipulate*, use this QR code or find the video at the URL https://vimeo.com/1058363187/1a72a018fd.

You can see another stellar example of Embedded Nonfiction in the clip *Emily Di Matteo: Manipulate*, which comes from Emily DiMatteo's eighth-grade English classroom at Cincinnati Country Day School in Ohio. Emily is teaching George Orwell's *Animal Farm* and demonstrates how Embedded Nonfiction can maximize the depth of student thinking about a text and how it can enrich class discussion. She and her students are reading the scene where Squealer attempts to manipulate the animals' memories of Snowball's role in the Battle of the Cowshed. The Embedded

Nonfiction, about false memories and the science of psychological manipulation, infuses the discussion with rigor:

Directions: Read the text below. Then, answer the questions that follow.

False Memory

Adapted from "Creating False Memories" by Elizabeth Loftus, Scientific American

A **false memory** is a recollection of an event that did not actually occur.

Misinformation has the potential for invading our memories when we talk to other people or when we read or view media coverage about some event that we may have experienced ourselves. False memories are typically constructed by combining actual memories with the content of suggestions received from others.

Researchers have learned a great deal about the conditions that make people susceptible to false memories. For instance, memories are more easily changed when the passage of time allows the original memory to fade. Also, false memories may occur when there are social demands on individuals to remember.

---

1. Explain how **false memories** are created.

_____

_____

_____

_____

2. In today's reading, Squealer will describe events from The Battle of the Cowshed. Return to pages 41 and 42 and refresh your memory on this battle. Then, summarize how the Battle of the Cowshed ended.

_____

_____

_____

In the video, Emily first asks her students to distill the article into three key takeaways about the ways memory can be manipulated. They will use this information to understand what Squealer does in the book, but they also now have useful background information about memory construction that they can apply to other texts for the rest of their lives. Emily has both built their background knowledge and used it to help them get more out of this book as well as future books.

Incidentally, they're also practicing reading scientific text, which is challenging in different ways from reading fiction. For example, key information is often conveyed in an undemonstrative passive voice as in this line: "For instance, memories are more easily changed when the passage of time allows the original memory to fade." The embedded article gives them important time reading—and comprehending—a nonfiction text, without taking up valuable class time on things like "finding the main idea" that actually distract from the reading itself.

Emily's transitions are particularly useful in helping students navigate between the fiction and nonfiction text, what's imaginary and what's real. "So, yes, this is a book about talking animals, and yet, false memories are things that we as humans experience." And "We don't want to be subject to these manipulations. We know what happened in the Battle of the Cowshed. What was Snowball's role?" Emily asks this question of Alex using a Cold Call, and Alex does an excellent job of summarizing most of what's important to know. But crucially, his answer leaves out Snowball's bravery and courage in battle—how he led from the front and was wounded. Many teachers would merely praise Alex's answer, but Emily goes back to him with a follow-up question: "Did he just direct people? Just supervising?" Emily prepared for this lesson (and this moment) by scripting her desired answer for key questions—including the knowledge that would be most critical for analysis. This is how she immediately notices a key gap in an otherwise strong answer. It's hard to see those kinds of gaps, unless you know what you're looking for. Now that the question has been answered completely, she's set the class up to reread the text and apply the lens of the article to study the technical details of Squealer's manipulation in Orwell's novel. Their discussion will be all the richer.

To watch the video *Brittany Rumph: Pout Pout Fish*, use this QR code or find the video at the URL https://vimeo.com/1058363013/5f6559ae9b.

Embedded Nonfiction can be powerful to use for our earliest readers as well. In our last example, *Brittany Rumph: Pout Pout Fish*, Brittany embeds a nonfiction article titled "North Atlantic Eel Pout" into her reading of the storybook *Pout Pout Fish*[26] with her kindergarten class. Brittany uses Overlapping Questions to illuminate the synergies between the texts she's chosen, while building useful background knowledge about the fish depicted in the story. She asks several great questions to help students make connections between the two texts: "What do you know about the water that this fish lives in?" "What is the same about the Ocean Pout and the Pout Pout Fish?" "Why do you think the author chose to use the Ocean Pout in her story?" These questions cause even our youngest students to rigorously engage with two texts in relationship to each other and apply the knowledge they've gained from the nonfiction to the fiction text and vice versa. Bloom would be proud.

One important thing to consider in Embedded Nonfiction, particularly for developing readers, is how important it might be to adapt nonfiction articles to make them more accessible or appropriate for younger students. We call this idea *Active Sourcing*. It's not enough just to source the articles that might be most relevant but also to adapt them as needed. Brittany replaced much of the domain-specific vocabulary that would distract and confuse students from the meaning of the text and planned instead to strategically reinforce key, high-utility words during reading that she knew would be valuable outside of the nonfiction text. Brittany also shortened the text significantly so that students were focused on the most relevant aspects of the nonfiction.

Brittany reads the nonfiction text expressively to bring it alive for her young students. Note that, appropriately, she does not read it quite as expressively as the fiction, but intentionally inflects on the words *Atlantic Ocean* and *freezing* to underscore the important facts she wants students to retain. And finally, Brittany asks students to respond in writing to a key Overlapping Question. This ensures that *every* student is engaged in thinking deeply about the question she asks and is therefore prepared to participate in discussion with a unique thought.

From these clips, we can distill some additional guidance on how to effectively incorporate Embedded Nonfiction into your lessons:

- Plan out the questions that you will ask during reading—questions that will help establish the meaning of the nonfiction text as well as Overlapping Questions that will push students to deepen their analysis of both texts.

- Consider briefly sharing the purpose of the Embedded Text with students to prepare them to effectively make connections. For example, "We're going to read this article about the Ocean Pout to see some of the similarities and differences between the actual fish that lives in Atlantic Ocean and the Pout Pout Fish from our story."

- Consider *how* the text will be read—aloud, independently, or using FASE Reading as described in Chapter Three. This decision relies on several factors including pacing, the difficulty of the text, and vocabulary, as well as the narrative voice of the Embedded Text—perhaps choosing to read aloud for students the sections of text that are more technical.

EMBELLISHMENTS AND KNOWLEDGE FEEDING

Embellishments are small visual or text-based enrichments that fill in the blanks of comprehension and knowledge for students. Add small pieces of key information during reading, much as you would with vocabulary, to explain references or allusions. Knowledge Feeding is the oral form of Embellishments.

When we're reading rich, complex texts we can't embed a nonfiction text for every network of knowledge that will help students get more out of the text. We don't need to tell you that it would be impractical to pause every other page to read an Embedded Nonfiction text. This is where our next tool, Embellishments, proves useful. *Embellishments* are brief knowledge-based supports for use during reading. They add small pieces of key information through visual or text-based enrichments, often to explain references or allusions. *Knowledge Feeding* refers to moments when we share bite-sized pieces of knowledge orally for students while reading.

Here's a sample visual Embellishment from our unit on *Narrative of the Life of Frederick Douglass*. In the early chapters Douglass describes sailing to Baltimore on a "sloop." Students can pretty reliably figure out that a sloop is a boat. But if we want them to really imagine Douglass's journey on the Chesapeake Bay a picture can't hurt. We place this one in our student materials along with a small caption.

A **sloop** is a sailboat, often used in the 1800s to transport goods for sale.

Similarly, here's a sample text-based Embellishment from our unit on *Catherine Called Birdy*. (It may look familiar; we discuss it briefly in Chapter Two.) It comes during a section of the novel that students read independently. In the midst of the passage, Catherine wonders about a group of lepers who pass by town and are shunned. "Then I wondered why Jesus used his miraculous powers to cure lepers instead of creating an herb or a flower so we could continue to use it even now when Jesus is in Heaven."

As a teacher you're damned-if-you-do and damned-if-you-don't. You can't embed an article about every detail in the novel. Is leprosy important enough that it's worth fifteen to twenty minutes of lesson time to read all about its history and causes based on that mention alone? Perhaps not. But neither can you ignore it if you want students to fully understand the scene. Some students might know that leprosy is a disease but likely not that it was a disease that caused brutal disfigurement and that lepers were shunned and isolated and often hated. If you don't know that lepers are the most marginal members of medieval society you don't really understand Catherine's musings. The solution is a text-based enrichment—half-way between a definition and an Embedded Nonfiction article. Our Embellishment here gives students the basics: "Leprosy is a devastating disease that causes skin lesions and nerve damage. Because the condition is so contagious, lepers were shunned and not considered part of society. In Medieval England lepers had to ring a bell like the one in this image to signal their presence in public places." There are no questions for students to respond to. It's straight information feeding. But the knowledge is in the lesson packet where students can read it and refer back to it. The Embellishment does its job in a few seconds, and now when they read the passage they'll better understand the allusion and the context.

Pages 93-96: On Your Own

Annotation Task: As you read, an otate details that help answer the following question

- Why is Catherine punished?
- Who is Geoffrey? What is Catherine's perspective on him?

> *Leprosy* is a devastating disease that causes skin lesions and nerve damage. Because the condition is so contagious, lepers were shunned and not considered a part of society anymore. In medieval England, lepers had to ring a bell like the one in this image to signal their presence in public places.

Notes

While Embellishments and Knowledge Feeding are related to Embedded Nonfiction, our colleague Jen Rugani recently described key differences in purpose, scale and format for how we think about each of these tools:

> We use embedding when we want to supplement student's knowledge about something in a text, to expand what they know beyond even what the text says. An Embellishment, on the other hand, is what we use to knock down knowledge barriers to comprehension. So, in reading Pam Muñoz Ryan's *Esperanza Rising*, a teacher might briefly say, "This is what 'crocheting' looks like," and show a brief picture. Our goal with Embellishments and Knowledge Feeding is to be fast and ensure clarity in

the reading. And we don't necessarily expect students to retain the knowledge taught through an Embellishment or Knowledge Feeding for the long term—they are used to prevent a stumbling block in the moment. Whereas Embedded Nonfiction is used for knowledge that is more critical to the book and also transferable to other texts and we therefore also want it to stick in long-term memory.

To watch the video *Jamie Davidson: Scalpel*, use this QR code or find the video at the URL https://vimeo.com/1058363337/9f170b783a.

One of our favorite examples of an Embellishment occurs in the video *Jamie Davidson: Scalpel*, when Jamie Davidson's class encounters the word *scalpel* while reading Roald Dahl's *Boy*. It's clear from the student's stilted reading of the word *scalpel* that she is unfamiliar with the term. This is one of the places where technology can assist us. It's easy to find images that quickly and easily augment student background knowledge as they read if we have the discipline to read in advance with a "curse of knowledge" lens—that is, asking ourselves what our students might not know and briefly projecting an image to supplement in a few seconds at exactly the right time. It's also clear that Jamie had done this effectively, as she anticipated and prepared for this moment with the image already posted on the overhead projector to support students in comprehending this scene so that all she had to do was point to the image and move on.

To watch the video *Knowledge Feeding Montage*, use this QR code or find the video at the URL https://vimeo.com/1058363514/3477c50da7.

Depending on pacing decisions, Jamie could have opted to briefly describe the tool as well, but in this case, with the context of the scene, this brief Embellishment was all that was necessary. In our discussion of vocabulary in Chapter Five we delve more into how Embellishments can assist in providing vocabulary definitions of words—itself a kind of knowledge building—as there is overlap between the idea of Knowledge Feeding and the ideas that we present in Implicit Vocabulary (an approach to vocabulary instruction that supports comprehension and increases students' attentiveness to the words they encounter as they read). The clip *Knowledge Feeding Montage* includes a few examples of a variation on Embellishments (you might recognize Doug guest teaching at his daughter's school). Knowledge Feeding is the oral form of Embellishments, and you'll notice in each of these examples that the teachers briefly provide small pieces of knowledge critical to understanding the text without breaking the thread of the narrative. Students interact, also briefly, with the new knowledge through Call and Response, annotation, or by connecting it to their own experiences. The knowledge that is fed enables students to more effectively Establish Meaning in the passage and therefore enables them to do richer levels of analysis.

Like Embedded Nonfiction, teachers can use Embellishments as an opportunity to ask Overlapping Questions about both texts. We see this in the clip *Christine Torres: Forest,* as she teaches *Number the Stars* using the *Reading Reconsidered* curriculum. Christine questions students about Lowry's author's craft through the use of an Embellishment on reading symbolically, shown here. She asks, "Why might Lowry have Annemarie journey through a *forest*, instead of, say, through a town or a field?"

To watch the video *Christine Torres: Forest,* use this QR code or find the video at the URL https://vimeo.com/1058363724/57026ca310.

Do Now

Reading Symbolically: The Woods

The forest is a mysterious place; in legends and fairy tales, the woods are usually full of mysterious creatures, symbols of all the dangers which young people must face if they are to become adults. Hansel and Gretel, Snow White, Little Red Riding Hood – in these and many more tales, the forest is a place away from civilization, a place of testing, an unexplored land full of the unknown.

The forest is often the home of the outlaws or a place where typical rules no longer apply. Since its trees obscure the light of the sun, it's often a place of literal and figurative darkness and mystery. Entering the forest can be seen as a metaphor for entering the unknown. Sometimes it is also a place of opportunity and transformation – the hero enters the forest and discovers something about him or herself.

---

1. Consider the final line of this text: *"Sometimes it is also a place of opportunity and transformation – the hero enters the forest and discovers something about him or herself."*

   a. What does the pronoun "it" <u>refer</u> to? _____

   b. What might Annemarie have discovered about herself during her journey through the forest?

   _____

   _____

   _____

2. Why might Lowry have chosen have Annemarie journey through a *forest*, instead of, say, through a town or a field? Underline any words or phrases in the text above that support <u>your</u> thinking.

Asking a question about symbolism without actually giving students a text or the relevant background knowledge from which to draw on usually results in a "guess what's in my head" type of back and forth with a teacher. The use of the Embellishment makes this exercise more rigorous and more knowledge-based, as students can draw on the knowledge they have just been given, thereby making that knowledge more likely to stick in their long-term memory.

KNOWLEDGE ORGANIZERS

A Knowledge Organizer is a one-page document that organizes high-priority knowledge for students to store in long-term memory. It may include key facts, literary terms, timelines of events, important quotations and historical background.

Our third knowledge-building tool, which is perhaps most underused by schools and teachers (at least in the United States), is *Knowledge Organizers*, or one-page documents that organize high-priority knowledge for students to store in long-term memory. Based on the content of the unit, these documents may include key facts, literary terms, timelines of events, important quotations and historical background. They are designed intentionally to be quizzable, usable documents. A two-column format with key terms on one side and the explanation on the other lets students cover up one side and quiz themselves on the other. The "quizzability" of Knowledge Organizers is important in leveraging the research on low-stakes assessment as described by Peter C. Brown and his colleagues in *Make It Stick:* "Retrieval strengthens the memory and interrupts forgetting. A single, simple quiz after reading a text or hearing a lecture produces better learning and remembering than rereading the text or reviewing lecture notes."[27]

See next for an example of a Knowledge Organizer for *Charlotte's Web*. We share this example because it's a well-known text and quite simply displays some of the relevant knowledge, both literary and contextual, that is important to understanding in order to discuss *Charlotte's Web* as a class.

Charlotte's Web by E.B. White

Story Terms	
conflict	the central problem in a story • **external conflict**: motivation + obstacle • **internal conflict**: negative thoughts and feelings or tough choices
motivation	what a character wants or needs (often causes the **conflict**)
obstacle	what stands in the way of a character reaching their **motivation**
perspective	the way a character views or thinks about a situation, another character, or themselves
setting	when and where a story takes place

Characters		
Fern		the **protagonist** (main character); a young girl who lives on a farm and loves animals
Wilbur		a pig raised by Fern
Charlotte		a barn spider who befriends Wilbur
Templeton		a rat who lives in the barn

Farming Terms	
livestock	animals raised on a farm to earn money for the farmer through their meat, eggs, milk, or other products
slaughter	the killing of animals for food
county fair	**livestock** competition and community event

Literary Terms	
personification	giving human characteristics to something that is not human
narrator	the voice telling the story in a novel
theme	the underlying message or big idea of a story

Knowledge Organizers help students by clearly organizing the most important information a student might need to be able to meaningfully engage with a new text. They make the most important knowledge transparent for students at the outset—instead of the knowledge being a destination point of the unit. They are given to students before reading a new text and they become a tool to study and use to inform their analysis, making it richer, more rigorous and therefore more lasting. The idea is that students work to encode these definitions and ideas into their memories throughout the course of the unit. Knowledge Organizers include a balance of knowledge that is necessary to understand the book (or unit) and that students should remember ten years from now. We borrow this idea from a great book out of the Michaela School in England called *Battle Hymn of the Tiger Teachers: The Michaela Way*, in which they refer to the ten-year rule: is this knowledge relevant to the text or unit that we want students to be able to remember ten years from now? If so, it should be included in the Knowledge Organizer.

When we introduce Knowledge Organizers in our workshops, teachers are usually equal parts apprehensive and excited. They are apprehensive because they worry that Knowledge Organizers will give away too much about the novel too early. There are, of course, ways around this—having students complete parts of the organizer that may include spoilers later in the unit, or having one organizer for early in the unit and another later in the unit. But teachers are also excited not only by Knowledge Organizers' power to build lasting knowledge for their students but also by the way they can act as key tools for differentiation—leveling the playing field for all learners so that all students can have access to the same key knowledge they may need to deeply understand the book.

To watch the video *Jasmine Morales: Counterculture*, use this QR code or find the video at the URL https://vimeo.com/1058363872/227e95c523.

The clip *Jasmine Morales: Counterculture* provides an excellent example of how Knowledge Organizers can support students in using key terms and ideas in their thinking, helping to raise the bar for understanding and analysis of a text. Jasmine Morales at St. Athanasius Middle School in the Bronx asked her students to take out their Knowledge Organizer for their Do Now as they read S. E. Hinton's *The Outsiders* using our *Reading Reconsidered* curriculum. Let's take a look at the Knowledge Organizer they are using:

The Outsiders Knowledge Organizer

Terms to Discuss Culture	
Culture is defined by the patterns of behavior and thinking that are shared by a group of people.	
Signifiers of Culture	People often show their culture through their language, clothing, food, music, arts, or religion.
Mainstream	The dominant ideas, beliefs, and values of a culture. Mainstream culture often dictates what is considered "normal" in society.
Counterculture	A way of living that actively rejects what is expected by mainstream culture, often in protest.
Stereotype	An assumption about a person or group that is overgeneralized or applied without reason.
Status	Many cultures categorize and rank people according to a hierarchy. Certain traits (like wealth or education) may make someone "higher status" or "lower status."

Understanding Socs & Greasers	
The Socs	• Wealthier, upper-class "status" • Live on the West Side of town • Identifiable by their madras clothing and nice cars
The greasers	• Poorer, working-class "status" • Live on the East Side of town • Identifiable by their long, slicked-back hair; jeans; t-shirts; and leather clothing

Nothing Gold Can Stay Author: Robert Frost (1923)	Key Motifs
Nature's first green is gold, Her hardest hue to hold. Her early leaf's a flower; But only so an hour. Then leaf subsides to leaf. So Eden sank to grief, So dawn goes down to day. Nothing gold can stay.	Family and Brotherhood Loyalty Belonging Chivalry and Heroism

Mainstream 1960s Culture
Throughout the 1950s and early 1960s, many people in society held strong beliefs about the importance of conforming to "traditional" family and societal roles. These included: • A married two-parent household • The expectation that women stay home to care for the children and the home • The expectation that children be quiet, polite, and do as they are asked • Anxiety surrounding juvenile delinquency and crime, and fear of cultural choices that suggested the rejection of tradition, such as jeans or leather

Jasmine first reminds the students that the bolded words in their Do Now are described in the Knowledge Organizer. As she circulates to support students during their independent work, she is able to direct students' attention to the key terms on the Knowledge Organizer that they need to reference in order to answer the Do Now question, "Describe the relationship between

mainstream culture and a **counterculture**." By doing so, she's providing access to knowledge her students will need to reference when reading *The Outsiders*. In reviewing the Do Now with the whole class, she asks students to annotate their questions using the information from the Knowledge Organizer. This entire process builds background knowledge, deepens students' analysis of *The Outsiders* and reinforces important vocabulary with which to think about and discuss the novel. Without having these terms captured in the Knowledge Organizer (and without frequently reviewing them), only a portion of the class might have been able to answer their Do Now question as thoroughly and thus, understand the book deeply.

One essential part of using Knowledge Organizers well in the classroom is to first teach students how to use them. Our colleague Sadie McCleary recently shared this sage guidance after reflecting on using Knowledge Organizers in her chemistry classroom. "Studying is a skill!" she emphasizes. "Just like with other skills in class, we need to teach students how to do it. This means studying (even simple vocabulary drills) needs to be modeled and students need lots of at-bats to practice."

The best way to model to students how to use a Knowledge Organizer for studying this might be conducting a Think Aloud—read out the term from the Knowledge Organizer and begin narrating your own thinking. From her chemistry classroom, Sadie gives this example of how she might use a Think Aloud with her students in their study of lab equipment and measurements: "Analog measurement—I know there are two types of measurements, and the second is digital. This means analog is nondigital, and I know there are special rules for these because the accuracy of analog measurements is not communicated." She follows this up with several minutes of students doing their own silent self-quizzing and an oral drill or recall quiz after modeling for them what these look like. Sadie recommends teaching students how to use Knowledge Organizers both as tools for self-quizzing and for partner quizzing, explicitly naming for students that this should be replicated at home with a family member or friend. This highlights another key benefit of Knowledge Organizers, which is their utility in supporting the school-home connection for the purposes of knowledge building.

RETRIEVAL PRACTICE

> *Retrieval Practice is a system for low-stakes quizzing to activate previously learned content to help encode knowledge into long-term memory.*

Knowledge Organizers are incomplete without our next Knowledge Building tool, *Retrieval Practice*. The Knowledge Organizer defines and organizes important information while Retrieval Practice is the tool for encoding that information in long-term memory. Setting aside a consistent time during class to ask students retrieval questions with the intention of having students access information from the Knowledge Organizer that they may be on the verge of forgetting, as well as knowledge that will be critical in the lesson, is important for encoding this information in long-term memory. It is an opportunity for us to activate existing knowledge that students have to prime their brains for future connection and learning, yet it is different from and more rigorous than Ms. Hoover's approach with the K-W-L chart at the opening of this chapter. Retrieval Practice asks students to retrieve information that they have already been explicitly taught with the key purpose of encoding it in long-term memory. It enables us to effectively support students' knowledge acquisition by activating their existing knowledge.

A great example of Retrieval Practice with the support of Knowledge Organizers comes from *Alonte Johnson-James: Night* in his seventh-grade classroom, as Alonte teaches Elie Wiesel's *Night*. As we have mentioned with other clips of *Night*, we want to prepare you for the emotionally charged content, just as Alonte did for his students throughout the unit. In this clip, Alonte works to make sure that students have a clear understanding of the facts of Elie's devastating life experiences in the Holocaust.

Before beginning Retrieval Practice, Alonte prepares students for the academic routine in two ways. First, he tells students that this is the first time the class will be expected

To watch the video *Alonte Johnson-James: Night*, use this QR code or find the video at the URL https://vimeo .com/1058364318/545f18aa24.

to recall knowledge from *any* part of their Knowledge Organizer: "Instead of telling you the section I am focusing on, we're going to look all over both sides of this organizer." In earlier Retrieval Practices, Alonte had narrowed students' focus, but here he begins to scale toward greater autonomy by expecting students to retrieve information from the entire organizer. This "randomized practice" is an important way of increasing students' ability to retain knowledge they have learned.

Alonte also tells students that he will take hands for some questions and Cold Call for others (varying formats and leveraging the idea of covert retrieval which we'll describe more next). His transparency makes Retrieval Practice feel predictable and low stakes. Note that Alonte is insistent on students' accurate pronunciation of proper nouns throughout the practice. This move is subtle, but crucial to help students avoid encoding inaccurate names and terms into their memory (and into their reading). While the majority of the questions in this practice are specific and factual ("What concentration camp are these men, in Chapter Three?" "How many concentration camps have they been to by the time they reach Buna?"), he shifts to a broader question at the end to increase the rigor ("What motif is being developed as they receive the tattoos?"). This question is challenging for his students, so he uses Turn and Talk (again varying the format in which students respond) and intentional discussion cues to help students arrive at an accurate answer. Alonte's tone is casual and quick, despite the seriousness of the material, to support pacing and keep students invested in Retrieval Practice.

After installing the Retrieval Practice routine in our classrooms, we want to gradually release students' reliance on looking at the Knowledge Organizer during Retrieval Practice throughout a unit of study. So, your first few Retrieval Practices will likely be done with Knowledge Organizers in students' hands, then eventually you'll build up to asking Retrieval Practice questions without them. You also may want to ask students to study Knowledge Organizers as homework or when they're done with classwork or writing as a way of self-quizzing.

Repeated use of Retrieval Practice is the key to addressing what Peter C. Brown and his colleagues call "a central challenge to improving the way we learn," which is finding a way to "interrupt the process of forgetting"[28]—in fact, a consistent cause for retrieval is the only tool we have to combat it. We often describe this idea of "forgetting" in our workshops as the most overlooked factor in learning. The following graphic illustrates how learners forget things over time and how Retrieval Practice can arrest this process.

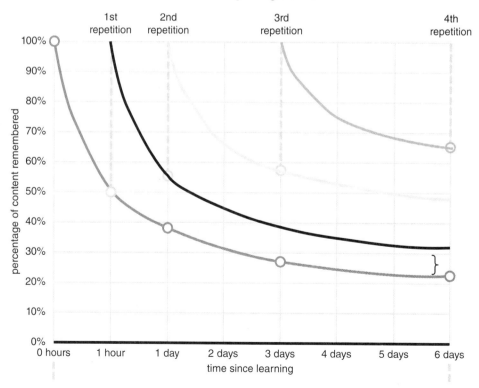

The Forgetting Curve

THE FORGETTING CURVE

The original Forgetting Curve was derived in the 1880s by the German psychologist Hermann Ebbinghaus. It plotted the actual rate at which he was able to remember a series of nonsense syllables after learning them. The general shape of the curve is broadly accepted by cognitive psychologists to capture the learning and forgetting processes. However, it's theoretical or hypothetical in any specific case—it cannot tell you exactly what the rate of retention will be for your students (or a specific student) at time A or time B for a specific topic you've taught. There are individual differences and factors in the learning environment, like how much attention students are paying and how new to students the information is. Differences in content also affect it, such as whether the ideas are abstract and complex or simpler and more concrete.

But while the Forgetting Curve cannot be applied to a specific situation, it illustrates several key ideas that point to the importance of Retrieval Practice. The first is that as soon as you learn something, you begin forgetting it almost immediately—and the rate of that forgetting is often shockingly high: a few hours after learning something, people routinely remember only a small fraction of it. But each time you practice recalling what you know, the rate and amount of forgetting is reduced. Retrieving something back into working memory slows the rate of forgetting, and how and when the retrieval happens is important—a concept we'll describe later as "spacing."

While the curve leaves open what the magic number of times is that students have to engage with something in order to learn it, other research gives suggestions to fill in these blanks. Education researcher Graham Nuthall, in *The Hidden Lives of Learners,* describes the three exposures rule: "We discovered that a student needed to encounter on at least three different occasions, the complete set of the information she or he needed to understand a concept. . . . We found we could predict what students would learn—and what they would not—with an accuracy rate of 80–85%."[29] The consistent use of Retrieval Practice is the key to giving students these frequent opportunities for retrieving knowledge and, therefore, as cognitive scientists tell us, creating stronger neural pathways in our brains so that the learning is more enduring and more likely to be encoded into long-term memory. As Ben Rogers recently stated in a guest post on the *Teach Like a Champion Blog:* "To comprehend a text, readers must apply what they read to what they already know about the world. Retrieving well-learnt knowledge is easy. Retrieving half-remembered knowledge is much harder."[30]

While some teachers might worry this sort of practice could be too rote or boring to engage students' attention, we've found the contrary to true. One teacher who uses the *Reading Reconsidered* curriculum recently shared her experience with Retrieval Practice and Knowledge Organizers. "Retrieval Practice helps us to harness the power of frequent low-stakes assessment; this is a way that students can practice in a consistent, authentic way, but without the stress of grades or high stakes," she said. "I found in my implementation of the curriculum, Retrieval Practice is really fun. My students really enjoyed the chance to share their growing knowledge, especially when it's so clearly defined in the Knowledge Organizer."

To watch the video *Spencer Davis: Anomaly*, use this QR code or find the video at the URL https://vimeo.com/1058364182/c60e1363ca.

We see this idea come alive in the clip, *Spencer Davis: Anomaly*. The Retrieval Practice in Spencer's sixth-grade classroom in the Bronx feels predictable and low stakes because of his warm and casual tone and his ability to make it conversational by asking students to build on and connect to each other's answers. He and his students are reading *Wonder* using the *Reading Reconsidered* curriculum, and he uses Retrieval Practice as a chance to reinforce accuracy and understanding of technical vocabulary by briefly praising and by transcribing their answers on the board. The glimpse into his classroom is anything but rote and boring.

We've distilled the following five key techniques for Retrieval Practice based on extensive literature review and a conversation with Bradley Busch, a leading expert in translating cognitive science into educational practice and the director of InnerDrive:

- Specific questions are better than general ones to cause students to retrieve information. They prevent students from talking generally about what they remember and push them to be more precise in their recall and explanation. Specific questions signal to the brain that the material is especially important and cause students to attend better and learn more from them.

- Retrieval responds to spacing. Spreading retrieval out and doing it in shorter bursts rather than big chunks can give students more frequent, lower stakes at-bats than doing it all in a single chunk. For example, asking students to practice five times for ten minutes per day over five days is better than fifty or sixty minutes of practice. This guidance is useful for any parents of a student studying for the SAT—more frequent, perhaps daily, but providing shorter bursts of practice is better than a few larger chunks of practice each week or month. We'll see a few examples of this type of spacing across our curriculum next.

- Ask students to answer in a range of formats (e.g., in writing, with a partner, via Call and Response, or using Cold Call). Different formats cause students to think about the material in different ways and encode the information better through building a stronger memory. This can cause students to use both *overt retrieval* (we see or hear them do it) and can cause *covert retrieval* (they do it silently). This is why both Cold Calling and Wait Time (inserting a short delay between posing your question and calling on a student) are so powerful as part of Retrieval Practice. When students know a Cold Call might be coming but there is a five- to ten-second pause before another student is called on (using what we call Question-Pause-Name in *Teach Like a Champion 3.0*), students will recall the information silently to themselves in preparation for a possible Cold Call. Covert retrieval can multiply the thinking in your classroom by thirtyfold, simply by adding a few seconds of Wait Time and being intentional about when you call on a student to answer.

- Retrieval Practice questions should be in what researchers call the *sweet spot*: difficult, but not so difficult that students are unable to be successful. A 70 percent to 80 percent student success rate on questions is a good rule of thumb to ensure that questions are challenging enough to push students to retrieve the information in a rigorous way so that it's more lasting.

- Use *elaboration* as a way of pushing students to retrieve by asking students to apply and expand on them or to explain why. This results in deeper and better organized memory. Elaboration is more than simply asking a follow-up question; rather, it's about asking interrelated questions that ask students to apply their thinking or connect between concepts and ideas.

An excellent illustration of elaboration, the power of Retrieval, and the way Knowledge Organizers and Retrieval Practice work together comes from Neha Marvania's sixth-grade history class at North Star Vailsburg Middle School in Newark, New Jersey. The clip *Marvania: Chronological Order* opens with Neha asking students to think metacognitively in a Turn and Talk to discuss with a partner, "the benefit of remembering events in chronological order when it comes to history." The students' conversations allude to putting important historical events in historical context and to better understand how they are related to one another. The

To watch the video *Marvania: Chronological Order*, use this QR code or find the video at the URL https://vimeo.com/1058364009/1c32330e0d.

second student gives his rationale by citing the chronology of the Haitian Revolution and John Locke's ideas. The consistent use of Retrieval Practice in Neha's classroom contributes to his impressive recall of these facts in his answer. Neha follows up the Turn and Talk question with some Retrieval Practice—rebranded in her classroom as a *Timeline Game*. This is not the competitive learning games of our own childhoods.

As you'll see in the clip, Neha clearly assigns roles and reviews the task so students are clear on what they are doing and why. She clearly connects the task to the historical thinking skill (causation and chronological reasoning), making it clear why students are doing this task and how it connects to their daily historical thinking. Students are instructed not to use their Knowledge Organizers, so it's about retrieving, applying, and elaborating. And once again, you need only to listen to the incredibly rich knowledge that students are sharing with each other in their Turn and Talk conversations to become a believer in the power that consistent retrieval can have on students' thinking.

To watch the video *Jen Brimming: Recap*, use this QR code or find the video at the URL https://vimeo.com/1058364471/52e476060c.

Two final examples that illustrate the five key principles of Retrieval Practice come to us from across the pond from Jen Brimming and Lia Martin—one of the original teachers from whom we learned about the power of Retrieval Practice. In *Jen Brimming: Recap,* Jen Brimming prepares her students for the lesson in which they'll be "zoom[ing] in on two really important details from what we read." Before diving into instruction, she makes time for a "brief recap" on the opening setting and characters in *Lord of the Flies*, so they are prepared for the day's reading. As you'll see, she leverages both overt and covert retrieval as she gives students significant Wait Time before sending them into a Turn and Talk to ensure that all students are engaging with and thinking about her questions. She then picks up the speed with the less rigorous retrieval questions before they dive into reading.

In *Lia Martin: Hamartia,* she and her year seven (sixth grade in the United States) students review the technical vocabulary—*hamartia, dilemma,* and *patriarchal*—needed to discuss the scene that they are reading in Sophocles' *Antigone.* You'll see how this brief review prepares students for a deeper level of understanding and analysis of the play with her question: "What element of stage craft could we talk about in this scene?" Just like in Neha's class, her students' responses reflect the deep knowledge building that Lia has done with them throughout the unit—not just in their use of technical vocabulary but in their ability to apply and explain it with sophistication.

As we plan Retrieval Practice, we should be thoughtful about planning questions about a given topic with a short delay after students have learned about it to combat the Forgetting Curve. These examples illustrate the idea known as *Interleaved Practice*—practice that occurs frequently and interspersed with other learning—as opposed to *Blocked Practice,* when a concept is drilled consistently and then the class moves on. Both are important when it comes to encoding knowledge into long-term memory. Blocked Practice can be particularly useful in early encoding as we see from Jen Brimming, as she and her students are early in the novel. Interleaved Practice is useful in ensuring effective retrieval, long after an idea has been initially taught as we see from Lia Martin's class.

THE RECURSIVENESS OF KNOWLEDGE: PUTTING IT ALL TOGETHER

In addition to having a consistent routine for Retrieval Practice, it's important for us to consistently activate knowledge in meaningful and authentic ways throughout our instruction. The following examples from the C. S. Lewis' *Magician's Nephew* illustrate how we can ensure that students can better recall knowledge with automaticity and how we can ask students to authentically apply their knowledge to enrich reading, writing, and discussion. Next you will see how the idea of "intrusive narration" continuously spirals and reappears throughout a unit on *The Magician's Nephew* from the *Reading Reconsidered* curriculum. Intrusive narration is a technique frequently used by authors in the eighteenth and nineteenth centuries, in which the narrator interrupts the story to provide commentary or information directly to the reader. It's a key feature in *The Magician's Nephew,* so it's one of the terms on the unit's Knowledge Organizer. Knowledge of this literary technique will transfer to other texts that they encounter and will be especially helpful in accessing and analyzing archaic texts. As part of their lessons, students first encounter the idea of "intrusive narration" in an embedded text in Lesson 1:

One form of an omniscient narrator is an **intrusive narrator**. Sometimes an omniscient narrator will interrupt the story to "speak to" readers directly, addressing them as "you," and providing background, commentary, or judgement. This **intrusive narrator** often expresses their own ideas about what is taking place in the narrative and can sometimes evaluate the action and characters of the story or give a view about the world in general. Even though a third person narrator is not a character is the story, an especially intrusive narrator can begin to blur that line. This type of narration can help establish a special relationship with the reader. When the narrator jumps in, it gives readers the feeling they are being *told* a story rather than just reading it on their own. This type of narration was very common in novels written in the 19th century.

It then is the focus of an annotation task in Lesson 2:

Pages 9-13: On Your Own

Annotation Task: As you read pages 9-13, underline any:

- Moments of **intrusive narration**

- Similarities between the novel and Lewis's life

And then appears in the Do Now in Lesson 3:

Do Now

Directions: Reread this excerpt from p. 13 and answer the questions below.

*It was shaped, of course, like an attic, but furnished as a sitting-room. Every bit of the walls was lined with shelves and every bit of the shelves was full of books. A fire was burning in the grate (**you remember that it was a very cold wet summer that year**) and in front of the fireplace with its back toward them was a high-backed armchair. Between the chair and Polly, and filling most of the middle of the room, was a big table piled with all sorts of things – printed books and books of the sort you write in, and ink bottles and pens and*

And twice again in Retrieval Practice in Lesson 7:

---

2. The line in bold is an example of:

    a. first-person narration

    b. intrusive narration

    c. an allusion

    d. C.S. Lewis's autobiography

Retrieval Practice

Make sure to use the words in your answer to show your understanding!

1. What is **fantasy**? Describe one aspect of the novel that shows it belongs in the **fantasy genre**.

2. What is **intrusive narration**?

3. Explain one element of **C.S. Lewis**'s life that is reflected in *The Magician's Nephew*.

4. What is an **allusion**?

5. Name one **allusion** used in the novel so far.

6. What is **suspense**?

7. Describe one **suspenseful** moment from the novel so far.

And to prepare students for a writing question later in the lesson:

5. Reread this line from p. 56:

I cannot excuse what he did next except by saying he was very sorry for it afterward (and so were a good many other people).

a. Who is "he"? What action is the narrator referring to?

_____

b. Why might Lewis have chosen to include **intrusive narration** in this moment?

_____

_____

And again, in Lesson 9 with another annotation task:

Pages 76-80: On Your Own

Annotation Task: As you read, annotate any examples of **intrusive narration**. Pay particular attention to the narrator's **tone** or attitude toward characters and situations.

Notes

Background knowledge, when it is encoded in long-term memory through consistent exposure at key times, is a significant driver of reading comprehension. It enables students to execute skills such as drawing inferences and seeing connections that are critical to reading. Our success as reading teachers relies on building students' relevant background knowledge and taking the necessary steps to help them encode it in an organized and connected way in their long-term memory.

CHAPTER RECAP

The importance of background knowledge to reading comprehension is well established by the research at this point. Yet even when teachers are familiar with the research, they still may have difficulties in applying the research to their own classrooms for a number of reasons. In this chapter, we aimed to present practical knowledge building tools that put the research into effect and enable you to effectively impart to your students the robust, lasting knowledge they need to be strong lifelong readers.

To build knowledge in your classroom:

- Incorporate Embedded Nonfiction throughout your unit. Map out what and when to embed, use Overlapping Questions to connect student thinking about the nonfiction and fiction text, employ nonfiction to maximize the value of discussion, and curate your nonfiction texts for your students through Active Sourcing.

- Employ Embellishments, or small visual or textual enrichments, to support Knowledge Feeding of key pieces of background information during reading to quickly ensure students have the necessary knowledge to understand textual references or allusions.

- Use one-page Knowledge Organizers to provide and organize high-priority information for students in a format that facilitates self-quizzing to aid in their storage of it in long-term memory and teach them how to use them successfully.

- Provide frequent opportunities for Retrieval Practice to encode knowledge into long-term memory and to combat the Forgetting Curve, remembering that students need to encounter something on at least three separate occasions to learn it. Ask specific questions, space out retrieval, ask students to answer in a range of formats to facilitate overt and covert retrieval, strive for questions that fall into the sweet spot of difficulty level of a 70 percent to 80 percent student success rate, and use elaboration to push students to connect, apply, and expand on ideas.

Notes

1. *How Do We Learn?* (Jossey-Bass, 2024).
2. Daniel T. *Willingham, Why Don't Students Like School?: A Cognitive Scientist Answers Questions About How the Mind Works and What It Means for the Classroom*, 2nd ed. (Jossey-Bass, 2021).
3. Ibid.

4. https://knowledgemattercampaign.org/statement-from-the-knowledge-matters-campaign-scientific-advisory-committee/.

5. Natalie Wexler, *The Knowledge Gap: The Hidden Cause of America's Broken Education System—and How to Fix It* (Avery, 2020), 35.

6. *How Do We Learn?*, 36–37.

7. Margaret G. McKeown, Isabel L. Beck, Ronette G. K. Blake "Rethinking Reading Comprehension Instruction: A Comparison of Instruction for Strategies and Content Approaches," *Reading Research Quarterly* 44, no. 3 (2009): 218–53. https://www.southingtonschools.org/uploaded/faculty/psmolinski/Rethinking_Reading_Comprehension.pdf.

8. E. D. Hirsch Jr., *The Knowledge Deficit* (Houghton Mifflin, 2006), 37.

9. *The Knowledge Deficit*, 3.

10. https://www.forbes.com/sites/nataliewexler/2023/08/27/to-make-progress-in-reading-we-need-to-monitor-it-differently/.

11. This is our experience-informed opinion. Yours may differ.

12. Thank you, Aristotelis Orginos, for this phrase! We wish you joyful lessons and brilliant readers.

13. https://fordhaminstitute.org/national/research/think-again-should-elementary-schools-teach-reading-comprehension.

14. https://cft.vanderbilt.edu/wp-content/uploads/sites/59/BloomsTaxonomy-mary-forehand.pdf.

15. https://substack.nomoremarking.com/p/skills-vs-knowledge-13-years-on.

16. *Why Don't Students Like School?*

17. Data from 2022–2023 New York State ELA State Test.

18. Adam Tyner and Sarah Kabourek, "Social Studies Instruction and Reading Comprehension: Evidence from the Early Childhood Longitudinal Study." https://files.eric.ed.gov/fulltext/ED609934.pdf.

19. This is a great example of the "curse of expertise," also called the "curse of knowledge": most teachers are so familiar with the basic framework of the Civil War—North versus South, Union versus Confederates—that it would never even cross their minds that many students would have no idea about this information. It's hard for an expert to spot things that are confusing to a novice.

20. *How Do We Learn?*, 36–37.

21. S. B. Neuman, T. Kaefer, and A. Pinkham, "Building Background Knowledge." *The Reading Teacher* 68, no. 2 (2014): 145–148.

22. The Radclyffe School moved from Ofsted's "requires improvement" rating to "outstanding" and enjoyed their best-ever English results in 2016. As a result of their recent focus on using academic language, building oracy and grammar skills, and generally reading more, they are now well above UK national average and they have attributed these gains in part to their approach to Embedded Nonfiction.

23. https://www.forbes.com/2009/06/18/julius-caesar-ambition-leadership-forbes.html.

24. https://macbethdelta2.weebly.com/macbeth-as-a-tragic-hero.html—Helen notes, "I altered this one before I shared with students to remove the spoilers!"

25. https://www.dailymail.co.uk/sciencetech/article-2778336/Power-REALLY-does-head-Giving-people-taste-authority-corrupt-honest-members-group.html.

26. Deborah Diesen and Hanna Dan, *The Pout-Pout Fish* (Farrar Straus Giroux, 2013).

27. Peter C. Brown, Henry L. Roediger III, and Mark A. McDaniel, *Make It Stick: The Science of Successful Learning* (Belknap Press, 2014), 3.

28. *Make It Stick*.

29. Graham Nuthall, *The Hidden Lives of Learners* (Nzcer Press, 2007), 63.

30. "03.02.17 Pairing Reading Reconsidered Techniques with Cognitive Science, Part I—A Guest Post from Ben Rogers." https://teachlikeachampion.org/blog/pairing-reading-reconsidered-techniques-cognitive-science-part-guest-post-ben-rogers//.

Chapter 5

Vocabulary Reconsidered

In Chapter One we write that of all the forms of knowledge, vocabulary might be the most important, and we argue that it should be taught as if it were a body of knowledge rather than a skill. Certainly, the research supports that. Vocabulary can seem secondary to teaching reading, perhaps, but there's almost nothing more important. In the closing paragraphs of his book *Reading in the Brain*, Stanislas Dehaene puts vocabulary development at the top of the list of factors that determine reading success, on par with decoding.[1] And as we mention in Chapter One, studies like Tannenbaum, Torgesen, and Wagner's 2006 analysis suggest that roughly half of what you comprehend when you read a text comes down to whether you have the vocabulary to understand it.[2] If that's not a compelling case for getting vocabulary instruction right, then we don't know what is.

A common suggestion for developing students' vocabulary is to simply require them to read a lot. And while we know that lots of reading is important in building vocabulary, it cannot be the only practice, especially because students are reading less than ever before.[3] Beck, McKeown, and Kucan's seminal book *Bringing Words to Life*, which we draw on extensively (with gratitude and admiration) similarly challenges this notion: "Depending on wide reading as a source of vocabulary growth leaves those children and young people who are most in need of enhancing their vocabulary repertoires with a very serious deficit." Relying on it exclusively "adds to the inequities in individual differences in vocabulary knowledge,[4]" they write. This warning makes sense in consideration of core principles of cognitive science. That we learn things by connecting them to our prior knowledge also means that those who start with the largest vocabularies learn more words as they read. And they probably then read more widely because they understand and enjoy what they read. Their vocabularies increase. Those with smaller vocabularies don't understand as much of what they read. They see new words but don't remember them. Their vocabularies don't increase. The gap gets larger.

What we need then is a clear path forward, one that describes how teachers can leverage the science to better develop all students' vocabularies and to make sure that every student progresses.

First though, let us briefly describe what we mean when we say vocabulary is often taught as if it were a skill. Two extremely common approaches we often see teachers use in reinforcing vocabulary are to ask students what they *think* a particular word might mean or, if the word has come up during oral or silent reading, to ask them to try to derive its meaning from Context Clues—the words and syntax of the text surrounding it. Really, *both* of these approaches involve asking students to use Context Clues. The first just relies on more distant Context Clues— maybe a student heard the word at home or used in a movie. Either way the basic premise is that students will use critical thinking skills to infer the word meaning from observing its use.

We understand why those two approaches are tempting. They seem like they are relying on critical thinking, which is a good thing. And inferring vocabulary from context is appealing because it seems natural. Why spend a whole fifteen minutes on vocabulary words that students might or might not need when you can just organically and naturally respond to words as they read them? And if nothing else, vocabulary is assessed on most statewide exams via questions that ask students to rely on Context Clues to find the meaning. Of course, teachers ask students to use Context Clues to derive word meaning then. They want students to feel prepared and confident for the questions they'll encounter on an important test. But unfortunately, while the test may push us in this direction, the science does not.

Even if words are assessed through Context Clues, teaching them that way—beyond perhaps practicing Context Clues a few times so students don't ignore relevant textual information—is a poor way to build and encode deep and lasting word knowledge, especially if used as the primary means of teaching vocabulary. Inferring, or guessing words from context, is often a waste of time and can result in faulty or incomplete encoding.

As parents ourselves, we each read nightly with our kids—we want to keep this ritual as long as we can—and a story from one of Erica's evenings with reading to her kids helps illustrate why Context Clues are a poor teaching tool.

Erica was reading *The Mouse and the Motorcycle* by Beverly Cleary to her then second grader, and they encountered this passage:

> marveled. "Why, it's a peanut butter and *jelly* sandwich and it even has butter in it."
>
> "I told you he would bring it." Ralph could not help boasting, even though his mouth was full.
>
> After sharing his feast with his squeaky little broth...

Lured by the Context Clues approach, she asked, "What do you think *boasting* means?"—partly to make sure that her son wasn't distracted by his brother's bedtime shenanigans, but also because she thought he might know the definition as he was familiar with the word *bragging*. She shouldn't have been surprised by his answer: "It means talking with your mouth full."

In fact, her son *was* using Context Clues—he was just using the wrong ones, and Erica quickly ceased this line of questioning. But in a classroom setting, teachers using the Context Clues approach sometimes tend to dig in more deeply, asking questions like "What clues from the text help us understand what *boasting* means?" or "Can you guess, based on this sentence or anything else you know about Ralph in this scene that might help you figure out what *boasting* means?"

The best-case scenario in that case would be that time would be spent guessing and that students would arrive at an incomplete definition of the word—passable but not perfect.

As we will discuss, a more productive use of time would be to say, "*Boasting* is when you talk a lot about something you're really proud of. Can you think of another word that we sometimes use to describe that?" Or, giving students a definition and then asking them to apply it in the text, "*Boasting* is talking too much about your own achievements or skills. Why is Ralph boasting in this moment?" In this way of questioning, kids are briefly given an accurate definition and then immediately have the chance to apply it to the text. This enables us to both support their vocabulary development and their comprehension of the text in a more efficient and effective way. When we give them a definition and ask them to use it to discuss the text like this, they are connecting the meaning of the learning object to other knowledge stored in their long-term memory, which is Héctor Ruiz Martín's definition of learning, which we cite in Chapter One and again in Chapter Four.

Using Context Clues to teach words assumes that vocabulary acquisition is a skill—that if you follow a set of steps, they'll help you arrive at an accurate definition, and that, just maybe, you will learn to be able to derive any definition to any word you encounter in the future. It assumes the skill is to infer meaning and the hope is that you will be more likely to learn new words. Classroom time is then spent guessing at a definition of an unknown word rather than spending time learning the word and applying it. The latter task is actually more rigorous, as we will discover, and more likely to result in encoding the definition of a new word into long-term memory. Approaching vocabulary as "micro knowledge"[5] enables us to follow the science of Retrieval Practice that we share in Chapter Four by giving students repeated opportunities to encounter and use a word in order to encode it in their long-term memory.

Our goals when it comes to vocabulary instruction should be lofty. We should want students to master a lot of words. But in *Speech to Print: Language Essentials for Teachers*, Louisa Cook Moats shares a daunting look at the numbers: "Of the 1,000 to 3,000 new words that fourth-through eighth-grade students encounter in the texts they read each year, teachers have time to teach directly only a few each day."[6] These numbers explain why it is so enticing to believe we might develop a skill students can use over and over to acquire knowledge of all those words independently. But the numbers could also be used to point out that the time we have for vocabulary instruction with students is finite and immensely valuable. We want to use it wisely.

That's why the story of a classroom we recently observed is another useful cautionary tale. Please let us say before we start that we share this story not to embarrass this teacher—we thought she was a very good teacher, and as Erica's story suggests, each of us has found ourselves down the Context Clue rabbit hole ourselves before. We tell the story with empathy and understanding, not with judgment.

Students encountered the word *salve* while reading Ralph Moody's *Little Britches* (right off the bat, we love this teacher's text selection from a knowledge-building perspective, a book set on a Colorado ranch in 1906). Here is the passage that students were reading and the questioning that followed:

> When Mr. Aultland came back, his horses were still running as fast as they were when he left. He drove around the circle, as he had before, and pulled up right beside the back steps. Father had gone to see if he could find the stakes that marked the corners of our land, so Mother went to the door. Mr. Aultland gave her a quart jar of blue-colored salve, a big square package, and a *Denver Post*. He said, "Tell Charlie to lay this stuff on over those sores good and heavy. It's got blue vitriol in it, but tell him not to be afraid of it. It'll dry those sores up quicker than anything else."

Student Reading:	"... a quart jar of blue colored salve, a big package and a *Denver Post*."
Teacher:	"Pause, what does that word *salve* mean? Look for Context Clues to help you out. [Wait Time] Marcos."
Student 1:	"Like a brush to brush clean."
Teacher:	"A brush, to what?"
Student:	"To like, a brush and you paint it?"
Teacher:	"Why do you think that? What words, what Context Clues, make you think that it's like a brush to brush to paint."
Student 1:	[Reading] "It's got blue vitriol in it ... it'll dry up those sores quicker than anything else."
	Note the student is pointing to the word vitriol *in it, which is likely a word that they don't know—pointing further to the problematic nature of the Context Clues approach when texts are filled with other unknown words.*
Teacher:	"Okay, because you're seeing that it dries. Um . . . Bryson your hand was up."
Student 2:	"I was going to say something else."
Teacher:	"What do you think it is?"
Student:	"The brush?"
Teacher:	"No, salve. What is a salve?"
Student:	"I mean, I was going to say I don't know what it is, but since I know *salvage*, I thought it was something like that."
Teacher:	"What's does *salvage* mean?"
Student 3:	"You know to like, to throw away, get rid of."
	This response is typical of one of the challenges of word guessing. Novices draw on flawed information to guess and this often makes the situation worse. Here Bryson knows a little about salvage *but his definition is wrong. It's the opposite of what he thinks.*
Teacher:	"Salvage. I went to the recycling place and I salvaged some really nice shoes before they could be thrown away. What does *salvage* mean?"
	At this point, the teacher gives an example to try to be more directive. But note that this Context Clue is actually for the word salvage *not the original word encountered in the text, which was* salve.
Student 4:	"To recycle?"

Teacher:	"To recycle, to save something. So what is *salve*? I like that you use that background knowledge of a word. What is a *salve*? If *salvage* means to save something, Mason?"
Student 5:	"I'm thinking a salve, if they're saying it's like a quart, maybe like a type of medicine."
Teacher:	"Where do you see that a salve is a type of medicine? Guys, let's all get our annotation devices ready. Where did you see those Context Clues?"
Student 5:	"Uh, I just use two pieces of Context Clues . . . So it's, um, between two, it says it's got blue in it and it says it'll dry the sores quicker. So, it's like the sores, or because Bill had like the thing on his stomach. So, I'm like, 'oh, okay, so it could be medicine because if it's a sore then that means it could be medicine' and another Context Clue that I use is like it's like um . . . a postage is like a stamp, so mostly I think it's like a little package. I think a notebook for example is a square and um, it's just like medicine. Depending on how it comes, like in a little pill package but back then it came like in a box so it's different."
	Here you may notice that the final student has used the "kitchen sink approach." He knows he's a little bit about a lot of the clues but he's really not sure so he throws the whole kitchen sink at the problem and says every relevant thing he can think of.
Teacher:	"So let's all annotate that together where it says 'it'll dry those sores up quicker than anything.' Sore can mean that something hurts. A sore is also if you get an injury like if you get a rug burn or something, or you get a cut and it gets infected and the blood crusts up, that's called a *sore*. When there's a dry open wound on your body, it's called a *sore*. So, remember that the horses got stuck and they like rubbed their bodies and they're bleeding. They're hurt now. So, they need to put something on the sore."
	Note here at the end of this three-minute sequence that she's now defining for sore, *another word she's realized students didn't fully grasp, rather than* salve. *It's one step forward two steps back.*

First, let us pause to celebrate some of the positive things this teacher was doing really well. Long stretches of the class were spent with students reading aloud getting lots of at-bats at fluency. At the start of the lesson, she built background knowledge intentionally using Embedded

Nonfiction and Knowledge Feeding like we discuss in Chapter Four. And she asked students retrieval questions to review the plot and details of the setting: 1906 in Denver, Colorado (a setting quite different from their own in the South in 2024). And when the student struggled to read the word *salve*, the teacher took this as important data to respond to by attempting to teach them the definition of the word. However, relying on the Context Clues approach never produced a correct definition of the word *salve*. In fact, it probably confused them more.

The sequence took more than three minutes and, apart from the fifth student who was able to successfully use his own murky background knowledge to loosely define *salve* as "medicine," no students emerged from this exchange with more vocabulary knowledge than they started. The remainder of the class was led first to believe that *salve* meant a brush that dried something. They then took a distracting foray to a recycling plant to define *salvage*. A salve is "an ointment used to promote healing of the skin"[7] but students still don't know that. In fact, they aren't likely to walk away remembering much from this passage at all since so much time was spent in a distracting traipse through several inaccurate definitions. If students stopped paying attention just for a little during this lengthy exchange, they may have walked away thinking one of the wrong definitions was correct.

In the Context Clues approach, the purpose of vocabulary instruction is to arrive at a viable definition of the word, and most of the instructional time is spent guessing at the definition of the word. This approach can be attributed to sins of enthusiasm (and hope!). As teachers we want to require thinking of the students rather than simply giving them a word meaning. But guessing isn't actually "critical thinking."

In the previous example, think of how much more efficient and effective it would have been to say, "A salve is a cream or ointment that heals your skin. Jot that definition in the margin. Turn and Talk to your partner: why did they need to use salve on the horse? Make sure you use the word *salve* in your answer." In this approach, students are given the definition and then immediately asked to use that knowledge and apply it to the text. This is critical thinking instead of guessing. And it is not only more efficient but will more likely result in students learning the correct definition *and remembering it*, given that they will have had to use it actively. It will also result in their understanding the story better. A word defined and used immediately, avoids distractions and prevents their losing track of the narrative.

Again, we can point to the research in Chapter Four to support this. As we know, when students aren't familiar with a topic they are reading about, they will struggle to comprehend it fully. Their working memories are likely to be overloaded as they try to understand new concepts. A short interaction limits time and attention diverted from the text and prevents unproductive distractions.

Ask any room of teachers about the biggest challenges they face in the classroom, and most will put "not enough time" at the top of the list. As this example shows, one problem with teaching vocabulary via Context Clues is that it wastes valuable learning time. Three to four minutes spent guessing what a word means would be better spent applying the knowledge of a word's meaning through problem-solving and then getting back to reading.

The difference between the two approaches can be seen in this figure:

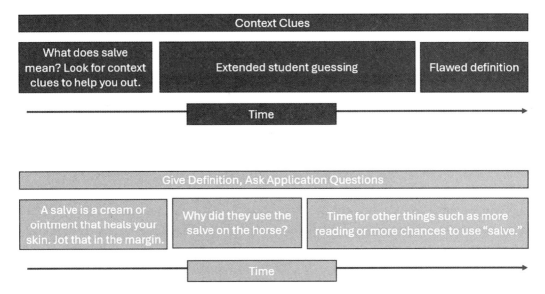

In the latter knowledge-based approach to vocabulary, students start with a clear, precise definition provided by the teacher, and the goal is that students become more confident and comfortable with it through application and exploration of the nuance and use of the word. This approach treats vocabulary as knowledge—here's the word, now let's help you learn and encode it through practice and play. So instead of spending a significant amount of time guessing at a word, we encourage teachers to give students the knowledge they need to learn the word and understand the text.

Isabel Beck and her coauthors explain one of the key reasons why Context Clues are so inefficient and ineffective: the majority of Context Clues students encounter are either non-directive (they don't give students the necessary information to infer the meaning of a vocabulary word) or are mis-directive, "rather than revealing the meaning of the target word, seem to direct the student to an incorrect meaning." Based on their research they conclude that "it is precarious to believe that naturally occurring contexts are sufficient, or even generally helpful in providing clues to promote initial acquisition of a word's meaning."[8] If students could learn to infer the meaning of almost any word by reading the clues around it, then all of our vocabularies might be more robust. But this is simply not how words work. Vocabulary is a body of knowledge to be taught and learned, not a skill to be universally applied.

Our colleague Jen Rugani recently summarized the research on Context Clues by sharing, quite simply, that in complex texts, Context Clues just don't exist. When the text is full of challenging words and unfamiliar context, even "directive" Context Clues are hard to use. The case of *salve* is a good example. If you know what *blue vitriol* is, it actually could help. But do you? We certainly don't.

In the end, the only argument for using Context Clues is that we still have outdated assessments, so students need at least some exposure to this approach, but this is not the way to teach vocabulary if we actually want them to learn new words and encode them into long-term memory.

We argue that using two simple approaches to knowledge-driven vocabulary instruction can be far better and that doing so will have an incredible impact on students as readers. These approaches can (and should) be used across content areas in order to support students in acquiring word knowledge that is both broad and deep.

The first of those two approaches is Explicit Vocabulary Instruction—a deep dive into the meaning and nuances of one to two words per day with many opportunities for student practice. This approach is intended to expose students to careful study of vocabulary so that they can have a deep and robust understanding of words and their meaning.

But if you do the math, you'll quickly realize that this approach on its own will only introduce students to 360 new words each year at most, which is not enough for them to acquire the breadth of word knowledge they need to be successful readers. That's where the second knowledge-based approach comes in—Implicit Vocabulary Instruction. Teachers use this approach with words that are encountered *during* reading in order to quickly build understanding and cause students to attend better to unfamiliar vocabulary. This causes them to learn more words but prevents distractions that can create a stumbling block to students' comprehension of the text. It supports students in learning a higher volume of words in briefer, lower dosage ways.

In the rest of this chapter, we'll share examples of each of these approaches from actual classrooms, then dive into the best practices for employing them.

EXPLICIT VOCABULARY INSTRUCTION

Use Explicit Vocabulary Instruction to teach important words with depth and nuance.

Christine Torres, a fifth-grade teacher and academic dean at Springfield Prep in Springfield, Massachusetts, is a teacher of truly epic skill and spirit. We recently captured her teaching two vocabulary words (*implore* and *caustic*) using the Explicit Vocabulary Instruction approach as part of our unit on *Number the Stars* by Lois Lowry. Before we turn to this video, let's take a look at the materials that Christine was using in her lesson:[9]

Word	Definition	Related Parts of Speech	Situations	Image
implore *verb*	to ask in a serious or emotional way; to beg	imploringly *adverb*	• She **implored** the firefighter to go back inside the burning house to rescue her trapped puppy. • _____	
caustic *adjective*	very harsh and critical	caustically *adverb*	• The judge's **caustic** remarks destroyed the contestant's confidence at the talent show. • _____	

Notice that Christine has provided a clear student-friendly definition for both words at the outset of the lesson. This is critically important. Too often, when we try to produce definitions *while* we are teaching, the result is a faulty and inaccurate definition. Anyone who's been asked to define a word on the spot has experienced this. It happens to us when we are training adults on vocabulary instruction—if we have not prepared thoroughly enough, we find ourselves grasping at incomplete and inaccurate definitions on the fly to use as examples.

With the word *caustic*, for example, a teacher who hasn't preplanned a definition might come up with the definition of *bitter* (as one of the authors did). But while *bitter* might be a synonym of *caustic*, it doesn't capture the degree or depth of what is intended by the word—its critical and harsh nature—and so therefore would be limited in building depth of word knowledge. We have watched hundreds of vocabulary lessons from excellent teachers in which we frequently encounter definitions that are lacking either in accuracy or student friendliness, despite the teachers' heroic efforts. Providing a good, clear student-friendly definition is a surprisingly difficult thing to do, but it's important if we truly want our students to acquire vocabulary knowledge critical for their reading success.

Christine's materials also include the vocabulary words' parts of speech, along with related forms of the word so that students can be exposed to a variety of parts of speech that a word might take. The situations and images she provides are particularly significant because they give students the opportunity to briefly apply the word in a variety of settings in order to support early encoding of the words and their meanings into long-term memory. And note that example sentences are also provided to extend understanding.

With these materials in mind, let's jump into Christine's classroom in *Christine Torres: Implore.* You can see in the first two minutes of teaching that her students are *very enthusiastic* participants in her vocabulary lesson. (It may look familiar because we watched excerpts from this lesson in Chapter One.) This enthusiasm might come as a surprise. You might think giving a definition and asking questions about it would feel more rote than asking students to come up with a definition themselves. Instead, what you see are eager students with their hands flying into the air, delighted to participate in the collective experience of building word knowledge.

To watch the video *Christine Torres: Implore,* use this QR code or find the video at the URL https://vimeo.com/1058364645/b23b050057.

In Christine's classroom, the definition is the *starting point* of the lesson, and class time is spent applying the newfound knowledge the teacher has provided in playful, challenging, and interesting contexts that deepen word understanding and also students' understanding of the book that they are reading. The "playfulness" is important here: when students enjoy playing with words, when we create opportunities for laughter and deep thought, we are "selling them" on words, language, and reading. We'll return to this idea later when we describe Active Practice as part of the Explicit Vocabulary Approach.

As Beck and her colleagues point out, *depth* of word knowledge correlates almost as strongly to reading skill and classroom achievement as breadth of word knowledge does. "People with more extensive vocabularies not only know more words but also know more about the words they know," the authors write. "Depth of word knowledge correlates almost as strongly to reading as breadth of knowledge."[10] Word play with multiple examples is fun and it builds depth of knowledge.

There is something else important happening as a result of Christine's decision to start the lesson by giving students the knowledge of the word's meaning: she has suddenly leveled the playing field. In the Context Clues approach, only some students can engage because only some students might know enough about the word in question at the outset.

When a teacher asks, "Who can tell me from experience what this word means?" perhaps half of the students in the room have no experience with that word—perhaps even less. They can no longer participate. In Christine's classroom, everyone has the knowledge they need to be able to engage in her clever and upbeat problem-solving activities. Suddenly everyone can join in. No wonder they all raise their hands. In this way, a knowledge-driven approach to vocabulary instruction is an equity tool as well—it gives all students in the class access to the content. And all students will know the word when it appears later in the novel.

We find this unexpected and important. Oftentimes, when people argue against teaching knowledge and facts, they do so because they think it will be boring to students and will reduce critical thinking. It clearly has the opposite effect in Christine's classroom. When rolling out the word *implore*, Christine first asks students to pronounce the word via Call and Response. Making sure that students can accurately pronounce a word is the first step to knowing the word and encoding it in long-term memory and, as we discussed in Chapter Three, it assists with orthographic mapping. It is also important because if students (especially English Language Learners) don't know how to pronounce a word, they are far less likely to try to use it, nor will they be able to read it aloud correctly to themselves.

Christine then has a student read the preplanned (and student-friendly) definition aloud, "loud and proud," and follows by immediately asking students to apply the definition of *implore* by describing a preplanned scenario ("She implored the firefighter to go back inside the burning house to rescue the trapped puppy."). She next asks (via a Turn and Talk so that all students can participate) how the projected image of clasped hands illustrates the word *implore*.

This whole series of questions takes less than two and a half minutes yet consider how many times students were able to hear or say the word *implore*. Our count was that Christine and her students each said it six times, meaning they heard it a total of twelve times in two minutes. This repetition is important in helping develop students' ownership of a word. The research varies on the number of times a student needs to interact with a word to learn it—on the low end for more proficient readers, it's about eight times and on the high end about fifteen to twenty-five times for more struggling readers.[11] So, making sure that there are repeated opportunities to hear and say a word initially and then spiraling back to it later with more opportunities increases the likelihood that a particular word will become a lasting part of students' word knowledge that they can pull from in reading, writing, and discussion with fluency and ease.

Compare for a moment the learning created in the two minutes of instruction on *implore* to the three minutes on *salve*. There's no comparison.

Note, too, that students are hearing and using the words in different ways, especially because Christine is using Cold Call and Turn and Talk to ensure that all students are engaged and thinking about the word. Having strong academic systems like these in place also makes the way Christine rolls out words in her Explicit Vocabulary Instruction predictable. Familiar routines focus students' working memory on the mental task of using a word in a variety of challenging settings.

That brings us to another vital resource that Christine is able to leverage in her lesson—the Active Practice questions, pictured next, that she asks her students after introducing each word. (Christine's questions are from the *Reading Reconsidered* curriculum, but we'll go into more detail on how teachers can come up with their own shortly.) This Active Practice enables students to apply their new word knowledge in a variety of ways, better increasing the likelihood that they will remember the words they have learned. You'll notice in the questions she asks that she is also revisiting words that have been taught earlier. Spiraling back to previously taught words employs Retrieval Practice, the idea we introduced in Chapters One and Four, to build stronger memory of the words. One interaction will not enable a student to use a new word easily.

Vocabulary Active Practice

As we apply our new word knowledge, be sure to use the vocabulary word in your answer!

1. Would you want to be friends with a person who frequently made **caustic** comments? Why or why not?

2. Finish this sentence: His fears started to **subside** when...

3. What might a teenager **implore** her parents to do?

4. Imagine there was a **commotion** at recess. What might have caused it? What could make it **subside**?

5. Would you be surprised if Mama spoke **caustically** to Kirsti? Why or why not?
   Challenge: include the word **exasperated** in your response.

   _____

   _____

   _____

   _____

6. Write a sentence that includes at least two of the following words:

In the cases of both new words and those she is asking students to retrieve from previous lessons, Christine asks questions that cause students to make connections to their knowledge about the novel that they are reading as well as other topics. They are thinking hard about the learning object and connecting it to other knowledge in their long-term memory.

Finally, it's useful to see how this introduction to the new vocabulary words prepares students to apply them critically during the lesson. Later, students will be asked to answer a Close Reading question (see Chapter Eight) that hinges on the meaning of *implore*. You can see the question here. Students need to have a nuanced and deep understanding of the word in order to be able to answer the question.

1. Consider these two versions of this scene from p. 116:

Original	Revised
Annemarie gave him a withering look. "You know we have no meat," she said insolently. "Your army eats all of Denmark's meat."	Annemarie gave him a withering look. "You know we have no meat," she said insolently. "Your army eats all of Denmark's meat."
Please, please, she implored in her mind. Don't lift the napkin.	**Please**, she **thought**. *Don't lift the napkin.*

a. **Turn and Talk**: How does the revision change the meaning of these lines?

_____

_____

b. In the original version, what contrast do you notice between Annemarie's thoughts and her actions? How does Lowry heighten this contrast? Why might she have done this?

_____

_____

_____

With Christine's example of Explicit Instruction in mind, we'll now dive into the best practices to follow using this approach in order to build depth and breadth of vocabulary knowledge.

Word Selection

Choosing which words to study carefully and deliberately for Explicit Instruction is a difficult but important decision. We need to be intentional about choosing words that appear in the text that are crucial to supporting comprehension and also useful for the future. We can also choose words that empower students to talk about the text in deeper ways even if they don't appear in the text itself.

Once again here, we have the brilliant guidance and research from Beck and colleagues to rely on. They identify a three-tier hierarchy that is useful when deciding which words deserve "instructional attention." Tier 1 words, they say, are those that are simple, familiar, and used in everyday speech. Their use is widespread and so they are not necessary to teach in a classroom setting. These include words like *imagination*, *communication*, and *realize* are more often known to students because they appear to commonly occur in spoken discourse. Students are likely to learn them and hear them in everyday conversation. Words like these are not well suited for Explicit Vocabulary Instruction.

Tier 3 words are technical vocabulary words, specific to a particular discipline or subject (for example, *chromosome*, *thoracic*, *fiefdom*). If we teach Tier 3 words in our literacy classes, we would likely select literary terms like *juxtaposition* and *analogy* to help students discuss and analyze texts. In these cases they would probably appear in a Knowledge Organizer (see Chapter Four). Otherwise, Beck and colleagues advise, Tier 3 words typically occur too rarely and specifically to have maximum return. They can be helpful in building domain knowledge, which is useful to being able to fully understand, discuss, and write thoughtfully about a particular topic, and so they can be taught using the Explicit or Implicit Instruction guidance in subject-specific classes like history, math, and science.

The most useful words to teach, according to Beck's team, are those in the middle: Tier 2 words. Tier 2 words are highly useful, likely to appear in multiple contexts or with varying meanings and are rare enough that they primarily appear in print (for example, *inflection*, *disparate*, or *boisterous*).

We find Beck and colleagues' framework for choosing words compelling. In our *Reading Reconsidered* curriculum, we teach a combination of rich Tier 2 words students will find useful in a variety of settings, now and in the future, and a few Tier 3 words so students will have a technical vocabulary with which to discuss, analyze, and write about the texts they read.

A deeper dive into words implies a greater time commitment, so word choice becomes even more important when selecting which words to Explicitly teach. Here are some characteristics of words to consider for Explicit Instruction:

- Words that appear in a text you are reading, that students may not know, and that are critical to understanding it.

- Words that relate to the content or themes of the novel or other content being taught. For example, when reading *Esperanza Rising*, you might consider teaching the word *exploit*. Although the word does not appear in the novel, students might use this word to describe the treatment of Esperanza and the other child migrant workers.

- Words that relate to other vocabulary words that can be compared, contrasted, or used as a group (for example, *tyranny* and *oppression*; *embellish* and *exaggerate*; *glance*, *gaze*, and *gawk*).

- Words that enable students to upgrade their word choice, replacing common words used in a book discussion or literary analysis. For the word *good*, for example, they might use *acceptable, favorable, satisfactory,* or *pleasing;* for the word *bad,* they could instead use *evil, wicked, atrocious, dreadful,* or *inadequate.*

Accurate, Student-Friendly Definitions

Once you have carefully selected the words that you will teach Explicitly, the next task is to craft an accurate and student-friendly definition. Please don't overlook this step. Our team has watched lesson after lesson to pick up best practices in vocabulary instruction and have found one single factor makes more lessons unusable as exemplars than any other: the definition the teacher uses.

We see teachers do brilliant things with a word but use a definition that's problematic, either because it's inaccessible—too jargony and circular to be useful—or inaccurate—even just not all the way right—far more often than we would have guessed. Though this may seem self-evident and self-explanatory, crafting definitions that are both accurate and student-friendly is one of the most challenging and overlooked aspects of knowledge-driven vocabulary instruction.

We see teachers fall into one of several different pitfalls when it comes to crafting definitions. Teachers can sometimes oversimplify a definition in an effort to make it student-friendly. For example, when defining the word *alacrity*, a teacher who hasn't thoughtfully prepared might say "if you do something with alacrity you do it quickly." While this is true, it's not complete. It's oversimplified to not include the idea that *alacrity* means doing something immediately with eagerness and pep. Another pitfall is not matching the definition with the part of speech of the word. *Alacrity* is a noun, not a verb, so a better definition (found in Oxford) might be "brisk and cheerful readiness." A third pitfall is using definitions that reference words that students don't know. In our example, if students don't know the word *brisk*, the definition won't help much. So then perhaps a better definition would be "quick and cheerful readiness"—far different than the original, spur-of-the-moment definition of "doing it quickly."

Another challenge that we often see in vocabulary instruction is when teachers introduce word pairs as synonyms. This oversimplifies precise definitions, inhibits accurate application, and ultimately hinders reading comprehension. Beck and her colleagues describe the flaws in the synonym model of teaching vocabulary, saying, "Although handy for providing a quick anchor point for a word, [the synonym approach] is a bankrupt way to teach word meaning. Building an understanding of language comes through developing knowledge of both the similarities *and the differences* among words and the precise roles they can play [emphasis added]."[12]

With all of these potential pitfalls lurking, it's no wonder that crafting quality definitions is something that teachers can struggle to do well. Here are a few guidelines to help:

- It's crucial to plan definitions in advance. Definitions that are provided spontaneously are often inaccurate or fail to capture a word's precise meaning.

- Definitions should be written in language accessible to students. A tidy and efficient definition gives students the best possible chance of understanding and recalling the definition of a new word. We suggest five to seven words generally, though there will be some vocabulary words you can capture in a three-word definition and some you can't capture in seven.

- The definition should use the same part of speech and tense as the word is used in the text. Definitions that inadvertently imply a word is a verb when it's shown as a noun can be confusing and sabotage students' application of the word.

- The definition should be double-checked for accuracy. It's useful to ask a colleague for a "peer review" to ensure your definition is correct and precise, keeping the described pitfalls in mind.

- If you opt to use synonyms as definitions, make sure that the two words have the same basic meaning, and if they differ in degree, articulate what the two words have in common but also why they should not be used interchangeably. (For example, *imitate* is similar to *mimic* but *mimic* implies that you are also doing so to entertain or ridicule.)

When Explicitly rolling out a new word, the definition and explanation should also capture a word's common use and its nuance. For example, it might be tempting to define a word like *respite* as "a short break." However, when you take a respite, you are taking a break from something difficult, and it's almost always used with a preposition (a respite *from* something). A strong definition would be something like "a rest from difficulty" and would note that it often appears with *from*.

Active Practice

If carefully selecting the words you will teach Explicitly, starting with an accurate definition and explaining its uses are essential foundational steps for building word knowledge, the last step, Active Practice, is the most fun. It also might be the most important step for ensuring students build and solidify deep word knowledge into long-term memory. Active Practice provides students with opportunities for playful and flexible application of a word in a variety of contexts and forms, requiring them to use the word in their answers. This is to increase the chances that they will understand the word fully and that they will use it on their own—verbally and in writing. We recommend aiming to include five to ten such questions in each session. We especially love Active Practice that requires students to use and apply their new words in playful ways.

The first few questions of Active Practice, especially, should enable students to feel successful. That way, you start with success and enjoyment and still provide useful Retrieval Practice. Just make sure students use the word in their answer, as it is a common misapplication for a student to talk *about* a word, without actually including it in their answer. A few examples of these Active Practice prompts from our curriculum include "If a classmate was described as 'easily *influenced*,' would that be a compliment? Why or why not?" or "Think of something a child might be *forbidden* from doing alone?" or "When might one sibling *smirk* at another? How would a sibling's *smirk* make you feel?" or "What might someone do to *spite* an annoying neighbor?"

One way to make Active Practice more playful (and rigorous!) is through combining words in questions to increase scenario difficulty. For example, "If I said my little brother had an *aptitude* for *disobedience*, what kinds of things would you expect him to do?" or "How might someone with an *aversion* to conflict respond to being *smirked* at?" or "Would a *noble* person ever *betray* a friend? Why or why not?" or "Could you *fret* about something and also *nurture* it?" or "Is it possible to *dread* making a *sacrifice*? Why or why not?" or "Imagine your friend is *petrified* of the dark. What might you do to *accommodate* him during a sleepover?" These questions, while playful, are also incredibly rigorous. Their level of deliberate difficulty is useful in intentionally encoding each of these words into long-term memory.

Notice that several of these examples don't have clear-cut answers to them. No problem—that is actually intentional. Active Practice questions can invite conversations and debates. We just need students actively applying and thinking about the words deeply as they use them. If a question is especially thought-provoking, try having students write their answers first to give them time to use their word well.

Word play is also good for teachers. Laughter makes everyone happy, including the boss. And it gives you the opportunity to show off your humor. The student laughter and sense of collegiality that was built in Christine Torres's classroom is an excellent example of this, especially when she playfully talks about how no one would *ever* make *caustic* remarks about her singing voice!

In addition to these playful word combination examples, it is useful to ask students to describe the small nuances in difference between similar words. This leverages the cognitive science research on how powerful "discrimination tasks" are for perception. Discrimination is required to describe the slight differences between similar things. These tasks are especially valuable when the differences are subtle because it takes perception to see how they are different. Developing this perception is critical to reading comprehension as well as to building robust word knowledge. For example, asking students "When might you *imitate* a teacher versus *mimic* a teacher? Which might be more offensive to your teacher?" or "If someone is described as a *voracious* eater, they might behave the same way as someone who is *ravenous*. But what is the key difference between the two descriptions?"

Active Practice is not only critical for students' encoding word knowledge but also enables teachers to Check for Understanding on words that they have taught Explicitly to ensure that students are using words correctly. For example, a colleague once rolled out the word *excerpt* to her students. When they got to Active Practice, she realized that she had not been clear enough on the definition of the word *excerpt* after she had to correct a student on incorrect use: "Ah, I can see why you might have said that, but you don't *excerpt* a slice of pizza; the verb form of *excerpt* typically applies to a text rather than to an object." Active Practice reveals how students are thinking about a word, enabling the teacher to refine the definition or correct mistakes as needed.

We'll repeat: it's essential in Active Practice (and throughout Explicit Vocabulary) that students use the words in their answers. In watching lots and lots of vocabulary lessons, we have often seen classes where students talk *about* a word and its meaning without using the word itself. Remember that using the word (multiple times) is critical to students' ability to encode it into long-term memory, and it also helps our ability to Check for Understanding for accurate pronunciation and application.

Active Practice is also an opportunity to start to increase students' fluency with the different ways that words might be used—literally and figuratively. For example, from our *Wonder* Unit we ask, "The word *contagious* is most often used to describe illness, but it can also be used figuratively. Why might Mr. Browne say kindness is *contagious*?" Or when reading *Bomb* we ask, "Would you rather face a *torrent* of rain or a *torrent* of criticism? Why?"

Another benefit of Active Practice is that it can give students a chance to apply different forms of the word and different parts of the speech. For example, "The word *emphatically* shares the same origin as words like *emphasize* and *emphasis*, meaning force or intensity of expression. How are the meanings of all of these words similar?" Or from our unit on *Haroun and the Sea of Stories*, "The opposite of *tactless* is *tactful*. If someone tripped in the hall, what might be a *tactless* response? What might be a *tactful* response?"

Asking students to apply newly taught vocabulary to a book is an important way to both reinforce comprehension and to support the likelihood that students will use these new words when writing about the book. For example, from *The Giver*: "What's something Jonas's father has an *aptitude* for?" From *Wonder*: "Why might Mom *regret* the choice to send August to school? Why might she feel the choice is *justified*?" And from *Heroes, Gods and Monsters*: "What did Prometheus do that Zeus found *reprehensible*?" Asking these types of book-based questions are a great way to build background knowledge or schema through Retrieval Practice for both the book and the new vocabulary.

While we have not discussed etymology much in our study of vocabulary, Active Practice is a great place to support students in understanding words roots, prefixes and suffixes, and how words are related to one another. For example, asking questions like "*Persecute* comes from a root word *sequi*, which means 'to follow' or 'to come after.' How does that root word help you better understand the meaning of *persecute*?" These types of questions can help students see that words don't exist in a vacuum but are interconnected. Roots, prefixes, and suffixes are more useful than Context Clues in supporting students in determining what a word might mean.

To watch the video *Jen Brimming: Reprehensible*, use this QR code or find the video at the URL https://vimeo.com/1058364815/a6420a605c.

A final piece of Active Practice is to consider not only what questions you ask but also *how* you ask students to respond to them. A great example of Active Practice comes from Jen Brimming's English lesson at Marine Academy in Plymouth, England, in the clip *Jen Brimming: Reprehensible*. As Jen teaches the word *reprehensible* to her students, she balances brief writing opportunities with Turn and Talks to build students' confidence and extend their thinking before they are called on to speak aloud. As a result, the room crackles to life when prompted to Turn and Talk because they have first had the opportunity to jot down their answers. Jen's cues for each form of participation are clear, crisp, engaging, and energetic—adding to the joyfulness of their Active Practice and setting students up for success because they know *how* to respond. Her multiple Means of Participation help Jen to achieve not only universal participation across the classroom but also render high-quality thinking about worthy questions. Although this clip lasted only five minutes, students had multiple opportunities to think about and understand the word *reprehensible*, applying it to examples from several of the books they'd read.

When you contrast the Active Practice portion of an Explicit Instruction class like Jen's with the example we gave at the outset of the chapter of a "guided inquiry" approach, it's easy to see how arming students with word knowledge *before* asking them to participate better enables them to engage with the word richly and deeply. As these examples illustrate, the Explicit Instruction approach does not mean that there is no student participation. Quite the contrary, unlike the guided inquiry approach, when students might enter the lesson with little word knowledge, Explicitly giving students the definition of a word better ensures active student participation.

IMPLICIT VOCABULARY INSTRUCTION

Use Implicit Vocabulary Instruction to support comprehension and increase students' attentiveness to the words they encounter as they read. Implicit vocabulary instruction also helps develop breadth of word knowledge.

If Explicit Instruction is carefully, deeply, and intentionally teaching two words per day, then the yin to its yang is Implicit Instruction, which encompasses a variety of ways that you can briefly (but accurately!) define words for students as you and your students encounter them in your reading. Much like Explicit Instruction, Implicit Instruction is an instructional tool that can and should be used across content areas.[13] And, like Explicit Instruction, it enables us to support both reading comprehension and vocabulary development.

Once again, it's helpful to jump into a classroom to see it in action. In *Hassan Clayton: Infuriated,* students are reading a nonfiction text that is embedded in his instruction of *Roll of Thunder, Hear My Cry*. Hassan asks students to circle the word and twice gives them the brief definition, "*Infuriated* means extremely angry," asking students to punch the word *angry* via Call and Response. As the clip rolls a little longer, you can see two students in the foreground who are annotating this definition in their texts.

This is a perfect example of Implicit Instruction because it doesn't detract from the flow of the narrative itself but rather adds to it. Hassan's brief description of

To watch the video *Hassan Clayton: Infuriated*, use this QR code or find the video at the URL https://vimeo.com/1058365161/750872842e.

the word *infuriated* supports students in understanding the text *and* goes a long way toward both building broad word knowledge and building students' attentiveness to vocabulary and word choice during reading. The whole thing takes a whopping twelve seconds.

Hassan does more than just pronounce the word; he goes a step further and defines it for his students. If he were to add a layer of practice to his Implicit Instruction he might have briefly asked, "Why were many in the north infuriated?," and then had students Turn and

Talk or raise a hand to share their answer while using the word *infuriated* in their answers. The choice to practice a word as part of Implicit Instruction or not is usually dictated by how many challenging words are found in the text. If a text is laden with new and challenging vocabulary, pausing to practice at every single word would disrupt the narrative too much. In that case, a teacher might choose to teach two key words from the text Explicitly first, and then choose one to three words to teach Implicitly, likely choosing the approaches that would take the least amount of time in order to not detract from the narrative.

As the example of Hassan's instruction shows, Implicit Vocabulary also starts with word selection and a student-friendly definition. After that though, there are several pathways that a teacher might take to teach a word *Implicitly*, depending on how much time she has or wants to spend on the word. Of course, there is a trade-off here: the longer you spend teaching a word during reading, the more in-depth your instruction can be, but the more you risk disrupting the narrative flow of the text. With that in mind, next are the best practices for approaching Implicit Instruction.

Word Selection

Pick any section of any book you teach in your classroom, and there's a good chance you can find at least one—if not several—words about which you think your students might benefit from Implicit Vocabulary Instruction. Some texts may include a high volume of potential implicit vocabulary words, as you can see from this example from the first lesson in our science fiction unit in which students read Isaac Asimov's *Robbie*. At the beginning of each teacher-facing lesson plan, we identify words students will encounter in the text that might be challenging, and we define them in a "Word to Watch For" chart so teachers can select the words they might need to teach Implicitly. This same type of planning can be done by teachers who might not be teaching from a curriculum by planning their own Implicit Vocabulary Instruction prior to teaching the lesson so that they can prioritize which words to teach and how to teach them.

- Words to Watch For:

Page	Word	Meaning in Context	Page	Word	Meaning in Context
1	recesses	secret or hidden places	2	resonant	deep, clear, and continuous in sound
1	profound	complete; deeply felt	3	ponderously	in a slow, serious way
1	incessant	continuing without interruption	4	irrefutable	impossible to prove wrong; indisputable
1	dismay	disappointment	5	alacrity	promptness or speed
2	basest	lowest or meanest	5	genial	friendly and cheerful
1	pantomime	to tell through movement rather than words			

As you are likely thinking, this is far too many words to teach Implicitly in five pages of text, with five potentially unfamiliar words on the first page alone. Our guidance is that teachers might consider choosing one to two words per page to prioritize based on their knowledge of their students' vocabulary. In a particularly complex text with lots of new vocabulary a teacher might guide students to mark up their texts with the definitions they provide before reading, much in the way footnotes might be provided in a vocabulary-rich nonfiction article or textbook.

When deciding which words to teach Implicitly, you can use the Tier 2 framework described previously much in the same way you would for Explicit Instruction.

Once you've chosen your words for Explicit Instruction, the main consideration for which words to teach Implicitly should be whether or not the words will be a barrier to comprehension for your students. Beyond that, here are some characteristics of words to consider for Implicit Instruction that you'll see applied in the following Lesson Preparation examples:

- Words that appear in a text you are reading, that students may not know, and that are critical to understanding it.

- Words that lend themselves to being taught briefly and therefore allow you to return quickly back to the text. These might include words that can quickly be taught using a picture—projecting a picture of a scalpel for a particularly gory scene in Roald Dahl's *Boy*, as we saw in *Jamie Davidson: Scalpel* in Chapter Four—but that don't require much discussion or practice to help make them stick.

- Words that have an accurate synonym that students know that can be briefly dropped in to provide a useful and brief definition.

- Words that have multiple meanings that students may be more familiar with but that differ from the author's intended meaning. For example, students might read the word *novel* and think it means *book* because that's the meaning they're most familiar with, but the author was using the word to mean "something new or original."

- Idioms or phrases that may disrupt comprehension because students are unfamiliar with them. For example, "that phrase 'by the skin of her teeth' means that she barely avoided something bad. Jot that note in the margin."

Word selection also involves the difficult yet equally important decision of which words *not* to teach. We call this *Selective Neglect*—knowing that a word may be unknown to students but intentionally deciding that you will *not* teach it is an important decision you'll make as part of Lesson Preparation (more on that later).

Approaches to Teaching Implicitly

There are five different ways you might address a word Implicitly. We list them here in order of the least amount of time you might spend on the word to the most amount of time.

The first approach is to simply *define* the word for students and continue reading ("That word *dismay* means 'disappointment'; let's keep reading.").

The second approach is to *define and pronounce* the word via Call and Response ("That word is *pantomime*. It means 'to tell something through movement rather than words.' Let's say it together: *pantomime*."). This is useful if the word is more challenging to decode and for Multilingual Learners, in case students encounter it again in the text, they'll know the pronunciation.

The third approach, which overlaps with the idea of Knowledge Feeding and Embellishments from Chapter Four, is *define and picture*, when the word that you are Implicitly teaching is more efficiently defined through the use of a picture. This is particularly useful for nouns and for providing a very quick definition and moving on.

The fourth approach is to *define* the word and *jot* the definition in the margin ("That word is *genial*. It means 'friendly and cheerful'. Take thirty seconds to jot that definition in the margin.").

And finally, the fifth approach is to *define* and briefly practice *applying* the definition. This is best done in the context of the book with a few brief comprehension questions so that the definition and the practice directly support comprehension.

To watch the video *Emily Badillo: Kin*, use this QR code or find the video at the URL https://vimeo.com/1058365290/cab362abb3.

As always, it's useful to see a few of these examples in action. In *Emily Badillo: Kin*, Emily and her students are reading Laurie Halse Anderson's *Chains*. She starts by asking if anyone knows the word *kin*. This is a brief attempt at trying to activate potential prior knowledge, but when she realizes that none of her students do, she defines it ever so briefly by saying, "It means she has family." She keeps it brief to maximize the time spent in the text. No use spending time guessing at the meaning of a word they haven't heard. If you listen carefully, there's a student near the front who says something like "Oh, my god" after she gives the definition of *kin*.

Suddenly a light bulb of understanding the text has gone off as a result of being given this vocabulary knowledge.

In the next example, *Rachel Harley: Curtsy,* the class is also reading *Chains.* After demonstrating a curtsy alongside a brief definition, Rachel briefly prompts students to practice using the word to increase the likelihood that the knowledge will stick. She asks, "Would you curtsy to someone in authority?" Impressively, and likely as a reflection of her emphasis on careful and intentional vocabulary instruction, her student's answer includes the word *propriety*—a word that was taught Explicitly earlier in the unit—demonstrating the impact that carefully executed vocabulary instruction can have on students. They love having great words at their disposal!

A final example comes from Erica Lim's ninth-grade history classroom in *Erica Lim: Sovereignty.* When her students encounter the word *sovereignty,* it's clear from the hesitancy in his reading that it's not a word that he is familiar with. Erica pauses her student's reading to deliver a short lesson on *sovereignty*'s meaning. You will immediately notice that she spends a bit more time than we might typically see with Implicit Vocabulary but it's justified. As Erica told us (and her students), it's a word that will come up again and again in their study of history (specifically in AP World History).

To watch the video *Rachel Harley: Curtsy,* use this QR code or find the video at the URL https://vimeo.com/1058364956/84c55eee47.

To watch the video *Erica Lim: Sovereignty,* use this QR code or find the video at the URL https://vimeo.com/1058365431/0568bc40d0.

Erica first makes sure that students can pronounce the word accurately since it isn't spelled phonetically. Her definition, "state authority or power," is brief enough that students can write it quickly in the margin and access it later. Then she gives her students one example and challenges them to give her another. She calls on Silas and reminds him to use the word in his sentence. She takes it a step further by asking her students to argue why certain countries would not be sovereign nations—further embedding the meaning of the word and deepening their understanding. Erica's example, while longer than the other Implicit examples, speaks to the power of vocabulary instruction across content areas as a way of using word knowledge to also build robust content knowledge.

THE VOCABULARY CASE FOR READING ALOUD (AND FASE)

You may already be realizing that our Implicit Vocabulary approaches are most suitable when the class is reading aloud together using FASE or Read Aloud (as described in Chapter Three). And in fact, the amount of new vocabulary that students will encounter in texts is yet another reason why reading aloud together is so important. Consider the data from Jim Trelease's *Read-Aloud Handbook*: a typical children's book uses almost thirty-one rare words per thousand. That's three times more rare words than adults use when they speak to children (9.3 rare words per 1,000) and also almost twice as many rare words as adults use when speaking *to other adults* (17.3 per 1,000). As students grow older, the percentage of rare words in books they read increases. A book written for an adult audience uses 52.7 rare words per 1,000. But when college-educated adults speak to other college-educated adults, they only use about seventeen rare words per thousand.[14]

Beyond telling us that it's important for students to read a lot to develop their vocabularies, these statistics tell us that the words that make reading challenging generally don't occur in spoken language. Functionally, they are exclusive to written discourse. For example, in one's night's reading from *Island of the Blue Dolphins*, Doug and his daughter came across the words *glisten*, *befall*, and *pelt*. Like other vocabulary words, they are rarely if ever used in oral conversation. They live almost exclusively in print. Therefore, it is critical not only to read a lot with our students but also to provide effective vocabulary instruction to support students in understanding those words that they won't hear through conversation.

A section of text that has a fair amount of new or complex vocabulary (given the previous discussion, we know that this is a very likely scenario) is ideal to read twice—once together as a class when you are briefly inserting Implicit Vocabulary instruction, generally asking students to annotate their text with the definitions that you drop in, and then a second time independently so that they can read for comprehension and fluency with their annotations to support them.

A great video example of this comes from Nashville Classical, as school leader Charlie Friedman is reading aloud *Esperanza Rising* to his students in the clip *Charlie Friedman: Condolences*. As he reads aloud, students are following along in their own texts. He briefly pauses to define several words while reading. We have put these moments together so that you can see them all at once. First they encounter the word *condolences*—"Condolences are what you say when somebody dies. You don't have

To watch the video *Charlie Friedman: Condolences*, use this QR code or find the video at the URL https://vimeo .com/1058365554/7f74356c4b.

to write that down, I just wanted you to know." He then resumes reading with emotion and vibrance until they encounter another word: *methodically*—"*methodically* means carefully." And again, later in the reading, "until Mama maintained her calm composure . . . *composure* means a calm demeanor, so it means she is maintaining her self-control." And then, "her uncle's papers were strewn. . . . when something is *strewn* it means it's tossed everywhere." This explanation was important to the plot of the story as it was a clue that he had been kidnapped. And finally, "a look of indignation . . . that means anger [whispered]." Each of these moments is a small but tidy example of how when reading aloud a rich section of text, teachers can very briefly define words in a way that doesn't detract from students' comprehension of the narrative but, rather, supports it. In our workshops we talk about the importance of teachers taking teaching techniques and making them their own. Charlie does this in a beautiful way, consistently lowering and slowing his tone to draw attentiveness to the words and the brief definitions that he has prepared in advance to both support students' comprehension and vocabulary. This string of moments illustrates the power of reading aloud and how diligent preparation for Implicit Vocabulary Instruction can make a world of difference.

Another useful observation by Isabel Beck and colleagues is worthy of discussion: "The source of later vocabulary learning shifts [as students get older] to written texts—what children read [as opposed to what they hear]. The problem is that it is not so easy to learn [vocabulary] from written context. Written context lacks many of the features of oral language that support learning new word meanings."[15] Beck and her colleagues' point is that hearing someone use a word helps students learn it better since the emphasis and inflection implicit in spoken language communicate a large amount of additional information about the word and how it is working in a given situation. It expands the amount of usable context for a student to learn from. When a teacher reads aloud, students get faster exposure to new words infused with expression to facilitate meaning making. In other words, hearing the way a teacher reads an unfamiliar word, as opposed to simply reading it on their own, adds to what students now know about the word.

An example of how another teacher uses intonation in a different way to support comprehension comes from Eric Snider as he reads Alfred Lansing's Shackleton's incredible voyage in *Endurance* in the clip *Eric Snider: Ominous* (an excerpt from the clip "Eric Snider: Epic Voyage" in Chapter Three). The passage opens with the sentence "The wind had an ominous sound." Simply

To watch the video *Eric Snider: Ominous*, use this QR code or find the video at the URL https://vimeo.com/1058358047/51838a3168.

through his expression, Eric is able to support comprehension of the word *ominous* even though he doesn't pause to define it.

This is why reading aloud to students is so important. If the hardest vocabulary, the words that are most powerful for students to learn, appear in textual settings that provide less context to help them learn than spoken words, we can easily remedy this by reading the text aloud. One of the great benefits of reading aloud to students is that they are exposed to vocabulary at maximum frequency—written text, especially difficult text, multiplies the number of rare words they hear; it ensures exposure to a much wider range of words, with particular emphasis on rare words that appear only in print. At the same time, students hear those words infused with inflection and expression, communicating more about the words and thus enhancing meaning. In fact, even hearing a word pronounced correctly is valuable in a way that's often overlooked: it increases the likelihood that a student will use the word, attend to it, and/or connect it to the previous time she heard it the next time she encounters it in print. If she doesn't know how to pronounce it, though, she may skip over it cognitively and therefore run the risk of misunderstanding the passage as result.

So, reading aloud to (or with) students puts you in the sweet spot for vocabulary development: it optimizes the maximum number of rare words that students can encounter per minute and gives them the maximum degree of additional information needed to expand and cement meaning.

This function—the sweet-spot-ness of reading aloud—*does not abate as students get older*. In fact, the more critical the vocabulary of a discipline, the more important for older students to occasionally hear its written discourse read aloud. If you teach high school science or history, one of the most valuable things you can do for students is to read aloud to them from the literature of the discipline with expression every so often. A dry, scientific sentence like this one from *Bomb*—"Their theories determined that atoms are made up of components called protons, neutrons, and electrons. The protons and neutrons are grouped together in the nucleus, or center, of the atom; the electrons move around the nucleus."—takes on new life when a teacher reads it aloud and imbues it with meaning.

LESSON PREPARATION

Lesson Preparation is key to supporting decision-making for teachers and it is perhaps one of the ways that our understanding and guidance has most evolved since the publication of the original *Reading Reconsidered* with the support of input and guidance from our colleagues at Teach Like a Champion. Choosing which word to teach Explicitly or Implicitly (which includes deciding which words to Selectively Neglect) causes us to make difficult decisions as teachers. We need to balance our desire to build vocabulary with the need to maintain the flow of the narrative in the text. Lesson Preparation is vital, as it can help us determine which words from a particular section of text should be taught Explicitly versus Implicitly; plan our accurate, student-friendly definitions that will support both breadth and depth of word knowledge; and anticipate words that might cause disruptions to comprehension and therefore suggest that a word should be taught Implicitly.

Following, you'll see a few examples of strong Lesson Preparation from teachers who use our *Reading Reconsidered* curriculum. They exemplify strong decision-making, which would be nearly impossible to do in the moment in front of thirty adolescents with a complex text in hand. This Lesson Preparation frees up teachers' working memory to be able to effectively teach new vocabulary in an accurate and rigorous way—whether that's Explicitly or Implicitly.

Active Practice for Explicit Vocabulary on Student-Facing Handout from Lesson 4 of our Sixth-Grade Freak the Mighty *Unit: Lesson Prep by Alyssa Erny at Nashville Classical*
A few things that you might note in reviewing the following Lesson Preparation:

- Alyssa scripts exemplar answers so she knows what she is listening for in student discussion and observing in student work.

- She plans for pacing, noting how long each section of instruction could take to make sure that vocabulary instruction doesn't crowd out the rest of the lesson.

- She stars the most important questions that she plans on asking to support prioritization of content if she is tight on time.

- She plans Means of Participation (more on this soon) to anticipate the best way to call on students to share their answers (CC = Cold Call, FF = Fast Finishers).

As we apply our new word knowledge, be sure to use the vocabulary word in your answer!

1. An **invincible** superhero meets an **unvanquished** supervillain. What might happen next?

   Hardcore fight scene.

CC ✱ 2. What might the **invincible** superhero's **demeanor** be like as he approaches the supervillain? How might he walk and talk? ✓

   Cocky, proud. Shoulders up, booming voice.

CC ✱ 3. What might your **demeanor** be like when your favorite sports team loses? What's your **demeanor** when you get an A+ on a test?

   Sad. Slouchy.   A= proud, tall

CC ✱ 4. Many books and movies feature the hero on a **quest**. What examples of (literary quests) can you think of?

   HP Horcruxes, Jonas to find answers.
   Odysseus

5. Explain a situation at school in which your **demeanor** might not match how you feel on the inside.

FF ___*If I am feeling upset about something*___
___*personal, I might act like everything*___
___*is ok and look fine, but actually*___
___*not feel fine.*___

FF 6. How would you describe the **demeanor** of a person who **struts**?

   Cocky, confident and proud.

Explicit Vocabulary Instruction on Student-Facing Handout from Lesson 3 of our Eighth-Grade Romeo and Juliet *Unit*

A few things that you might note in reviewing the following Lesson Preparation:

- Again, the teacher has planned for how long Explicit Instruction should take (in this case, five minutes) so that it doesn't crowd out the rest of the lesson.

- She has annotated the definition in order to explain it with common uses (e.g., "fulfilling it, like 'quench your thirst' means to stop being thirsty.").

- She has scripted follow-up questions for the situations so that students can get immediate practice applying and using the word. This gives students the first of many at bats required for them to start to use the word, increasing the chances that the word will stick. As we've noted, it's critical when you ask questions such as these that students use the words in their answer rather than talking about the word and its meaning (as often happens).

- She has scripted questions to ask students to describe how the picture illustrates the meaning, again asking students to immediately apply the word they have just learned.

			Vocabulary: Valiant, Quench	
Word	Definition	Related Parts of Speech	Situations	Image
valiant *adjective*	showing courage and determination	valiantly *adverb*	• Although the team made a **valiant** effort to score in the second half, they could not overcome their opponents' large lead. *– What might the team do to show a valiant effort?* • _____	*How does the image illustrate the word valiant?*
quench *verb*	to eliminate or end something by *filling it – like quench your thirst means to stop being thirsty. water can quench your thirst* satisfying or decreasing it		• The firefighters hauled water hoses over to the old barn to **quench** the fire. *What do the firefighters do to the fire?* • _____	

Teacher Annotations for Implicit Vocabulary Excerpted from Lesson 1 of our Seventh-Grade I Am Malala *Unit (page 1 and 4 of Prologue by Malala Yousafzai and Christina Lamb)*

A few things that you might note in reviewing the following Lesson Preparation:

- The teacher planned directly into the text so that he can effectively support Implicit Vocabulary Instruction with his accurate and preplanned student definitions.

- The words that the teacher circled and defined briefly in the margin to prepare for Implicit Instruction were *cricket*, *cheeky*, *prime minister*, and *cross*. These are useful words to drop in Implicitly because of the multiple meanings that each of these words might have, and to support student comprehension of the text. Students in the United States would probably think of other definitions for these words than the way they are used in the text based on their background knowledge. For instance, when they see the word *cricket* they'll likely think of the insect, and for *cross* they might think of the *t*-shaped structure.

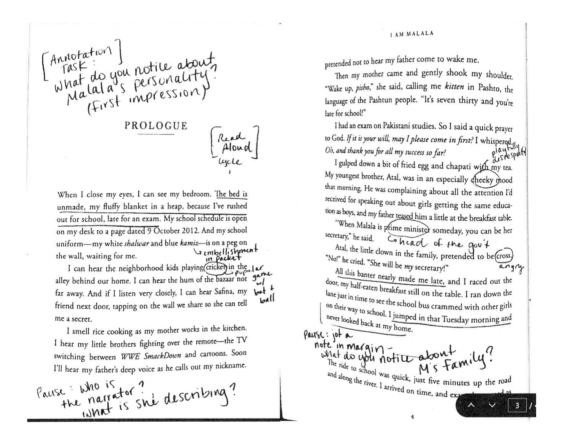

[Annotation Task: What do you notice about Malala's personality? (First impression)]

PROLOGUE

[Read Aloud cycle]

When I close my eyes, I can see my bedroom. The bed is unmade, my fluffy blanket in a heap, because I've rushed out for school, late for an exam. My school schedule is open on my desk to a page dated 9 October 2012. And my school uniform—my white *shalwar* and blue *kamiz*—is on a peg on the wall, waiting for me.

↳ embellishment in packet

I can hear the neighborhood kids playing (cricket) in the alley behind our home. I can hear the hum of the bazaar not far away. And if I listen very closely, I can hear Safina, my friend next door, tapping on the wall we share so she can tell me a secret.

popular game
bat + ball

I smell rice cooking as my mother works in the kitchen. I hear my little brothers fighting over the remote—the TV switching between *WWE SmackDown* and cartoons. Soon I'll hear my father's deep voice as he calls out my nickname.

Pause: who is the narrator? what is she describing?

I AM MALALA

pretended not to hear my father come to wake me.

Then my mother came and gently shook my shoulder. "Wake up, *pisho*," she said, calling me *kitten* in Pashto, the language of the Pashtun people. "It's seven thirty and you're late for school!"

I had an exam on Pakistani studies. So I said a quick prayer to God. *If it is your will, may I please come in first?* I whispered. *Oh, and thank you for all my success so far!*

playfully disrespectful

I gulped down a bit of fried egg and chapati with my tea. My youngest brother, Atal, was in an especially (cheeky) mood that morning. He was complaining about all the attention I'd received for speaking out about girls getting the same education as boys, and my father teased him a little at the breakfast table.

"When Malala is prime minister someday, you can be her secretary," he said. ↳ head of the gov't

Atal, the little clown in the family, pretended to be (cross). "No!" he cried. "She will be *my* secretary!"

angry

All this banter nearly made me late, and I raced out the door, my half-eaten breakfast still on the table. I ran down the lane just in time to see the school bus crammed with other girls on their way to school. I jumped in that Tuesday morning and never looked back at my home.

Pause: jot a note in margin— what do you notice about M's family?

The ride to school was quick, just five minutes up the road and along the river. I arrived on time, and exa...

3

RECURSIVENESS OF VOCABULARY

We'll leverage the expertise of Isabel Beck and her colleagues one final time in this chapter to stress the importance of spiraling back to previously taught words. They assert,

> Vocabulary research strongly points to the need for frequent encounters with new words if they are to become a permanent part of an individual's vocabulary repertoire. Those encounters should not be limited to the week in which words are the focus of instruction. Rather, students should have opportunities to maintain their vocabulary learning and elaborate their understanding of words by meeting words they have learned in contexts beyond the instructional ones.[16]

In our curriculum, teachers often note how much they appreciate how our treatment of vocabulary is recursive in that we frequently spiral back to previously taught vocabulary words in multiple ways—not just in the Active Practice portion as previously described, but in other ways as well. In our lessons, vocabulary words are a living, breathing part of our lessons, critical to helping kids comprehend and analyze the books they're reading. In our lessons, Explicitly taught vocabulary words form a shared bank of word knowledge that students can leverage throughout a unit in writing and discussion.

We try to make vocabulary recursive in a variety of ways, through having them frequently reappear in Active Practice; through appearing in question stems for discussion and writing, in key ideas/student responses, on assessments, on word walls; and through the reminder to teachers in our professional development to praise and acknowledge when students push themselves to accurately use a new vocabulary word in writing or in discussion. Next, we provide an example of how the word *idyllic* appears first in Explicit Instruction, then in question stems in that lesson, then in future lessons (along with the word *deplorable*, which was also previously taught), and then also in an Embedded Nonfiction text in another lesson. These repeated exposures help to address the challenges of the Forgetting Curve outlined in Chapter Four. Through repeated exposure to new words across several lessons throughout a unit, students are less and less likely to forget these words with each intentional exposure.

Word	Definition	Related Parts of Speech	Situations	Image
idyllic *adjective*	peaceful, happy, or pleasing in a simple, natural way	*idyllically* adverb	• The island was an **idyllic** spot before it was discovered by all the tourists. • _____ _____ _____	

3. Would it be accurate to describe Charn as **idyllic** before Jadis used the **Deplorable** Word? Why or why not?

___

c. How might the contrast between London and the new world make Narnia seem even more **idyllic**?

_____

_____

_____

Genesis 3:1-6, 22-24

Excerpted from the New Revised Standard Version

*In this excerpt from Genesis, Adam and Eve, the first man and woman God created, are living in the Garden of Eden, an **idyllic** paradise. As you recall, God has told Adam and Eve they may eat from any tree in the Garden except the tree of the knowledge of good and evil.*

Now the serpent was more crafty[1] than any other wild animal that the Lord God had made. He said to the woman, "Did God say, 'You shall not eat from any tree in the garden'?" The woman said to the serpent, "We may eat of the fruit of the trees in the garden; but God said, 'You shall not eat of the fruit of the tree that is in

---

If you are using a curriculum that doesn't intentionally spiral previously taught words into your instruction, there are several key ways you can do this yourself.

The first is through using a classic word wall (often with a compelling or "sticky" image that will be lasting for kids), so the words live in the classroom in some way. Having words posted (you might have noticed this in Christine Torres's video, the bright yellow bulletin board on the right side of her classroom) makes it more likely both students and teachers will notice and name the words when they appear in other settings, such as questions. We bold vocabulary words in the students' packets and lesson plans for the same reason. This also makes it easier to consistently prompt students to use words in their written responses or in revision—sometimes you may make this an Explicit part of the questions ("Use the word *caustic* in your response"), but other times you'll want to encourage students in the moment to stretch to include a vocabulary word or to revise to add one in.

Another way to ensure that vocabulary is recursive is through praise and celebration—noticing when students include those rich words in writing and speech and recognizing their efforts. Students often feel so proud and excited to use their juicy words, which can go a long way in helping students love the words they're using and eventually start to own them.

Finally, to ensure those words remain an active part of students' vocabulary, we want to notice and name when they appear in other texts. "That's one of our vocabulary words! Who can remind us what it means?" With careful attention to vocabulary, through using both Implicit and the Explicit Instruction, students often will light up themselves and throw their hands in the air to show you when they've found one of their new words.

CHAPTER RECAP

In conclusion, to briefly capture all of the guidance from this chapter here, remember to do the following:

- Avoid teaching vocabulary through the use of Context Clues.

- Provide students with an accurate student-friendly definition.

- Support vocabulary acquisition and comprehension before reading with Explicit Vocabulary Instruction on one or two words each day.

- Support vocabulary acquisition and reading comprehension during reading through Implicit Vocabulary Instruction.

- Give students lots of rich opportunities to apply a word's meaning.

- Spiral back to previously taught words.

Notes

1. ". . . although decoding is essential for beginning readers, vocabulary enrichment is equally important." Stanislas Dehaene, *Reading in the Brain: The New Science of How We Read* (Penguin, 2010), 328.
2. K. R. Tannenbaum, J. K. Torgesen, and R. K. Wagner, "Relationships Between Word Knowledge and Reading Comprehension in Third-Grade Children," *Scientific Studies of Reading* 10, no. 4 (2006): 381–398. https://doi.org/10.1207/s1532799xssr1004_3
3. https://pmc.ncbi.nlm.nih.gov/articles/PMC4122318/.
4. I. L. Beck, M. G. McKeown, and L. Kucan, *Bringing Words to Life: Robust Vocabulary Instruction* (Guilford Press/Childcraft International, 2002), 6.
5. As we note in Chapter Four, Nikki Bridges, our colleague and CEO of Lit recently coined this idea for us.

6. Louisa Cook Moats, *Speech to Print: Language Essentials for Teachers*, 3rd ed. (Brookes Publishing, 2020), 233.

7. *Webster's Third New International Dictionary, Unabridged.*

8. *Bringing Words to Life*, 4.

9. The materials are from the *Reading Reconsidered* curriculum.

10. *Bringing Words to Life.*

11. H. E. Lemoine, B. A. Levy, and A. Hutchinson, "Increasing the Naming Speed of Poor Readers: Representations Formed Across Repetitions," *Journal of Experimental Child Psychology* 55, no. 3 (1993): 297–328. https://doi.org/10.1006/jecp.1993.1018.

12. *Bringing Words to Life*, 85.

13. We recently worked with an affluent school district in Massachusetts that believed in this so deeply that they offered our reading-based professional development to all content teachers across the district.

14. Jim Trelease, *The Read-Aloud Handbook* (Penguin, 2013), 8.

15. *Bringing Words to Life*, 3.

16. *Reading Reconsidered*, 109.

Chapter **6**

Using Writing to Develop Readers

Writing—the task of describing complex ideas in precise verbiage and clear syntax—is hard work, a source of what UCLA cognitive psychologist Robert Bjork calls "desirable difficulty."[1] It requires the sort of deliberate, effortful thinking that encodes knowledge in long-term memory and leads to deeper understanding. To write—if the task is done properly—is to ask, "What exactly am I trying to say? Have I said exactly what I mean? Have I said exactly what I thought I said?"

The desirable difficulty writing creates is one of its primary attributes from a learning point of view. Writing is (or can be) an iterative process in which meaning is sought, reflected on, and refined. To write and to revise, and sometimes revise again, is to come to understand what you want to say and how to say it best. In that sense it is among the most meta-cognitive tasks we can ask of students.

"Aren't all those things also true of speaking?" you might ask.

Not in the same way. For one thing, writing is durable. Unlike speech, which disappears as soon as it emerges, written words remain fixed on the page (or in some cases on a whiteboard)[2] where they can be examined, reconsidered, and revised. The permanence of writing creates the opportunity for both reflection and accountability.

"They're wealthy boys. They have everything already, so they turn on themselves and start fighting," your student opines in a discussion on *Lord of the Flies*.

"But Golding is writing about human nature," you say. "A key idea is that the 'savage' in all of us is just below the surface."

"Yeah," your student responds. "That's what I said."

And there endeth the discussion.

But if the student had written the thought down, you might reply, "The way you've written it makes it seem like when they 'turn on themselves' it's only because of their wealth, whereas if you said 'despite all their schooling' or added 'there's something within them' you could suggest the issue was broader, maybe human nature."

"The permanence of writing creates an external record . . . that can be readily critiqued and reworked," the Carnegie Corporation of New York's landmark 2010 report, *Writing to Read: Evidence for How Writing Can Improve Reading*, opined.[3] Written work enables a teacher to effectively point out where meaning breaks down:

"This word is vague."

"Can you see that this reference is unclear?"

Or, to paraphrase Inigo Montoya from the *Princess Bride*, "You keep on using that word. I don't think it means what you think it means."

Similarly, students can develop a habit of asking of their own writing, *Does this sentence say what I think it says? Is there a better way to say it?* If that habit develops, they may just develop a sensitivity to language and an ability to create, refine, or perceive it at a higher level of nuance than most. Durability has immense value when the goal is thinking.

Another simple but profound fact is that we write far more slowly than we speak. This gives us the opportunity to use words and phrases we otherwise might not. In Chapter Five, we mention that rare words appear much more frequently in writing than they do in speech. Many words, in fact, occur almost exclusively in print. "Why?" we might ask. "Do writers set out to use a different lexicon when they write?" Likely not. More likely, they set out in search of meaning, to express an idea as well as they can. Writing at one-tenth the speed of speech enables them to ask and then revisit: "Which exact word here? Why?" They may even consult a thesaurus for a word they recognize but cannot recall unaided—a word they know, but not well enough to access it instantaneously. Using the word requires deliberation or prompting.

Call that the *thesaurus effect*: when we slow the process of thinking down enough to allow ourselves the chance to think consciously about words and ideas, as writing does, we expand the pool of available words, phrases, and concepts we can use, including, especially, those we are in the process of mastering. This is relevant both to professional writers and to students at every level. You've experienced it yourself if you've tried to use a language you have not fully mastered while traveling. Given a few minutes (and perhaps a bit of artificial intelligence), you can craft a credible email to the hotel asking for an early check-in on the day of your arrival. But showing up to the desk in person and having to express the same thought to the busy desk clerk with no time to think or double-check your use of the conditional tense, you find you do not speak half as well as you thought. To recall something into working memory as quickly as speech demands requires you to have used it many, many times.

This is highly relevant for students, whom we have a particular interest in causing to use ideas and language they are in the process of learning and understanding. Speaking at 150 words per minute, Jason cannot access a phrase or idea that he has read about but never used in the fraction of a second he has available to find it in his memory. But if Jason is writing, he can glance back at his notes or take the time necessary to use the new and precise phrase (*representative democracy*) not the vaguer approximate he is more familiar with (*voting*).

In other words, writing not only enables a student like Jason to use more of the words and ideas he knows well but it also expands the pool of ideas and phrases available to him to include those that he is in the process of mastering.

You can see an example of this in the video *Arielle Hoo: Conjectures Part 1*. The sequence begins with Arielle's students writing (in math class!) in response to this prompt: "When we are solving systems of equations, how will we know when we will have infinite solutions and no solutions?"

At 1:05 in the clip, Arielle calls on a student named Sahdie. "If you graph it and your lines intersect at every point," Sahdie begins, "which means that they're . . . . coincidental . . . . then you know that there are infinite solutions."

To watch the video *Arielle Hoo: Conjectures Part 1*, use this QR code or find the video at the URL https://vimeo.com/1058365847/ce8207f417.

Except Sahdie doesn't say *coincidental* exactly. He says it slowly, in syllables, as if it were a question: "*co . . . in . . . ci . . . DEN-tal*?"

This is almost assuredly the first time Sahdie has said that word—an excellent and precise piece of mathematical vocabulary—aloud. It takes him several seconds. He checks his notes as he speaks—what was that word again?—to make sure he's got it. Halting, not sure how to pronounce it, he voices the word as a question.

We are seeing something beautiful and important: a student expanding his vocabulary and his knowledge in real time. The word *coincidental* is being mapped in his brain. Next time he will use it a little more easily, a little more confidently. And he will begin to accrue more knowledge about the idea.

In part it happens because of the supportive classroom environment. No one shouts out during the pause as Sahdie struggles to access this new word. But he also uses the word because he has had the time to write it first, to think carefully about the word and how it applies and to insert it into the sentence he shares with the class. If this sequence did not begin with Arielle asking her students to write their responses, there's little chance Sahdie would have used the term. By asking the class to write, she has given him the chance to use it and to encode his nascent understanding of a crucial idea.

There are benefits to writing beyond the advantages of durability and slowness. Writing is an optimal tool to craft "arguments": logical progressions of linked ideas, presented in sequence. Through writing, we can create an argument that is longer and more carefully wrought than anything we could hope to hold in our working memory and express merely verbally. The resulting construction of logical, evidence-backed arguments gives humans the capacity to make breathtakingly complex and abstract ideas comprehensible and transmissible—for example, how a system of representative democracy can work, or how cooling systems can allow jet turbines to function at temperatures far higher than those at which the component metals typically melt.

Years of experience reading arguments that are more cohesive and organized than what could be created without written text also attunes us to expect written discourse to be thoughtfully crafted and worthy of study. With written text, our standards as readers are higher, which in turn influences the actions of the writer. One of us admits to jotting a reminder to our spouse on a sticky note and pasting it to the fridge, only to take it down and rewrite it. What was sufficient when spoken is not clear enough in writing.

The medium shapes the message. Though we occasionally jot things down off the top of our heads, we generally expect, in what gets put down on paper, a level of intentionality that is higher than what we verbalize. *We are supposed to think deeply when we write.* Your audience will read it as if you have done so. Nothing creates a more disciplined thinker.

Writing creates a unique opportunity to think about the highest levels of meaning and precision, not only of thought but of expression. But of course, like reading, writing—at least attentive, focused, thoughtful writing—is less likely to happen outside the classroom these days. The letter your student would have once written to a friend at summer camp is now an emoji-laden text—"luv U miss U [heart, smiley face, puppy]."

Finally, when we speak, we can compensate for lack of clarity in our words and syntax via gestures, voice inflection, and facial expression. It's much easier to be funny or ironic—or darkly funny or lightly ironic—when speaking. A roll of the eyes or the inflection of a word does the trick. And our audience is visible so we are always getting feedback on whether they seemed to grasp what we said. If they didn't, we can try again and punch up an eye roll or the inflection on a word a little bit. None of that is available to us when we write. Perhaps this, too, is a reason for the multiple drafts of the sticky note on the fridge about taking out the trash. We have to make meaning solely out of word choice and syntax, before we see if our audience is picking up what we are putting down.

These difficulties are mostly a good thing. Because writing is more difficult, it causes us to think hard and to remember more. Note-taking, for example, is often effective *even if students never reread what they write* (though it's better if they do, obviously). When we cause people to write, and especially to write thoughtfully and with intentionality, they are more likely to remember and understand.

When the subject of that writing is also the thing we have asked students to read, we can cause them to learn more about it, remember more from it, and, in doing so, achieve greater mastery of the communication code they will use both productively in writing and receptively in reading. They become more adept and perceptive readers as well. As the eighteenth-century polymath Georges-Louis de Buffon put it, "Good writing is good thinking, good awareness and good execution, all at once."[4] All of those things are valuable to a student, but the awareness—the mastery of the code of language in all its nuance—is particularly useful to them when they open a book and begin to read.

"WRITE DOWN SOME IDEAS FIRST"

You can see many of the beneficial aspects of writing play out in the clip *Jen Brimming: The Weight of His Clothes.* The video was shot during the second lesson of Jen's unit on *Lord of the Flies* (for which she used our *Reading Reconsidered* curriculum).

In the lesson, Jen wants to draw her students' attention to the importance of William Golding's word choice and symbolism at the beginning of the novel,[5] so she asks them to reread a passage from the first chapter in which Ralph, finding himself stranded on the island in which the book is set, rips off his clothing.

To watch the video *Jen Brimming: The Weight of His Clothes,* use this QR code or find the video at the URL https://vimeo.com/10583 66039/281679aa18.

Golding describes the "weight" of Ralph's clothes in the passage. Ralph feels a burden in the trappings of civilization now that he has been set free in a more "natural" state without rules or grownups. The impulsive "fierceness" with which Ralph rips off his clothing offers a dark foreboding. If you know the book, you know how important these themes are and so how ripe and important for deeper analysis this passage is.

Jen starts by rereading the passage aloud, infusing it with expression and emphasis (see Chapter Three). But she also reads to students a second, slightly altered version of the sentence in which a few words have been changed from the original. In the alternate version, Ralph becomes aware of the "inconvenience" of his clothes not the "weight" of them. He kicks off his shoes "eagerly" instead of "fiercely." The changes dilute the intensity of Ralph's reaction as described in the original. Here's the page from the *Reading Reconsidered* curriculum that Jen is teaching from:

Pages 9-10

 3. Reread this line from p. 10:

> He became conscious of the weight of his clothes, kicked his shoes off fiercely, and ripped off each stocking with its elastic garter in a single movement.

Compare it to the version below:

> He became conscious of the **inconvenience** of his clothes, kicked his shoes off **eagerly**, and **removed** each stocking with its elastic garter in a single movement.

a. What do you notice about the differences between each version? What does the first reveal about Ralph?

_____

_____

Jen is using a technique called *Sensitivity Analysis*, which we describe in Chapter Eight on Close Reading. In a Sensitivity Analysis question, small changes are introduced into a line of text and students study the resultant shift in meaning.

Jen asks, "What's the difference between those two [sentences] and what does that reveal about Ralph?," a question that warrants deliberate careful reflection. Many students won't be able to see and describe right away the shifts in meaning wrought by the changes. And, of course, thinking deliberately about a challenging question is hard work. Some students— far more, perhaps, than the two or three who at first volunteer to answer—might choose not to think that deeply and sit quietly instead, letting more eager classmates carry the cognitive load.

But Jen asks students to "write down some ideas first," to respond to the question in writing before anyone shares their thoughts aloud. This causes every student, even the reluctant, to answer the question. And it causes her students to think more carefully and deliberately. They are slowed to the pace of writing and there is time to consider, to go deeper than the first impulsive thought that comes to them.

Write first; then discuss. It's a simple change in the sequence of activities with far-reaching consequences.

Since we are noting subtleties of Golding's language, let's observe Jen's, as well. As a smattering of students volunteer to answer, she sends the class to write with the phrase: "Write down some ideas first." She asks for *ideas,* not *answers.* The presumption is that students likely won't know the answers for sure yet and perhaps even that their first responses are unlikely to capture the full nuance of a complete answer. They should start by using the writing process to generate ideas—even if they are not complete yet. In fact, her assumption is that they will be *both* valuable *and* incomplete. Some questions are deep enough that we would not expect to understand them fully right away, and the word *first* suggests this—that the writing is an exploratory activity, a preamble to the analysis to come.

She is asking her students to use writing not so much to explain what they already think about the text—to justify their opinion and/or support it with evidence—but as a tool to generate ideas. They are writing to discover what they think.

This is a valuable practice for students to learn. Writers often talk about the fact that they frequently don't fully know what they are going to say and where it will take them when they start writing.

"I write entirely to find out what I'm thinking, what I'm looking at, what I see, and what it means," Joan Didion writes.

Daniel Pink strikes a similar note: "Writing is an act of discovering what you think and what you believe."

So does Bruce Springsteen, who writes in his autobiography: "First, you write for yourself ... to make sense of experience and the world around you."

In fact, writing often generates ideas that authors didn't know they had or cannot explain the genesis of. Authors frequently describe themselves in the process of writing as being like a conduit. Ideas emerge that sometimes don't even feel like their own at first. That's likely what Ernest Hemingway meant when he said, "Sometimes I write better than I can."

But if professional writers are keenly aware of the fact that the order is often (1) begin writing and then (2) discover the idea you are writing about, rather than (1) conceive of an idea or an argument and (2) write to explicate it,[6] teachers can be less attuned to this process. Opportunities to let students use writing as a tool of discovery are often overlooked.

We call writing to discover what you think *Formative Writing*, and we distinguish it from *Summative Writing*, which is writing to explain or support a coherent idea—both of which we'll discuss shortly. A key difference is that, in the latter case, writers have to know what they are going to say before they begin, but in the former case they do not.

Jen's students are practicing Formative Writing here—jotting down their initial ideas to discover what they think.

There's a second, subtler application of writing in Jen's class that shows up while students are sharing and discussing their ideas. Its purpose is made most visible by looking at the student packet from the lesson:

(This moment occurs just after the sensitivity analysis on the previous page)

b. **Turn and Task** How might we read this moment, Ralph's undressing, symbolically? Jot down some notes in the space below. (Hint: You might reread the entire paragraph it is excerpted from on the bottom of p. 10.)

Notes

Notice there is space for students to take notes while their peers are speaking. When we socialize note-taking, as we will discuss, we help students listen and remember.

A few minutes later, after they have discussed the ideas that emerged from the initial reflection, Jen asks her students to write yet again. But this time, she says she wants students to "really craft this one carefully," noting that she will share some examples on the document camera (called a *visualizer* in the United Kingdom). Their goal is to revise and improve their initial thinking based on the ideas they've heard. "What might the removal of Ralph's clothes symbolize?" the prompt asks.

Writing, we noted, can be one of the richest metacognitive tasks we can ask of students. Here they look at their initial thoughts and revise: *Did I say what I meant? Do I still think that?*

That kind of reflection isn't automatic. We have to make space for rethinking and rewriting. Teachers often ask students to revise and improve their thinking as part of writing longer essays but find that students struggle with this task. Their revisions often don't change much.

If that's the case, we might ask why. One explanation would be that we don't teach them how. Another might be that they don't practice it much. Rewriting short pieces of writing, just a sentence or two in length, as a regular habit is a great way to address both of these issues, improving students' capacity to reshape their ideas when they rewrite. You can see students doing that here.

While the primary task is to adapt their initial writing based on what they have learned from their peers, Jen adds a challenge: "See if you can get an appositive phrase in there." She is deliberately trying to expand their mastery of syntactic tools, an idea called *Developmental Writing* that we will return to. No amount of discussion about the book will help students understand not only how to use appositives but also how to read them when the texts they encounter do so. It's a great example of how intentional writing exercises can support reading comprehension.

You can see the payoff of from Jen's decision to ask her students to revise their thoughts in writing in the final answers to the question are the ideas in. "After realizing the weight of his clothes, Ralph symbolically rejects his civility and rips off his clothes fiercely," one student has written. "After realizing there are no adults, Ralph, the fair boy who is disciplined, symbolically rejects the formal life and immediately takes his clothes off," pens another.

The sentences are notable for their complexity of construction, and the second student has done an excellent job of using an appositive phrase ("Ralph, the fair boy who is disciplined").

In the bigger picture, Jen's students have described multiple related ideas at once and have used complex syntactical forms. Not only their writing of high quality and reflective of complex thinking but the writing also shows incipient mastery of sophisticated syntactic forms—the sort Golding uses in *Lord of the Flies* and which they will now be more likely to comprehend fully as they read.

But Jen doesn't stop there. In the companion clip *Jen Brimming: Add to Your Sentence* we can see her further refining her students' thoughts and providing feedback to increase the level of sophistication in their writing.

With the first sentence, Jen praises the use of an exact word from the passage in the novel and encourages students to use quotation marks to make this clearer. She notes this on the board and names it—"use quotes from novel as part of sentence"—to turn a one-time correction into a replicable rule of thumb.

To watch the video *Jen Brimming: Add to Your Sentence*, use this QR code or find the video at the URL https://vimeo.com/1058366270/f7486b6762.

Jen quickly moves to another sentence, Riley's, and again she has praise for the use of specific words from the text and for the use of an appositive. She provides a bit of feedback about how to make the appositive and the writing generally a bit stronger, adding to her list on the board. She then sets her students up to learn from the study of their peers' work by immediately asking them to apply one of the proposed list of improvements to their own sentence.

Note that she is projecting the sentences as the class discusses them. If she simply read them aloud, the improvements she suggests would be abstract and students would not be able to see specifically how they might be made. But now, they have an exact model of how to make their writing more sophisticated. Additionally, if she had merely read the sentences and critiqued them, students would have to retain the memory of what their classmates had written in their working memory, using much of their thinking capacity to do this. But because they can see the sentences being revised, they don't have to use their working memory to recall the original. They can use all of their capacity to think, remember, and learn.

This concept is called the *transient information effect* (a corollary of cognitive load theory). We mention it briefly in Chapter One, but it tells us that when the object of study remains in view, students can sustain their focus on it and remember it better. So when you study writing as a class, always project it. (We call this *Show Call* in *Teach Like a Champion 3.0.*) This is also a benefit of editing small pieces of student writing—often a single sentence at a time. It makes it easier to see, study and focus on precise improvements.

It's worth noting that because Jen's writing exercise consists of a single sentence, it is not only easier to study but easier to rewrite quickly and simply. And it's easier for her to keep the pace of her class moving. The whole process takes less than five minutes. She can simply and easily make the study of written language a topic of her classroom because she studies it in small chunks.

This suggests one of the key principles of intentional writing exercises, the kind that make students not just better writers but better readers: they are often short, relying more on intentionality than volume. This is interesting in light of Judith Hochman and Natalie Wexler's observation that teachers often mistake *assigning* writing for teaching kids *how* to write.[7] The two are not the same; in fact, they often conflict.

Another key point: all of the writing students are doing is embedded in the content of the lesson—in the service of reading and understanding the novel. We can see Jen here teaching the technical details of creating clarity and meaning through writing, but the exercise would only be half as valuable if it weren't embedded in content. This is another point Hochman and Wexler emphasize. Writing is a powerful classroom tool because it causes students to master content as they do it, and it is more powerful and more interesting for students when they use it to unlock greater understanding of what they are studying.[8]

We are not saying that students should never write personal narratives and descriptions of their summer vacations, but we do note that our own children have in their first fourteen years on this planet written about eight such pieces each—but precious few trenchant analyses of a book or a historical period—the sorts of writing that not only improve their professional success but their professional learning will rely on. We'd be okay with a few less personal narratives and a few more discussions of what William Golding is saying about the nature of human behavior in the absence of societal influences.

WRITING FOR READING: PRINCIPLES OF WRITING TO BUILD LITERACY[9]

We saw evidence in Jen's classroom of some broader principles that can help build students' capacity not just to write effectively but to learn more from what they read and become better readers.[10] (These last two ideas are connected. As Harry Fletcher Wood writes, "What students know dictates what they can learn";[11] in other words, learning more from what you read is also a means of becoming a better reader.) There are six principles in all:

- Students should "think in writing."
- Students should write to expand their "syntactic control."
- Students should write to support and explain arguments.
- Students should write beforehand to improve discussion.
- Students should "stamp" ideas in writing.
- Students should revise their writing regularly in shorter, deliberate bursts.

We'll spend the rest of the chapter discussing how to translate these principles into daily practice and studying examples from classrooms.

Students Should "Think in Writing"

Use short Formative Writing prompts midstream to integrate deliberate reflection into the process of reading.

Let us introduce our discussion of this first idea by means of a video.

To watch the video *Formative Writing Montage*, use this QR code or find the video at the URL https://vimeo.com/1058366400/12136891ee.

In this video, *Formative Writing Montage,* you'll see three teachers, Will Beller, Spencer Davis, and Maggie Johnson. Each of them uses the key idea slightly differently, of course, because the text they are reading is different, their own styles are different, and their purposes in the moment differ. But you'll also see some common themes.

First Will, at Our Lady Queen of Angels in New York. The book is the classic World War One novel, *All Quiet on the Western Front.* As the clip opens, we hear a student reading aloud. Will is using FASE Reading (see Chapter Three) to build student fluency and to bring the book to life. Note also the Embellishment (see Chapter Four) on the screen—an image of a mask-wearing machine gun team in 1916—to help students envision gas masks. Just before he pauses, Will "bridges," that is, he reads himself for a few sentences. You can hear him bring a bit of extra emphasis to the book and also punch certain ideas—the ironic tone Jayden uses in making reference to the Kaiser ("*him*??"). He knows he's about to ask students to process in writing and is subtly priming them.

He pauses and, just seconds after he stops reading, says, "Answer the Quick Write in a sentence of your own words. Just describe: what was the narrator's impression of the Kaiser? Give it a go . . . ."

We love that students are writing midstream here. Just seconds after reading about the narrator's perspective on the Kaiser, students are reflecting on it in writing. To put this in the language of a cognitive psychologist, Will is asking his students to reflect on the ideas in the book while the recollection of them remains clear in their working memory. A pause of just a few seconds to say, for example, "Oh. So interesting. I'm wondering about *x*. Let's all take out our notebooks . . . and a pencil . . . and write for a moment . . . ." might be enough to let some of those vivid thoughts slip out of working memory. The proximity and speed of transition matter.

We love that Will has given this activity a name: it's a *Quick Write*. The more you name it, the more students become aware of the activity as a distinct and familiar routine. They know what to do and how to engage from experience. And we love that the name emphasizes the brevity and low-stakes nature of the writing. Even his start cue, "Give it a go," emphasizes this low-stakes vibe: it's all in the effort, in getting going.

The purpose, again, is to encourage students to process the experience of reading the book and reflect on it in writing before they know for certain what they think. So, coming out of the Quick Write, we like that Will tells students that he's "not going to react" to their responses. It's too early to comment or correct. It's enough for now to hear their thoughts and to cause the class to hear a bit of one another's thinking. We like that he emphasizes this listening—"check your answer against theirs."

But we also love the supportive accountability he brings to the activity. He's going to "call on a few people" to share their responses. That is, he's making it explicit that he is going to Cold Call after the Quick Write and thus make certain that everyone completed the task and made the effort required.

Will calls first on Ricardo, and asks him not to *explain* his answer but to *read* it. Subtle difference: if Ricardo was listening while the book was read aloud, he would be able to describe some ideas credibly when called on *even if he'd done a poor job of writing*. It would not be clear that he had actually written, and so he and his classmates would not be incentivized to write with intention. If that happened, desirable difficulty would be sacrificed. But asking students to read their responses defends against this possibility. A culture in which you are often (but not always) asked to share *what you actually wrote* puts the emphasis on the writing itself and, not incidentally, causes students to reflect on their words when they hear themselves read them aloud. *Hmmm, that doesn't quite sound right.* The writing is safe and low-stakes in terms of students' weddedness to what they say, but they're incentivized to put in real effort and reflection. It's a lovely balance: you only have to give it your best and you have succeeded, but you *do* have to give it your best. You are accountable for that.

Second is Spencer (University Prep, Bronx, New York). His class is reading R. J. Palacio's modern classic *Wonder*. You can see that Spencer's class, like Will's, has been reading the book together. Books are out. The girl in the foreground still has hers open in her lap.

Having heard two characters' perspectives, Spencer wants his students to reflect on what's similar and different. There's a T-chart for them to fill out. In his directions, he uses the word *jot* several times—"jot down the similarities . . . jot down the differences." It's a word that stresses informality: writing for personal purposes, writing that might change. We love that word in this setting so much that although we are all-in for Will's name of Quick Write, our preferred name (and we do think you should name this activity) for a *midstream-think-in-writing* activity is a *Stop and Jot*.

Spencer then reduces the stakes even more. Students' thoughts "do not have to be [in] complete sentences," he says. "You can absolutely have bullet points." This is a great variable to play with as you use Formative Writing. Are complete sentences often useful? Yes. Are they always optimal? No. Is it interesting to have variation? Probably. Is it beneficial to tailor format expectations to intentions? Surely. Here, we suspect, Spencer wants students to be able to process multiple ideas quickly and to build more of a "notes on the text" vibe than a "putting this together in thoughts" vibe. In other words, it's probably early in the process of idea formation.

Finally, there's Maggie (Troy Prep, Troy, New York). Her students are reading *To Kill a Mockingbird*. Again, we hear Maggie reading aloud as the clip begins.

We love the playfulness of Maggie's question and her "hmmmm . . . strange . . . " as she models reflection. She's building engagement and curiosity, obviously. We love that she lets students raise their hands first as if they will answer aloud. To raise your hand in class is to send the teacher a signal—"I'd like to answer"—but it is also to send your classmates a signal—"I want to talk about this book; I am all-in"—that is likely to make positive engagement the norm.

"Thoughts? I bet you have them, but you have to write them first," she says, smiling playfully. The word *first* builds anticipation—they'll get to share their thoughts soon enough. "Sorry. Can't help it!" she adds before students pick up their pencils and get started. The implication is that she values writing especially. You "can't help it" when you indulge in something you love.

All three clips show midstream writing. In all three cases, the writing comes just seconds away from the experience of reading. The book closes, and pencils start scribbling. It is a tool students use to process the experience of text.

This kind of writing also provides a valuable tool for teachers to gain insight into what students are thinking immediately after they read, and how much they are comprehending. There is almost assuredly assessment gold in student writing when it is generated directly (and solely) from a reading of the text and before it is influenced by hearing what other students and the teacher have seen.

When employing Formative Writing in your own classroom, keep the following guidelines in mind.

Keep Formative Writing Short

Formative Writing should be brief—a minute or two, perhaps, sometimes even less, as we saw in all three examples from the video. It's supposed to be embedded in reading, which means that reading comes right before it and starts again soon after (sometimes with discussion first, as well). As we will discuss later, one immense benefit of writing is that it helps students prepare for the next thing they will do in class. It's a preliminary step. Short is usually sufficient. In most cases we want to *start* the thinking, not exhaust it fully.

Short is also important because it means it is easy to drop in multiple times over the course of a lesson. We can build the habit of universal and thoughtful reflection in writing and still accomplish other things. In many classrooms, writing happens in a single long block. It's separated from reading like it's on the other side of a firewall. Here it is integrated. Brief bursts of writing allow for frequent writing, which makes a familiar habit of thinking deliberately about the text as you read it and therefore remembering more and more potent thoughts about it.

It's also important that Formative Writing be short because, by its very nature, it's happening before students have fully "baked" their thoughts. The goal is to get students writing earlier in the thinking process, which will both improve their thinking about the text and ultimately help strengthen any Summative Writing they do later, but the duration of a task need not always match its importance. In many ways we keep the stakes low—and the pace engaging—by keeping Formative Writing relatively brief most of the time.

Use Intentional Language in Prompts

One of the things we've dwelled on in our discussion of these examples is the subtleties of language—how telling students to "jot" their ideas or that you can't "help" asking them to write frame the purpose of the task.

We'll dig a bit deeper into language by showing you another video. This one shows a teacher using Formative Writing not embedded in reading but during a vocabulary lesson. We note that the idea of Formative Writing can be applied almost anywhere. If you read *Teach Like a Champion 3.0*, you can see examples of it in a variety of subjects and grade levels. So, while our focus here is on embedding Formative Writing *in the task of reading*, there are lessons we can take from applications of Formative Writing in other settings.

To watch the video *Jen Brimming: Reprehensible*, use this QR code or find the video at the URL https://vimeo.com/1058366585/edb2d727c6.

The teacher in the clip, *Jen Brimming: Reprehensible*, will look familiar since we saw Jen teaching *Lord of the Flies* at the beginning of this chapter. Here we see her at the beginning of a lesson with younger students—year 6, or fifth grade—in which students are discussing the vocabulary word *reprehensible*.

"Why is stealing form a charity reprehensible?" Jen asks. It's a great example of vocabulary Active Practice as we discuss in Chapter Five. As she asks this question, there are perhaps three or four hands in the air. This isn't bad, but it's not yet the kind of high engagement Jen seeks from her class. So, Jen asks her students to write first before they share their thoughts with the class. Seconds later, everyone is answering the question.

Note the phrasing she uses: "Jot down your first thoughts."

We think almost every teacher could and perhaps should borrow that phrase at some point in their teaching. It makes it so easy and safe to start writing. It communicates: it's thoughts we're after, not answers yet, and even better *first thoughts*, implying that you will have the chance soon to develop them further. You don't have to be perfect right now. We are reminded of the quotation, attributed to various sources, that "the key to success is to start before you are ready. It doesn't have to be perfect. You just have to get going."

And you can see how it affects the class. They write briefly and several new hands pop eagerly up even before she's asked for volunteers. And the Turn and Talk "pops"—you can hear that students are eager to share those "first thoughts." By the time Jen wraps up the Turn and Talk, just before she calls on Terry-Anne, almost every hand in the room is raised. Writing informally about a question that students have the knowledge to engage in but cannot easily resolve is a great way to start class.

What you're seeing is in part the result of Jen's language—how open it is, how it lowers the stakes, and how it suggests the idea that students are not wedded permanently to what they write.

This key feature of Formative Writing is something Ashley LaGrassa, an eighth-grade teacher in Rochester, New York, at the time, reflected on with us. Ashley wanted to experiment with adding more Formative Writing questions to her lessons in hopes that they might, as she put it, "make my classroom feel safer for students," and "lead them to take risks and engage more deeply."

After her students read a poem by Alice Walker, Ashley dropped in a quick Formative Writing prompt to get her students thinking about the connections between Walker's biography and her writing. "How *might* Alice Walker's experiences . . . have influenced her writing?" she asked.

The word *might* was critical. She had included it because it suggested both challenge—no one knows for certain—and that there were multiple potential answers. The result was dramatic. "Students began quickly jotting down their thoughts," Ashley said. She sensed instantly that they were feeling "more comfortable with risk." She saw the difference in the discussion as well. Within moments, students were analyzing the symbolism of a scar Walker mentioned with depth and candor.

Ashley was struck by how such a small change—shifting the wording of a question from "What is the theme?" to "What might be a theme be?"—led to such significant changes.

"Students need to feel that wrestling with a difficult text is a low-risk adventure—they don't always have to have a final argument about the theme to discuss the story," Ashley said.

Little things often have a big influence, and the words we use to introduce a task can make a challenging prompt more accessible. The following tips can help:

- Use modal verbs like *might* or *could* to imply possibility rather than certitude. For example, rather than "How are the figs symbolic in this chapter?" say: "Why *might* the figs keep appearing in the chapter? If they were a symbol, what *could* they be symbolic of?"

- Make words like *reason* or *explanation* plural, for example, "What might be *some of the reasons why* figs keep appearing in this chapter?" Or use an indefinite article rather than a definite article before those words, as in, "What's a reason why the figs keep appearing in this chapter?"

- Use words that explicitly tell students you're asking them for their initial thoughts, such as *conjectures*, *hypothesis*, or *working theory*, as in, "Jot down an initial hypothesis. What is happening to the boys on the island and why?" Or, you could use the word *notes*, as in, "Take a few minutes to jot some initial notes on the changes we're starting to see in the protagonist."

Here are some examples from our *Reading Reconsidered* curriculum in which we were especially attentive to Formative language. The first is from a unit on the book *Heroes, Gods and Monsters of the Greek Myths* by Bernard Evslin.

b. Think back to the gifts Pandora received from each god. Why might Pandora be so tempted to open the box? Try to come up with more than one reason.

_____

_____

_____

By now the word *might* should stand out. Students don't have to know for sure what they think before they start writing. There's also a nice little reminder to "think back to the gifts Pandora has received" that can help students know where to direct their thinking to start generating ideas if they come slowly. And there's the phrase, "Try to come up with more than one reason." This too communicates the idea that a range of answers may suit—but also that thinking doesn't stop for a student at the first answer they generate.

Here's another example from our unit on C. S. Lewis's *The Magician's Nephew*. We hope it shows how language that remains open and allows students to play with an idea is especially useful for exploring symbolism. It starts by pulling a key line of text and asks students to reread it.

7. Reread this moment from p. 148:

The Cabby gave one glance at the Lion and took off his bowler hat: no one had yet seen him without it. When it was off, he looked younger and nicer, and more like a countryman and less like a London cabman.

Suppose that the removal of the Cabby's bowler hat is a symbolic gesture. What might it represent? Why?

_____

_____

_____

_____

This prompt suggests a sort of thought experiment. We're not even at "The gesture is symbolic, why might that be?" yet. The prompt starts with *Let's just suppose for the moment that it is . . .. .* It's such an easy and safe way to play with an idea that can be intimidating for students, while leading them to deeper, analytical understanding.

Connect Formative Writing Prompts to What Comes After

Another reason we love Jen Brimming's phrase "Jot down your first thoughts" is that it implies that students will expand and extend their thinking. There will be second thoughts. That suggests another useful bit of advice for creating Formative Writing prompts: connect them to what comes after.

For example, a page or so ago we shared an example of a Formative Writing prompt: "Why might Pandora be so tempted to open the box? Try to think of more than one reason."

Here now is a second prompt from later in that same lesson:

10. Look at the image from your Do Now again. How would you describe Pandora in this moment? How would you describe the contents of the box?

_____

_____

_____

This question does not contain *mights* and *coulds*. It's the last question from the lesson in fact and it asks students to now interpret the image of Pandora in the moment of her temptation, to do some explaining. Answering it will require students to draw on their reflections in the initial question. Perhaps they will think about her temptation differently now. Perhaps they will affirm or expand their initial thinking and connect it. Either way the question is asking for "second thoughts" and students will almost assuredly have them.

Here's another example of a Formative Writing prompt leading to further thoughts. This sequence of activities is from our unit on John Steinbeck's *Of Mice and Men*:

b. Consider how the following clauses change when revised into active voice.

Passive Voice (Original)	Active Voice (Revised)
A path <u>beaten</u> hard by tramps who come wearily down from the highway	The tramps who come wearily down from the highway <u>beat</u> a path
The limb is worn smooth by men	Men wear the limb smooth

Why might Steinbeck use passive voice in this paragraph, discussing the relationship between the **migrant workers** and the natural world?

Initial Ideas:

_____

_____

_____

_____

Discussion Notes

Additional Insights or Revisions:

_____

_____

_____

_____

The activity begins with two passages from the text extracted for closer analysis to show what passive voice is (see Chapter Eight on Close Reading) and quickly asks students to think in writing: "Why might Steinbeck use passive voice in this paragraph. . ." Again, the word *might* is doing yeoman work, supported by the heading above the lines where students actually write: "Initial Ideas." The subsequent brief "Discussion Notes" section, followed by the "Additional Insights or Revisions" writing lines, asks students to revise their initial thoughts after articulating them, discussing them, and taking notes on ideas their classmates share. This Formative prompt leads ultimately to students being asked to develop second thoughts and perhaps a firmer opinion.

Students Should Write to Expand Their "Syntactic Control"

Use short Developmental Writing prompts to cause students to think deeply about text and to expand their knowledge of the tools of expression that appear almost exclusively in writing and that are critical to perceptive reading.

To write sentences that capture the nuance and complexity of an idea, or to reflect meaningfully on different ways one might express an idea, requires something called *syntactic control*, which is the mastery of grammatical structures such as the ability to subordinate one idea to another (using any of a dozen subtly different conjunctions) or the ability to use introductory phrases of the prepositional, participial, infinitive, and conditional variety (to name a few).

The sentence "Running through the forest, she fumbled for the key she knew was in her satchel, all the while glancing over her shoulder" demonstrates more syntactic control than: "She ran through the forest. She fumbled for the key in her satchel. She was glancing over her shoulder." A writer with syntactic control might *choose* to capture the idea the second way, in short choppy sentences, but to *only* be able to write the second way is to be limited as a writer and ultimately as a reader.

As writers, students with poor syntactic control will have a limited capacity to express ideas on the page. They will often produce a string of wooden, repetitive sentences: "I think *x*; I think *y*; I think *z*." Subject-verb-object, repeat. And as we hope to have shown, writing is central to the development of complex thoughts, so a student lacking syntactic control is also less likely to think as deeply.

As readers, students with poor syntactic control will have a limited capacity to decipher complex and nuanced text. They will not read as well as they might, and they might perhaps not be able to read some authors or texts at all—Steinbeck or Toni Morrison, not to mention the Constitution of the United States of America.

That's because syntax is a bit like vocabulary—a body of knowledge composed of mastery of discrete expressive units. With traditional vocabulary, familiarity with a range of words helps us select the right one when writing and also correlates strongly with reading comprehension. As we discuss in Chapter Five, combining Active Practice—using new words in playful and challenging exercises—with lots and lots of reading—because rare words are far more likely to appear (only) in print—is the best way to expand students' vocabulary.

So too with syntax, which involves mastery of individual structures instead of individual words. And as with vocabulary, most of its less common forms appear only in writing. When was the last time you heard an appositive phrase, a phrase that, like this one, redefines and explicates a noun, used in conversation? It is a form of expression that appears overwhelmingly in print.

A student with poor mastery of different types of clauses and phrases will struggle when reading the sorts of forty-word Dickensian-benders we describe in Chapter Two. Because learning how to write using complex or unusual syntax is one of the best ways to learn how to read it, writing can be a means of expanding the range of syntax students recognize and make sense of easily when reading.

We call this type of writing *Developmental Writing*. It often consists of short exercises—perhaps asking students to write only a single sentence—that create intentional challenges to push them to expand the range of syntactic tools they use. As these exercises are short, they facilitate deliberate practice—the opportunity for the regular and intentional application of feedback.

We divide these Developmental Writing exercises into two groups: Art of the Sentence prompts, which asks students to create sentences using specific syntactic tools, and Sentence Expansion, which asks students to expand an existing "kernel" sentence in a variety of ways.

Let's dive into how each of these work.

Art of the Sentence

Here's a good example of how the first type—Art of the Sentence—might be used in a reading context. It's from our study of *The Magician's Nephew*. Question b is the relevant one.

1. a. **Turn and Task**: Answer the following questions with your partner:

- Which characters are currently in the Wood between the Worlds? How did they get there?
- Why does Polly say, "Quick...Greens!" to Digory on p. 103?
- What happens as a result?

Notes

b. Explain the events of these pages in one carefully crafted sentence. Begin with the word, "After."

_____

_____

_____

The prompt causes students to start with the introductory prepositional phrase *after* and, implicitly, to practice writing a sentence that delineates the sequence in which key events occur.

Scarcity is also a key idea here. The prompt limits students to a single sentence with which to answer a rich question about which they will have lots to say (their writing is seeded with three separate ideas from the book to reflect on). If they could answer in more sentences, they could spread their ideas out: "Polly says *x*. Digory does *y*." With just one sentence and lots to say, it has to be: "After Polly says *x*, Digory does *y* despite Uncle Andrew saying *z*."

The prompt also reminds students to write intentionally and seek quality: "In one carefully crafted sentence . . ." You can see an extension of that idea in this prompt from our unit on *Romeo and Juliet*:

c. In one artful sentence, explain how Shakespeare presents the feud as both serious and humorous. Begin your sentence with "Although..." **Challenge:** Include a quote from one of the servants.

_____

_____

_____

_____

The prompt asks students to write an "artful" sentence. We have occasionally seen teachers substitute the word *beautiful or carefully written* in similar prompts to remind students that one of the things a sentence can do is try to express an idea in a stylistically appealing way—which is, of course, something they will routinely experience as readers but might not otherwise be as attuned to.

Again we see a single sentence in which students have to combine two complex ideas but also begin with a subordinating conjunction, *although*. There's a challenge for students who enjoy the puzzle-like aspects of Developmental Writing prompts: including a quotation from one of the servants.

Here's a slightly more complex example from a unit on short stories.

4. In one artful sentence, describe the woman and her **conflict.** Try to begin your sentence with the phrase, "While the woman believes..."

_____

_____

_____

Rather than a single word like *although* or *after*, it ask students to begin with a more complex subordinate clause. It both increases the challenge and the sophistication of what successful students will write and shapes the content of what students reflect on more deliberately. Everyone in the class will attend to the gap between what the character believes and what she does.

Teachers often think of sentence starters as tools to make writing *easier* for students, but we see it as the opposite: a fun and challenging exercise that raises the level of difficulty. We—and many teachers we've observed—have experimented with causing students to practice using some really rich and unusual pieces of syntax. For instance, we might ask for sentences with the abstract subject of "one," as in: "Start your sentence: 'When one considers . . .'" or a participial phrase: "Considering the situation. . ."

Or you could try something like this prompt, from a lesson on the short story, "The Necklace," which lets students start the sentence any way they want except the simplest and most common approach:

1. Write one beautiful sentence that describes Madame Loisel. Use a form of a vocabulary word in your response and do <u>not</u> start your sentence with "Madame Loisel."

_____

_____

_____

We should note that sentence prompts aren't limited to asking students to *start* with an idea—they can simply ask for something to be *included*, such as "use an appositive phrase," "use a compound subject," "use the word *juxtaposition*," or "use the phrase *intrusive narration*."

This example from our unit on Mark Haddon's novel, *The Curious Incident of the Dog in the Night-Time,* breaks a complex developmental task into steps. Students first summarize a key scene in the novel starting with the subordinating conjunction *although* and then revise to add a key vocabulary word as an additional parameter.

b. Write a sentence that describes Christopher's experience in Paddington Station. Begin your sentence with the word "Although."

_____

_____

_____

c. Revise your sentence by adding a form of the word "**compensate**" or "**wary**" to your sentence. **Challenge:** Add both words!

_____

_____

_____

This last example is useful for another reason. One challenge with Art of the Sentence prompts has to do with the curse of expertise. It takes time, practice, and often a bit of explicit instruction to master syntactic forms. An adult who writes regularly can often write a rich sentence in response to a complex prompt, but for students who are less experienced as writers, the struggle to create could be so challenging that it might result in failed sentences or in students writing sentences without not really attending to developing understanding about the book, that is, with all their working memory focused exclusively on syntax.

For instance, if we were to ask students to describe the narrative structure of Zora Neale Hurston's *Their Eyes Were Watching God* in one sentence beginning with the phrase, "Throughout the novel . . ." some students might process their understanding of the text and develop syntactic mastery at the same time, but others might seek merely to satisfy the rules of the game. So while we love how creative these questions can be, we've found that we've had to scale back our playfulness a little at times.

This also speaks to the need to be intentional about the scope and sequence you follow in teaching students using Developmental Writing.

We learned this lesson the hard way. We included a wide range of developmental prompts in the first round of our lesson plans. Teachers and principals reported back to us that they loved the prompts but that students often struggled to answer them—they just didn't have sufficient knowledge about language and grammar to construct artful sentences. It was hard, even for eighth graders, to include an appositive in their writing when they had just a vague notion of what an appositive was. We realized that in order to support students (and teachers) in using our Developmental Writing prompts, we needed to be explicit and logical in our introduction of grammatical knowledge.

In fifth grade, we started by ensuring that students knew the difference between a subject and a predicate before teaching compound sentences and complex sentences. Next, we added simple Art of the Sentence prompts to practice this knowledge through book-relevant examples.

Cycle 1: Pages 11-13

Annotation Task: As we read, annotate details that help you answer these questions:

- What is Annemarie doing in this chapter? Why?
- Who is King Christian?

King Christian X on his horse in Copenhagen, 1940

Notes

 1. a. Write one **simple sentence** that explains what Annemarie is doing on pp. 11-12. Underline the **subject** and circle the **verb** of your sentence.

_____

_____

Cycle 3: Pages 14-16

Annotation Task: As we read, annotate any additional details you learn about the German **occupation** of Denmark and other European countries.

A **trousseau** (pronounced troo-SO) is clothing, linens (sheets, pillowcases, etc.) and other items collected by a bride for her marriage.

4. In each sentence, the **subject** and **verb** are provided. Complete the **predicate** to finish each **simple sentence**:

Annemarie wonders _____

_____

_____

Papa explains _____

_____

4

Our last step was to layer in a new skill. We focused on using a wide range of conjunctions, introducing more complex forms of syntax in each subsequent year. The results were happier students and, in most cases, better sentences.[12]

Sentence Expansion

The second form of Developmental Writing prompt we call *Sentence Expansion*. It's a concept we have borrowed and adapted from Judith Hochman and Natalie Wexler's *The Writing Revolution*.[13] As with Art of the Sentence, the unit of writing in Sentence Expansion prompts is the single sentence.

One key difference between the two is that in Sentence Expansion prompts, students are given a kernel sentence with which to start. They expand this kernel sentence in multiple ways, either by adding additional information or by extending the sentence in specific ways.

They might be given a very short sentence and be asked to practice embedding key details (who, when what, where, and why):

5. Expand the following sentence:

They were weeping human tears.

Who: ....

Where: ....

Why: ....

Expanded Sentence:

_____

_____

_____

Or they might be given a simple sentence and be asked to extend it using three different conjunctions:

6. Complete each of the following sentences:

- Annemarie and Ellen think Kirsti is naïve **because**

_____

_____

- Annemarie and Ellen think Kirsti is naïve, **but**

_____

_____

- Annemarie and Ellen think Kirsti is naïve, **so**

_____

_____

The first example helps students embed a wider variety of information in their sentences. The second builds mastery of important conjunctions and helps students see the different ways they can build a compound or complex sentence out of a simple one. And both let students start out with a complete thought *about the text* they are reading. This causes these writing exercises to place a greater emphasis on understanding the text.

Consider this example of the sentence expansion activity we use most often: Because But So[14]—so called because it asks students to expand the original sentence with those three conjunctions. It asks students to respond in writing to a scene in *The Curious Incident of the Dog in the Night-Time*.

Here, the kernel sentence states, "Christopher is overwhelmed in Paddington Station." Let's imagine for a moment what students might write:

- Christopher is overwhelmed in Paddington Station **because** it is so busy and loud, and he is sensitive to noise and confusion.

- Christopher is overwhelmed in Paddington Station, **but** he somehow still manages to get to the underground.

- Christopher is overwhelmed in Paddington Station, **so** he starts to think maybe he shouldn't have come to London after all.

Or

- Christopher is overwhelmed in Paddington Station **because** there are so many signs, and he doesn't understand that he's supposed to ignore them.

- Christopher is overwhelmed in Paddington Station, **but** he is brave and asks a woman in a shop for help.

- Christopher is overwhelmed in Paddington Station, **so** he makes his hands into a tube to focus on one thing at a time.

In addition to developing their capacity to write about multiple ideas in a single sentence, students are summarizing the scene in important ways. A sentence with *because* asks students to explain why something is happening. A sentence with *but* asks them to explain how the outcome is not simple— there are contrasting outcomes. *So* asks them to describe something that results. It is, in other words, an ideal activity to cause students to think about an important idea or scene in a text, to process it and connect it to other things they know about the story.

Consider what the students had to do to complete the *Because, But, So* activity in light of cognitive psychologist Héctor Ruiz Martín's definition of *active learning*—that is, learning that results in the growth of student knowledge. Active learning, Ruiz Martín writes, occurs when "students actively seek meaning in what they are learning, trying to relate it to their prior knowledge, reflecting on its implications for what they already know."[15]

In a sense, this is exactly what students are caused to do here. The kernel sentence directs them to a worthy learning object, and the writing activity causes them to seek meaning in it and connect it to other things they know in multiple ways.

Of course, sentence expansion activities need not exclusively focus on Because But So. We could easily use a wider range of connectors and conjunctions, as in this example from *The Magician's Nephew*:

1. Complete each of the following sentences:

- Jadis threw the bar at the Lion **in order to** _____

  _____

  _____

- Jadis threw the bar at the Lion, **but** _____

  _____

  _____

- **After** Jadis threw the bar at the Lion, _____

  _____

  _____

Or take this slightly more complex example from our unit on Laurie Halse Anderson's *Chains,* which is a bit of a fusion of Art of the Sentence and Sentence Expansion. It's a Sentence Expansion in that it provides students with a kernel sentence, but, like Art of the Sentence, it asks students to employ specific syntactic tools when expanding it.

10. Develop the kernel sentence below using the following guidelines to describe this scene.

Bellingham searched the chest.

a. Begin with the word "When."

   _____

   _____

b. Include the phrase "even though."

   _____

   _____

c. Add the conjunction "but" and explain what happened next.

   _____

   _____

A key feature of the two types of Developmental Writing activities we've described here is their combination of intentionality and brevity. They enable us to shape student thinking and writing carefully and productively but at small cost to instructional time. We can use the activities frequently and elicit very thoughtful and beneficial writing from students in short pieces—building strong habits and enabling us to do other important things in class. A second benefit of their intentionality and brevity is that they can be easily and quickly reviewed and revised. Short exercises are ideal for deliberate practice, where students quickly apply focused, intentional feedback to improve their work.

Students Should Write to Support and Explain Arguments

Use a range of prompts that cause students to build logically coherent arguments with interconnected ideas supported by evidence.

Spare a thought for the five-paragraph essay or, as we like to call it, the *5PE*. Frankly, it needed that rebrand. No one, and we mean no one, dances for joy when "begin five-paragraph essays" shows up on the agenda. 5PEs are hard to write and harder to teach. They're good for learning, sure, but also unpopular with students—and a lot of teachers.

We understand why. There's plenty of gibberish and nonsense out there parading around as next-century wisdom. With the gang over at National Council of Teachers of English advocating for "decentering book reading and essay writing," it's easy to be persuaded to "reinvent" or "reimagine" something as hard as the 5PE and have students create concept maps to make videos (or videos to make concept maps) instead. Desirable difficulty aids learning, but that doesn't mean people want to choose it, especially when it requires mastering things like topic sentences.

It doesn't take a lot of imagination to see how a large stack of essays crying out to be graded every evening could make one very receptive to the argument that the tedious work of teaching students to frame a thesis, support it with clear distinct arguments, back those with evidence, and connect them via transitions—*Ugh, just saying all that is tiring, never mind grading it*—is something worth tossing in the dumpster behind the building.

Even our catchy rebranding won't fix that.

So, 5PEs' reputation isn't great. Yet it remains a constant presence. Skeptics aside, it's still hard to graduate from most high schools without having written at least few of them. It's certainly hard to survive in college if you can't.

This is perhaps because essays—five-paragraph and otherwise—ask students to communicate in a sequence of clear, connected arguments, diligently explained and supported by evidence—a skill that has resulted in the expression of most of society's most valuable and durable ideas. The written word, assembled into long-form argument, is the "coin of the realm." It is society's primary device for expressing and transacting valuable ideas. Almost every foundation of our lives today—intellectual, philosophical, or technical—has been understood, described, and shared thanks to some slogger (Watson and Crick, say. Or Thomas Jefferson) getting it down in a sequence of clear, connected arguments, diligently explained and supported by evidence. So, it's a teacher's job to ensure students can work in the coin of the realm. There's value, it turns out, in being caused to do things we don't necessarily love to do and in being taught to do things that are hard to do. Things like writing topic sentences, assembling evidence, and connecting ideas, for example.

We call the sort of writing that asks students to explain an important idea or to support it with evidence *Summative Writing*—writing to explain and describe a complete, coherent argument. You might think of it as the baby brother or sister of the five-paragraph essay, the short form practice by which students prepare to be able to create something larger.

It is also true that students generally don't do it very well, especially in its longer forms. Not much can break a teacher's spirit like a stack of poorly written essays! But by employing the following practices, the savvy teacher can stave off this scenario by better teaching students the art of Summative Writing.

Break Essays Down into Skills and Practice

One likely reason for the stack of subpar essays so many teachers face is that the skills required to write longer-form expository are many and difficult to master. To complete an essay about a text is to engage with all of those skills at once while also trying to think about the text in question. Thus it can easily become an exercise in long-form working memory overload.

We described Summative Writing as short-form practice. This is important, as Daisy Christodoulou points out in her book *Making Good Progress?*: "Chess players don't practise [sic] by playing entire games, but by studying decomposed problems and textbook openings and endings . . . . Game situations do not offer the potential for diagnosis and improvement that practice situations do because the place such a burden on working memory."[16] Chess, like writing, requires the simultaneous execution of a complex skill set under challenging and changing circumstances. In such contexts, Christodoulou writes, "Cognitive psychology tells us that [repeating] the end task isn't always helpful for learning."[17]

In other words, one of the keys to teaching students to execute important and challenging tasks like long-form expository writing is to break the complex down into component parts. Unlike the chimerical "transferrable" skills associated with reading that we discuss in Chapter One, such as "finding the main idea" or "making an inference," expository writing really does rely on real skills, and these should be broken down and practiced discretely. This ensures that working memory is focused, not overwhelmed, and attention is maximized.

Interestingly, because working memory overloads are not just inefficient from a learning point of view but are also unpleasant for the learner, this is also likely to result in more engaged and motivated students. As Carl Hendrick reminds us, successful learning leads to motivation more than motivation leads to successful learning.[18] Making something that seemed impossible feasible to accomplish has a surprising effect on motivation. And, of course, a more effective model of teaching the complex and interwoven skills implicit in expository writing will, in helping teachers to teach it more successfully, also perhaps cause them to dislike it more themselves.

Decompose the task into subtasks: the best way to teach students to write an essay—five-paragraph or otherwise—is to design practice exercises that break down the skills involved, and let students practice the pieces one at a time rather than just repeating the task in final form. This applies to both the writing of sentences themselves, which are the building block of any writing task, and to the execution of other tasks like summarizing an idea, stating an argument, or assembling and narrating evidence. Otherwise, the result of writing essays will be students who dutifully complete multiple essays but whose writing does not improve.

Let us decompose that argument into two parts that we think teachers should apply:

- Teachers should use Developmental and Formative Writing exercises to anticipate and prepare for Summative Writing—to rehearse both the sorts of thinking and the sorts of expression it will require. This is, we hope we have shown, especially valuable at the sentence level because the sentence—the "complete thought"—is the building block of the vast majority of idea creation. But it's also valuable because students who have wrestled with an idea in a Formative Writing prompt—"What might Jonas's reaction to this memory be?"—are students who are prepared to express that idea or a similar one in a Summative format. When they do so, they will more or less already be on their second draft of the idea and more likely to be attentive to the nuances of how they discuss it.

- Teachers should use narrower and more focused Summative Writing exercises to build up to larger composite Summative Writing tasks. Yes to longer essays, but also yes (several times over) to a regular diet of shorter Summative prompts where students practice discrete skills like the creation of arguments and the assembly of evidence.

When breaking down complex tasks into component parts, it's important to actually *teach* the component parts, not just name them, "practice" them in the abstract, and then hope to watch the insightful essays pile up. Consider this story from a visit to a school we recently made, where we observed a teacher in a fourth-grade class pause in the midst of reading aloud (beautifully) a story about the role of food in an author's family and ask students to use "RACE" to respond to the question: How and why was food especially important in the author's family? RACE, as many readers will know, is an acronym for a process of responding to open-ended questions about texts. **R** for "Restate the question"; **A** for "Answer the question"; **C** for "Cite text evidence"; **E** for "Explain and extend the evidence."

It quickly became clear to us, though, that the students were overwhelmed. They were trying to understand the passage and create a response in a four-step process that was only semi-familiar to them. It was too many things for working memory to do well. Their answers were illogical and superficial: they didn't know what they were trying to say yet, but were gamely trying to use the RACE framework to come up with something.

Part of the problem was that RACE doesn't actually break a complex task down into component parts (this is one reason why we aren't a huge fan of it and don't include it, or any similar acronyms, in our curriculum). Yes, good writing usually answers the question, cites evidence, and explains it, but those steps are hard to execute well for novices. Knowing that I should cite evidence is a long way from choosing the right evidence and being able to weave it thoughtfully and clearly into an answer. And needing to restate the question likely isn't the key skill students are missing from strong writing.

Our first suggestion was that students have the opportunity to answer a similar question in a Formative Writing prompt first. For example: "Why might the author have described the foods her family cooked in the way that they did? Do any words strike you as particularly important?"

After that they might refine their ideas by discussing—just a minute or two would likely be enough to help. Then the teacher could move to RACE or, even better, ask students to answer the question but narrow the focus to executing one of the skills implicit in, say, "explaining the evidence." For example: "Choose a sentence from the essay and explain how it is typical of the author's perspective on food." Or "Choose one of the author's family members and explain how one statement they make is typical of their perspective on food." Those skills, in contrast to repeating the question, will become the building blocks of a clear argument.

Here are some classroom examples that illustrate what we mean by these two ideas: aligning Formative and Developmental Writing prompts to later Summative prompts and designing Summative prompts so they enable students to master component skills one at a time.

One of our favorites is from our unit on Lois Lowry's *The Giver,* in which students are asked to reflect on Lowry's description of Gabriel's eyes:

 3. Reread these lines from p. 26:

> *Now, seeing the newchild and its expression, he was reminded that the light eyes were not only a **rarity** but gave the one who had them a certain look—what was it? Depth, he decided; as if one were looking into the clear water of the river, down to the bottom, where things might **lurk** which hadn't been discovered yet. He felt self-conscious, realizing that he, too, had that look.*
>
> **rarity**: something that almost never happens
> **lurk**: to hide in a threatening way

a. Why might Jonas compare looking into Gabriel's eyes to looking into a river? Think literally and figuratively.

Literal	Figurative

Note that students first reread a passage and write formatively about it: "Why *might* Jonas compare looking into Gabriel's eyes to looking into a river?" The prompt and the two-part space in which they answer it pushes them to think on both a literal and figurative level. Now, having reflected about eyes in a low-stakes way and having been encouraged to think about the idea on two levels (literal and figurative), students are asked to complete a very simple Summative prompt: "How does looking into Gabriel's eyes make Jonas feel? Why does it make Jonas feel this way?"

b. How does looking into Gabriel's eyes make Jonas feel? Why does it make Jonas feel this way?

_____

_____

_____

Students are asked merely to execute the single task of explaining a character's reaction. But they've already rehearsed it, so now they are able to think about crafting it more intentionally. They're given one round for the initial thinking; another to refine it.

Here's another example from our unit on *Freak the Mighty*, by Rodman Philbrick. Again, the prompt starts by asking students to reread and analyze a piece of text. This is a discrete skill in itself, one they are practicing repeatedly. Here, there isn't an explicitly Formative Writing prompt. Instead, there is a two-part Summative prompt. First, explain what Max is saying, then how the unexpected context influenced him. Separating the thinking into parts lets students go step-by-step. And presenting a piece of text helps them just focus on interpreting, not sourcing text.

5. Consider the descriptions of the two people Max and Freak meet on p. 65:

Loretta Lee	Iggy Lee
Now she's standing in the doorway, this scrawny, yellow-haired woman with small, hard eyes and blurry red lips. She's wearing this ratty old bathrobe and she's smoking this cigarette and squinting at us and making a face.	Next this there's this big hairy dude in the doorway, he's got a huge beer gut and these giant arms all covered with blue tattoos and he's got a beard that looks like it's made out of red barbed wire.

a. What is Max emphasizing about each person in the descriptions above?

_____

_____

b. What were Max and Freak expecting from this quest? What have they found instead? How might that contrast influence the way Max describes Loretta and Iggy?

_____

_____

_____

Here's a third example. It's actually of a Developmental Writing prompt—a Because But So—but notice its purpose: to cause students to practice incorporating direct quotations into their sentences smoothly. This is a discrete skill students are often quite poor at. They drop in a quotation with little framing. So here, students are building familiarity with skills they will use in their essay writing, piece-by-piece.

5. Complete the following sentences:

- "Slaves," Douglass writes, "almost universally say they are contented, and that their masters are kind"

  because _____

  _____

- "Slaves," Douglass writes, "almost universally say they are contented, and that their masters are kind,"

  but _____

  _____

- "Slaves," Douglass writes, "almost universally say they are contented, and that their masters are kind,"

  so _____

  _____

Here's a final example, again from our unit on *The Giver*. It's similar to the others we've shared in that it asks for Summative Writing while narrowing the topic to focus on a single task, but notice that it includes five different short excerpts pulled from across six pages. Instead of writing about a single moment in the text, students have to construct a very short argument that considers and summarizes multiple examples and multiple pieces of evidence.

8. Consider the following lines from today's reading:

- *He wanted to share them, but he wasn't eager to begin the process of sifting through his own complicated emotions, even with the help that he knew his parents could give.* (p. 6)

- *Lily's feelings were always straightforward, fairly simple, usually easy to resolve.* (pp. 8-9)

- *"Oh no," Mother murmured sympathetically. "I know how sad that must make you feel."* (p. 9)

- *One by one, they comforted her. Soon she smiled, thanked them, and murmured that she felt soothed.* (p. 12)

- *This evening he almost would have preferred to keep his feelings hidden. But it was, of course, against the rules.* (p. 12)

How would you describe this **ritual**? What purpose does it seem to serve?

_____

_____

_____

_____

We've discussed the benefit of smaller iterations of writing for students, which enables them to write more frequently, to be more intentional and to think about what quality looks like at a smaller task. That's true of Formative and especially Developmental Writing—the whole point of the latter is to build mastery of the sentence—but also of Summative tasks. Smaller exercises done with greater intentionality make it easier for teachers to fit lots of writing into their lessons.

Connect Summative Prompts to Each Other to Build Skills Back Up

We talked previously about connecting Formative Writing prompts to what comes after, including Summative prompts. But you can also link Summative prompts to one another, often in progression, "building up" the skills they "break down." The idea is to have students practice these skills more discretely, then ask them to use them to organize larger arguments. It's important to make sure that students practice building full arguments—our short Summative prompts don't replace longer tasks like the five-paragraph essay; they prepare students for them. In light of that, building the pieces back up is important.

We try to do just that in this example from our unit on the *Magician's Nephew*. You'll notice that we've identified this as a Summative prompt. We want students (and teachers) to be consciously aware that they are now beginning to link skills that they will need to connect to write longer pieces.

Here there are two questions to answer—what was the emotional state the music evoked in each character; why was it different and what does that show—and also evidence to provide.

Summative Writing

Prompt: Recall this quote from George Whitfield Andrews in the article we read previously:

Other arts have power to act thus upon the soul, but probably none so intensely and universally. [...] Music born of intelligence and imagination and fired by emotion has rare power to create emotional states.

Contrast the "emotional states" caused by the music in Digory and Uncle Andrew. Given what we know about these characters, what might this contrast tell us about the new world? Include at least two pieces of evidence in your response.

Note that the prompt asks students to do something both difficult and characteristic of five-paragraph essays—to apply an external quotation to their discussion of the text, to use it as a lens. If you've taught a lot of expository writing you know how hard a task like that can be for students—of course it is, they rarely have the opportunity to practice it anywhere else! Here they get that practice.

There are still elements of practice in this task, then, but there are also elements of something more complex. If students have been doing writing "drills" throughout the unit, they're now "scrimmaging." This isn't a full-on essay yet—that would involve creating a full argument about the full text or at least a chapter of it, or it might ask students to compare Digory and Uncle Andrew more extensively. Perhaps, *How do Digory and Uncle Andrew act and react during their time in Narnia? What does this reveal about the differences between Narnia and the real world?* Perhaps the response to this Summative Writing prompt or one like it would comprise a paragraph within that larger argument. If so, students would likely be more successful at writing that essay, having practiced the component parts in a slightly simplified setting.

Students Should Write Beforehand to Improve Discussion

Writing before discussion helps students refine what they will say and participate with confidence. It also frees their working memory, enabling them to listen more effectively to their peers. Finally it enables a teacher to "see" the ideas students are generating and select participants intentionally.

Our purpose in this chapter is to describe the ways that the strategic use of writing in classrooms can help make students better readers. Given the importance of discussion in most English and reading classes, it's worth pointing out some of the ways that writing, especially when it occurs just beforehand, can make discussion more productive and inclusive.

Let us introduce this idea via two tiny moments from the video *Jessica Bracey: Writing and Memory* in which we can see how students experience discussion from a cognitive perspective. Jessica Bracey was a fifth-grade teacher at North Star Academy in Newark, New Jersey, at the time of the video, which starts while she is holding a brief discussion with her class about *Circle of Gold* by Candy Dawson Boyd. At the start of the video she calls on a student named Omar. Just before that, however, Omar and all of his peers wrote briefly in response to Jessica's question about the book. The writing happened immediately after the reading, before discussion, directly from the text. This is important.

To watch the video *Jessica Bracey: Writing and Memory*, use this QR code or find the video at the URL https://vimeo.com/1058366710/8db8b46e5f.

Omar doesn't strike us as one of those highly verbal students who raise their hand over and over. He's a bit hesitant, a little nervous—he's willing to raise his hand but perhaps not always. He's a student we want to encourage to participate more and cause to participate successfully.

But observe some things about his answer. First, note that despite his hint of nervousness, his answer is pretty thorough: "I think Toni's plan is to act like she's not Mattie's friend anymore so she can find out who stole the bracelet and to find out if Angel is pulling a game on who stole the bracelet." He could be done the first time he says, "who stole the bracelet." He's shared a complete thought about the book at that point and has done what might typically be expected of him. But he keeps going and shares a second insight—Angel might be deceiving Toni. He's not yet 100 percent comfortable doing so but he *wants* to contribute to the discussion.

But also watch his eyes as he's answering. He looks at Jessica at first and then glances down as he speaks, then back at Jessica again. He's not reading his answer, he's describing it. But he looks down to remind himself of what he wrote, to refresh his working memory.

Having written an answer first, before discussion, has caused several beneficial things to happen for Omar. First, it's ensured that he has thought deeply so he has something to say. But also writing it out aids his confidence. If he forgets, he can glance down and remind himself of his point. He doesn't have to worry about freezing or about losing track of his thoughts—an easy thing to do, we all know from experience. The writing provides a safety net.

This reveals a simple but useful insight: students—especially students who might otherwise be hesitant—are likely to say more and participate with more confidence if they have written first. Writing democratizes and improves participation in discussion. It's no coincidence that almost every student in the class has raised their hand to participate.

Now watch Danielle, the second student to speak. If you liked Omar's answer, you'll love Danielle's—it's full of thoughtful earnestness. She wants to show in her response how much the question and perhaps the book matter to her.

"I agree and I would like to add that Toni's plan is to also [show] that she's not Mattie's friend any more, she says, but I would like to add that she is also doing this because, like Omar said, she wants to figure out who stole the bracelet, and I think she's also doing this to try to trick Charlene and Angel into thinking that they're not friends and they're separated now so she can really see what they're really thinking inside of them really deeply to think who really stole the bracelet or if it's a trick," she says.

Look at Danielle's affect. Her answer reveals a sincere desire to capture the experience of the characters in the book. Danielle is giving her absolute best, not just in her effort to answer the question but also, importantly, to work in collaboration with Omar, to talk to, not past, her classmates and connect her ideas to theirs.

She notes at the outset that she agrees with Omar and would like to add to his idea. She circles back and drops another reference to Omar's remarks in the middle of her comment: "like Omar said." Her actions say: "I listened to what Omar said. His words matter to me. He has my respect."

This is made possible, in part, perhaps, because Jessica has written a brief summary of Omar's comment on the board, and because Jessica has reminded the class to use Habits of Discussion—that is, to build off of and make explicit reference to one another's remarks.

The short-form notes on the board are valuable. They make it easier for subsequent participants like Danielle to remember what various classmates have said. That's smart. How many times in a meeting have you forgotten who said what? One of the primary reasons students—and adults!—don't connect ideas well in a discussion is because they forget them. The notes on the board help students to remember. And they socialize students to take notes themselves. Jessica is modeling behaviors that will help students remember what they talk about. That's not insignificant. Teachers often invest a lot of time in discussion, but as we explain in Chapter One, much of the "understanding" they achieve goes the way of most things in working memory. It is forgotten.

You can read more about the Habits of Discussion technique in Doug's book *Teach Like a Champion 3.0*, but it's important to note here how central the technique's purpose—fostering listening behaviors—is to a productive discussion. How well participants listen is at least as important as what they say. When Danielle references Omar's comments while making her own, she reminds him that his words matter to his peers in the class. She makes it more likely that he will want to speak again. And he is more likely to be honest and thoughtful, to say what he really thinks. People only do that when they feel psychological safety, "a shared belief held by members of a team that it's okay to take risks, to express their ideas and concerns, to speak up with questions, and to admit mistakes—all without fear of negative consequences."[19]

Psychological safety occurs when participants in the group give and receive constant "signals of connection" between and among them writes Daniel Coyle.[20] Those signals of connection include eye contact and body language—if there are heads nodding, if people look interested, if someone jots down your idea. But perhaps the biggest signal is whether people's subsequent comments place value on what you have said. If they make reference to your ideas, especially by name—"it's like Omar said"—you are far more likely to speak and far more likely to say what you really think.

Psychological safety is profoundly important in any group context. According to Amy Edmonson, professor of organizational behavior at the Harvard Business School and the first to coin the term, "it shapes the learning behavior of the group and in turn affects team performance."[21]

The "learning behavior of the group" is important everywhere in classrooms but especially in discussions, particularly discussions of books that present important and challenging ideas. There's not much point in having them if people don't want to speak and to share their opinions and observations. There's no way to know if the kind of honesty and openness to ideas we imagine being a part of our discussions exists in a given classroom, but we do know that it does not generally occur in most spaces in American public life more broadly. The majority of Americans disguise their opinions when they discuss them in public because they feel social pressure and fear they will be criticized or misunderstood.[22]

But when people signal that they are listening to us and value our words, we feel safe to speak and take risks. This is what is appears to be happening in Jessica's classroom, so it's worth asking how and why Danielle is able to send those *I am listening and I take your words seriously* signals so effectively. Surely much of that is down to Danielle and her individual character and effort. But there are other factors.

Consider how a less thoughtful student than Danielle might have started her remarks. She might have said, "What I was going to say is. . ." Tacitly this says to Omar: *What you just said is mostly irrelevant to me. I'm going to say exactly what I was going to say before you spoke. Your words did not influence me at all.* If that happens often enough, Omar will learn to stop speaking.

Students begin their comments in class this way all the time, and we're confident they don't intend to send a negative message. Most likely they say things like "What I was going to say is . . ." because, while their classmates are speaking, they are not listening. They can't. They are trying not to forget what they wanted to say. Working memory is tiny. We can only hold one or maybe two ideas there at a time. It is often a choice between listening well and remembering something you want to add to the conversation. When students begin their comments with phrases like "What I wanted to say is . . ." they are mostly expressing their relief that they can finally let go of the idea they've been anxiously holding in their working memory.

But since Jessica has asked her students to write down their thoughts, Danielle's are there in front of her. She knows that she can glance at them at any time to refresh her memory of them. Having written first, she does not have to choose between remembering her ideas and listening to Omar.

You can literally see the evidence of this in the video. Notice Danielle's eyes while she is speaking. She starts talking and then glances down at the page where she has written her thoughts. She does this several times, refreshing her working memory of her ideas, combining them with what she's heard from Omar.

That is a simple but profound fact about human cognition: when we write things down, we free ourselves to listen better.

If the purpose of discussions in reading and English classrooms is to share insights and observations about the text, the fact that writing first allows more students to participate confidently and with more to say causes people to listen better and therefore learn more from one another. We suddenly have a very powerful tool.

But in fact there's more. One downside of discussion is that duration often exceeds value. We make this observation lovingly but based on many, of hours of observation in classrooms. Discussions can go on for a long time with the value added by the ongoing comments uncertain at best. In fact we have seen more than one teacher try to cure a discussion that just isn't going anywhere by letting it go on longer! Maybe something interesting will be shared. If nothing else, talking for a long time will express that the topic is important.

We are big fans of a short and highly valuable exchange of ideas. A discussion of two or three minutes can accomplish a lot. And what happens in minutes four through ten may be largely redundant. We're not against longer discussions, mind you, but if they are going to happen we should make sure they result in learning.

One issue we often see with discussions is that the topic is unclear. More than once we have wondered from the back of the classroom, are we talking about something specific, or are we just talking here? One reason students lose sight of the topic is that they literally lose sight of the topic. It's surprisingly easy to forget what exactly the question is, especially when participants have to hold it in their working memory. In that case, the more they think about the topic the more the memory of the exact question is likely to get driven out of working memory. So our department of super simple teaching hacks suggests writing or projecting the question where participant can see it throughout the discussion. That way they can remind themselves of it. Or you can subtly remind them with a gesture.

We also think it's important to remember that discussions need not end in resolution. In fact one very useful thing to do in a discussion—especially if it is midstream while you are reading a book—is to merely surface ideas: "Let's hear three or four possible explanations for Madame Loisel's actions and then we'll pick up reading."

Look at us! Digressing ourselves as we discuss the topic of digressions. So let us return to the theme: how writing can help.

Writing can help teachers both achieve more value—insight shared per minute of duration—and more transfer—the degree to which what we talk about gets remembered—from discussion:

- **More value.** Asking students to write briefly before a discussion not only enables students to prepare, it enables teachers to prepare. You can circulate while students are jotting down their ideas and gather insights about what to talk about and who, perhaps, should do more of the talking. You could for example ask for a volunteer to start discussion. Jessica Bracey does this, and Omar does an admirable job. But if we want to maximize value—we know we only have four minutes to discuss and we want some important observations to emerge—why not walk around as students do their prewriting and choose intentionally? For example, if Angelique has noticed something really important that no one else noticed, we could start the discussion by asking her to share. What might have taken five minutes to emerge has now started the conversation. Or perhaps you noticed that while the majority of students think Monsieur Loisel is a fool, Thomas sees it differently. Instead of asking, "Does anyone have a *different* opinion?" possibly three or four times, you could simply say, "Thomas, you disagree. Tell us more . . ." and away we go, having skipped three or four not-as-productive answers to "does anyone have a *different* opinion?"

- **More transfer.** In Chapter One we discuss the fact that most of what we think about in our working memory gets forgotten. Understanding—and insight in the midst of discussion while the ending of Chapter Twelve is still in everyone's working memory—is not yet learning. Action is required after discussions or they will often be for naught. Happily, one of the most effective ways to encode ideas in long-term memory is to write them down. So the perfect thing to do after a discussion is to say something like "Great discussion. Take thirty seconds to jot your two most important takeaways in your notes." That way the time you've invested in discussion will be more likely to result in learning. The topic of writing at the end of discussion and other activities is one we will discuss further in the final sections of this chapter.

Students Should "Stamp" Ideas in Writing

We call a short, written summary employed to build the writer's memory of a key concept from class a stamp, *a term we borrow from Paul Bambrick Santoyo, author and Chief Schools Officer for Uncommon Schools.*

Stamp can be a noun or a verb. At the end of reading, discussion, or analysis, we "stamp" our takeaway, describing what we've learned briefly, prioritizing deliberately as we go and seeking to encode it in our memory. Its purpose is to cause us to remember important things we've thought about. (And, if we're honest, we like the word *stamp* over *summary*, because it avoids the confusion with Summative Writing.)

Stamping builds memory because of the desirable difficulty experienced by students when they write. The generation effect, you will recall from Chapter One, is a principle of cognitive psychology that tells us that actively producing arguments during encoding acts to improve later memory".[23] As Daniel Willingham writes in *Why Don't Students Like School*, "Memory is the residue of thought."[24] Writing, leads to strong encoding. When we work hard to think about a learning object—a passage from a novel, say, or our interpretation of it—we remember it better, especially if we are caused to describe it in spoken words or, even better, in writing.

This is one reason why writing notes by hand generally leads to better memory and subsequent understanding than does taking notes on a computer, as we preview in Chapter One. Handwriting is effortful and slow. When taking notes while listening, we can't directly "transcribe" as we would when typing, which means we have to prioritize what we write down, to think hard in the moment about what the information we are hearing means and about what's actually important.

This helps combat one of the primary defects of discussion: the fact that much—probably most—of what is said and thought in them is lost. "Learning," Paul Kirschner, John Sweller, and Richard Clark tell us, is a "change in long-term memory."[25] During discussion, working memory can be engaged in thinking, even deep thinking, without any of that insight being retained in long-term memory. Students can be listening well, connecting ideas, and understanding without any of that learning sticking. Stamping the insights at the end of a discussion is particularly important: without it, much of the benefits of discourse will be lost.

Similarly, when we ask students to write summaries of what they have read or discussed, we are combining the deliberate effort of writing—hammering ideas into words—with the challenge of prioritization, of choosing what matters. The Carnegie Corporation of New York's 2010 report, "Writing to Read: Evidence for How Writing Can Improve Reading," notes, "For students in grades 3–12, writing summaries about text showed a consistently positive impact on reading comprehension." They point out that this is especially true for lower-achieving students: "In twelve studies involving such students, the average weighted effect size for writing about a text was 0.63."[26] Using stamping to summarize can help break a complex narrative into manageable chunks for memory.

Successful stamps tend to share the following qualities. View these as general rules of thumb rather than strict guidelines:

- **Brevity is beneficial.** Prioritization is thinking about meaning, which we know is central to encoding ideas in memory. A short stamp is often as good—or better—than a long one. You might say, "Glance back over the notes on the board and take a minute to stamp the most important ideas from our discussion in just one or two sentences."

- **Cause students to shape their thoughts in new verbiage.** Peps McCrea observes that the power of summary lies in "reworking the main ideas in one's own words to deepen comprehension."[27] So, a key element of a stamp is to cause students to shape their thoughts in new verbiage and not just parrot words and phrases from the text. This ensures they have to reflect deliberately on the words they choose. For instance, you might say, "Take a moment now to try to describe the lesson of the myth. Try not to borrow too many phrases from what we've read. Try to put it in your own words."

- **Connect the stamp to previous writing and thinking tasks.** If you can make a record of the previous tasks visible so that students don't have to try to hold them in their working memory while also writing and thinking, all the better. This is one reason why teachers—or students—making visible notes on discussion points is so important. It enables students to refer to one another's ideas as they discuss and also to glance back at them later and use them in a summary. A good stamp prompt could be "Glance back over the notes on the board and take a minute to stamp the most important ideas from our discussion." Another is "Glance back at your original response and now revise it in light of our discussion."

To watch the video *Arielle Hoo: Conjectures Part 2*, use this QR code or find the video at the URL https://vimeo.com/1058366865/a25026e79b.

Previously in the chapter, we showed you a video from Arielle Hoo's math classroom. In *Arielle Hoo: Conjectures Part 2*, Arielle concludes the discussion about coincidental and parallel lines with an exemplary use of a stamp that applies the three characteristics of a good stamp. Even though this occurs in a math classroom, we think it shows us how to use a stamp effectively in a reading classroom.

Right before the stamp, Arielle asks students to summarize what they've heard in the discussion and put it all together: "Who can give me a statement talking about what they hear from . . . each of your peers and make one nice statement?" She's asking them to connect multiple arguments, to summarize the key points in the discussion. Note also the element of Developmental Writing: asking Kaylyn to begin "If you algebraically solve a system . . ." means she will have to use advanced syntax to stamp the idea.

Kaylyn's stamp is public—that is, Arielle asks Kaylyn to craft it in real time. Note that, as Arielle transcribes her answer and supports with clarifications and amplifications, everyone else is writing it down, too. She could just as easily have had students write their stamps privately, with everyone writing their own version in their notes. In that case, she would certainly have spread the thinking more. But there's often a trade-off between precision and universality of thinking; this way, Arielle is able to make sure a very high quality, precise summation of the concept exists in students' notes.

Note, too, that Arielle has kept a version of the problem the students had discussed on the board as students stamp so that it remains in their working memory, causing students to focus on sense-making rather than mere remembering.

We can think of a few similar ways to support working memory and thus better analysis and long-term memory in reading class: you might project the passage from the text you are discussing (annotated from the discussion, perhaps) on the board. Or you might project a series of shorter excerpts taken from different places in the text on the board, and ask students to weave them together. (We'll share more examples of what this might look like in the final chapter of this book on Close Reading.)

Students Should Revise Their Writing Regularly in Shorter, Deliberate Bursts

Revision and rewriting are powerful, creating opportunities for metacognition and idea improvement, but while many teachers mostly ask for revision of longer pieces of student writing, we argue here for more frequent rewriting of very short pieces.

Revising their writing, going back to change it based on new information or to refine it based on greater awareness of what it communicates, is one of the most metacognitive and demanding tasks students can engage in. Seeing one's ideas grow and improve is powerful and gratifying—visible progress leads to motivation as much or more than motivation leads to progress, Carl Hendrick reminds us.[28] And the message that your first impression—your first "hot take," to put it in the language of social media—is probably not fully and completely correct, especially when engaging in something as complex as, say, a novel that has stood the test of time, is a good one for students to internalize.

So, there is gold to be had in regular revising. Yet, it's something we think our schools could get a lot better—and a lot more efficient—at. We outline two common pitfalls in how teachers often think of revising, then suggest some better ways to incorporate revision into the classroom.

Pitfall 1: Conflating Editing and Revising

One challenge is that we often conflate editing and revising. The former task is about mechanics and the latter is about meaning making, which makes it the harder of the two by far. It's important to remember that distinction; otherwise, it's easy to default to simpler mechanical editing tasks and not require of students the more demanding metacognitive aspects of revision.

Hochman and Wexler describe revising as "clarifying or altering the content or structure of a draft." That could mean simple ideas like varying sentence structure, replacing a passive verb with an active one, using a more precise term of an idea, or inserting an additional clause or sentence or paragraph—or, as Hochman and Wexler note, the opposite: "For many writers it may mean eliminating unnecessary verbiage."[29]

These tasks are difficult and technically demanding and require the student to think deeply about meaning. That phrase, "think deeply about meaning," is important because it is essentially the definition of learning. "Active learning could better be defined as learning by thinking . . . in which the student actively thinks about the learning object, seeking meaning and comparing it to their prior knowledge," Héctor Ruiz Martín writes.[30] When students revise writing about something they are in the process of learning, they are engaged in some of the most effective "active learning" possible.

Editing, by contrast, rarely causes students to think about what their sentence means and the ideas they were trying to communicate. Instead, it involves tasks like "correcting errors in grammar, punctuation capitalization, syntax and spelling," Hochman and Wexler write. Although these tasks are still important, especially to the presentation of ideas, they are not as cognitively demanding.

One result is that "most teachers focus on editing, probably because they are more comfortable with the mechanics and rules of writing. Similarly, if you ask students to improve on a piece of writing they're likely to make mechanical changes," Hochman and Wexler point out. But "adding a comma . . . isn't nearly as complex as imagining what a reader needs to know."[31]

Pitfall 2: Only Revising Essays

Revising gets crowded out for other reasons as well. One is that it is often exclusively applied to longer essay writing. The good news is that we rarely have students write longer essays without invoking "the writing process"—the idea that students will write drafts in the course of finalizing. But the bad news is that the essay is a massive unit of analysis in which to revise and refine one's thinking. This dilutes the quality and frequency of the task.

When you give students feedback on a five-paragraph essay, for example, it takes a long time to get the information back to them. They may not remember well what they were thinking when they get the feedback three or four weeks later. It's also hard to use that feedback intentionally. Rewriting an entire essay in order to use a key piece of guidance—active verbs!—is inefficient and time-consuming. And there's likely to be lots of nonspecific guidance given but not taught. Feedback like "This sentence is unclear" or "You've used the wrong word here" might be true, but they are mostly useless to a student paging through your notes on their essay. Most of what you've written will be neither applied nor understood. The amount and quality of the student's actual reflection on meaning is often quite low, a point a teacher we know emphasized in this recollection: "I'd write scores of comments. They'd take an hour minimum. And when I asked my students to revise, they'd fix a comma splice, change one word, and turn it back in saying, 'There. I revised it.'"

In fact, it's hard to *not* give excessive and unusable amounts of feedback on essays. If my student spends weeks—or even hours—making an argument about Lorraine Hansberry's *A Raisin in the Sun* and my feedback only notes her passive verb tenses, she's going to feel a bit cheated. But I can't only comment on her argument if her verb tenses are a mess, so I have to comment on both. This is all to say that the incentives for how we give feedback often push us to overload student working memory.[32]

Revision, Revised

To address these pitfalls, we suggest instead something unorthodox: revision should be focused on shorter, more informal forms of student writing, often even a single sentence, that happen more frequently. This way, feedback is easier to give and apply, and it can be used right away. When the unit of analysis is small, it can be projected on a screen and studied. Bruce Sadler writes that every sentence is a composition in miniature.[33] By revising those miniature compositions as they occur, multiple times a week, we can make a robust habit of it. An additional bonus: giving feedback on lower-stakes writing often means students are more receptive to taking feedback or experimenting with its application.

Rather than trying to talk about everything at once, shorter pieces of revision enable us to draw on the science of deliberate practice, which tells us that intentionality matters. "Let's work on precise word choice"; "Let's work on active verbs"; "Let's go through and take out all the extraneous words": those are powerful ways to prompt students to revise.

To watch the video *Jen Brimming: Add to your sentence*, use this QR code or find the video at the URL https://vimeo.com/1058367274/e0cfa584e0.

Jen Brimming does this in the video *Jen Brimming: Add to your sentence*, the second half of the *Lord of the Flies* lesson we saw previously in the chapter. She intentionally derives a few key skills by sharing examples of student writing on the visualizer moments after they've written them, then she asks the class to apply the feedback to their own answers right away.

You'll notice how technical and concrete Jen is able to get because she is projecting the sentences she is discussing to the class on the visualizer. Because the students can look at the sentences while thinking about them or while the teacher guides them through an explanation of them, they can constantly refresh their working memory about what's being said. They don't have to remember, and so they can just think. If you want to maximize the revision process, you have to make the object of study visible to everyone.

To watch the video *Britt Carson: Stored*, use this QR code or find the video at the URL https://vimeo.com/1058367756/538f5c99b6.

You can see the value of revising short units of writing in a way visible to everyone in the video *Britt Carson: Stored*. Britt is editing student writing in her science class at Memphis Rise Academy in Memphis, Tennessee, but everything she does can be applied to writing and revising in English and reading classes.

The writing prompt she's using is short—just one sentence: "Describe how the book's energy changed from position one to the position you drew it in." She asks students to use the word *stored* to refer to energy and to include either *more* or *less*. As students write, it's easy for Britt to assess their ability to capture this idea clearly because she doesn't have to look at whole paragraphs. She's quickly able to choose a few examples of student work that will be useful to study then project them to the class.

One student has written, "The book's energy changed from position one to position two because position two is higher than position one."

"This response told us how the energy changed," Britt says. "Let's see what we can add on to this sentence to make it even better."

Melissa suggests adding "It stores energy in its height," a much more accurate and technical description of what's happening to the energy, but a phrase that may be difficult to add to the sentence—particularly for the poorest writers in the room—so Britt models how to incorporate the phrase, marking up the sentence on the screen as she speaks so that students can see where and how and make a similar change to their own sentence.

"We're missing a comparison word like *more* or *less*," she says before asking, "Where could I put a comparison word in this sentence?" Note that she's pointing to the exact sentence she is referring to, directing students' attention to focus on the thing they need to think about.

"Dasha, where should I put it?"

"After *stores*," Dasha relays, and everyone understands the revision she's proposing because they are all looking at the same sentence and can see Britt make the change: "We could say it 'stores more energy in its height.'"

"Circle the word *more* if you wrote it in your sentence. If you didn't add it in like I just did in this sentence," she continues, and every pencil in the room is scribbling away. Within about a minute's time, the students who did not write correctly now understand and have made the change.

PUTTING IT ALL TOGETHER

Let's turn to the clip *Emily Fleming: Why Is Homily Worried?* to see an excellent example of how many of the principles from this chapter can be incorporated at the same time.

The clip begins with Emily's year 4, or third-grade, students reading aloud from Mary Norton's *The Borrowers*. After Emily has students participate in an initial Formative Writing task that has them all scribbling away—"Stop and Jot: What could be the reason as to why Homily is so worried about Pod?"—the students share their thinking in a Turn and Talk, then engage in a beautiful, whole-class discussion in which they carefully listen to and build off of one another.

To watch the video *Emily Fleming: Why Is Homily Worried?*, use this QR code or find the video at the URL https://vimeo.com/10583 67904/0e665f3679.

Chanshelle starts it: "Homily is worried about Pod because Pod has not been back from his visit to the second floor," she begins. (She has a lot more to say on the topic. Writing first tends to do that.)

As she speaks, Emily makes notes about her comments on the SMART Board. (She could just as easily write it on the board in pen.) This makes it easy for students to remember key points made by their classmates in the discussion—to refer to them if they speak, and to use them in their stamp later.

"Who can build?" Emily asks as some students signal with a fist-stacking gesture that they want to respond to Chantelle's comment. When Tyler and Daisy respond, deliberately trying to connect their insights to Chantelle's original idea, Emily again makes note of their observations on the SMART Board where students can see them.

After Emily asks a follow-up question—"What will the impact be on the family if Pod doesn't survive?"—and Ernie weighs in with another thoughtful and expansive remark, Emily directs the students to update their notes to incorporate key ideas from the discussion. By doing so, Emily both socializes listening and communicates that writing down insights from classmates is important. They have a space on their student packets dedicated to that purpose, and Emily's notes are still posted on the board to help them remember what was said.

Next, Emily asks the students to rewrite their answers to the original prompt—to stamp what they have learned during the discussion.

What Emily is doing in this clip combines several of the principles we've described in this chapter. There's Formative Writing to start—a low-stakes, think-in-writing prompt to cause everyone to reflect. There's eager participation and careful listening to peers by students who have written first and unburdened their working memory. There's visual note-taking of comments to facilitate revision, and then there's the chance to revise based on the discussion.

This sequence is so powerful that we've tried to capture it in this template:

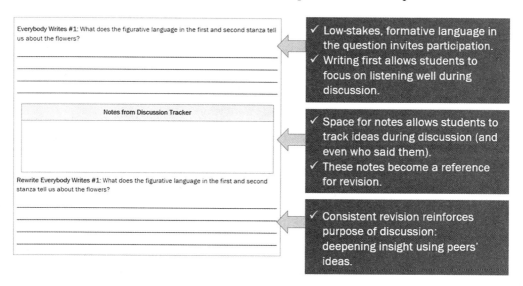

It puts together key ways to make writing about a text more powerful and to unlock more synergies with discussion.

CHAPTER RECAP

- **Students should "think in writing."** Writing is more than a technology for expressing what we already think. It is a tool for discovery—powerful, not despite the fact that it is slow, deliberate and iterative, but because of these attributes. We call writing that students do before they know what the answer is *Formative Writing*.

- **Students should write to expand their "syntactic control."** "Syntactic control," Bruce Sadler[34] writes, is "the ability to create a variety of sentences that clearly express an intended meaning." Exercises and activities that improve syntactic control in writing—that help students use a variety of subordinating conjunctions effectively, say—also help students make sense of those same elements of syntax when they are reading. We call writing that intentionally challenges students to use and develop mastery over a range of syntactic forms *Developmental Writing*.

- **Students should write to support and explain arguments.** Writing, as we've noted, is the means by which people craft "arguments": logical progressions of linked ideas, presented in sequence. We call writing that causes students to practice the craft of creating arguments to explain a complex thesis or to support an idea with evidence *Summative Writing*. It is valuable and important to distinguish from Formative and Developmental Writing, especially because the diet of the typical student is likely to contain a lot more of it than the two other types.

- **Students should write to improve discussion.** Writing beforehand is a key way to maximize the benefits offered by discussions of texts, including developing shared interpretations and creating the chance for students to reconcile their own perceptions of a text with those of others. Writing first optimizes discussion by freeing students' working memory and enabling them to listen more effectively. It enables more students to participate with confidence. And it enables a teacher to see the ideas students are generating and select intentionally where to begin discussion or who can bring a key observation at a critical time.

- **Students should "stamp" ideas in writing.** Writing is one of the most effective ways to build memory of a topic. Think intentionally or even talk about a concept you have studied and you may remember bits and pieces, but write about it and you are likely to remember far more. Writing about what they read is especially critical for students as it helps to encode their growing understanding in memory so it is retained rather than lost. We borrowed the term *stamp* from our colleague Paul Bambrick Santoyo to refer to writing that is used to briefly encapsulate takeaways from a discussion or other class activity while reading.

- **Students should revise their writing regularly in shorter, deliberate bursts.** When writing is an iterative process involving both drafting and revision, it allows the greatest opportunities for metacognition and idea improvement, and is most likely to result in attentiveness to and mastery of the craft of writing. That is, it is most likely to result in students' understanding of how text makes meaning and thus how to be better readers.

Notes

1. R. A. Bjork, "Memory and Metamemory Considerations in the Training of Human Beings," in *Metacognition: Knowing About Knowing*, J. Metcalfe and A. P. Shimamura, eds. (MIT Press, 1994), 185–205.

2. We say "in some cases" because we like the potential of mini whiteboards for daily use in class, but we are often struck by how much the details of their use erodes their benefit. If students scrawl a first thought quickly, even haphazardly on them without deliberation and effort, much of the good is lost. What is written on a whiteboard also tends to disappear. Sometimes that's an advantage but it also means it will be hard to go back to and edit or examine. See our following discussion on durability.

3. Steve Graham and Michael Hebert, *Writing to Read: Evidence for How Writing Can Improve Reading* (Carnegie Corporation of New York, 2010), 15.

4. Quoted in Jason Roberts's biography of Buffon and Linnaeus, *Every Living Thing: The Great and Deadly Race to Know All Life* (Random House, 2020), 6.

5. If you're not familiar with it, knowing a bit about the *Lord of the Flies* will help as you read the following section. The book tells the story of a group of well-educated English schoolboys who are stranded on a desert island without adults. They descend into brutality and chaos, revealing the worst of human nature despite the efforts of a few well-intentioned characters. In the state of nature, goodness is overrun by the inhumanity within all of us. Since we have your attention and since if you're reading this and you probably haven't read *Lord of the Flies*, can we say there are very few books we feel confident saying that every single young person who graduates from school should have read. *Lord of the Flies* is one of them.

6. The journals authors keep give testament to this fact. Like artists and their sketchbooks, writers explore ideas in journals merely to see where they go, sometimes repurposing what emerges in final copy. Experimental writing is central to the process of generating insight. So is the habit of writing regularly, even when you are not sure what and whether you have something to say.

7. https://www.edweek.org/teaching-learning/q-a-the-writing-revolution-encourages-focus-on-crafting-good-sentences/2017/06.

8. Hochman and Wexler's comments on the importance of writing being embedded in content are taken from this article, https://www.aft.org/ae/summer2017/hochman_wexler, but are discussed more extensively in *The Writing Revolution* (Jossey-Bass, 2017) and *The Writing Revolution 2.0* (Jossey-Bass, 2024)—both books we love and highly recommend.

9. By *writing* here we are focusing on the writing students do to process ideas in class, rather than creative writing and poetry. It should go without saying that we think those things are valid, too, and the fact that we don't talk about them here doesn't mean we don't think they're important. That said, we think being a better writer in the ways we describe here probably makes students better at creative forms of writing, too.

10. We hope we have shown elsewhere in this book that background knowledge—what you know—supports comprehension—what you learn.

11. Harry Fletcher-Wood, *Responsive Teaching: Cognitive Science and Formative Assessment in Practice* (Taylor & Francis, 2018), 6.

12. We would often give students who were ready for more advanced practice optional "challenge" prompts.

13. *The Writing Revolution* is truly one of the most important books on education written in the last ten years. It is with immense guilt and self-recrimination that we acknowledge that we define *sentence expansion* slightly more broadly than Hochman and Wexler do. We hope they will forgive us.

14. Another idea we stole from *The Writing Revolution*!

15. Héctor R. Martín, *How Do We Learn? A Scientific Approach to Learning and Teaching* (Jossey-Bass, 2024), 40.

16. Daisy Christodoulou, *Making Good Progress? The Future of Assessment for Learning* (Oxford University Press, 2017), 40–41.

17. Ibid., 73.

18. https://carlhendrick.com/2017/05/06/five-things-i-wish-i-knew-when-i-started-teaching/comment-page-1/.

19. https://hbr.org/2023/02/what-is-psychological-safety.

20. Daniel Coyle, *The Culture Code: The Secrets of Highly Successful Groups* (Random House, 2018).

21. https://hbr.org/2023/02/what-is-psychological-safety.

22. https://populace.org/research.

23. Zachary A Rosner, Jeremy A. Elman, and Arthur P. Shimamura, "The Generation Effect: Activating Broad Neural Circuits During Memory Encoding," *Cortex* 49, no. 7 (July–August 2013): 1901–1909.

24. Daniel T. Willingham, *Why Don't Students Like School?: A Cognitive Scientist Answers Questions About How the Mind Works and What It Means for the Classroom*, 2nd ed. (Jossey-Bass, 2021), 61.

25. Paul A. Kirschner, John Sweller, and Richard E. Clark, "Why Minimal Guidance During Instruction Does Not Work: An Analysis of the Failure of Constructivist, Discovery, Problem-Based, Experiential, and Inquiry-Based Teaching," *Educational Psychologist* 41, no. 2 (2006): 75–86. DOI: 10.1207/s15326985ep4102_1.

26. Steve Graham, and Michael Hebert, "Writing to Read: Evidence for How Writing Can Improve," *Carnegie Corporation Time to Act Report* (Alliance for Excellent Education, 2010), 15.

27. See Peps McCrea's blog, *Evidence Snacks*, November 7, 2024. https://snacks.pepsmccrea .com/p/elaboration.

28. https://carlhendrick.com/2017/05/06/five-things-i-wish-i-knew-when-i-started-teaching/comment-page-1/.

29. Judith C. Hochman, and Natalie Wexler, *The Writing Revolution 2.0: A Guide to Advancing Thinking Through Writing in All Subjects and Grades* (Wiley, 2024), 159.

30. *How Do We Learn?*, 40.

31. *The Writing Revolution 2.0*, 159.

32. Some teachers propose peer feedback as a solution to this problem. We all admit that we used it on days when we needed a break. And, yes, it's nice to make students read one another's work and think about it. It's no sin but it does not serve the same function as feedback from an expert teacher who understands the text (students are novices reading it for the very first time) and whose job it is to teach students how to express ideas. It's not going to build knowledge of how language captures ideas effectively. A better labor-saving device, we think, is group feedback. Read all the drafts, distill three or four key examples that apply to everyone; teach them to the group. Note places in individual essays where they should be applied.

33. Bruce Saddler, *Teacher's Guide to Effective Sentence Writing* (Guilford Press, 2012), 6.

34. *Teacher's Guide to Effective Sentence Writing*, 9.

Chapter 7

The Power of the Book

We are unapologetic advocates for the book, the whole book, and if not quite *nothing but the book*, certainly a lot of books, thoughtfully chosen, read together and discussed as a class.

Among many other reasons, which we'll delve into in this chapter, we think a well-chosen book, at least one with a narrative structure, is a sustained and deep reflection from which the protagonist or narrator almost never emerges with the same thoughts and beliefs he or she began with. It models a type of thinking that is slow, reflective, deep, and thoughtful—an antidote to a fast, impulsive, and often froward world.

Allow us to linger for a moment on that word: *froward*.

It means *difficult to get along with, contrary, inclined to be argumentative*. It's an obscure word. Our spell-check doesn't know it. It keeps on trying to change it to *forward*!

We're not just trying to be fancy though. We learned *froward* from reading Charles Dickens's novel *Little Dorrit*. In the very last scene, the book's heroes are married. They leave the church and go "quietly down into the roaring streets, inseparable and blessed." The last line of the book is, "As they passed along in sunshine and shade, the noisy and the eager, and the arrogant and the froward and the vain, fretted and chafed, and made their usual uproar."

And so the book ends. But we have remembered that word *froward* long after, in part because the *passage* is so meaningful to us. If you have not read the book, perhaps you read those lines quickly and thought, "Ok, nice enough . . . kind of, you know, wordy . . . typical Dickens . . ." but were not moved by what you read. It has little context. It's just a passage.

But to us, those lines are profound the concluding thoughts in an extended reflection on a set of ideas with which, having read the book, we have developed a sort of a relationship.

And then as we were writing *this book* and thinking about how teaching books might help us sustain attention on what is important in a fractious world, something reminded us of that chaotic London street, and the word *froward* demanded to be used.

It is an example of the way encountering a word, a scene, or an idea in a meaningful context, one where a relationship between reader and narrative has been built, can make it richer, more memorable, and more useful. We remembered *froward* not only *better* but also *bigger*—connected to other ideas—because it came to us in a book.

It doesn't hurt that the passage is beautiful. This too makes it memorable and reminds us that the way things are written can create understanding beyond the strictly semantic. Words are more than mere tools of barter and transaction. Beauty evoked by mere print on a page is a powerful reminder of what the careful, attentive selecting and sequencing of words can do, which not incidentally is a very good reason to ensure that students consistently read texts that allow them to experience the highest levels of expression of which people are capable. Beauty is underrated—not least as a teaching tool.

There's science and research behind our memory of that odd word we read in an obscure novel. Stories tend to make us remember things better—they are cognitively privileged.[1] This is one of the primary reasons why books are so worthy of study. We learn from them deeply. If you have read George Orwell's *Animal Farm* in a setting that does it justice, you are likely to remember for perhaps your whole life your outrage at Napoleon's craven willingness to betray every principle he has espoused in the pursuit of self-interest. And what better thing for a citizen of a democracy to remember?

However, we have never remembered an unusual word like *froward* nor its role in the expression of values by which we wish to live, nor had a realization we will carry with us all our lives like our realization of Napoleon's perfidy, after reading one of the hundreds of short text passages or excerpts that students are given to read in lieu of books in many classrooms. Certainly, we have never experienced anything in those passages as being beautiful and therefore a statement about the power of language.[2]

Imagine, though, if most readers had read *Little Dorrit*, too, and perhaps recognized the use of the word *froward* as a reference to Dickens and just maybe recalled his depiction of that London street 170-odd years ago. The allusion might have evoked a recognition of the a similarity between two eras and offered a reminder that people worried about a distracted and quarrelsome world then as well as now.

To be clear, we are not arguing that *Little Dorrit* should be read far and wide. We're happy we read it but honestly, it was pretty tough sledding at times. Our point is that when we have read stories in common, we—citizens, students and teachers—suddenly have the power to refer to complex ideas that we know in common. We create the possibility of allusion, comparison, and conversation. The more we have read in common, the more we can do, connect with make meaning out of that shared knowledge.

Think for a moment about the possibilities that might provide from a teaching point of view. Imagine you are reading George Orwell's *1984* and you know your students have read *Animal Farm*, Lois Lowry's *The Giver*, and Aldous Huxley's *Brave New World*. Perhaps Suzanne Collins's *The Hunger Games* or Ji-li Jiang's *Red Scarf Girl*, too. Or even just one of them. You can now compare the vision of totalitarianism or the coercion of the individual in *1984* to the depiction in one of those other books and know that every student will be able to join you in that comparison. Discrimination activities—those in which we ask students to compare two similar portrayals of an idea and discuss the important ways they are similar and different—are especially powerful teaching tools. We will apply this concept in a micro sense in Chapter Eight on Close Reading. But it also applies in a macro sense. Students will see more deeply if they can compare not only similar portrayals of totalitarianism but also differences in narrative voice, the use of suspense and irony, or the depiction of heroes and heroines across books.

Compare that to the reality in which most teachers take on *1984*. They can assume nothing about the other books their students have read and so cannot hope to compare narrative voices or portrayals of totalitarianism to any other book and be sure the great majority of their students will have read it. When there is no body of shared texts students can be presumed to have read, every book exists in a vacuum. And books are most certainly not written nor intended to be read in a vacuum.

Network effects is the term used to describe the phenomena whereby the benefit to users of a product or technology corresponds to how many other people use it as well. Your fax machine is only useful when everyone else has a fax machine. If you could only fax 10 percent of the people in the world, the machine's functionality, what it can do, would be the same, but its value would be much lower because you couldn't rely on it as a means to connect to other people. Suddenly a fax is not worth having. The value is in the network.

Knowledge, too, has network effects.[3] The value of many ideas we seek to teach in schools corresponds to how many people can discuss them. The book *1984* is a decent example. It is one of the few books with broad network effects. Most teachers—most people—can presume that many students will know a bit about the idea of Big Brother. But think of how much more powerful our discussions about society would be if the network effects were deeper—if we could presume understanding of not one concept from the book but a dozen, if we (English teachers, history teachers, parents, colleagues, etc.) could talk about New Speak and the way constraining language is a means of achieving censorship and a dozen other Orwellian ideas across a broad network of people.

Can we note that we tried to draw on network effects in the first line of this chapter? We alluded to the phrase "the truth, the whole truth and nothing but the truth," which of course is what witnesses pledge to tell in a court of law. Naturally, most readers will know that, so we tried to echo it and suggest, a bit playfully, that we were just maybe "testifying" ourselves. Common knowledge enriches communication.

If we know the same books, we can refer to *Big Brother* or *star-crossed lovers* or Napoleon's hypocritical assertion that *all animals are equal but some animals are more equal than others*, and know that Napoleon's statement is an allegory for the way people abuse principles. In referencing these things, we connect our words to larger ideas as we share them. We will return to this idea when we discuss *cultural capital* later in this chapter.

The memorable ideas that books have brought to life—Big Brother, star-crossed lovers, and the idea of all animals being equal when it is convenient to the one doing the talking—represent important insights handed down through generations. Societies have spent hundreds of years stocking the library with worthy books that have been the storehouses of almost every idea worth sharing, often expressed in its most memorable terms. Almost every important idea has been defined or became broadly known by virtue of a book. Books are the place where what we thought most profoundly was made legible to others. The best of them represent the shared accumulated insight of humankind. We should want to socialize young people to value books and seek them out.

There's another, more quotidian reason why we ought to read whole books in classrooms. The tools of effective teaching are made more powerful when directed at the objects most worthy of study.

Recall as an example a video we showed you in Chapter Six on writing. In the video *Formative Writing: Montage* we saw three teachers—Will Beller, Spencer Davis, and Maggie Johnson—using short formative prompts to allow students to "think in writing."

There's much to appreciate about the language all three teachers use to lower the stakes and prompt students to start writing before they know the answers. It's even better that the Formative Writing happens midstream, at a pause in the process of reading. The teacher says something like, "Pause. Close your books and take a moment to jot your thoughts: what do you think is happening and why might it be happening?" With no distraction and a speedy transition from reading to reflecting, the thoughts in students' minds about the text remain fully present in their working memory as they seek to put thoughts to paper. And in all three cases, we find the class in the midst of reading aloud together, bringing the text to life to the fullest degree possible and sharing the experience of it.

It's a video of very good teaching.

But it's far better because all three classes are reading *books*. The thinking students do happens not just in the midst of a text they are reading *that day*—an article or an excerpt, say, something they have a brief transactional relationship with—but one they have come to understand deeply. They will have seen the protagonist's views and understandings change. They will have grown to understand the context with some depth. They will probably have come to care about the characters they are reading about. They will have a relationship with the book.

In addition, all three classes are reading not just books but *important, highly regarded, and widely read books*. As they write, students are thinking deeply about Erich Maria Remarque's *All Quiet on the Western Front*, R. J. Palacio's *Wonder*, and Harper Lee's *To Kill a Mockingbird*, stories that people by the millions have handed to friends and, in two cases, handed down across generations. They are stories that are especially worth thinking deeply about, that will reward reflection (and therefore make reflection seem worth the trouble), and that will enable students to connect with other people who have also read and thought deeply about those same books. These are books that will withstand the test of time. (We'll share guidelines on text selection and the rationale behind our selections for our own curriculum later in this chapter.)

Why is the test of time so important? We think enduring interest is likely to be a good measure of quality, for one thing, but we also think that if a key goal of reading is to think deeply about stories and understand them from multiple perspectives, the perspective of how people thought about things in the past is one of the most important and undervalued forms of diversity we can expose young people to. Understanding how people conceived of things in the past—that they thought of their society as "froward"; that they went to war out of a sense of duty; that they felt more connected to place and faith than most people today; that they were more amenable to hierarchy; that they stereotyped and often discriminated based on culture, race, and religion; that they experienced the loss of loved ones with shocking regularity and went stoically on with their lives—is one of the best ways to contextualize ideas in the present. The beliefs and values of the past are more than just quaint relics and deserve inquiry, regardless of whether we agree with them.

We hope it's clear by now how strongly we believe that books are the most important form of writing that young people can engage with if we hope to help them succeed as readers and as members of society.

But, as we've alluded to, this isn't just based off of our feelings (or our deep love for books). As in other chapters, we will ground our argument for books in research—in the ideas that stories are cognitively privileged, that the medium of long-form narrative is a form of message, and that they provide "cultural capital" that is useful to students throughout their lives, to name a few.

And we will argue not only that the choice to build reading classrooms around books in general is important, but also that the choice of the specific books themselves is critical—far more so than is often thought.

At this point, though, we want to recognize that some readers may be wondering why we even feel the need to make the case for books. "Aren't they already a staple of the English classroom?" Others may have seen their decline, but want to understand better how classrooms ended up here. So, we'll kick things off by exploring some of the reasons why our belief in books has become a dissenting opinion and what books have been replaced with.

WHY HAVE ALL THE BOOKS GONE?

Recent debates about what books to allow and restrict in schools might lead you to imagine that reading books is a core activity of students, that teachers are carefully choosing and assigning them, one after the other, while a few subversive instructors perhaps sneak tattered copies of edgier texts into eager students' hands, and that, on balance, books are shaping the worldviews of American students.

Sadly, though, the notion that books are central to the intellectual life of schools is, as many of our readers will know, an increasingly anachronistic one. First, there's the clear and overwhelming data we share in Chapter Two that few students read books on their own anymore. But even in classrooms, books are few and far between. And when they do appear in curricula, they tend to be valued less for their content than for their potential as a vehicle for a process. As we noted in *Reading Reconsidered*, there are many schools in which reading has come to be tacitly defined as "the act of asking and answering questions about a text," a process that consists, at its core, of asking students to practice a set of skills inherent in readership. Florida State University associate professor of education Sonia Cabell pointed out in a recent issue of *Education Week* that reading comprehension instruction has become increasingly "content agnostic," and focused on practicing "skills."[4] In other words, it doesn't really matter what you read, so long as you use the text as a vehicle to develop universal and fungible skills that can applied to almost any other text. Even if they are illusory.

If teachers believe that what students read doesn't really matter, the incentives tip toward selecting texts in the hope that something "appealing" or "accessible" or "relevant" will prompt reluctant students to actually read them. Doubly so if teachers lack the tools and support to cause students to actually read. When that happens, the incentive is to choose things to read that are less challenging—but often, ironically, less worth reading.

In other words, while the books we assign in school are more and more likely to be the only ones many students read in their formative years, they are less and less likely to be challenging or chosen for their enduring value.

And, more likely than not, there are no shared books at all in the classroom. Instead, they've been replaced by some combination of the following:

- A series of "passages" of one to three pages, often designed to forefront a specific "skill" or demonstrate representation of a viewpoint

- Shorter "extracts" from longer texts designed to give students a "taste" of them

- A selection of largely forgettable texts that someone presumes will be instantly engaging to the most reluctant students (The argument is not that students will value them most *after* having read them but that they will appear interesting *beforehand*, so there's a chance students will actually try to read them. You could call this the *Captain Underpants* theory.)

- Choice books, selected by students themselves based on their limited knowledge of what is available for them, and read independently on the presumption that this too may motivate them to read—but guaranteeing that discussion and shared experiences are few and far between

- An array of videos and other digital media "recentered" in our children's learning (we see you, National Council of Teachers of English) in lieu of the things it is too often considered tedious to try to get them to read

We acknowledge that there's little data to prove this replacement has occurred, though this fact in and of itself suggests that what gets read has not struck many people at, say, state departments of education or schools of education, as being worth tracking.

It could also be an issue of policy. In the United States, "standards" are determined by state education departments, but curriculum, at least in English and reading, very rarely so. What to read is mostly a decision that devolves to the school or, more likely, each individual classroom teacher, who must come to terms alone with changes in student attention and wrestle with trade-offs: does she want to be the one teacher who asks students to do what they are not inclined to do, what they may find hard and perhaps will resist, what she may have to grade them poorly for not doing, but that is in their long-term interest?

Unfortunately, it seems many teachers are answering those questions in the negative. Recall Rose Horovitch's *Atlantic* article, "The Elite College Students Who Can't Read Books,"[5] which we briefly mention in Chapter Two. It begins with the story of a Columbia professor whose struggling student sought him out. Unable to keep up with the reading load in his class, the student professed that "she had been assigned excerpts, poetry, and news articles, but not a single book cover to cover" in high school. She was alarmed now to find herself asked to read *several* in the course of one semester! That certainly resounded with readers, if the reaction across both social and legacy media is any indication.

But beyond an informal survey of college professors conducted by Horovitch, the evidence in the article that this is a widespread issue was mostly anecdotal, the one exception being an EdWeek Research Center survey[6] of third- to eighth-grade educators. Of three hundred teachers interviewed in that survey, 17 percent said they primarily teach whole texts. About half (49 percent) said they use some whole texts and combine them with shorter pieces. If that means a book or two per year, it could be worse: about a quarter of the teachers interviewed reported that books were not an important part of their curriculum. Of course, a survey of grades 3–8 tells us nothing about high school. That said, our own experience visiting hundreds of schools a year gives us little reason to think Horovitch is wrong.

The most common explanation for the rise of the text passage as bulwark of reading classroom is that it is the fault of testing, but this is a bit of a straw man. It's true that state reading comprehension tests are made up almost exclusively of text passages, so of course some schools try to prepare students by having them read lots of passages. But this practice is itself a result of the erroneous belief that reading is composed of transferrable skills. As we note, "standards" are determined by state education departments but curriculum rarely so. And standards are almost always transferable skills like "students will be able to draw conclusions and make inferences from texts." The fundamental problem is in the purpose people perceive in reading.[7]

If nothing else, we hope we have given the lie once and for all to the unscientific notion that we can teach transferable critical thinking or reading skills (see Chapter Four). We have to develop critical thinkers and deep readers book by book and realize that what we read is impossible to separate from what students learn. We dissent from book-free classrooms, and we think this is more than a matter of taste. We think the science is with us! Let's dive into exactly why.

STORIES ARE COGNITIVELY PRIVILEGED

Because of how humans have evolved, stories have a special power in helping us to remember facts, develop knowledge and emotional capacity, and build connections with each other.

One of the most important things to know about stories is that we learn especially well from them. "The human mind seems exquisitely tuned to understand and remember stories," Daniel Willingham writes. "They are treated differently in memory than other types of material."[8] They are *cognitively privileged.*[9]

Researchers find that people remember ideas and insights better when they encounter them in a story. We remember the facts because they are connected to a story—the more memorable and compelling the story is, and the deeper our relationship to it, the better.

Evolved for Stories

The privileged nature of stories from a cognitive perspective is almost assuredly evolutionary in origin. Long ago in the mists of human prehistory, stories conferred a double selection advantage on groups that told them, William von Hippel argues in his book, *The Social Leap.*

The first advantage is that stories contained information that taught group members how to survive. The second is that sharing stories bound individuals into close-knit groups that increased the likelihood of everyone's survival. "Once night falls, communal fires are lit and people gather in small groups, conversations blend into stories and stories often reveal important lessons about how to live one's life and follow cultural rules," von Hippel writes.[10] If you know how to follow the cultural rules, to understand what the group values and believes, you know how to belong. And belonging is very important: a human in a group is a much more adept creature from an evolutionary point of view than a human by him- or herself.

In fact, von Hippel writes, it was only when we formed reliable groups for hunting and defense that we went from prey to predator. He argues that developing the ability to use projectiles, beginning with rocks, to attack or defend from a distance, as a group, was one of the most important developments for humans evolutionarily. Using projectiles allows a group of less adept creatures to engage a superior individual in battle at reduced cost. Humans can compete with a lion, for instance, only if they can do battle without coming into close contact with its claws and teeth. To do that we need ten or twenty of us—all of us reliable, trustworthy, and with the ability and desire to coordinate—throwing rocks to drive it away or hunt it. If and only if we are able to form these close-knit, reliable groups, we are apex predators.

This is why group formation is so important: it turns us from a weak species into the dominant one and makes the groups that bond best into supergroups. And this is also why stories are so important; they not only communicate knowledge of evolutionarily valuable information—say, how to hunt or drive off of lions—but they also communicate the norms and culture that bind us into the groups that give us power. The experience of telling stories together is a form of glue that bonds the group.

The oral narratives humans developed to store their knowledge of how to live and survive didn't die with the people who originally came up with them. In fact, humans are the only species on the planet to have "cumulative culture," which is the process by which innovations are progressively remembered, communicated, and incorporated in the knowledge and skills of a group.[11] Other animals are limited to very simple processes they can see and copy. With stories, humans are able to remember and communicate progressive layers of information. Each of the details of how the lion was hunted were added to the story as it was learned. If you listened, you were in on cumulative knowledge- generations' worth. If not, it was a very short stay in this world. So, we evolved to listen very carefully and to remember what stories told us.

Myths attest to this. They are stories that we told from the beginning to frame who we are. To be a culture is to have unique stories that define an "us." Without stories, we struggle to form cultures. The universality of this—the fact that every culture has myths—suggests that their creation cannot be an accident evolutionarily. It shows how privileged their status is, and how central to our group evolution they were.

Knowledge and Empathy Through Stories

Another reason for the privileged status of stories in accelerating learning may be what the psychologist Raymond Mar and colleagues call "close parallels" between their narrative structure and how we "communicate our own experiences" internally. A story is a series of "temporally ordered causal events organized around personal goals," and that mimics the goal-oriented internal narrative unfolding each day in a person's mind. It's a form that is intuitive to us because we live it, and so we are especially receptive to the ideas we encounter in this manner. Habits hack working memory, and a habitual way of narrating and thinking about the world is presumably ideal for optimizing the portion of working memory focused on content—intrinsic cognitive load—versus format and conventions—extrinsic cognitive load. In other words, stories make sense because they are familiar to our minds, which maximizes our working memory's capacity to think about meaning and to remember.

Mar also argues that exposure to narrative fiction appears to "improve or maintain social skills, especially skills of empathy and social understanding." Stories improve people's capacity and desire to understand what other people think and feel. The longer and deeper the story, the greater the benefits. This also has implications for thinking: when you build a relationship with a character and care about him or her, you are primed to build memory and understanding. Emotional events are often called "flash-bulb memories," Mar and colleagues write, and become "deeply imprinted in the mind," whether they happen in fiction or in reality.[12]

Experiences gleaned from reading are in fact closer to "real" experiences than some might think. Recall Annie Murphy Paul's statement from Chapter Two that "the brain, it seems, does not make much of a distinction between reading about an experience and encountering it in real life." She continues, "In each case, the same neurological regions are stimulated. Indeed, in one respect novels go beyond simulating reality to give readers an experience unavailable off the page: the opportunity to enter fully into other people's thoughts and feelings."[13]

So, if you want students to remember what they read and learn as much as possible about the world, give them long-form narrative—doubly so if you want to help them build empathy and listen well to the perspectives of others.

Keith Oatley, emeritus professor of cognitive psychology at the University of Toronto, notes that fiction is a "vivid simulation" of the real world that is especially useful in building empathy and emotional depth among young people "because negotiating the social world effectively is extremely tricky, requiring us to weigh up myriad interacting instances of cause and effect. Just as computer simulations can help us with complex problems such as flying a plane or forecasting the weather, so novels, stories and dramas can help us understand the complexities of social life." They give us lots of safe but valuable practice with emotional experience.[14]

In fact, Mar used MRI imaging to show that the areas of the cortex used to react to and process stories are the same ones used to process interactions with other people—in particular, those that are about predicting and understanding what others think and feel and those related to the deeply and exclusively human ability to recognize that others think differently than we do—a concept called "theory of mind."[15]

"Narratives offer a unique opportunity to engage this capacity, as we identify with characters' longings and frustrations, guess at their hidden motives and track their encounters with friends and enemies, neighbors and lovers," Murphy Paul writes.[16] By "this capacity" Murphy Paul means the experience of recognizing and perhaps even reconciling the difference in perspectives between ourselves and others. As parents and as educators we are all for students getting plenty of such experience.

Of course, while stories are ideal for developing empathy and fostering "theory of mind," not all experiences with stories will be equal. Disconnected reading, in which students do not develop a relationship with text and characters, is more likely to model simplistic and transactional experience rather than real empathy. For a character they don't care much about or understand well, students might breezily say, "I'd just tell him to quit that job" or "She should leave him," when the point may be to weigh the many intense and unforgiving trade-offs the character would have to consider. A reader who is connected to the story and sees all the angles is less likely to practice snap judgments in response to the challenges others experience.

Enriching a book with background knowledge (as we discuss in Chapter Four) is also likely to deepen depth of emotional response among readers. A student who knows nothing about the economic prospects of a woman living alone with a child in Victorian England and the social stigma that would be heaped on her if she left her marriage, no matter how horrible, can easily announce, "She should leave him!" A student with knowledge of history sees the depth of the problem. One of them is reading a costume drama and practicing the sorts of oversimplification common, in exaggerated form, on social media, while the other is reading historical fiction and is building knowledge and developing empathy.

Better Together

Another benefit of reading stories is that we can experience them together. People who read together experience the "simulation" that Oatley describes *in a shared manner*. For a social species, that is critical. People who experience a story together are far more likely to be bonded emotionally by the experience, especially when the reading of it happens in real time; that is, when students and teacher are reading the text aloud together and it is unfolding for them in synchrony. In that case, they hear their peers laughing or gasping and laugh or gasp themselves as well, and think: *We experienced that emotion together* and so build a shared connection. To us, this is one of the most profound arguments for shared oral reading during class: it connects readers and makes them feel a sense of belonging.

You may recall the story from Chapter One of Doug watching a movie with his family. and glancing around to see if his wife and children were laughing, too. He and his family chose the shared experience of a story as a way to reconnect and solidify bonds, but it was also important to confirm that they indeed were sharing a similar version of the experience.

All three of us have in fact done this, with laughter and with other emotions experienced during stories—perhaps a brief flash of eye contact when a character does something that seems foolhardy and doomed. Maybe you have as well. This raises the question: why would we look around at other people during a movie or when reading a story to see their reactions?

The answer is that the emotions we feel, be it laughter fear or disapproval, are not as meaningful if others don't share the experience. We are looking around for confirmation and connection. Did you think that was funny, too? If so, it is a bonding experience. If we were teenage boys, the next step would be to replay the joke ad nauseum in every conversation for the next six months. It's a funny little quirk of a subset of the population that reveals our tendency to replay and remind ourselves of the stories we share over and over. Quoting movie lines to one another is really people saying, "Remember we saw that together?" or "Remember we both love that movie?" A shared story connects us.

Stories bind us together not just in the culture and knowledge they communicate but also in the experience of listening together. Experiencing the tale of the lion together around the campfire is less powerful than actually hunting together, but only slightly so, and we can share it with a lot more people.

Stories, then, are meant to be shared—to cement belonging and instill knowledge. They work optimally that way. (So, perhaps it's not a coincidence that teenage boys, who are at the most sensitive period of their lives in terms of the influence of peer-to-peer bonding and acceptance, are so inclined to engage in shared text allusions in a way that seems excessive to the rest of us.)

If sharing stories leads to a sense of belonging, then stories gain even more power when they are brought to life by reading aloud, a point we make in Chapters Two, Three, and Five. In fact, the sense of belonging created by shared reading may be the book's primary chance of salvation. If the book is going to survive its death struggle with the isolating and disconnecting technology of the smartphone, its best hope will be social reading—causing students to read books together in proximity and time, laughing and gasping together, and in so doing creating meaningful connections and shared experiences that, we hope, they will seek to recreate by reading more and further.

Even though people in contemporary America now tend toward individualism, we are still wired to want to form and belong to groups. As we note in Chapter Two, this may be one reason why, despite the book's state of decline in terms of overall readership, book clubs are more popular than ever. "Life satisfaction is achieved primarily by being embedded in your community," von Hippel writes.[17] Sharing stories teaches us better but also binds us together in communities, and this, too, is important. Social scientists find that people who lack social connections have poorer physical health, with social isolation having an impact comparable to smoking fifteen cigarettes a day. In the long view, those who were drawn to stories were more likely to survive, enough so that the tendency was selected for. We are the heirs of that process.

THE MEDIUM IS THE MESSAGE

> *Reading is a slow, deliberate, thoughtful process—providing an antidote to a fractious world.*

The phrase "the medium is the message," we mentioned in Chapter One, comes from the social theorist Marshall McLuhan's 1975 book *Understanding Media*. It has proven to be one of the most enduring and important observations about information in the era of mass communications. The phrase refers to the idea that every means of communication shapes the way the people using it see the world.

"Every time a new medium of communication comes along," Johann Hari writes in *Stolen Focus*, "it is gently guiding us to see the world according to a new set of codes."[18]

The internet shapes our perception of the world because it democratizes information, for example. We can find out almost anything we want at almost any time. In 1970, say, we'd have been reliant on network news or print newspapers. We'd have to wait until 6 o'clock to find out what happened in Vietnam. We'd be limited to the three-minute story we heard, and we'd have to take the network's word for it. Nowadays, we're not taking anyone's word for it and we're not waiting to find out. It's almost hard to imagine what that was like then.

But the internet has other less positive effects. It elevates impulsiveness, anger, and dissent, for example. The implicit message of social media platforms, for instance, is that "the world can be understood in short simple statements of 280 characters," Hari writes, which in turn means that the world "can be interpreted and confidently understood very quickly."[19] All around us we see evidence of this message. Hasty views are shouted back and forth in cacophony. For many young people, especially, this model for interpersonal communication is the most commonly experienced format of social interaction. It's their normal. And, of course, this model—judge quickly, fire off a hot take, assume you understand almost immediately—becomes increasingly normal for students, even when they are not on their phones. It shapes their relationships. Ask any school principal where and how most of the arguments and fights in their school start these days.

By contrast, Hari writes, "the medium of the book tells us, that. . . the world is complex and requires steady focus to understand; it needs to be thought about and comprehended slowly."[20] First impressions often turn out to be wrong. The truth is nuanced and often not simple. A protagonist never understands fully at the start; a book always involves a change in thinking about the world. This is an act of intellectual humility. If there is a hope for our increasingly fractious and judgmental society, it lies in part in the sustained and evolving understanding a book can help model and foster.

With a book, we can return to phrases over time and see how their meaning changes. In reading Chapter Seven, we can reexamine a line from Chapter Two. How does seem different now, knowing what we've learned since? What did we miss the first time we read it? We can revise our original thinking, call attention to the fact that our understanding is changing, draw attention to the fact that wisdom accrues slowly and deliberately.

For instance, let us revisit an idea that we present in Chapter Two: that while the fleeting flashes of shallow pleasure brought to us by our phones have shortened our attention spans, reading books can help us to retrain them, rewarding us with deeper, longer-lasting pleasure. This chapter helps us to deepen our understanding of why that's the case, recognizing that the medium of the book shapes the way we encounter the world.

This is why we prefer books to "multimedia texts" such as videos or films. While other storytelling tools such as movies may provide similar experiences of emotions that we discussed previously, the book is deeper, more thoughtful, more inclined to cause reflection. In film, a scene requiring emotional depth from the viewer is likely to be immediately followed in rapid succession by additional scenes of tension, of intense suspense, of emotional intensity of some different type, or maybe just highly explosive car crashes. The rate at which these subsequent distractions from the original reflection occur and reoccur is far slower in books. Also, there tend to be fewer cars exploding and plunging off freeways in books, generally speaking. And, we note, books lend themselves to being set down after a particularly emotional scene to allow the reader time to process. Movies and TV shows, however, tend to wrap the viewer up in the cinematic experience, sweeping them along onto the next scene. We're guessing you haven't ever paused a movie mid-watch to process what happened. In a book, readers have time to think and reflect more slowly and for longer. The medium—slow, reflective, deep, and thoughtful—shapes the message and the thinker.

BOOKS PROVIDE VALUABLE CULTURAL CAPITAL

The knowledge that books contain is some of the most important and relevant that we can offer students, in no small part because it has been treasured by others and has the potential to open doorways of opportunity.

In the 1960s, the French sociologist Pierre Bourdieu sought to explain the disparity in achievement and outcomes for French students from lower social classes. Like any self-respecting 1960s French intellectual, Bourdieu was a Marxist, so he coined the terms for what he observed in terms of "capital." He observed that there were two forms of important and valuable things that could be converted into what he called "economic capital"—what we non-Marxists might call *opportunity*.

If you knew well-positioned people, that was *social capital*. If you knew certain useful things, that was *cultural capital*.

A person with social capital might get first chance at a job because they knew the person who was hiring through their parents, say, or they might be invited to the swanky cocktail party where the deal was struck because they went to college with the host.

But even if you got in the door, certain things about you such as the way you dressed, the way you spoke, and the things you talked about signaled whether you *belonged* in that room. There was an invisible velvet rope. If you nodded when the person you were talking to mentioned something they thought was important—if you knew Marx well enough to know that the word *capital* was synonymous with economic resources, say, or if your familiarity with early James Bond films allowed you to smile and nod at the idea of deal-making at swanky 1960s cocktail parties—you ducked under the rope. Before anyone said, "You know, I have an investment opportunity that might really interest you," they were sizing up whether you seemed to think and know things that were valuable.

As a Marxist, Bourdieu told a fairly cynical version of this story. "Symbols, ideas, tastes, and preferences . . . can be strategically used as resources," he wrote. They are "disguised forms of economic capital."[21] The wealthy self-identify and ally themselves through a hidden code written in allusions: Monet's paintings and quotes from Shakespeare. But this is a fairly simplistic portrayal as well.

People might very genuinely ask you about a book they've read or make an allusion to a favorite film because they like and value it and want to talk to you about it. They might not be testing you or evaluating you or seeking to enforce some class barrier. They might just be talking to you—just possibly across barriers of class or some other apparent difference with hopes of breaking them down. If you got the joke (and so made it seem like you thought they were funny), well, they quite naturally liked you a little more. If you understood their comment and said something smart about Monet they thought, "Wow, she's so smart and interesting." They might be looking for a way to connect with you, with shared knowledge opening the door.

As we discussed in Chapter Four, critical thinking is empowered by knowledge. In fact, it requires it. To have someone notice the power of your thinking, you have to know some things in common. Chatting it up at a party, you could of course go on a long and insightful monologue about an obscure sci-fi film you love, but unless you were also talking to someone who loved and valued obscure sci-fi films, it probably wouldn't help much in connecting you to people. Reading what other people also read is a tool to break down barriers and connect.

But imagine being like Cedric Jennings, the subject of Ron Suskind's book, *A Hope in the Unseen*. Jennings arrives on campus at Brown University, having grown up in one of Washington, DC's most impoverished neighborhoods and having worked tirelessly in schools that did not always try to enrich his store of shared knowledge or that were unable to do so for other reasons (mostly chronically poor behavior). New to the world of privileged classmates, he does not know the things they know by virtue of their hundreds of museum visits and by having grown up in houses where their parents talk about the things they read in college. So, as Suskind chronicles, walking through the bookstore, he sees posters of Monet and books by Marx and *he knows he should know who they are and why they are important*, but he doesn't. He lacks cultural capital. The things people talk about when they talk about ideas and tacitly assess someone's ability to contribute to projects of the mind are hidden from him. The result is that it is hard to connect with people; he often feels like a loner. And when his classmates talk about those things and a thousand others and he gives them a blank stare, they assume he isn't very smart, even though he is—even though the difficulties he's overcome on the path he has taken to Brown would crush most of them. If that was you, and you had enough of those blank-stare conversations, you too might start to question yourself and whether you belonged.

People are connected in a variety of ways through the knowledge they share. The knowledge contained in books is among the most important and relevant. It makes up the majority of the ideas that are and have been communicated via an education and represents the library of important ideas people have developed across the world. Of course those ideas change, and of course they need updating; but, as a body, important books remain a critical touchstone, something it is a profound disservice not to provide students access to because, among other things, not doing so excludes them from conversations and communicates that we don't think they are worthy of reading the very best.

"We really weren't sure about teaching Shakespeare," a colleague told us about the time when her school added *Romeo and Juliet* to their curriculum. The school was in a socio-economically disadvantaged community and most of the students had immigrated to the

United States, many of them quite recently. "So, we asked the kids: 'We're thinking of reading Shakespeare. It will be really hard,' we told them. 'You might struggle and you might not even like it, so we want to give you the choice.' But we never really got to finish letting them choose. Kids were nodding and turning around right away. They were adamant," she said, "Adamant. They thought they could do it and they wanted to know what the fuss was about. And I think they wanted to feel like they were the kind of kids who the system took seriously enough to give the best to read too. I still think about that reaction sometimes. How emphatic it was. To a kid, they were sure that they wanted the things that society said were best and were what the students at the top got."

There are certainly ways in which today's students manufacture their own cultural capital, a currency of worth only to themselves—one of the reasons why it's so hard for them not to be up on the latest social media trends, vernacular, or movie references. But there's also a reason why certain books comprise the curated cultural inheritance that has been handed down to us through the ages, forming the veritable "war chest" that offers a unique cure to the allure of today's digital world, as we touch on in Chapter Two. It's up to us as educators to ensure that students are offered the chance to encounter these treasured texts, which contain things long deemed worth thinking about and knowing.

Bourdieu focused exclusively on the economic power of cultural capital, but cultural capital can be used to connect to other people socially and converted into opportunity—or even happiness and belonging. There is real and legitimate value in knowing things that other people think are worth knowing and being able to understand the things that are relevant to other people, particularly those whose education puts them in a privileged position to do and create things. People who have certain linguistic and cultural knowledge—of which books are the primary means of delivering—will have a greater chance of success in school and a better chance to pursue their dreams.[22] It's hard to be cynical about that.

ALL BOOKS ARE EQUAL, BUT SOME BOOKS ARE MORE EQUAL THAN OTHERS

Given the finite number of books our students will read, we need to be selective in what we put before them.

When it comes to selecting which books to read in a classroom, we think the selections we make are is important and that there is a wide range of worthy choices. But we should also recognize the power of common narratives: no culture emerges without a corpus of shared and valued stories, myths, and fables that define it. No culture endures without shared stories to tell. We should recognize the importance of books in building knowledge that ought to be commonly shared.

There are some forms of knowledge that are especially critical in a democratic society, one in which schooling is both an individual and a societal good. For example, we think every citizen of a free society should have read at least one book that describes the means by which totalitarianism can emerge and sustain itself. And we think the book that does that should be great. Storytelling, we hope to have shown, is one of the most important aspects of any society. It has communicated the rules and values of societies since long before governments existed. Students should read books that communicate what matters most in the most compelling and vivid way. Craft and quality matter. A mediocre argument about the dangers of totalitarianism isn't sufficient.

Fortunately, there are multiple books that can satisfy these criteria at once. George Orwell's *1984* is one example. Arthur Koestler's *Darkness at Noon* is another. The latter is a novel about how people can be made to believe in what they know to be wrong. The narrative is mostly internal, marked by recollection and deep reflection—much like thinking itself, as Raymond Mar and colleagues point out and as we discussed previously in this chapter. Koestler's prose is haunting and powerful. It is surely one of most important books of the twentieth century.

In an ideal world, then, students would read both *Darkness at Noon* and *1984*. But the books we can choose for students are finite. Hard choices must be made.

And so, it is difficult to say, but we would choose *1984*. It's "difficult" because, in many ways, we (or at least one of us) prefer *Darkness at Noon*. It speaks to us; we find it unforgettable. The protagonist of *Darkness at Noon*, Rubashov, is more psychologically real to us than Winston Smith, the main character of *1984*. But personal preference is not the most important factor in selecting what texts to teach in classrooms. Choosing for ourselves, we choose *Darkness,* but choosing on behalf of students, we choose *1984*. It offers more cultural capital. It is more widely read. Its value is in part due to the network effect. If you know *1984* you will understand the allusions and references to it that will inevitably inform your participation in civil society. People will talk about "Big Brother," "thought police" and "Newspeak" a lot more than they will talk about Rubashov. Perhaps our students will read *Darkness at Noon* in college (if college English programs are able to find their way back from increasingly arcane course offerings that probably help explain the dramatic decrease in English majors), but it's more important that they read *1984* now.[23]

It's hard to let go of your darlings, and hard to say that the book you like best isn't the best choice. But doing so is implicit in the responsibility of being a part of an institution as important as a school.

The purpose of reading and of English as a discipline, we have tried to say in this book, is not to merely socialize students to ask and answer questions about a text, with the texts more or less interchangeable. Teaching reading is choosing wisely what to read and giving students the opportunity to experience the best stories and understand how they have been made, to know the stories and arguments that others will also have read and valued.

Not *every single book* must do this. We can choose an occasional book because it is special to us, but teachers should recognize that a selection of books that is too idiosyncratic, too heavily skewed toward personal passions, is a disservice to students. Yes, you should admire the books you teach. That will probably help you teach them better. But it is solipsistic to make that the dominant factor. The books students will read with us in English and reading classes are finite in number. Not every book is worth selecting. Even ones we like immensely. And a teacher of reading should be able to admire and teach a wide range of books.

In his 2020 book *A Time to Build*, the political theorist Yuval Levin describes a broad shift in how people view institutions in American society. People have become increasingly less likely to prioritize their role in serving the functions of the institutions they are a part of and more likely to see institutions as platforms for expressing and amplifying their own ideas. One result of this is that stakeholders in institutions who see them used to amplify the personal interests of individuals tend to develop a distrust in those institutions. Among other things this makes the institutions harder to run.

Schools are exposed to this trend as well, and the risks are much the same. A teacher serves the long-term learning needs of students and the interests of the families who send them there. The risk is that we choose not the texts that best facilitate becoming richly informed, capable readers and citizens in a meritocratic and democratic society, nor those that model the most admired examples of the craft of storytelling, but those that provide a platform to our own personal interests and political or social beliefs.

When we select books, we should discipline ourselves to ask:

- Are these books truly great?

- Do they model the craft of meaning making at its highest and most influential level?

- Will they stay with students forever?

- Will they enable students to talk to others about the important ideas that have been communicated across time and place?

- Are they likely to be relevant in twenty years?

The good news, is that choosing a great book and bringing it to life for students is also a good way to cause them to want to read more books on their own and perhaps more books on a similar theme. If we get *1984* in the curriculum, the odds that we're going to be able to get some students to go off and read *Darkness at Noon* are probably higher.

That's what our colleague, Sean Morrisey, found. Sean is a fifth-grade teacher outside Buffalo, New York. He spent six weeks teaching Lois Lowry's *Number the Stars* and bringing it to life—reading it aloud, infusing it with background knowledge, asking students to reflect on it in writing. When they were finished, he encouraged his students to read other books that took place during World War II on their own, but it didn't take much pushing. Students lined up for his copy of Anne Frank's *Diary of a Young Girl* and other books set during World War II. They couldn't wait to find out more.

This is one reason why we think building your class on student text choice is a mistake. It results in students merely reading what they already think they like, a choice often made based on very limited information. It also results in students reading in isolation, without connection and discussion. We think getting students to value reading is more likely to result from a knowledgeable teacher choosing a truly great book that students have never heard of and bringing it to life. If it's on a topic students never would have guessed they would be interested in, all the better. That, after all, is kind of the point of school. And if they can experience the book as a group so they share the experience and feel connected, well, then there is hope still for the book.

Please don't take our argument for shared books, carefully chosen by the teacher and read as a group, as an argument against choice. It isn't. We are full believers in independent reading and choice therein. We just think independent reading and class reading are different things—connected, yes, but different. That's why Sean's story is such a useful one: increasing young people's knowledge increases their curiosity. The more you know about a topic, the more you perceive when you read more about it, as we discuss in Chapter Four on knowledge. A brilliantly illuminated shared read, carefully orchestrated, is the ideal jumping-off point to more and more enriching independent reading.

But let us return to one of our key arguments in this chapter: that it matters what we read.

Book selections are difficult but they are among the most important decisions we make—and are growing more important by the day as students read less and less outside of school. We say this not just from a theoretical point of view. We had to choose books—specific books, a finite number of them, when we wrote our own curriculum. So let us share with you the books we chose and tell you a bit more about why.

Reading Reconsidered Curriculum Units

Grade 5	Grade 6	Grade 7	Grade 8
• *A Single Shard* by Linda Sue Park • *Bud, Not Buddy* by Christopher Paul Curtis • *Inside Out and Back Again* by Thanhha Lai • *Number the Stars* by Lois Lowry • *Once Crazy Summer* by Rita Williams-Garcia • *The Magician's Nephew* by C. S. Lewis • *Where the Mountain Meets the Moon* by Grace Lin • *Wonder* by R. J. Palacio	• *Bomb* by Steve Sheinkin • *Boy: Tales of Childhood* by Roald Dahl • *Brown Girl Dreaming* by Jacqueline Woodson • *Chains* by Laurie Halse Anderson • *Esperanza Rising* by Pam Muñoz Ryan • *Freak the Mighty* by Rodman Philbrick • *Heroes, Gods and Monsters* by Bernard Evslin • *The Birchbark House* by Louise Erdrich • *The Giver* by Lois Lowry • *The Outsiders* by S. E. Hinton	• *Catherine Called Birdy* by Karen Cushman • *Haroun and the Sea of Stories* by Salman Rushdie • *I Am Malala:* Young Reader's Edition by Malala Yousafzai • *Lord of The Flies* by William Golding • Narrative Short Story Unit by various authors • *Roll of Thunder, Hear My Cry* by Mildred Taylor • *The House on Mango Street* by Sandra Cisneros • *The Poetry Collection* by various poets	• *Animal Farm* by George Orwell • *A Raisin in The Sun* by Lorraine Hansberry • *Of Mice and Men* by John Steinbeck • *Narrative of the Life of Frederick Douglass* by Frederick Douglass • *Night* by Elie Wiesel • *Romeo and Juliet* by William Shakespeare • Science Fiction Short Story Unit by various authors • *The Wanderings of Odysseus* by Rosemary Sutcliff • *To Kill a Mockingbird* by Harper Lee • *The Curious Incident of the Dog in the Night-Time* by Mark Haddon

First, you will notice that there are a lot of books here—eight to ten per grade level. That's far more than most teachers could teach in a year—especially if they are reading as deeply as a great book deserves.

This is because we believe in "constrained choice," a process in which you: 1) assign a group of people to think deeply about balance and value. 2) Develop a corpus of best books from which to choose. 3) Let people choose from within that group.

Having a group to decide the booklist was important. There were eight or so of us in our selection group. We read and discussed more than hundred books in all. We debated, sometimes over weeks, as we considered each book's individual merits and the balance reflected in the larger group of books we chose. Were they rich in vocabulary? Were they examples of excellent writing? Did they cover diverse areas of knowledge?

We chose *Catherine Called Birdy* for grade 7, for example, because we thought the writing was outstanding—arch, ironic, funny, but not too modern. Another reason we love the book is because it offers students an opportunity to read about an important time and place they might otherwise know little about: England in the Middle Ages. We wanted to go deep on building historical knowledge on life in that distant era and thought the book's sparkling and headstrong narrator would be a good way in, causing students to build a relationship with the text so they cared a little more when we embedded nonfiction articles about hierarchy or food in the Middle Ages. But it was important that the book didn't go too far and become ahistorical in its treatment of the era. There is a difference between true historical fiction that is steeped in knowledge and a book that is described as historical fiction but where characters with twenty-first-century sensibilities wander through historical context without taking on the ways of thoughts and beliefs that might have been characteristic of the times. In the end, we agreed that the book was very good and would stand the test of time.

We chose *A Raisin in the Sun* for eighth grade because it describes quintessentially American tensions about identity and self, not to mention race and class. And because it is a play—how many plays will students read on their own?—and because we thought the play was very, very good. The writing is brilliant. The portrayal of characters is subtle. We know it will stand the test of time because, well, it already has. And we chose it because students will likely see Hansberry's work referenced throughout their lives.

The idea from the start was to make the curriculum modular—to let schools and teachers make choices from within the larger group of books about what would best serve their students. Will the best books for students in a rural Texas district be the same best books as those for students in Brooklyn? Probably not. Or not exactly. Certainly they should overlap.

At your school, you may not have a committee like ours selecting a booklist from which individual teachers can choose their texts. But we think schools should use constrained choice. In *Reading Reconsidered*, we discuss the idea of the internal canon: that, within a school, there should be a body of books that teachers can know all students will have read and so can refer to and discuss in subsequent years. A school might choose four books that every sixth grade teacher will teach and then let each sixth grade teacher choose one or two from the list that reflect their tastes and interests.

GETTING THEM TO READ

At this point in the chapter you may be thinking, "Okay, sure, I'm on board philosophically with the importance of teaching books in the classroom—but you don't know my students! They're just not going to read a book unless we do it in class together, but even with the techniques you've presented in other chapters on how to do that, we just don't have enough time to read aloud several entire books in a year."

If you feel like getting your students to read on their own is a Sisyphean task, know that you're not alone. In a recent article in *Education Next*, Fordham Institute's Michael Petrilli[24] took up the question of students not reading books in school and pointed out another potential causal factor than the ones we've mentioned so far: how easy it is, now, to cheat. "Perhaps the most surprising part of these discussions is how few people mention the many ways that kids can get away with not doing the reading and still get a good grade. This is not exactly new—we had *Cliff's Notes* back in my day. But now kids have *SparkNotes*—in their *pockets*—along with YouTube videos that summarize book plots, ChatGPT to write their essays (or at least first drafts), and if push comes to shove, plenty of papers for sale on the open market," Petrilli wrote. "The problem, then, may not be that schools aren't assigning books, but that students (even high-achieving ones) aren't reading them, in part because cheating has become pervasive and socially acceptable."

One of our favorite books, Chip and Dan Heath's *Switch: How to Change Things When Change Is Hard* makes a compelling case for the idea that the size of a solution does not need to match the size of a problem. Small fixes can have cascading effects, especially in complex organizations. So, Petrilli's observations led us to think about one of our favorite things: small, straightforward things teachers can do to begin addressing complex problems like actually getting their students to read.

In the case of there being lots of tools that make it easy to not read and still succeed if you are assigned a book, we think one of the best solutions is the *reading check*. A reading check is a very quick, teacher-written, pencil-to-paper mini quiz given at the beginning of class.

We suggest adhering to the following design principles for your Reading Checks:

- Keep them short so that you can give one every day without taking time away from the lesson. Five question per check is usually sufficient.

- Give them frequently. Each individual Reading Check should be small stakes, but twenty or thirty added together should provide a significant incentive.

- Ask specific questions but not trivial question—things that a student would know relatively easily if they'd read the book attentively, but not if they'd only read a commercial summary. (It might be worth skimming a commercial summary or two of your own to see the kinds of details they point out, then avoid including those on your Reading Checks.)

- Keep the questions factually based on what happens in the text. The point is not to test interpretation. The question is, did they read it?

- Don't make the questions too hard. The questions should not be so obscure that they will trip up kids who have read well.

- Generally, open-response questions are better. One- or two-word answers are fine.

Here are two Reading Checks we wrote for books we love so that you can get a sense of how you might go about asking specific questions that are straightforward but not trivial.

For each, we've imagined that a section of a chapter had been assigned as the previous night's reading. We have put the answers in brackets so you can see how specific the answers we expect are. Note that we have avoided using first chapters of books because we typically start the book together in class then assign the second or third chapter as the first homework assignment.

This first Reading Check is for the first seven or so pages of the third chapter of *The Magician's Nephew*, "The Wood Between the Worlds":

- Who is "he" in the following sentence? "His clothes were perfectly dry. He was standing by the edge of a small pool." [Digory]

- In the wood between the world, Digory meets a girl and asks her, "Have you been here long?" "Oh, always," she says, "at least—I don't know—a very long time." What is the girl's name? Where has she come from? [Polly, though Digory doesn't recognize her at first.]

- In the chapter, Digory finds an object taped to the back of a guinea pig. What is it? Bonus point if you know the color. [a ring; it's yellow]

- Looking at something he finds in the wood between the worlds, Digory says, "We want to go down, don't we?" What is the thing he is looking at? [a pool]

- "Suppose there were dozens," Digory says to Polly. And Polly replies, "You mean this wood might be only one of them?" What are they referring to? [other worlds]

This second Reading Check is for the first five or so pages of the second chapter of *Animal Farm*:

- On whose ideas is animalism based? Name at least two of the four animals who develop it as a belief system. [Old Major, Snowball, Napoleon, and Squealer develop it.]

- Who asks "the stupidest questions" and is very concerned with whether she will be allowed to wear a ribbon in her mane? [Mollie]

- What is Sugarcandy Mountain and where does Moses say it is located? [It is the place where you go when you die, like heaven. It is just beyond the clouds.]

- Who are Boxer and Clover? Are they on the side of the pigs or against them? [They are the two work horses. They are the most faithful disciples of the pigs.]

- Who went to Willingdon on Midsummer's Eve and got very drunk? [Farmer Jones]

To be clear, we don't recommend solely employing at-home reading followed by in-class Reading Checks for a book. Rich reading in class, as we discuss in Chapter Two and Chapter Three, provides many robust opportunities for learning—and it's the easiest way to get students to read (though of course you can't usually read the whole book in class, especially with books of significant length). In the end, though, we want to socialize students to build the habit of reading on their own. We want both the joy of a great book brought to life by a thoughtful and research-informed teacher and the accountability of "and you have to read when you get home every night and I will check to make sure you do."

The consequences of this are not trivial. When you can cause students to read books (in part through a system of thoughtful and caring accountability) you can cause them to read great books—even if they are skeptical at first—and experience them in a way that brings out their meaning. In so doing, students can come to be persuaded that books are worth the trouble. If you can't *cause* students to read books, you are left trying to *convince* them to do so, perhaps by promising that the books will be short or there will be a reward (a movie!) for reading them, or by choosing what you think will be "appealing" or "relevant" but which may or may not be and which is actually not calculated to inspire during the course of reading but to appeal to students before they've actually read a book. It's selling a concept, not an actual text.

A last note: some teachers eschew the book because it is hard and because students will struggle. We agree that books can and often do imply struggle for students but think this is a good and highly beneficial thing. Students should learn that understanding does not come easily. Learning to be able to struggle—to read a challenging text, and to persist with it—is one of the greatest gifts an education can give students. Our next chapter on Close Reading and complex text is about reinforcing that connection explicitly.

CHAPTER RECAP

We firmly believe that books—entire books, thoughtfully chosen, discussed and experienced as a class—should form the bulk and backbone of what reading and ELA classrooms study, for the following reasons:

- **Stories are cognitively privileged.** Humans have evolved both to learn knowledge from stories, whose structure parallels the way our mind produces internal narratives, and to form group bonds and a sense of belonging through sharing stories.

- **The medium shapes the message.** A book's medium is inherently slow, reflective, deep, and thoughtful. It shapes the way its readers see the world and offers a much-needed antidote to today's hot-take, fast-paced, impulsive world.

- **Books provide valuable cultural capital.** People who have certain linguistic and cultural knowledge will have a greater chance of success in school and a better chance to pursue their dreams. Books contain some of the most important and relevant knowledge we can offer students.

Because books are so important in the classroom, it greatly matters which books we choose to put in front of our students—even more so now that students tend to read less on their own. When selecting which books to teach, consider the following criteria:

- Are these books truly great?
- Do they model the craft of meaning making at its highest and most influential level?
- Will they stay with students forever?
- Will they enable students to talk to others about the important ideas that have been communicated across time and place?
- Are they likely to be relevant in twenty years?

Finally, we advocate for a blend of in-class reading and assigned at-home reading of books. To ensure students do their assigned reading, we suggest employing Reading Checks that are

- **Short:** about five questions each
- **Frequent:** each Reading Check is small stakes, but together they provide a significant incentive to read
- **Specific, but not trivial:** focus on details that only someone who read the book—not a summary of it—would know
- **Factually based:** don't test interpretation of the book, but what happens in the book
- **Easy:** at least, for anyone who has read the book attentively
- **Open-ended:** one- or two-word answers work well

Notes

1. See Daniel T. *Willingham, Why Don't Students Like School?: A Cognitive Scientist Answers Questions About How the Mind Works and What It Means for the Classroom,* 2nd ed. (Jossey-Bass, 2021). Willingham uses the term *psychologically privileged* but we think he means the same thing and is using the term *psychologically* in a more technical sense than the typical lay use.

2. We should add the disclaimer that we are not speaking about shorter forms of literature—poetry, short stories, essays—here. We believe those are important to read in their own right (obviously). When we write a curriculum, we include units on poetry and short stories and embed poems and essays in many of our book-based units of study. But perhaps we could best describe these as important seconds: worthwhile, necessary to understand and experience, far better than what often gets taught, a must-have supplement to a curriculum of books—but still not as central and important to students as the book, for reasons we hope to make clear in this chapter.

3. You probably figured this out but the "networks" in network effect are different from the "networks" we reference in Chapter Four when we talk about networks of knowledge, but we thought we'd be doubly clear.

4. https://www.edweek.org/teaching-learning/what-is-background-knowledge-and-how-does-it-fit-into-the-science-of-reading/2023/01.

5. https://www.theatlantic.com/magazine/archive/2024/11/the-elite-college-students-who-cant-read-books/679945/.

6. Apparently it's here: I can't see around the paywall though I know Stephen well enough to ask: https://www.edweek.org/teaching-learning/how-to-build-students-reading-stamina/2024/01.

7. That said, a change in assessment wouldn't hurt. In the United Kingdom, the English Literature General Certificate of Secondary Education exam is not content agnostic. It is understood that the exam will ask for analysis of important books and genres. You can choose which Victorian novel or which play from Shakespeare to read, but you know students will be asked to write about at least one of each—and, consequently, these types of texts are taught in every classroom. A national (or state) curriculum that sets expectations for the types of texts students will read and be assessed on appears sufficient to make a significant difference.

8. *Why Don't Students Like School?*, 71.

9. Willingham uses the term *psychologically privileged*. We prefer the term *cognitively privileged*. While the enhanced role stories play in building memory is certainly a psychological phenomenon, we think *psychology* is a broad term and that *cognitively privileged* helps teachers see more clearly the memory benefits we are referring to here, as opposed to some other advantage.

10. William von Hippel, *The Social Leap: The New Evolutionary Science of Who We Are, Where We Come from, and What Makes Us Happy* (Harper, 2018), 46.

11. Christine H. Legare, "Cumulative Learning: Development and Diversity," *PNAS* 114, no. 30 (2017): 7877–7883.

12. Raymond Mar, Keith Oatley, and Jordan Peterson, "Exploring the Link Between Reading Fiction and Empathy: Ruling Out Individual Differences and Examining Outcomes," *Communications* 34 (2009): 407–28. 10.1515/COMM.2009.025.

13. Annie Murphy Paul, "The Neuroscience of Your Brain on Fiction," *New York Times* (March 18, 2012), https://www.nytimes.com/2012/03/18/opinion/sunday/the-neuroscience-of-your-brain-on-fiction.

14. Ibid.

15. Raymond A. Mar, *Stories and the Simulation of Social Experience: Neuropsychological Evidence and Social Ramifications*, Doctoral Thesis, University of Toronto, 2007: https://utoronto.scholaris.ca/server/api/core/bitstreams/b7c3639e-2a9a-4248-a01b-21a7e433b286/content.

16. "The Neuroscience of Your Brain on Fiction."

17. William von Hippel, *The Social Leap: The New Evolutionary Science of Who We Are, Where We Come from, and What Makes Us Happy* (HarperCollins, 2018), 248.

18. Johann Hari, *Stolen Focus: Why You Can't Pay Attention—and How to Think Deeply Again* (Crown, 2023), 83.

19. Ibid., 84.

20. Ibid., 85.

21. P. Bourdieu, "Cultural Reproduction and Social Reproduction," in *Power and Ideology in Education*, J. Karabel and A. H. Halsey, eds. (Oxford University Press, 1977), 487–511.

22. https://www.oxfordreference.com/display/10.1093/oi/authority.20110803095652799.

23. You should read *Darkness at Noon*, though, if you possibly can.

24. https://www.educationnext.org/seven-thoughts-about-elite-college-students-who-cant-read-books/.

Chapter 8

Close Reading

In Chapter Seven we argue for the importance of reading rich and worthy books that will expand students' understanding of the world. In this, our final chapter, we explore how students can be taught to read such books (and other texts) with depth and acuity, even when they prove challenging.

This is profoundly important. All students deserve to be prepared to master texts that will open doors for them—as college students, as professionals in the workplace, and as citizens.

Choosing texts that are sufficiently challenging and worthy, as we discuss in Chapter Seven, is one critical step in this process. But merely exposing students to harder texts will not by itself cause them to understand what they have read fully, nor instill in them the confidence to struggle with further texts.

The work lies in helping students make meaning when meaning is not evident on the first read and in developing their comfort with struggle. We want students to know what to do when a text proves difficult—and just maybe to relish the challenge such a text provides.

In Chapter Seven, we describe a group of students in a colleague's school who were offered the opportunity to read Shakespeare and embraced it. The story is inspirational only because they were right: they read *Romeo and Juliet*, almost entirely in the original, and in so doing showed not only their teachers, but perhaps themselves, that they could make sense of what so many students find intimidating and often almost indecipherable.

Exposed to challenge without the tools to master it, they could just as easily have decided that difficult reading was beyond them. Many students have. Exposed to challenge with the mastery of those tools, their prospects are unlimited.

To unlock meaning in something that initially appears confusing or disorienting can be a bit like solving a puzzle—which is to say, pleasurable—if we make the steps legible. Not every student will come to find uncovering hidden layers of meaning a gratifying experience, but we note that many people enjoy reading Toni Morrison, Shakespeare, or Gabriel García Márquez for just this reason. And, to provide just one example of the broader relevance of this, we note that many a lawyer has made his or her career with an insightful reading of an excessively complex law or statute.

Close Reading, then, is the name we give to the important and empowering process in which we ask students to seek the fullest meaning of complex texts and in so doing access books above their comfort level. It helps students to do these things by, in particular, helping them to understand and apply the power of rereading.

In Chapter Six, we showed you video from an outstanding lesson on William Golding's *Lord of the Flies* that Jen Brimming taught to her year 6 students at Marine Academy in Plymouth, England. Our purpose then was to highlight the writing her students did and to study why it was so productive, but the moments of thoughtful writing are only part of what's so effective about Jen's lesson.

We want to start this chapter by taking you back to her classroom to watch a different view of that lesson. This time, we'll focus on the way Jen rereads short, carefully selected sections of the text to build an ethos of careful and attentive reading and to study how meaning is made.

Individually, each section of text that Jen rereads with students is useful in causing them to engage deeply with *Lord of the Flies*. Because it is a worthy text, they are interested and motivated by the process of discovery. But more broadly, each section of text that Jen rereads contributes to an overall ethos that in many ways expresses the purpose for teaching English.

To experience the most meaningful reading of the worthiest books is often enjoyable, we've noted, and often something we strive as teachers to make pleasurable for our students. We argue in Chapter Two about how this pleasure helps provide an incentive for reading, an antidote to the fleeting pleasures of the digital world. But enjoyment is not the purpose of the English classroom: the purpose is to teach students to understand the full depth of what has been written in books and valued by societies. We hope students will learn to love doing that, but their skill at doing so, not their emotions, is our focus in this chapter.

In many ways, this chapter is the end point of our teaching, and the end point of the journey students take in studying reading in school. As we'll see with Jen's lesson, the power of Close Reading is in the repetition of the experiences, the building of habits. This is one of our greatest recognitions since writing *Reading Reconsidered*. We looked at the lessons we wrote in our curriculum and realized they were often exercises in Close Reading without our realizing it, with the goal achieved through the steady aggregation of exercises on a theme.

With that, let's jump in.

JEN BRIMMING'S CLOSE READING OF *LORD OF THE FLIES*

The video *Jen Brimming: Close Reading Part 1* shows you some of the key moments in one such lesson focused on helping students make meaning of the opening pages of *Lord of the Flies*. It starts with Jen asking her students to open their copies of *Lord of the Flies* to page One. Moments later, a student pauses her; he thinks she's made a mistake. "Didn't we get to page six [last time]?" he asks.

To watch the video *Jen Brimming: Close Reading Part 1*, use this QR code or find the video at the URL https://vimeo.com/1058368042/4853560405.

His expectation is that they will pick up from where they left off and keep reading. This is a revealing assumption. Many students have come to believe from experience that reading is a one-and-done phenomenon. But Jen points out that they are going back to reread to look at some important details.

We're glad to see Jen's students reading a shared book together, in hard copy. We're ecstatic to see that FASE Reading, which Jen has been using, has already made the reading of the book and the development of her students' fluency a pleasure—seen in the fact that she reassures the class that the reward for their hard work will be that they'll soon continue reading aloud together. But the fact they are rereading, with intention, differently than the first time through, might be the most important fact for us.

A first read-through of a text is almost always what we call a *contiguous read*. We read the story as it appears on the page. It would be odd *not* to do this. It's *made* to be read that way. But when we have made a first pass and then reread, we can consider alternative ways to approach the text, finding opportunities to cause students to orient their attention differently, to focus less on some things and more on others.

This is important because we know that attention is selective. We can only pay attention to a small number of things—probably just one or two—at once. So, in the complex cognitive environment that a text like *Lord of the Flies* presents to us, we are always making choices. If attention is selective, then to pay attention to *x* is to ignore *y* and to ignore *x* is to allow us to pay better attention to *z*.

Note that Jen tells her students what to direct their attention to as they reread, instructing them to make note specifically of any references to "the scar." Asking students to trace a specific image, pattern, or idea across a segment of text is a great way to reread and reorient attention to focus on that recurring image or idea.

From a cognitive point of view, Jen is placing the three references to the scar that occur in that part of the text in an attentionally privileged setting: the students experience all of the references in close proximity because they are skipping over other things in the text. The references to the scar can be held and compared in working memory more easily without the other details of the first pages to distract. This sounds simple, bordering on simplistic, even, but we will see this principle again and again. A key part of Close Reading is comparing important passages, in the most attentionally privileged settings: placed next to each other where students can see them throughout and so perceive and compare them with the full force of their working memory, and presented in units of analysis small enough for students to be able to think about each word.

Making a habit of rereading key pieces of challenging and important text in an attentionally privileged environment while orienting students to focus on specific, critical details is in fact a good starting point for a practical definition of Close Reading.

But there's more to notice in Jen's class. There are three questions she asks students to be thinking about as they reread for two-and-a-half minutes:

- What is the scar?

- Why might it be called that?

- What might it symbolize?

"Firstly," Jen says, after students have had a few quiet minutes to think and make notes, "Let's think about the scar actually is. What it *literally* is. . . ."

We call this sort of question an Establish Meaning question because it requires students to make clear that they understood the text on a literal level: who did or said what to whom.

Such questions are often deceptively tricky. With a complex text, it can be quite easy to miss the literal. If you do, you're going to be confused for the rest of the story.

Unfortunately, teachers often skip the Establish Meaning step. They want rigor. They want to get to the "good" stuff right away. But students aren't likely to tell us they didn't get the basics; in fact, they probably won't even realize that they didn't understand something important. As a result, their subsequent "analysis" is likely to have gaps. The more challenging the text, the more likely this is to occur.

This is evident in the example from Jen's classroom. Understanding what the scar is literally at the outset of *Lord of the Flies* is very tricky. It refers to the strip of damage the wreckage of the crashed plane has cut into the jungle. But you wouldn't know it from its initial appearance in the book's first paragraph where, among other problems, readers don't yet know there's been a plane crash. They don't know who the boy is or how he got there (emphasis added):

> *The boy with fair hair lowered himself down the last few feet of rock and began to pick his way toward the lagoon. Though he had taken off his school sweater and trailed it now from one hand, his grey shirt stuck to him and his hair was plastered to his forehead.* **All round him the long scar smashed into the jungle was a bath of heat**.

The metaphor is implicit. A more explicit version of the text might have said "The long scar where the plane had smashed into the jungle was a bath of heat." But here the *referent*, the thing a word or phrase refers to, is omitted. And there's no indication yet that this confusing off-hand reference is even worth paying attention to.

"What literally is the scar?" is doubly difficult because the first appearance of the phrase comes in the first paragraph, when students are already disoriented by the abrupt *in medias res* start to the book. Who is this boy? How did he get here? Where exactly is he? To pay attention to one thing is always to pay less attention to something else. Students trying to figure out the context—what's going on here?—are less likely to be able to pay attention to subtle signs of foreboding in a detail of the setting—if they notice it at all. Situations such as this where we find high attentional demands and working memory overload, as we discuss in Chapter One, tend to lead to reduced perception.

The second appearance of the scar doesn't provide much help: "The undergrowth at the side of the scar was shaken and a multitude of raindrops fell pattering."

Only in its third appearance does Golding reveal (subtly) that there has been a plane crash, giving a the reader a more direct clue as to what he means by the scar (emphasis added):

> "When we was coming down I looked through one of them windows. I saw the other part of the plane. There were flames coming out of it."
> ***He looked up and down*** the scar.
> *"And this is what the cabin done."*

Three times now this word has appeared in the first few pages. But still, students might not attend to or even follow it. A teacher, however, realizes this recurrence is no accident.

We consider Establish Meaning questions "deceptively simple" because of what's known as the "curse of expertise." What is important and confusing to a novice—a student—is very easy for an expert—a teacher—to overlook, especially when the expert presumably has read the whole book, or at least the passage in question, multiple times—enough to know how rich in symbols it is and how much Golding's use of the term *scar* reveals. Enough not to be trying to hold multiple threads in their working memory at once—"Wait, who is this boy? What does it mean that he is picking his way toward the lagoon? How did he get there?"

"Oh! The scar is what Golding is calling the place where the plane crashed!"

You could easily miss that—and a lot more—as a young and developing reader.

Jen, having taken a critical moment to establish this, moves on to analysis: why that word for it instead of some reasonable alternative? What might *scar*, with its implications of damage and injury and permanence and disfigurement, suggest about what's in store?

We especially love the writing task she gives students: write a sentence describing what the scar is literally and what it is figuratively. This helps students to see multiple levels of meaning and how they are connected. To ask students to describe both the literal and figurative at the same time not only ensures that students attend to both but also helps them see the connection between the two. As Jen's students now understand, the scar is the place where the plane has crashed and it suggests permanent damage to the island and dangers yet to come.

Jen next glances ahead: they're going to study how Ralph's removal of his clothing might also be imbued with meaning and suggestion. But first, there's a brief interlude where Jen takes the time to invest in background knowledge. As we discuss in Chapter Four, inferences about symbolism, like other inferences and examples of analytical thinking, are knowledge-based more than skill-based.

Reading any text is the process of disambiguation, and what resolves ambiguities is knowledge. Sometimes there's enough in the text to resolve the ambiguity with an Establish Meaning question, but sometimes students need additional knowledge to do so. The latter is the case here, so Jen sets out to make sure her students have the background knowledge necessary to read key sections of the text deeply.

They start with an Embellishment (see Chapter Four for more): this picture of students from an English boarding school in the 1950s, the background from which the boys in the novel appear to have come.

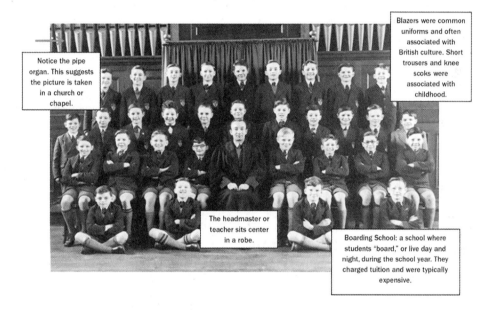

Notice the pipe organ. This suggests the picture is taken in a church or chapel.

Blazers were common uniforms and often associated with British culture. Short trousers and knee scoks were associated with childhood.

The headmaster or teacher sits center in a robe.

Boarding School: a school where students "board," or live day and night, during the school year. They charged tuition and were typically expensive.

Her students note the orderliness of the group and the importance of their uniforms in communicating belonging and status. They note the way the teacher—the "grown up," of which there are none on the island—is at the center of the picture and how the organ in the background is a clue that they have taken the picture in the school chapel because religion is an important influence on their actions.

To watch the video *Jen Brimming: Close Reading Part 2*, use this QR code or find the video at the URL https://vimeo.com/1058368172/b3dc7abc5a.

Suddenly Jen's students understand a lot more about the characters' backgrounds and, more importantly, what Golding might have wanted that to communicate. They are boys steeped in order and civility, the heirs to society's institutions and to the upper tiers of the domestic hierarchy.

Armed with that knowledge, they return to the text and reread, using FASE, the section from page One where Piggy and Ralph meet. As we pick up the video in *Jen Brimming: Close Reading Part 2*, you can hear the pleasure they take in the reading. Jen then tells her students that they are going to reread another key line.

First, Jen projects the line, which describes Ralph, for students to see and reread: "The fair boy stopped and jerked his stockings with an automatic gesture that made the jungle seem for a moment like the Home Counties."

She recognizes that her students probably won't get what Golding has implied by the phrase "Home Counties" and so she takes some time to Knowledge Feed again to help them understand what Golding would have assumed his readers would intuitively grasp. Then she asks her students to apply the knowledge to the text:

"When he says 'with an automatic gesture that made the jungle seem for a moment like the Home Counties', what's that telling us about Ralph? Write down your first thoughts!"

Note that Jen first feeds her students important background knowledge, then asks students to analyze the text, much as we saw with vocabulary in Chapter Five. This is far more interesting, rigorous, and equitable than asking students to guess something about a passage without the knowledge that might be required of them, especially for students who haven't been exposed to this knowledge previously.

You'll also probably notice another theme from our discussion of knowledge in Chapters Four and Five: the enthusiasm of students in knowledge-rich environments. Jen asks students to write, but they are eager to talk. With knowledge to apply to an interesting question, their curiosity has been awakened.

But notice also the structure of the task: the key line is projected to students *so they can look at it and sustain their focus on it*. If they forget it, if they miss a detail the first time through, they can reread it again and refresh their working memory.

In Chapter One, we explain the transient information effect—the idea that when students can see the object you have asked them to think about, they can analyze it more successfully and more deeply because they won't have to divide their working memory. Instead of using some of it merely to remember the learning object they seek to analyze, all of their working memory can be used to think deeply.

Close Reading is a perfect example of a time when this is especially useful. If we want students to think deeply about a sentence, or to perceive subtle details in a sentence, keeping the sentence in view is a boon to critical thinking. It enables students to sustain focus, refresh their memory of details they originally saw, and even notice new ones.

This is another example of reading an important and short excerpt in an attentionally privileged environment—and of how positively students respond. Here's what that looks like in the student-facing materials:

Annotate as you read and answer the following questions in your annotations:

- What is the scar? Why might it be called that?
- Consider how the two boys are different. How do they seem to get along?

2. Reread these two details. Compare Ralph's behavior in each of these two moments.

Detail 1	Detail 2
The fair boy stopped and jerked his stocking with an automatic gesture that made the jungle seem for a moment like the Home Counties. (p. 7)	"Aren't there any grownups at all?" "I don't think so." The fair boy said this solemnly; but then the delight of a realized ambition overcame him. In the middle of the scar he stood on his head and grinned at the reversed fat boy. "No grownups!" (p. 8)

_____

_____

_____

_____

_____

Now, Jen projects a second sentence on the board next to the first one, making it easy for students to compare both in close proximity and refresh their memory of the details of either sentence as necessary.

The first sentence, in which Ralph's actions reflect his internalization of the order of the Home Counties (an idea beautifully explicated by Jen's students) is taken from *before* the moment in the text when the boys realize for certain there are no grown-ups alive on the island. The second sentence is from *after* the boys' realization that there are no grown-ups.

Jen wants her students to look carefully at the contrast between the two. She leads them through a brief discussion and follows with a lovely Developmental Writing prompt asking them to summarize ("Describe the change in Ralph's behavior in the two passages in one sentence. Start with the word *initially*.").

Again, the structure of the close comparison and the study of the differences between the sentences is enabled by Jen's attention to students attention: to the manageable size of the passages, to their projection, to their being in proximity, to their being both on the board and on the materials they are using at their desks, pictured here, so they can easily transfer observations from board to paper and vice versa.

Reread Pages 7-9: On Your Own

Annotate as you read and answer the following questions in your annotations:

- What is the scar? Why might it be called that?
- Consider how the two boys are different. How do they seem to get along?

 2. Reread these two details. Compare Ralph's behavior in each of these two moments.

Detail 1	Detail 2
The fair boy stopped and jerked his stocking with an automatic gesture that made the jungle seem for a moment like the Home Counties. (p. 7)	*"Aren't there any grownups at all?"* *"I don't think so."* *The fair boy said this solemnly; but then the delight of a realized ambition overcame him. In the middle of the scar he stood on his head and grinned at the reversed fat boy.* *"No grownups!" (p. 8)*

Then, there's a last bit of rereading. It's the Sensitivity Analysis we discuss in Chapter Six: a key sentence is selected and projected to maximize attention and working memory. This time, though, an alternative version of the sentence, edited by the teacher, is also projected and students are asked to compare.

Here's the question with the original at the top and the alternative, with subtly diluted intensity and fewer hints at savagery, here:

Pages 9-10

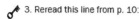 3. Reread this line from p. 10:

> He became conscious of the weight of his clothes, kicked his shoes off fiercely, and ripped off each stocking with its elastic garter in a single movement.

Compare it to the version below:

> He became conscious of the **inconvenience** of his clothes, kicked his shoes off **eagerly**, and **removed** each stocking with its elastic garter in a single movement.

a. What do you notice about the differences between each version? What does the first reveal about Ralph?

_____

_____

As we've seen in the previous video, the students, having compared the original to an alternate version, do a beautiful job of analyzing how the language in Golding's prose shows how quickly Ralph's primal nature emerges when he realizes there are no adults and no hierarchy to maintain the trappings of civilization.

Several of the activities we suggest in Close Reading rely on a principle of cognitive psychology called the *law of comparative judgment*, which tells us that people are able to make more accurate and reliable judgments about objects of analysis when they compare multiple examples than they are able to do when they look at one thing alone and try to interpret it in isolation (what's called *absolute judgment*).[1]

It's why Jen's Sensitivity Analysis question is so effective. It's hard to make an absolute judgment about the semantic decisions in this line from *Lord of the Flies*:

> He became conscious of the weight of clothes, kicked his shoes off *fiercely* and ripped off each stocking with its elastic garter in a single movement.

It's much easier to make those judgments when you can compare how Ralph kicking off his shoes *eagerly* is different from *fiercely*, for example.

In fact, you can almost see Jen Brimming draw on this law with her students in the video. "What was the difference between Christina and Riley's answer and Jack's answer?" she asks to enrich the students' discussion of what the scar symbolizes.

It's worth noting that students are making this comparison not by looking at the responses in question but only from listening. In other words, they have to use their working memory both to remember what Christina and Riley and Jack wrote, and how those answers are different. Their working memory is heavily loaded by this task, so it's not surprising that they don't notice right away the key difference Jen wants them to see: that Jack has pointed out that this forbodes bad things to come, while another student has merely pointed out that the word *scar* signifies permanent damage. It's a helpful reminder of how projecting the answers so all of the students' working memory can be focused on comparative analysis can make a large difference.

Let us pause here to take a look at some of the commonalities among the three exercises of rereading Jen uses:

- They are all **focused and detail-oriented.** They involve short passages of text that students can maintain intense focus on—manageable chunks that they can process fully with working memory. Perhaps later she might project longer pieces but at this point, early in the book, quality (of analysis) and quantity (of text) are inversely related.

- They are all **arranged to maximize attention.** The text under analysis is always in view, both on the board and in students' materials. Extraneous material is removed or de-emphasized so everyone is studying deeply the crucial moments to the best of their capacity.

- They end with the **generation effect,**[2] most often writing. Students have to describe what they've seen and observed in their own words, which encodes it more fully in their long-term memory.

In the rest of this chapter, we'll take a look at how to successfully engage in Close Reading with your own students. We'll discuss the importance of doing Close Reading in short bursts followed by opportunities to encode, how to select quality text for Close Reading, how to Establish Meaning in a text, how to create an attentionally privileged environment, share four types of effective Close Reading questions, and describe the role of knowledge in disambiguation, before closing with an example of Close Reading bursts in the context of an entire lesson.

SHORT BURSTS AND OPPORTUNITIES TO ENCODE

Close Reading works best in short bursts so as not to overburden students' working memory, followed by opportunities to encode to ensure the learning makes it into their long-term memory.

Close Reading asks students to reread, but there's more technique to it than saying "Okay, students, time to reread that passage." We have many times heard teachers *tell* their students to reread, but the teachers who have taught us the most have *shown* their students how to reread, differently and in a focused and attentionally privileged way so they see more and better the second time through. After all, merely repeating the same process a second time will not likely result in many aha moments that make going back seem worth the struggle.

Close Reading, as we define it, is the *focused, detail-oriented rereading of short sections of text in an attentionally privileged setting, ideally followed by an opportunity for encoding such as a Stop and Jot or a Turn and Talk.*

After writing a curriculum's worth of Close Reading questions for our *Reading Reconsidered* curriculum and working with teachers who have taught them to students, we've learned that Close Reading actually doesn't work as well when it's a lengthy reread all at once. Instead, a series of smaller "bursts" of Close Reading, often several in a lesson and linked by a shared focus on an important theme or idea, are especially impactful.

This idea jibes with much of what cognitive science tells us about what accelerates learning—particularly with novice learners like the readers in our classrooms when they are exposed to challenging texts.[3]

In his *Principles of Instruction*, educational psychologist Barak Rosenshine observes that presenting new content is best done in small, manageable steps and that this is especially the case when the content is dense and challenging. "Our working memory, the place where we process information, is small . . . [and] too much information swamps our working memory," he writes.[4]

Short bursts of careful rereading enable students to study challenging text with the full capacity of their working memory available. This not only prevents working memory overloads but also allows them to see more deeply and so come to value the process more.

This is the case because one result of working memory overload is that perception is degraded.[5] We see less and understand less of what we see when our brains are overloaded with things to think about. This is why driving a car while talking on your cellphone is dangerous—helping your spouse think about where their car keys might be causes you to be less adept at judging the rate and distance of another vehicle. It's also why fluent reading is so important, as we discuss in Chapter Three. If you have to think about what a text you are reading says—what the words mean or how they fit together—you can't think about what it means.

Much of what we saw Jen Brimming do (and much of Close Reading) is about building students' perception. Jen wants students to notice and perceive the subtle difference between *fiercely* and *eagerly* in the description of Ralph removing his clothes. So, just as important as choosing a rich and interesting line of text with something worthy to perceive is what she chooses *not* to present in order to prevent distraction and working memory overload.

Again, Close Reading is in large part about improving perception and, from a perception standpoint, it's optimal to read short passages deeply, with working memory entirely devoted to noticing subtleties within passages and differences between passages.

It's also worth noting that working memory overloads are often unpleasant for learners. Students feel the frustration of not being able to complete a task and the anxiety of trying to remember more than they can process. The feeling that you cannot keep up is no fun. And yet this feeling must be balanced with the reality that students *must struggle*. We don't want to remove struggle, in other words—we want to manage it, to make it so students struggle successfully. The key to that lies in ensuring manageable doses.

To have students read well—perhaps even surprising themselves with their insights—for a short period of time makes the process of Close Reading feel motivating and exciting but not overwhelming. Using shorter bursts of Close Reading enables us to increase the challenge and the load on working memory over time. It's an effective structure to build students' confidence and perseverance at challenging tasks.

A story about the renowned cellist Yo-Yo Ma provides an analogy. As you probably know, Ma is among the most gifted musicians in the world, known for his ability to interpret music in a unique and expressive manner. Put another way, he sees a bit more than almost anyone else in the music that is written on the page—Close Reading of a different variety, but Close Reading just the same.

Ma's father was a musician as well and began teaching his son to play at a very young age. He gave him complex texts to learn to play and interpret: Bach cello suites. But the elder Ma simplified the learning process for his son by asking him to study and play only two measures at a time—as a very rough estimate (none of us is musical!), that's about five seconds of music in each burst of study!

He would practice those with intensity but, because of their reduced size, he could do this with full focus and within a short amount of time—especially important for a five-year-old whose working memory is still developing. Each time he played he was fresh; his working memory and attention were fully engaged. He practiced playing with maximum insight and quality and this became a habit, one he was soon able to apply to longer stretches of music. And so, the young Yo-Yo Ma learned to play very difficult music beautifully, deeply, insightfully because his father focused on deeper, not more.

An additional benefit of shorter, more frequent bursts of Close Reading is that more frequent practice makes key ideas more durable. As we mentioned in our discussion of Retrieval Practice in Chapter Four, there is an ideal number of times that you need to be exposed to an idea to ensure that it's encoded into long-term memory. The repetition of key ideas about a text makes the learning, knowledge, and themes that we're hoping to elucidate and reinforce more durable.

Our vision of Close Reading is built on this idea: careful study of short passages of text, often just a sentence in length, done with maximum focus and attentiveness, spaced throughout a lesson. Rosenshine's guidance that teachers should teach new and complex material in small steps is useful, but it also begs the question of what happens in between those steps. Rosenshine recommends that students "practice" once they are exposed to a new idea, but the examples he provides are primarily from math—a more skill-driven endeavor than reading, in which knowledge is by far the greater factor. Could a teacher try to use practice after a burst of Close Reading? Perhaps. Jen Brimming might ask her students to write a Sensitivity Analysis sentence of their own introducing changes to some other sentence, but it's not clear what overall goal this would serve.

Instead, it's worth reflecting on why the practice Rosenshine recommends is useful. One purpose of it is to begin encoding, a process that is facilitated by active learning. This unburdens working memory, preparing students for more new information or perhaps another Close Reading burst.

So, a bit of active learning after a dose of new content might also achieve the process of encoding and unburdening of working memory. But what exactly is active learning? As we discuss in Chapter Six the cognitive psychologist Héctor Ruiz Martín describes *active learning* as a "learning experience in which the student actively thinks about the learning object, seeking meaning and comparing it with their prior knowledge."[6] Daniel Willingham describes it similarly. "Memory is the residue of thought," he writes. Think deeply about what you just discovered and you will remember—and encode—it.[7]

We can get the most active learning by understanding the generation effect, which we discuss earlier: you begin encoding ideas in your memory when you create a version of what you are learning in your own words. Active learning on your own is hard to sustain. It requires more focus and self-regulation than most people can easily muster during learning. But the learning environment can socialize it. If we ask students to talk briefly to a peer or to write briefly in a notebook in response to a question that causes them to seek meaning in the object of study and connect it to other things they know, we can cause active learning—thus both beginning the process of encoding the ideas students learn from Close Reading in long-term memory and priming their working memory to be ready for more.

Again, you can see Jen doing this in her lesson. A bit of Close Reading yields an insight—the word *scar* implies permanent damage! It's followed by a question that asks students to think about what this means—what might this imply about what is going to happen?—and they are asked to talk and/or write about it for a few seconds to cause them to benefit from the memory-building advantages of the generation effect.

SELECTING COMPLEX TEXTS FOR CLOSE READING

Close Reading only works with complex text, carefully selected, aimed at supporting students in arriving at a larger understanding about the book.

As you may recall from Chapter One, one of our key research-backed arguments is that the ability to read complex text is the gatekeeper to long-term success. The report from a 2006 study by the makers of the ACT revealed that only about half of ACT test takers were prepared for college based on their reading abilities. Test makers concluded that "performance on complex texts is the clearest differentiator in reading between students who are likely to be ready for college and those who are not."[8] Being able to read what is difficult, it turns out, is the gatekeeper to further study.

We hope this reinforces why Close Reading is so important. When students encounter complex texts, they need tools to help them succeed and they need experience succeeding in the face of adversity to help them persist.

But Close Reading is not just the set of tools to help young people master complex text, it also *requires* complex text. Without text that stands up to analysis, it is an empty exercise. Jen's questions about *Lord of the Flies* are worth asking because the book is so challenging and rich in symbolism. The answers revealed by a second look at the text are worth discovering. Not every text offers that.

Five Types of Text Complexity

In *Reading Reconsidered,* we presented five forms of text complexity[9] that are especially challenging to developing readers. We revisit them here because they are especially good indicators of a text that are well suited for Close Reading:

- **Archaic text.** The first line of Charles Darwin's *Origin of Species* reads, "This Abstract, which I now publish, must necessarily be imperfect." Today we would say something like: "The essay I am publishing is imperfect."

  The first line of Jane Austen's *Pride and Prejudice* reads: "It is a truth universally acknowledged, that a single man in possession of a good fortune, must be in want of a wife." Today we would more likely say: "It is a universally acknowledged truth that a wealthy single man needs a wife."

  A key sentence in the first paragraph of *Narrative of the Life of Frederick Douglass* reads, "By far the larger part of the slaves know as little of their ages as horses know of theirs." Today we would say something like: "Most slaves know as little about their own ages as horses do."

  Texts written in the past used different words, different phrasing, and different syntax. This poses unique challenges to modern readers—and to a society that values older texts. Imagine a world in which only a tiny minority of students could read the three mentioned books, never mind the works of Shakespeare, the Constitution, and the Bible. Imagine arriving on campus having never read anything older than fifty years in age and being handed one of these texts to read.

  Unpacking older text is an ideal topic for Close Reading, and skill at Close Reading makes older texts viable to teach.

  Fortunately, as we also point out in *Reading Reconsidered,* there are dozens of books that offer manageable exposure to archaic language. We call them *pre-complex texts* because they offer a version of the challenge we seek to help students master but at a level appropriate for younger readers. C. S . Lewis's *The Magician's Nephew,* P. L. Travers's *Mary Poppins,* L. Frank Baum's *The Wizard of Oz,* and Kenneth Grahame's *The Wind in the Willows* are examples of engaging texts that even young students can read that gradually expose them to older and rarer forms of written expression.

- **Nonlinear texts.** Simple texts tell the story in chronological order and make any flashbacks or jumps forward in time obvious with transitions (e.g., "a few weeks later . . .").

More complex, nonlinear texts move arbitrarily and suddenly throughout time, often without telling the reader. The reader must figure it out. James Joyce's *Ulysses* is perhaps one of the most famous of these texts, but there are a myriad of more accessible books for young people that can prepare them to study about the linearity of narration. Donald Crews's book *Bigmama's* is one of our favorites.

- **Complexity of narrator.** Narrators can be unreliable, meaning readers must learn to find the story behind the inaccuracies and biases of the storyteller. Narrators can be invasive. They can, in the midst of telling a story in the third person, suddenly address the reader directly with a germane point—as C. S. Lewis is wont to do in *The Magician's Nephew*—or an obscure one, as Lemony Snicket (the nom de plume of Daniel Handler) is wont to do (a phrase which here means he tends to do it)[10] in his A Series of Unfortunate Events books.

- **Complexity of plot.** Texts can be rich in symbolism like *Lord of the Flies*, offering a deeper level so that the explicit narrative is only a partial version of the story. Or, they can tell multiple intertwined and sometimes not apparently connected stories at once, leaving it up to the reader to track the moving pieces until they all come together.

- **Intentionally resistant texts.** These texts can use the tools above and others to deliberately try to disorient and confuse the reader—perhaps for experimental reasons, perhaps to try to create for the reader the psychological experience of the thing they are reading about—the confusion of war, say, as in Kurt Vonnegut's *Slaughterhouse-Five*, or living in a dystopian future, as in Ray Bradbury's *Fahrenheit 451*.

Complex Text and Student Persistence

In her book *Reader, Come Home*, Maryanne Wolf uses the term *cognitive patience* to describe the nexus of mindset, self-discipline, and self-regulation required to sustain focus on a difficult text. If one of the goals of reading in school is to ensure that students read regularly from complex text that is at or above grade level, some of the skills they need are these "softer" skills.

As Wolf writes, in the age of the device, increasing numbers of college professors have expressed their concern about students' "impatience with older, denser . . . literature and writing"—a topic we also discuss in Chapter Two and Six. Wolf shares the observation from professors that "students have become increasingly less patient with the time it takes to understand the syntactically demanding sentence structures in denser texts and increasingly averse to the effort needed to go deeper in their analysis." Reading dense and difficult texts requires cognitive patience, and in the age of the device, that's in steep decline—for students of all ages.[11]

As teachers of literacy and English, we must consider how we can strategically build the cognitive patience required to persist through challenging reading. Close Reading is one such tool (or part of a set of tools) to help students learn to persist, even when it's hard.

We do want to be clear that Close Reading isn't the only tool to support students in developing cognitive patience. In Chapter Two, we talk about rebuilding attentional skills via sustained bouts of reading with annotation. In Chapters Four and Five, we talk about using background knowledge and vocabulary to help students to understand more and see more in what they read—which also makes them more likely to persist. Close Reading is another critical tool in that toolbox.

SELECTING TEXTUAL EXCERPTS

This brings us to an important point about choosing text for Close Reading bursts. A rich and complex text offers an unlimited number of passages worthy of concerted focus and depth of analysis via Close Reading. We have to be disciplined about selecting the moments for Close Reading so that the analysis we do within our bursts supports kids in arriving at the larger understanding we're aiming for.

The goal for closely reading a text is to help students arrive at a holistic understanding of the section of a text they're reading. It's not just Close Reading for the sake of practicing "the process of Close Reading," but for the sake of a deeper reading of a hard or important section of text that culminates with more thorough understanding than one can glean in the first reading of challenging text. The analysis from Close Reading should link back to our essential understanding or key themes for the day or unit. While it can be tempting to pause and closely read every beautiful and ornate decision an author makes, it can also distract students from a cohesive reading of the text or overload working memory, diminishing the very perception and decision-making skills we seek to build. Choosing sections of text to closely read without considering the desired takeaways from the text can lead to a magpie approach that proves confusing and distracting for students.

One of our curriculum writers, Emily Badillo, describes her sequential process for thinking about the best moments within a text for Close Reading:

- As planners, when we approach a complex text, our first questions are always:
  - What do students need to understand from this section of text?
  - What lines or passages are most critical for developing that understanding?
- Once we have a clear sense of the central understanding that we want students to walk away with, we think about which of the lines that we identified might require Close Reading to unlock. Within those lines, Establishing Meaning is especially important. We ask ourselves:
  - What questions can we ask about this section of text that will help students develop a shared, accurate understanding of the text's literal meaning?
- Then, we consider any vocabulary or knowledge stumbling blocks that might interfere with understanding. We ask:
  - Where might we define a word or phrase or activate students' prior knowledge?
- Finally, we think about additional layers of analytical meaning:
  - Is there figurative language, symbolic meaning, or other craft moves we want to draw students' attention to?
  - Are there phrases that can be interpreted multiple ways?
  - Is there language that connects to other analysis students have done within the lesson or unit?

Emily's process makes clear that Close Reading is one part of a larger equation that adds together the various methods we've discussed in this book to result in a better foundational understanding of the text as a whole. And, by intentionally selecting the passages that will best contribute to students' understanding of the texts, teachers can help students to realize the connection between Close Reading of a text and their overall understanding of the work.

Here's an example of a Close Reading excerpt and questions from a lesson on Malala Yousafzai's *I Am Malala* that we selected and crafted to help students reach an important lesson objective: to analyze evidence of Malala's growing maturity and shifting role. The burst also ties into broader unit key understandings, as we'll explain.

3. Reread these lines (p. 119):

[The campaign for girls' education] was my calling. Some powerful force had come to dwell inside me, something bigger and stronger than me, and it had made me fearless. Now it was up to me to give my father a dose of the courage he had always given me.

a. **Turn and Talk:** In your opinion, what is the "powerful force" that makes Malala "fearless"? Try to think of several possibilities.

b. In a carefully crafted sentence, explain how these lines reveal a change in Malala.

c. Revise your response by including a form of the word **advocate** or **fortitude**.

You'll notice that Part A asks students to think of several possibilities. This is a good passage for a Close Reading because there is not one right answer—kids can recall many previously read details from the memoir to come up with multiple possible answers.

The question in Part B requires students to do some Developmental Writing—they're thinking about how, in the writing of her memoir, Malala has selected lines to reveal changes in her perspective. It's designed to deepen their understanding of the objective of the day, but also to reinforce one of the key understandings of the unit: *Malala Yousafzai selects memoir as the form to relate her personal experiences. In her memoir, Malala intentionally selects events from her past and shapes them through the lens of her present experiences to communicate her particular perspectives about her family, faith, culture, and her passionate belief in education for all.*

Part C requires students to think about their response to Part B on a deeper level—this time including a previously taught vocabulary word (*advocate* or *fortitude*). It's a great question for reinforcing knowledge and increasing the depth of student responses, and it connects to another essential understanding from the unit: *Fear plays different roles in motivating actions. It can be used as a tool to prevent people from acting or speaking their minds, but it can also generate acts of courage and inspire people to greater achievements.*

By looking at three lines from the text, students have a greater understanding of some key understandings of the unit as well as the intentional decisions Malala made in crafting her memoir to convey critical ideas about her life and experiences.

Here's another example from our unit on Lorraine Hansberry's play, *A Raisin in the Sun*. The lesson objective is for students to examine Mama's decision to spend insurance money she has been paid on a house for her family. The burst we chose includes lines from multiple scenes that will cause students to notice that plants are recurring symbols in the play and to think specifically about what they represent to Mama, which will help them to better understand her decision.

2. In the excerpt from pp. 44-45, Mama mentions outdoor space twice when she dreams of a house. Contrast these references with lines earlier in the play:

Dream House	Kitchenette Apartment
• with a yard where Travis could play in the summertime (p. 44) • fixing it up and making me a little garden in the back (p. 45)	• The sole natural light the family may enjoy in the course of a day is only that which fights its way through this little window. (p. 24) • MAMA Lord, if this little old plant don't get more sun than it's been getting it ain't never going to see spring again. (p. 40) • MAMA Well, I always wanted me a garden like I used to see sometimes at the back of the houses down home. This plant is as close as I ever got to having one. (p. 53)

Why might a garden be an important part of Mama's dream? What might it represent to Mama?

Notes

These examples are linked to essential understandings about the play that are sustained over time. They are about sharpening focus on what's important. Without this critical anchor, Close Reading can become a scattershot experience where students "go deeper" into the text without making real sense of the book in the end.

THE CRITICAL IMPORTANCE OF ESTABLISHING MEANING

Students cannot engage in higher-level analysis until they first understand what a text is literally saying.

Before Jen Brimming asks her students "big" analytical questions like what the scar might symbolize or what it might foretell about events on the island, she asks "small" literal questions: What exactly is "the scar"?

The importance of this step to Establish Meaning is easy to overlook. As we noted, most teachers want to be rigorous, and bigger, figurative, abstract questions feel more rigorous than literal questions. Sometimes they are. And asking literal meaning questions feels so, well, literal. Additionally, as we discuss in Chapter Four, many teachers have taken knowledge's place at the bottom of Bloom's taxonomy and analysis's place in a higher tier to mean that they should skip over any knowledge-building questions in favor of analysis.

But you can't think deeply about something you don't quite get, something you're confused about or something you haven't noticed. And as the example of the scar showed, literal questions are often far from easy—especially with complex text. What percentage of students in Jen's class would have had only a vague idea of what the scar was if she hadn't Established Meaning first?

Or, take the following example from Edgar Allan Poe's *The Tell-Tale Heart*, which asks simply what "the idea" the narrator refers to is. If you know the story, written from the point of view of a narrator who is not just unreliable but unhinged, you know how hard this question is. Part of the point of the story's early narration is the gradual emergence of the answer: The "idea" is to murder his neighbor. All of which illustrates how hard it can be to answer literal Establish Meaning questions in complex texts.

3. Reread this line from the second paragraph:

It is impossible to say how first the idea entered my brain; but once conceived[1], it haunted me day and night.

[1]**conceived**: thought of

a. What is "the idea"? _____

b. What causes the narrator to decide on this idea? What *doesn't* cause him to decide on it?

Notes

One of the most common and easy ways to overlook ways to Establish Meaning is what we call a *pronoun reference question*: What is *it* in that sentence? Who is the *he* the main character is referring to?

You can watch Jen Rugani asking one such question in the video *Jen Rugani: What Does* It *Refer To?* In the lesson, Jen and her students encountered this passage on the opening page of Natalie Babbitt's *Tuck Everlasting*:

The road that led to Treegap had been trod out long before by a herd of cows who were, to say the least, relaxed. It wandered along in curves and easy angles, swayed off

To watch the video *Jen Rugani: What Does It Refer To*, use this QR code or find the video at the URL https://vimeo.com/1058368372/ad9183f62c.

and up in a pleasant tangent to the top of a small hill, ambled down again between fringes of bee-hung clover, and then cut sidewise across a meadow. Here its edges blurred. It widened and seemed to pause, suggesting tranquil bovine picnics: slow chewing and thoughtful contemplation of the infinite. And then it went on again and came at last to the wood. But on reaching the shadows of the first trees, it veered sharply, swung out in a wide arc as if, for the first time, it had reason to think where it was going, and passed around.

Jen pauses at this point and rereads the last sentence with her students:

But on reaching the shadow of the first trees, it veered sharply, swung out in a wide arc as if, for the first time, it had reason to think where it was going and passed around.

She asks: "What does *it* refer to?"

Her tone is playful as she asks; her countenance smiling as if to confirm it was a bit of a puzzle.

The sentence, as we're sure you noticed, is describing a road wending its way through the countryside. The road has taken on the personality of the cows that made it. But of course, that is not likely to be clear to all readers—certainly not on first reading. And so, "What does *it* refer to?" while a literal question, is far from an easy one. After all, it's unusual to see such extended a personification of any object, never mind a road—several sentences worth in which it ambles, widens, pauses, and goes on again, veers, and so on. Even an experienced reader might begin to doubt whether the author was still talking about the road. By the time the passage refers to *it* in the sentence Jen chose, the last explicit mention of the noun *road* to which it refers has occurred *six sentences* prior. In between, there's the mention of cows—maybe one of them is the *it*?—and plenty of complex syntax and purplish prose to overwhelm working memory.

Jen will ultimately ask students to analyze the passage, to discuss why the path the road takes is important and what it might suggest about the setting, but first she recognizes that this is a doozy of a sentence for a developing reader. With complex text, the literal is easy to misconstrue, and if students don't follow that this long description is about the road, they cannot consider why it is described as if it were a character in an almost timeless drama. Students can't move on to symbolism and meaning if they don't recognize the actual image that is being referenced in the text.

You'll notice that Jen's students give a range of answers to her question, illustrating their confusion about the meaning of the word *it* (and the sentence itself) and underscoring the importance of her decision to Establish Meaning during reading.

In fact, given the complexity of this text, it's probably worth asking a series of Establish Meaning questions before expecting students to be ready to explain the significance of the path of the road. Some additional questions Jen might have asked to prepare her students for analysis include these:

- Who or what originally made the road? (cows)

- When does the road "veer sharply"? (upon reaching the wood)

- Does the road go through the wood? (no; it "swings out in a wide arc" and passes around)

- What reason does the text give for why the road might have avoided the wood? ("it had reason to think where it was going, and passed around")

- Follow-up analysis question: What does that make you think or wonder about the wood?

These questions are not only rigorous but also help to establish the full meaning of the paragraph. Before we wrote them, we ourselves got the "gist" of the paragraph: this is a last road wending its way through the countryside; it has taken on the personality of some cows that first made it. But we did *not* notice the sudden fear the road shows when it nears the woods—the way an otherwise tranquil and contemplative road "veered sharply" and suddenly became aware "as if for the first time" of where it was going. In trying to write questions to Establish Meaning more clearly, we ourselves became aware of how much there was to analyze in the passage.

This is really our key point. *Establishing Meaning comes first and it works in synergy, not competition, with more analytical questions.* Otherwise, students are likely to get frustrated when their teacher goes off on a tangent about symbolism while they're still trying to figure out what's what.

In the video *Erin Dziak: Houses in the Hills*, seventh-grade teacher Erin Dziak at St. Thomas Aquinas Middle School in Cleveland, Ohio, pauses in the midst of reading Sandra Cisneros's *The House on Mango Street* to ask her students a couple of questions about the section her students have just read.

To watch the video *Erin Dziak: Houses in the Hills*, use this QR code or find the video at the URL https://vimeo.com/1058368533/e52151e74a.

Cisneros's book, as many readers will know, is written as a series of short vignettes that are often a bit like prose-poems with writing that is both rich and challenging.

The passage Erin's class is reading is from the beginning of a chapter called "Bums in the Attic":

> *I want a house on a hill like the ones with the gardens where Papa works. We go on Sundays, Papa's day off. I used to go. I don't anymore. You don't like to go out with us, Papa says. Getting too old? Getting too stuck-up, says Nenny. I don't tell them I'm ashamed—all of us staring out the window like we're hungry. I am tired of looking at what we can't have. When we win the lottery . . . Mama begins, and then I stop listening.*

Erin starts with two seemingly basic questions:

"Where did Esperanza used to go with her family?"

"What's special about these houses?"

These might seem like obvious questions, but as we've seen, literal does not always mean easy, especially when the writing is complex as Cisneros's prose is here. It's hard to tell who is saying what. Quotation marks are not included. The time sequence is nonlinear—Cisneros describes in the present tense ("I stop listening") what used to happen because she doesn't go anymore. Unfamiliarity and unconventional writing are often a recipe for working memory overload, and even bright students suddenly must engage their thinking in figuring out who is speaking and when the events described have happened. This increases the likelihood that they will fail to perceive things they would otherwise have noticed.

And, in fact, the students' answers reveal that they are confused. They have read carefully, we know, because their answers contain accurate details from the text, but they can't put it all together: Esperanza and her family used to go look at houses on the hills, nicer than their own, and her mother used to daydream about the houses.

Erin handles the moment beautifully, calmly fielding multiple student responses, but this clip is a reminder of how difficult it can be for students to make basic meaning of texts. Erin's diligence about Establishing Meaning pays off because, as the clip ends, we see that students are quickly able to answer the more analytical question about why Esperanza no longer wants to look at these houses on the hills.

Once literal meaning has been established, students are ready to analyze. But it is a mistake to presume that students have automatically understood literal meaning on a first read with complex text. When we don't effectively Establish Meaning like Jen and Erin do, students may be reluctant to respond to the analytical questions we pose. Who hasn't had a time when they asked a beautiful and thought-provoking question only to get crickets in response? In cases when students do attempt to answer, they often share inaccurate, overly narrow, or incomplete responses. They say something true about the text but fail to answer the question. It's more effective (and a better use of students' time) to Establish Meaning first.

Establish Meaning questions don't have to come at the end of a section of reading. We think they can be effectively interspersed into the reading as this next clip shows. The clip *Jonathan Gallegos: Mr. Yakota's Market* was shot in Jonathan's fifth-grade classroom at Creo Prep in the Bronx, a school that is pervaded both by a hard commitment to reading whole books of merit and by a collective diligence about Establishing Meaning in the course of reading. Before his lesson on Pam Muñoz Ryan's *Esperanza Rising*, Jonathan identified key lines in the text that would be important for later analysis and that he knew might be challenging for students to comprehend. In order to support meaning making during

To watch the video *Jonathan Gallegos: Mr. Yakota's Market*, use this QR code or find the video at the URL https://vimeo.com/105836 8678/6e80c60a08.

reading, he planned pause points to define unfamiliar words (as we discuss in Chapter Five) and asks a series of Establish Meaning questions to check students' literal understanding ("What does she mean by who would be next?" "What does that tell us about how she's feeling?" "Who's asking this question?" "What is Esperanza asking Miguel, in your own words?"). Jonathan uses annotation to give students a chance to process their thinking, creating a record of key ideas they can refer to in their written analysis.

In Chapter One, we explain the role of disambiguation in comprehension. Authors always make assumptions about what readers know and assume they will fill in gaps. This is always true, even when authors aren't deliberately leaving blanks and ambiguities for stylistic or artistic reasons. Meaning making relies on resolving ambiguities. In a complex text the process of disambiguation can be more challenging. Knowledge plays a big role in supporting disambiguation, as we'll discuss later in the chapter.

In Jen Rugani's *Tuck Everlasting* lesson, which we discussed previously, students were able to read the sentence with ease, but it was only after she stopped to question them on its referent that it became apparent that they didn't actually know that *it* referred to the path of the road. They were missing key information about the subject of the sentence. As experienced or expert readers, we naturally or automatically disambiguate in these moments, so it can also be harder for us to identify those moments as stumbling points for our students. It's critical to mine the text for these potentially ambiguous moments and then pause to ask questions like "Who's speaking?" "What does that pronoun refer to?" "What additional information do we learn from that appositive?" They're important for supporting meaning making and for providing models of the kinds of questions kids should ask themselves when they read.

In the video *Eric Snider: Snow*, Eric Snider and his sixth-grade students are reading Lois Lowry's *The Giver* when they encounter an especially tricky paragraph:

To watch the video *Eric Snider: Snow*, use this QR code or find the video at the URL https://vimeo.com/1058368845/709c9ba65d.

Climate Control. Snow made growing food difficult, limited agricultural periods. And unpredictable weather made transportation almost impossible at times. It wasn't a practical thing, so it became obsolete when we went to Sameness.

Eric's ultimate goal is for students to understand Lowry's conception of Sameness and the measures that Jonas's community takes to achieve the seemingly utopian state of Sameness. Like Jen Rugani did with her second graders, Eric realizes how disorienting but critical the pronoun *it* is in context of this paragraph, so he asks students to annotate by drawing an arrow to its referent. When he sees that students are confused, he asks a student to reread and drops in a quick definition for *agricultural* (another possible stumbling point for students). After a reread, it's still evident that not all students are sure that *it* refers to snow, so Eric asks an additional question to support them ("What became obsolete?") and rereads to test out a couple of their responses ("Did transportation become obsolete?"). Once they arrive at *snow*, Eric is careful to link this back to their holistic understanding of the text by jotting it on the board as part of a list of what they're starting to learn about "this program of Sameness." Understanding that community members eliminated snow is one piece of a puzzle they're putting together to understand the concept of Sameness, a critical but dangerous feature of their dystopian community.

This excerpt from Lowry's novel includes an example of grammatical ambiguity at the level of the individual sentence, for which Eric deftly asks Establish Meaning questions to support students in disambiguating.

Teachers often ask us if Establishing Meaning deflates rigor. We hope this section has shown that it's actually the opposite: Establishing Meaning creates a pathway to support students in successfully analyzing meaning in complex texts. Otherwise, we are asking students to develop real insights about a text that they don't understand—resulting in students giving answers that are essentially guesses, leaving us to provide a more rigorous answer ourselves.

We also hope this section has made clear the value in following up with questions that cause students to Analyze Meaning. When you don't offer opportunities to Analyze Meaning, students don't develop sensitivity to word choice, phrasing, or figurative language, and they risk gaining no or limited insight into an author's intentionality.

The most effective bursts, then, include opportunities both to Establish and Analyze Meaning, constantly toggling back and forth between the concrete (Establish Meaning) and the more abstract (Analyze Meaning). For some students, the hard work of Establishing Meaning is justified by the insight that comes from the subsequent Analyzing Meaning—seeing text in a new, surprising or symbolic way.

ATTENTIONALLY PRIVILEGED ENVIRONMENTS

We set students up for successful Close Reading when we reduce distractions and increase the availability of their working memory.

Another key to successful Close Reading is ensuring it occurs in "attentionally privileged environments." We use this phrase to mean students studying text where distractions are reduced and where the presentation allows for the maximum possible proportion of student working memory to be made available for careful reading, perception, and analysis.

One of the things we know about human cognition is that working memory can be drawn to extraneous or distracting tasks very easily. Holding ideas in working memory is hard to do and even small distractions can allow the contents of a student's thinking to dissipate.

When comparing two key sentences in a book, for example, it's very easy for students' working memory to become absorbed by other tasks. Students have to hold the memory of line A in their heads. Just the task of remembering that first line requires a significant amount of working memory. If students cannot refresh their working memory of line A, they will have to choose between remembering it and studying line B deeply. It's even more challenging if they have to hold the memory of line A in their minds while they flip ahead or back through the book and find line B, perhaps reading or skimming the text on a new page to find it. How well do they remember line A at this point? Probably not as well as we'd like to think. How easily can they refresh their memory of it, without looking back at it? Not easily at all.

These seem like mundane problems—in fact, they are mundane problems—but they are problems nonetheless, ones that are especially relevant when what we are asking of students requires their full working memory. This is why it's important to design Close Reading tasks with awareness of the *transient information effect*, which, as we discuss in Chapter Six and the introduction of this chapter, reminds us that when we want to maximize working memory available for a cognitive task, the object(s) of analysis should remain constantly in view.

Creating an attentionally privileged environment often involves taking lines we want students to study and placing them where they can see them as they study and analyze them. We saw this previously in the chapter when Jen and her students were studying key lines from *Lord of the Flies* and she projected the lines on the board. They were looking at the lines as they talked about them. If the students forget—because cognitive science tells us they will forget some aspects of the lines as they study others—they can simply glance at the projected lines and quickly be reminded.

The lines of text on the board were also a mirror of what was on their desk in their notes packet. No matter where Jen's students directed their gaze—to the board or to their desks—it was easy to see the lines in question. And if they generated an insight while looking at the board, it was easy to transcribe it directly onto their paper because the images looked the same.

Here's another good example from our *Reading Reconsidered* curriculum's student packet for our unit on *Lord of the Flies*. During instruction, it would also be projected on the board:

5. Reread the following details:

Detail 1	Detail 2
The fat boy waited to be asked his name in turn but this proffer of acquaintance was not made; the fair boy called Ralph smiled vaguely, stood up, and began to make his way once more toward the lagoon. The fat boy hung steadily at his shoulder. (p. 9)	*"He dived into the sand at Piggy's feet and lay there laughing."* *"Piggy!"* *Piggy grinned reluctantly, pleased despite himself at even this much recognition.* (p. 11)

In each of the details above, underline specific words or phrases that capture Piggy's behavior toward Ralph. Then, describe the relationship that seems to be growing between the two.

The lines are clearly presented so that they are easy to see and study. Notice also that there is very little else on the page—or projected on the board—to distract students' attention. Creating an attentionally privileged environment means a simple visual presentation of the relevant text—no emojis or extraneous images!

When asked to "underline specific words and phrases that capture Piggy's behavior toward Ralph," a student who starts reading from the board—or who is attending to the teacher pointing to a line or phrase that might be worth looking at—can easily find this on their page because the student packet looks the same as what the teacher is projecting on the board.[12]

If there are more than one lines to be studied, as in this example, they are placed next to each other for ease of comparison. No flipping back and forth between page 9 and page 11 to compare the two passages.

If there are required supports such as vocabulary terms, they are subtly included so students can access them without diverting their attention elsewhere, as they are with the definition of *minstrel* in this question from our unit on Bernard Evslin's *Heroes, Gods and Monsters of the Greek Myths*:

8. Reread this excerpt from p. 111:

> *The ship was searched, and Arion's property restored to him. He insisted on dividing the rich gifts with the king. When Periander protested, Arion laughed and said, "Treasures are trouble. You're a king and can handle them. But I am a minstrel[1]. I must travel light."*
>
> **[1]minstrel:** traveling musician

a. Why do you think Arion decides to share his treasure with Periander?

_____

_____

_____

b. What does this suggest about Arion's values?

_____

_____

_____

This kind of attentionally privileged presentation can be supported by asking perception-based questions, which ask in a relatively open-ended way for students to make observations about details they notice in the text. For example: "What do you notice about the difference (or similarity) between the two lines?" The goal is to make it easy for students to look carefully and perceive things of importance as they study how meaning is made by the language in the text.

This question from our *Lord of the Flies* unit offers an example:

4. Reread this moment from p. 14:

"We may stay here till we die."

With that word the heat seemed to increase till it became a threatening weight and the lagoon attacked them with blinding effulgence[1].

[1] **effulgence**: so bright it's hard to look at

a. What do you notice about the way heat is portrayed?

_____

_____

b. Why might the phrase *"the lagoon attacked them with blinding effulgence* [brightness]*"* be particularly important?

The question "What do you notice about the way the heat is portrayed?" is a perception-based question. Notice also the ease with which the definition of *effulgence* is provided and how easy the mirror image of the two formats makes it for students to translate what they may be thinking as they look at the passage on the board to the writing they do in their packets in response. All of these things contribute to students' attention being focused on the instructional task, rather than the mundane distractions surrounding it.

MORE EXAMPLES OF EFFECTIVE CLOSE READING QUESTIONS

We know that Close Reading starts with the careful selection of portions of complex texts presented in an attentionally privileged environment. And, we know that Close Reading should occur in frequent, short sequences of questions, or bursts, which enable students optimally to focus their working memory on the perceptive and analytical work—preventing working memory overload and enabling them to understand the text more deeply through questions that ask them to establish and analyze meaning.

One of the things Close Reading bursts do is prompt students to build a habit—to look for and attend to lines of special importance, to think about them deeply so that, over time, they will internalize the process of doing so, the capacity to do it well, and the perception to notice when heightened attention is warranted.

We think there is pleasure in this process when aimed at brilliant and worthy books, and we think students in classrooms are likely to want to read more brilliant and worthy books as a result. But we also note that these skills transcend fiction texts. If the students who do this kind of Close Reading become our doctors, lawyers, or government officials, we are confident in their ability to pay keen attention to the information in the texts they read and to unlock the maximum meaning from them.

As we have developed our *Reading Reconsidered* curriculum and worked with teachers who use it, we have found ourselves relying on four kinds of bursts in particular. Of course, bursts aren't limited to just these four types, but they are the ones we find most effective.

Key Line Questions

Key Line Questions facilitate the deep study of a critical single line or short passage of a few sentences to seek to fully understand it, often with a special focus on unpacking how meaning is made.

You can see those design elements in these two examples, one from our unit on *The Giver* and the previous example from our unit on *Lord of the Flies*:

 3. Reread these lines from p. 26:

> *Now, seeing the newchild and its expression, he was reminded that the light eyes were not only a **rarity** but gave the one who had them a certain look—what was it? Depth, he decided; as if one were looking into the clear water of the river, down to the bottom, where things might **lurk** which hadn't been discovered yet. He felt self-conscious, realizing that he, too, had that look.*
>
> **rarity**: something that almost never happens
> **lurk**: to hide in a threatening way

a. Why might Jonas compare looking into Gabriel's eyes to looking into a river? Think literally and figuratively.

Literal	Figurative

🗝 4. Reread this moment from p. 14:

"We may stay here till we die."

With that word the heat seemed to increase till it became a threatening weight and the lagoon attacked them with blinding effulgence[1].

[1] **effulgence**: so bright it's hard to look at

a. What do you notice about the way heat is portrayed?

_____

_____

b. Why might the phrase *"the lagoon attacked them with blinding effulgence* [brightness]" be particularly important?

Both of these questions enable students to focus deeply on a single critical line and then simply and easily translate their thinking into writing. Since the writing tasks involve multiple steps, it's important that it's easy for students to go back to reread and reconsider it as they write, and this is easily and simply accomplished since students merely need to glance up to do so.

Comparison Questions

Comparison Questions are questions where two pieces of contrasting text are presented in proximity so that subtle or important differences or connections can be studied. They leverage the law of comparative judgment, which we describe earlier in this chapter OR drop this additional information entirely, which tells us that people are more insightful when they compare examples directly than when they try to make abstract observations about the quality of an object of study.

Here are two examples, one from our unit on *Heroes, Gods and Monsters of the Greek Myths*, the other from Mildred D. Taylor's *Roll of Thunder, Hear My Cry*:

Example 1

b. Compare Icarus's thoughts during his flight to Phaethon's thoughts during his ride in Apollo's chariot.

Icarus	Phaethon
"How I should like to get a closer look at the sun. Once and for all I should like to see for myself what it really is... I think I shall go a bit closer, anyway. The old man seems to be napping. I can be up and back before he opens his eyes. How splendid if I could get a really good look at the sun and be able to tell my father something he doesn't know."	*"Just imagine," Phaethon thought, "how many people are now looking up at the sky, praising the sun, hoping the weather stays fair. How many people are watching me, me, me... But I'm too small to see... How can they know it's me, me, me?... I must show (them) that it is I driving the chariot of the sun, I alone. Apollo said not to come to close to earth, but how will he know?"*

How is Icarus similar to Phaethon? What might this tell you about Icarus's **hamartia**?

_____

_____

_____

Example 2

1. Reread the following comments from Mr. Granger:

- *"Been hearing 'bout your teaching, Mary, so as members of the school board we thought we'd come by and learn something."* (p. 183)

- *"You must be some kind of smart, Mary, to know more than the fellow who wrote that book."* (p. 184)

What do you notice about Mr. Granger's tone in these lines? What is his hidden or unspoken meaning?

_____

_____

_____

The two examples enable students to draw connections between scenes that are separate—in the first case, from different stories, and in the second, from different places in the same story. The first instance leverages the more obvious pride of Phaethon to draw out for students the more subtle pride of Icarus, something they may not have attended to without the comparison—perhaps taking Icarus's words about wanting to tell his father something he doesn't know as altruistic. The second builds up evidence that the speaker, Mr. Granger, is hostile toward Mary, believes she thinks she is smarter than everyone else, and resents that—a nuanced attitude students would be highly unlikely to pick up in the first line without seeing the second. It also prepares students to string evidence together in an analysis, much as they will do when writing an essay. Again, students can focus intently on the given task and quickly and simply translate their thoughts into writing.

Another example, from *Lord of the Flies,* focuses on the emerging relationship between Ralph and Piggy and is one of our favorites:

5. Reread the following details:

Detail 1	Detail 2
The fat boy waited to be asked his name in turn but this proffer of acquaintance was not made; the fair boy called Ralph smiled vaguely, stood up, and began to make his way once more toward the lagoon. The fat boy hung steadily at his shoulder. (p. 9)	"He dived into the sand at Piggy's feet and lay there laughing." "Piggy!" Piggy grinned reluctantly, pleased despite himself at even this much recognition. (p. 11)

In each of the details above, underline specific words or phrases that capture Piggy's behavior toward Ralph. Then, describe the relationship that seems to be growing between the two.

_____

_____

_____

_____

_____

_____

It assembles two passages that are separated by several pages in the book and places them in proximity to facilitate analysis. Seen together, they offer much insight about Piggy: his subservience, his need to be accepted, the weakness Ralph perceives in him that other boys will soon exploit. But it would be easy to miss the connection because they occur several pages apart. It is a case study in why assembling things in proximity is a powerful analytical tool. And, of course, it is what students will do on their own when they write a paper analyzing the book: assemble disparate connected pieces and describe the ideas they bring to life.

Pattern Questions

Pattern Questions take related information that occurs in different places in the text—images or words that recur, references to a similar idea, statements by or about a given character—and place them in close proximity for easy analysis. They are similar to Comparison Questions but often trace examples through more than two moments.

In the video *Emily Badillo: Mist* you can see Emily using a Pattern Question with her sixth-grade students in a lesson on Laurie Halse Anderson's novel, *Chains*. Emily has lifted four short excerpts from the novel in which the main character, Isabel, thinks about the mist that is present in a field as she seeks to commune with her dead mother. Here's the section from the student packet to the lesson:

To watch the video *Emily Badillo: Mist*, use this QR code or find the video at the URL https://vimeo.com/1058369001/4229d47fb5.

1. There are four different mentions of mist in these pages. What do you notice about these descriptions? Why do you think it comes up so often?

   - *The morning mist twisted and hung low over the field.*
   - *I stared without blinking at the mist, looking for the curve of her back or the silhouette of her head wrapped in a pretty kerchief.*
   - *"Please, Momma," I whispered urgently. "I need your help." I squinted into the ash grove, where the mist was heaviest.*
   - *The sun had popped up in the east like a cork and was burning through the morning mist.*

   _____

   _____

   _____

   _____

We love the way Emily begins by having students reread the four excerpts aloud in sequence to bring them to life a bit (and practice their fluency!). We love that she narrates her rationale for the exercise: "I noticed they mentioned this mist a lot. That makes me think it's important, and I want to figure out why." She's modeling for them her decision-making process and what makes her think something is worth rereading.

Notice how quickly students spring to life when Emily sends them to a Turn and Talk to discuss. There's lots to talk about and it's easy to build toward a deeper discussion—particularly because students can refresh their memory of the phrases as they think about them and hear their classmates' insights. Notice doubly how eager students are to write down their thoughts after the Turn and Talk. We think this excitement is the outcome of effective thinking. They've generated lots of new insights and feel like they've discovered something. We also think Emily's warm, supportive demeanor encourages students to take intellectual risks and grapple with a difficult question. That's critical when we're asking students do something as challenging as Close Reading. Finally, her use of discussion and writing keeps engagement high and ensures that all students have the opportunity to develop their ideas in response to her question.

The next example from *Lord of the Flies* assembles in close proximity three references to the "creepers," the name Golding gives to the thick vines and brambles of the island. Notice also how, in addition to its narrow focus on this small recurring detail, the question leverages the transient information effect to maximize attention and working memory.

Do Now

1. Reread these three details from the opening of *Lord of the Flies* (p. 7). Then answer the questions bulleted below.

Detail 1:	Detail 2:	Detail 3:
He was clambering heavily among the creepers and broken trunks when a bird, a vision of red and yellow, flashed upwards with a witch-like cry; and this cry was echoed by another.	I can hardly move with all these creeper things.	The naked crooks of his knees were plump, caught and scratched by thorns.

- The creepers are probably vines or ground plants. Why call them "creepers"?
- What might this be an allusion to? (Use your Knowledge Organizer.)
- What might this suggest about the island?

_____

_____

_____

_____

_____

_____

Later in the same *Lord of the Flies* lesson, this Pattern Question draws students' attention and focus to a different detail of the early interactions of the boys: Piggy's fearful anxiety and Ralph's lingering faith in the influence and power of the civilization the boys have left behind:

3a. In one carefully written sentence, explain what these details reveal about the difference between Ralph and Piggy's mindset. You might choose to begin your sentence with "While Ralph..." or "In spite of Piggy's..."

When'll your dad rescue us? "Soon as he can."	"How does he know we're here?" Because, thought Ralph, because, because.	"They're all dead [...] an' this is an island. Nobody don't know we're here. Your dad don't know, nobody don't know—" His lips quivered and the spectacles were dimmed with mist.

_____

_____

_____

_____

_____

Again, three diverse but connected ideas—a pattern—are presented in close proximity, always visible and with extraneous details removed to direct and focus attention optimally.

This example from *Roll of Thunder, Hear My Cry* shares seven examples in all to help students see how tiny details—each perhaps seeming unimportant by itself—coalesce over the course of a section of the novel to tell a powerful story about Mama's hidden emotions:

6. Consider these descriptions of Mama from pp. 183-184 and pp. 185-186.

pp. 183-184	pp. 185-186
• Mama seemed startled to see the men but [...] she merely nodded and went on with her lesson. • But Mama did not flinch • Mama, her back straight and her eyes fixed on the men, answered, "Because all that's in that book isn't true."	• Mama did not answer immediately. When she did, her voice was muffled. • Mama bit into her lower lip and gazed down the road. • [Papa's] eyes settled on Mama; the pain was in her face. • Her voice cracked.

What contrast do you notice in her actions and body language in these two scenes? Why might this be?

_____

_____

_____

_____

Here's a last favorite example, from Christopher Paul Curtis's *Bud, Not Buddy*. In this case the Pattern Question presents three examples of figurative language in which the narrator, Bud, compares the music he hears to a storm:

5. a. Reread these lines from pp. 200-203 and annotate any examples of figurative language:

- *The Thug was brushing his sticks across the round gold metal thing next to his drums and making it sound like a soft rain was commencing to fall on someone's tin roof. (p. 200)*

- *Steady held the note for a long time, then made the sax drift away from the rest of the storm of music. It swirled and floated back and joined the rain sound that the Thug and Dirty Deed kept going. (p. 201)*

- *Or it seemed like [Herman E. Calloway] was the thunder, soft and far away but getting closer all the time. (p. 200)*

What **extended metaphor** do you notice developing in Bud's description of the band's music?

Notes

b. **Turn and Task**: With your partner, skim pp. 200-203 and find any other lines that contribute to the **extended metaphor**. Jot any phrases you notice in the box above.

c. What does this **extended metaphor** show about Bud's experience of the music?

The goal for students by the end of the lesson is to describe Bud's response to the band and their music. Earlier in the unit, students learned the term *extended metaphor*—in fact, it's a term on their Knowledge Organizers (which we discuss in Chapter Four). This question gives them a chance to apply their knowledge of this literary term, but they have to look more carefully at some key details first.

The first step simply requires students to notice three key lines they read in several pages of text. These lines are arranged to maximize attention to the moments where Bud is describing the band's music.

After they have reread Bud's descriptions of music, students have a chance do some Formative Writing (see Chapter Six). They develop an initial hypothesis and then work with a partner (Turn and Task) to go a bit deeper searching for more evidence themselves. This is the power of Close Reading. In a first reading, students could easily read each of these details without noticing the emerging pattern, not considering how Christopher Paul Curtis had thoughtfully crafted each sentence, using the metaphor of a storm, to convey how mesmerized and fascinated Bud is by the band's music.

We especially like the last task here as it asks students to go back to the text, having now thought deeply about the extended metaphor, to find other examples on the theme. We like this task because much of what we are doing in asking Pattern Questions is preparing students to write papers and conduct analyses of their own where they trace an idea across a text. We start by making the first step—the meaning-making part—easier to focus on. But, over time, we will want students to be able to notice and assemble evidence of their own patterns. This question begins students on that latter task and makes a sort of bridge to assembling an argument.

Sensitivity Analysis

Sensitivity Analysis is a special type of Comparison Question. Rather than comparing two lines from the text, the teacher presents an original line from the text and an alternative, which she has slightly altered, to demonstrate the nuance of the choices made by the author. These questions work best when the differences are subtle, not obvious, and when the number of changes introduced is small.

At the beginning of this chapter, we shared an example of Sensitivity Analysis in Jen Brimming's classroom, one that involved her asking students to compare a line of text not to another line but to a slightly altered version of itself. In that case, the implications of William Golding's symbolically weighty description of Ralph removing his close fiercely was made more evident to students by comparing it to a version where he removed his clothes "eagerly," a subtle change that removes some of the powerful implications of the boys incipient savagery. Here's the question again:

Pages 9-10

3. Reread this line from p. 10:

He became conscious of the weight of his clothes, kicked his shoes off fiercely, and ripped off each stocking with its elastic garter in a single movement.

Compare it to the version below:

*He became conscious of the **inconvenience** of his clothes, kicked his shoes off **eagerly**, and **removed** each stocking with its elastic garter in a single movement.*

a. What do you notice about the differences between each version? What does the first reveal about Ralph?

_____
_____

Here's an another example of a Sensitivity Analysis question from our unit on *The Giver*:

7. Compare the lines from p. 99 to the altered version:

Original	Altered
He rested for a moment, breathing deeply. "I am so *weighted* with them," he said.	He rested for a moment, breathing deeply. "I am so *full of* them," he said.
Jonas felt a terrible concern for the man, suddenly.	Jonas felt a terrible concern for the man, suddenly.

a. What does "them" refer to? _____

b. How is the meaning of the altered version different from the original? What does the language in the original suggest about the Receiver and his role?

_____

This Close Reading burst asks students to reflect on a line in which a character called the Receiver discusses the burden of memories. Notice that it starts with an Establish Meaning question: "What does *them* refer to?" Then, it presents in an attentionally privileged environment the original line from the text and a slightly altered version in which the speaker describes being *full* of memories rather than *weighted* by memories. There is a perception-based question to support the analysis: "How is the meaning altered by this change?" Finally, there is an Analyze Meaning question: "What does this suggest about the Receiver and his role?"

KNOWLEDGE, DISAMBIGUATION, AND CLOSE READING

Building students' knowledge is an essential factor in enabling them to disambiguate the text while Close Reading.

As you've observed in the clips in this chapter, Close Reading is not a stand-alone tool or skill but an amalgamation of multiple techniques. Recall Scarborough's Rope from Chapter Three. Because knowledge is so central to comprehension, its role within Close Reading—when the text is particularly challenging—is paramount. As a result, it's likely that Close Reading in bursts will be central in each of your lessons—something we saw for ourselves when writing our *Reading Reconsidered* curriculum. We were constantly asking kids to reread critical excerpts, providing bits of key knowledge and vocabulary and then asking them to read again with a new lens to perceive the text, with more information to ensure literal understanding as well as a strong foundation for analysis.

University of Virginia cognitive psychologist Daniel Willingham gives a fantastic explanation of the role of background knowledge in reading comprehension on an episode of the *Melissa and Lori Love Literacy* podcast that he appeared on with Barbara Davidson of Knowledge Matters.[13] Willingham explains, "The key feature of not just written but oral language is that language is sometimes ambiguous. And frequently a good deal of information that the speaker or writer intends their audience to understand is actually omitted. And it is in resolving this ambiguity and replacing that missing information that [makes] reader knowledge is so important." The term for resolving this inherent ambiguity is *disambiguation*, something we are always doing with the language we read and hear.

To illustrate his point, Willingham makes up a sentence: "Lori tore up Melissa's art work. She ran to tell the teacher." He goes on, "The second sentence is ambiguous. *She* could refer to Lori or Melissa. But clearly if you're an experienced reader you're not going to see that as ambiguous. You're going to understand that you run and tell the teacher not when you are the perpetrator of a crime but when you are the victim of a crime. So that's how *she* gets disambiguated. That obviously depends on some knowledge of the world. But pretty much everyone listening has that knowledge so it [*the disambiguation*] is simple."

You may recognize this type of unclear-pronoun-referent disambiguation from previous mentions in the chapter, when we used the term in discussing the importance of Establishing Meaning. But sometimes the knowledge needed to disambiguate is not contained within the sentence or text itself. Willingham explains that once you get to making inferences across sentences, knowledge is even more important. He provides an example sentence: "Tricia spilled her coffee. Dan jumped up to get a rag."

"If all you understood was the literal meaning of the two sentences, you probably would not have understood everything the author intended. The author intended for you to draw a causal connection between the sentences: Dan jumped up because Tricia spilled her coffee," he says.

"You need to have the right knowledge to build that causal bridge. You have to know that when you spill coffee, it makes a mess. You have to know that rags can clean up a mess. And so forth. All of this is just stuff that the writer left out. The reason authors write this way is that if you actually gave all that information, the text would be impossibly long and boring. 'Tricia spilled coffee. Some of it went on the rug. She did not want coffee on her rug. The rug was expensive.'"

Willingham notes this would be absurd.

"Knowing your audience means tuning what you say and write to provide as much information as your audience needs, but not more."

In other words, every author is making assumptions about the optimal knowledge of readers required to disambiguate and then understand at a substantive level what he or she is saying.

We think Willingham offers a really elegant and clear description of the role knowledge plays in comprehension of text. We often focus more on the role of background knowledge in bigger inferences in the text—the ones an author might deliberately place to exist in a text—which is why we've included an entire chapter in this book devoted to tools to build and reinforce background knowledge. But given the critical role that knowledge plays in the constant and perpetual process of disambiguation, we'd be remiss if we didn't mention that knowledge building tools work in support of Close Reading.

In our lessons, knowledge works in synergy with Close Reading bursts. After experiencing or reading the text for the first time as part of the daily reading, we then provide (or reactivate) some key knowledge for students (vocabulary knowledge or contextual knowledge), and ask them to more deeply analyze a given word, phrase, or excerpt from the text. It's a chance to reconsider its meaning with the lens of new knowledge.

Planning for Close Reading includes not just planning a series of questions but also considering the knowledge that will be necessary for successfully accessing and unpacking the text.

In Chapters Four and Five, we share a variety of tools to build knowledge to support comprehension. Those same tools—Embedded Nonfiction, Embellishments, Knowledge Feeding, Explicit and Implicit Vocabulary, as well as retrieval of key knowledge—are useful in supporting students in Close Reading.

CLOSE READING IN THE CONTEXT OF A LESSON

Let's close by looking at how Close Reading works within a lesson and how the process of Close Reading relies on tools we've described in previous chapters. The lesson we'll study is the second lesson in our *Reading Reconsidered* Curriculum English Language Arts unit on *brown girl dreaming* by Jacqueline Woodson.

Before we jump into the lesson, it's important to know about the overall goals of the unit so that we can be sure the moments of Close Reading we select are in support of more deeply understanding the text and in consideration of the overall goals for the unit. Jen Rugani and Emily Badillo, cowriters of the unit, give the following description of the unit: "In this memoir written in verse, Jacqueline Woodson shares what it was like to grow up as a Black child in the 1960s and 1970s, living with the remnants of Jim Crow and developing a growing awareness of the civil rights movement. Woodson's poems examine her family history, explain the 'in-betweenness' of her childhood in Ohio, South Carolina, and New York, and describe the joy of finding her voice through writing. This unit exposes students to the complexities of memory and storytelling as well as the unique benefits and challenges of analyzing poetry."

Essential Understandings. This unit is designed with repeated exposure to the following conceptual understandings and themes:

- Memoir gives authors an opportunity to share meaningful personal stories about their lives in the context of a specific time and place; through *brown girl dreaming*, we learn about both Woodson's personal history and the events in history she lives through.

- Poetry is a different type of writing than prose, so some of our vocabulary and processes as readers change when we read poems.

- People are complex; their young life, experiences, and family history shape their worldview as they grow. Part of growing up and developing one's beliefs is understanding the perspectives and beliefs of those around you.

- Woodson writes her memoir by combining the stories and memories of others with her own. Memory is subjective and unreliable, so it can be both beautiful and challenging to try to recount stories from memories.

In Lesson 2, the objective for students is to be able to describe how Woodson connects herself to her family's history in the first poem of her memoir (on pp. 1–2). You'll notice this objective closely connects to the first and third essential understanding. Readers will learn more about Woodson's personal history as described in her memoir and begin to understand how her family history has shaped who she is as a person.

After reading an embedded text on the Mason-Dixon line to acquire knowledge about two key locations within the United States that are important to Woodson's story and her family history, students learn two new vocabulary words: *emancipate* and *evocative*. Both will be critical to understanding the poem they read in the lesson and doing a Close Reading of it. See the embedded text and vocabulary portion of the lesson next:

Embedded Text

brown girl dreaming (1-2) "february 12, 1963"

> **Lesson Objective:** Describe how Woodson connects herself to her family's history.

Do Now

Directions: Review the map and the text below, then answer the questions.

Mason Dixon Line

The map (left) shows the location of two important places in Jacqueline Woodson's life: Columbus, a city in Ohio, and the state of South Carolina. The line stretching across the middle of the United States represents the **Mason-Dixon line**, which dates back to the 1700-1800s when slavery was still legal in much of the country. The Northern states above the line were "free" states, where slavery was outlawed, and the Southern states below the line were slaveholding states. Even though slavery has been illegal in every state since 1865, people still refer to the Mason-Dixon line as an imaginary divider between the region of the U.S. known as the North and the region known as the South.

1. What did the Mason-Dixon line divide in the 1800s?

_____

2. The Mason-Dixon line is still referred to today as an "imaginary divider" between North and South. Why might it continue to impact the way people perceive different regions of the U.S.?

_____

_____

Vocabulary

Vocabulary: Emancipate, Evocative				
Word	Definition	Related Parts of Speech	Situations	Image
emancipate *verb*	to set free, especially from a figure of authority	emancipation *noun* emancipated *adjective*	• The factory workers decided to **emancipate** themselves from the unfair restrictions of their bosses.	
evocative *adjective*	bringing to mind strong images, memories, or feelings	evoke *verb*	• The flower's **evocative** smell made her think of her first family vacation.	

Vocabulary Active Practice

Use a form of the vocabulary word as you respond to each question.

1. What images or feelings does this picture **evoke** for you? Use the sentence starter, "This picture **evokes**…"

2. Consider the information you learned from the map in the Do Now. In the early 1800s, do you think you would be more likely to find a supporter of **emancipation** in the North or the South? Why?

3. When in a movie might a director include a particularly **evocative** song? Why?

4. The musician Bob Marley has a song that includes the famous lyric, "**Emancipate** yourselves from mental slavery." What do you think this means?

_____

_____

_____

_____

5. Why might poetry be a particularly **evocative** form of writing?

_____

_____

_____

Students then begin the first cycle of the lesson, in which they listen to a Teacher Read Aloud of the poem while they annotate for words, phrases, or lines that they find evocative. Here's a copy of the poem annotated by a teacher as part of her Lesson Preparation:

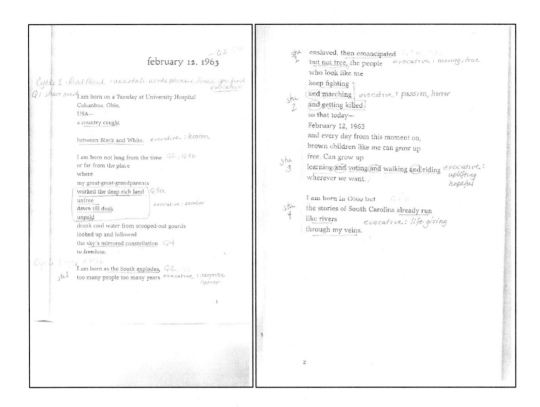

Pictured next is the student packet for this poem. Note that in question two, students respond to a question that ensures that they've Established Meaning for the poem and its title. Knowing that this poem describes when and where Woodson was born will be critical to later analysis.

Annotation Task: *brown girl dreaming* is a **memoir**, meaning it is a collection of memories written about important moments and events in a person's life. As we read the first poem in Jaqueline Woodson's memoir, circle the words, phrases, or lines that you find most **evocative**.

1. **Turn and Talk:** Share your annotations with a partner. Why did you choose these moments? What images or feelings do they **evoke** for you?

2. What is Woodson describing in this poem? Why is it called "february 12, 1963"?

Notes

After the literal understanding of the poem is stamped, students are ready to go a bit deeper. They begin their Close Reading of just one stanza from the poem, included in question three, following. It's a great opportunity to reread and practice their own fluent reading after hearing their teacher read aloud. Once again, students are asked to demonstrate solid literal understanding with responses grounded in evidence from the text, this time on just a few key lines (in question three a). In question three b, students zoom in on the phrase "not long from the time," considering not just its meaning, but how it helps us better understand Woodson and her connection to her family's history. Notice how there's a critical piece of Knowledge Feeding about the ending date of slavery. For students lacking this knowledge, the phrase "not long from the time" might not have much meaning, but knowing that Woodson was born nearly a hundred years after slavery will help them better understand that Woodson uses the phrase to convey a feeling of connection to this part of her family's history even though it was many years before her birth. It's not exactly what you'd expect someone to feel about something that happened one hundred years before their birth.

3. Reread this stanza from p. 1:

> I am born not long from the time
> or far from the place
> where
> my great-great-grandparents
> worked the deep rich land
> unfree
> dawn till dusk
> unpaid
> drank cool water from scooped-out gourds
> looked up and followed
> the sky's mirrored constellation
> to freedom.

a. **Turn and Talk**: What is Woodson sharing about her great-great-grandparents in this stanza? How do you know? **Challenge**: How might the **rhythm** of the poem emphasize this idea?

b. Slavery was declared illegal in 1865, almost 100 years before Woodson was born. What might Woodson be suggesting when she says she was born "not long from the time" of her great-great-grandparents' enslavement?

Notes

Before students study another reference in the poem more deeply, they'll do some more knowledge building via an Embedded Nonfiction text, titled "Follow the Drinking Gourd," to prepare them to analyze the line "the sky's mirrored constellation" to explain its meaning and consider why Woodson might make this reference. Without this knowledge, the line and Woodson's deliberate decision-making would be inaccessible to all (or most) students. But with the addition of this small piece of knowledge, students can understand and appreciate Woodson's deliberate (and beautiful) decisions in crafting her memoir.

"Follow the Drinking Gourd"

A drinking gourd is a spoon- or cup-like container that can be used to scoop and serve water. In slaveholding states in the American south, the term "drinking gourd" is thought to have been used as a code to refer to the Big Dipper constellation, a formation of stars that looks like a water dipper. This constellation points to the North Star, so it can be used as a navigation tool to help travelers—or escaping enslaved people—find their way north. The American folk song "Follow the Drinking Gourd," popular during the Civil Rights movement of the 1950s and 1960s, describes enslaved people using the "drinking gourd" of the Big Dipper as a guide to help them flee north to freedom.

An illustration of the Big Dipper constellation, which points north and looks like a drinking gourd.

4. On p. 1, what is Woodson referring to when she describes the "sky's mirrored constellation"? Why might she include this reference in the poem?

Notes

The next questions in the lesson will require students to use knowledge built early in the lesson. For question five, they'll need to rely on their new understanding of the word *emancipate* in order to explain how emancipation is different from freedom, then use that understanding to make inferences about life in the South the year Woodson was born.

Cycle 2

5. Reread these lines from pp. 1-2:

> *I am born as the South explodes,*
> *too many people too many years*
> *enslaved, then emancipated*
> *but not free*

a. **Turn and Talk:** How could a person be "**emancipated** but not free"?

b. What is Woodson suggesting about life in the South in 1963?

<table>
<tr><td>Notes</td></tr>
<tr><td>

</td></tr>
</table>

The Close Read in question six once again emphasizes how Woodson artfully conveys her feelings of connection to her ancestors, who were from South Carolina.

6. Reread the final stanza:

> *I am born in Ohio but*
> *the stories of South Carolina already run*
> *like rivers*
> *through my veins.*

a. **Turn and Talk:** What does it mean that Woodson has "the stories of South Carolina" in her veins, even though she was born in Ohio? Why might this be?

b. Complete the following sentences:

- Woodson is connected to South Carolina **because** _____

_____

- Woodson is connected to South Carolina, **but** _____

_____

- Woodson is connected to South Carolina, **so** _____

_____

Not all of the lessons we plan include as many Close Reading bursts as in the lesson we shared from the *brown girl dreaming* unit—poetry naturally lends itself to more Close Reading because of its intentionally resistant nature—but they follow a similar pattern or process of rereading key lines and using text-dependent Questions and Knowledge Feeding to elucidate both literal and analytical meaning.

A last theme that's worth noting: as we discussed previously in the chapter, the generation effect tells us that when students create a version of what they are learning in their own words, they begin encoding the ideas they are discussing and thinking about in memory. So, it is not coincidental that almost every example of Close Reading you see in the lesson on *brown girl dreaming*—and, in fact, almost every Close Reading question in this chapter— ends with some version of writing or talking to a peer to process and internalize the insights students have worked so hard to arrive at. If we're going to ask students to work hard to understand complex texts, and we want them to see the results of their efforts, we should end by making sure the learning is durable.

CHAPTER RECAP

Close Reading enables students to read complex texts for their fullest meaning, helping them to understand the depth of what's been written in books and valued by societies perhaps for thousands of years. To effectively engage in Close Reading in your classroom, remember the following:

- Close Reading works best in short bursts, so as not to overburden students' working memory, followed by opportunities to encode to ensure the learning makes it into their long-term memory.

- Close Reading only works with complex text, carefully selected, aimed at supporting students' arriving at a larger understanding about the book.

- Taking time to Establish Meaning and ensure students understand what a text is literally saying is an essential prerequisite before students can Analyze Meaning.

- We set students up for successful Close Reading when we create Attentionally Privileged Environments that reduce distractions and increase the availability of their working memory.

- Building students' knowledge is an essential factor to help them disambiguate the text while Close Reading.

The following types of bursts are highly effective tools for Close Reading:

- **Key Line Questions.** Questions that require deep study of a single-line or short passage to seek to fully understand it with special focus on unpacking how meaning is made.

- **Comparison Questions.** Questions where two pieces of contrasting text are presented in proximity so that subtle or important differences or connections can be studied.

- **Pattern Questions.** Questions in which students look at a recurring idea, phrase, or image from across the text, but with the examples culled and presented in proximity.

- **Sensitivity Analysis.** A special type of Comparison Question in which an original and a slightly altered alternative are presented to demonstrate the nuance of choices made by the author. These questions, we note, are best when the differences are subtle, not obvious, and when the number of changes introduced is small.

Notes

1. The original work on the Law of Comparative Judgment was done by L. L. Thurstone. See L. L. Thurstone, "A Law of Comparative Judgment," *Psychological Review* 34, no. 4 (1927): 273–86. More recently Daisy Christodoulou has pointed out how much more efficient and accurate it is to ask people to look at two similar things and say, "Which is better?" or "What are the key differences?" She describes its applications in simplifying teacher marking in this post, for example: https://researched.org.uk/2018/07/06/comparative-judgement-the-next-big-revolution-in-assessment-2.

2. See M. P. McCurdy, W. Viechtbauer, A. M. Sklenar, A. M. Sklenar, A. N. Frankenstein, and E. D. Leshikar, "Theories of the Generation Effect and the Impact of Generation Constraint: A Meta-Analytic Review," *Psychonomic Bulletin & Review* 27 (2020): 1139–65, https://doi.org/10.3758/s13423-020-01762-3. "The generation effect is the memory benefit for self-generated compared with read or experimenter-provided information," the authors note.

3. One of the key applications of cognitive load theory is the realization that experts and novices learn differently. Experts are far better able to learn from unguided experience and exposure to challenges. Novices learn better from direct instruction. This is especially relevant because English majors in a university setting are, if not experts, then at least far closer to being so than students in middle or high school. So, what makes for

an inspiring lesson in a senior seminar as an undergrad is not what recent graduates should try to replicate in their classrooms as teachers, no matter how much they loved those seminars and were inspired by them. It is easy to see why they might want to do this, but it overlooks the key difference in how novices and experts learn.

4. https://www.aft.org/sites/default/files/Rosenshine.pdf.

5. https://www.nature.com/articles/s41562-019-0640-4 and described in lay terms here: https://medicalxpress.com/news/2019-07-perception-memory-deeply-entangled.html.

6. Héctor R. Martín, *How Do We Learn? A Scientific Approach to Learning and Teaching* (Jossey-Bass, 2024), 40.

7. Daniel T. Willingham, *Why Don't Students Like School?: A Cognitive Scientist Answers Questions About How the Mind Works and What It Means for the Classroom*, 2nd ed. (Jossey-Bass, 2021), 58.

8. ACT, "Reading Between the Lines: What the ACT Reveals About College Readiness in Reading" (2006).

9. In *Reading Reconsidered* we called these—tongue-in-cheek—The Five Plagues of the developing reader.

10. This is an (hilarious, thank you) inside joke. If you've read the series you know Handler is constantly dropping in definitions for words in this charming but intrusive way, for example: "As they peered over the side of their ruined boat, the children saw that the water was not much deeper than a puddle, and this enormous puddle was littered with **detritus**, a word which here means "all sorts of strange items.""

11. Maryanne Wolf, Reader, *Come Home: The Reading Brain in a Digital World* (Harper, 2018), 92. Wolf shares a second observation from the professors that is worth attending to, even if it is less germane here: students' diminishing patience with writing: "In our epoch, we must ask whether students' diminishing familiarity with conceptually demanding prose and the daily truncating of their writing on social media is affecting their writing in more ways than in the past." The same students who lack the cognitive patience to untangle the sophisticated and dense syntax written by others are also losing their own ability to write.

12. We should note that we use packets for our middle school curriculum. For our high school curriculum, we think students should begin taking notes on their own on blank paper so we would be less likely to provide a copy of the text like this every day. Still, there might be days on which we would discuss a line or series of lines extensively enough that we would want students to have a copy on their desk that mirrored what was on the board.

13. https://podcasts.apple.com/us/podcast/ep-139-knowledge-and-comprehension-with-daniel/id1463219123?i=1000594218421.

Appendix A:
Full Sample Lesson, Seventh Grade

Name: _____   Date: _____

Catherine, Called Birdy (pp. 87–103) "It bodes not well"

> **Lesson Objective:** Consider Catherine's experiences during the season of Lent.

Do Now

Directions: Reread this excerpt from p. 86 and answer the questions.

---

*I was partnered for [Robert's wedding] feast with an ugly shaggy-bearded **hulk** from the north. My father sought to honor him because his manor lies next to my mother's, and my father **lusts after** it. I fail to see how sitting next to me and sharing my bowl and goblet honored him—and it certainly did me no good. The man was a pig, which dishonors pigs. He blew his red and shiny nose on the table linen, sneezed on the meat, picked his teeth with his knife, and left wet greasy marks where he drank from the cup we shared. I could not bring myself to put my lips to the slimy rim, so endured a dinner without wine.*

Worse than this, he proved himself near a murderer. As the dogs burrowed under the rushes for bones and bits of the wedding meat, Rosemary (the

---

(continued)

> *smallest and my favorite but for Brutus) mistook his skinny foot for a bone and nipped it. The shaggy-bearded pig howled and kicked the dog, who, of course, defended herself by biting. Then Shaggy Beard, pulling his knife from the table, tried to skewer the dog as if she were a joint of meat.*
>
> **hulk:** giant
> **lusts after:** wants

1. Who is Shaggy Beard? What are we meant to understand about him based on this diary entry?

Notes

---

2. Why might Catherine's father have seated Catherine next to this visitor?

_____

_____

_____

Vocabulary: Melancholy, Vile				
Word	Definition	Related Parts of Speech	Situations	Image
melancholy *noun*	a feeling of deep sadness or depression that usually lasts a long time	melancholy *adjective* melancholic *adjective*	• The boy was in a **melancholy** mood for days after the argument with his friend.	
vile *adjective*	1. highly offensive or immoral 2. repulsive, disgusting, or exceptionally bad	vileness *noun* vilely *adverb*	• The **vile** queen tried to hide her stepdaughter in a tower, but the girl bravely escaped.	

Vocabulary Active Practice

Use a form of the vocabulary word as you respond to each question.

1. What **vile** smells might force you to leave a room?

2. Catherine's father is often in a **vile** mood. How does he act when he is in this mood?

3. What song might you listen to if you were feeling **melancholy**? Explain why.

4. Why might someone who doesn't show **remorse** be considered **vile**?

5. Why might Aelis and George be feeling **melancholy?**

_____

_____

_____

_____

Pages 87–91

Annotation Task: The next several diary entries take place during a time in the **religious calendar** called Lent. Read this text and annotate details that help you understand how medieval Christians observed Lent.

Lent

Christians believe that Jesus Christ died to forgive Christians of their sins and was **resurrected** on Easter Sunday. Lent is the 40-day period before the holiday of Easter and is a time when people reflect on their sins and practice self-discipline.

The season of Lent begins with Ash Wednesday, a celebration of Mass that includes being marked with ashes on the forehead. The ashes are meant to remind each believer that "you are dust and to dust you shall return" (based on the book of Genesis) and begin the period of Lenten reflection.

During Lent, medieval Christians **abstained** from indulgence and focused on reflection and prayer. Scholar Martha Daas explains, "For people in the Middle Ages, Lent was a time of both physical **fasting** and **spiritual renewal**."[1] Medieval people typically ate just one meal a day during Lent, and often stopped eating meat, alcohol, and dairy. Lent was seen as a **somber** period of waiting, self-examination, and self-denial to prepare for the joyful and hopeful celebration of Easter.

Image of Ash Wednesday Mass c. 1260–1270

resurrected: brought back to life
abstained: prevented oneself from doing or enjoying something
fasting: going without food for religious reasons
spiritual renewal: recommitting to one's faith and religion
somber: serious

Annotation Task: As we read pp. 87–91, annotate details about how Catherine and her family observe Lent.

1. **Turn and Talk:** Share your annotations with your partner. How are Catherine's descriptions of Lent similar to the information in the article? How does Catherine seem to feel about Lent?

> **Notes**

2. Consider these lines from Catherine's entries:

    - *Today my father questioned me about the bearded pig. I said he affected my stomach like maggoty meat and my father laughed and said, "Learn to like it."* (p. 87)

    - *It **bodes** not well. [. . .] I fear they are planning a match between me and Stephen. I will not. To be a part of Shaggy Beard's family and have to eat with him every day! If my father does not drive him away, I will, as I have done the others.* (p. 87)

    - *No further words from my father about Shaggy Beard, so mayhap the trouble has passed and these plans, too, come to nothing.* (p. 90)

    bodes: indicates something to come

What does Catherine fear? Why does she think "the trouble has passed"? Include at least two of the following words in your response:

initially   at first   however   but   after

_____

_____

_____

_____

Pages 91–93

Annotation Task: In these entries, Catherine describes her interactions with Agnes of Wallingham, a guest at the manor. As we read, annotate details that show Catherine's perspective on Agnes.

3. **Turn and Talk:** How is Agnes different from Catherine? **Challenge:** Why might Cushman have included this character?

Notes

Pages 93–96: On Your Own

Annotation Task: As you read, annotate details that help answer the following questions.

- Why is Catherine punished?
- Who is Geoffrey? What is Catherine's perspective on him?

Leprosy is a devastating disease that causes skin lesions and nerve damage. Because the condition is so contagious, lepers were shunned and not considered a part of society anymore. In medieval England, lepers had to ring a bell like the one in this image to signal their presence in public places.

Notes

Pages 96–100

Annotation Task: As we read, annotate details that answer the following questions.

- What message does Catherine's father receive?

- How does Catherine respond?

4. **Turn and Talk:** Share your annotations with a partner. Are you surprised by these developments? Why or why not?

Notes

5. Reread Catherine's reflections on Lent.

p. 97	p. 98
I think Lent is all about hope. No matter how bad we feel about Jesus dying or how sick we get of fish, Easter Day always comes. We just need to hope and believe.	*It seems so long ago that I wrote a Lenten song and spoke of hope and the promise of Easter Day. Now I would that Lent would last forever.*

    a.   Why have Catherine's feelings about Lent changed?

_____

_____

_____

_____

b. **Challenge:** Why might Cushman have chosen the season of Lent as the setting for Catherine's **betrothal**?

Notes

---

6. Reread this excerpt from p. 100.

> In the solar with my father this morning: "Daughters and fish **spoil** easily and are better not kept. You will, Lady Birdy, be wed. If this new suitor is stubborn enough to outlast your willfulness, he will be your husband. If not, I will find another, mayhap even less to your liking. Accept it."
>
> Will I then be caught in this marriage trap? If I must be wed, I'd rather it be to someone young and comely like Geoffrey.
>
> **spoil:** lose value or usefulness by being kept too long

a. **Turn and Talk:** What is Catherine's father trying to get Catherine to understand?

Notes

---

b. Recall Catherine's earlier thoughts about this betrothal on p. 98:

*I must make a plan, for I will not, of course, wed the pig. Deus! I cannot even conceive of such a fate. Could it be? Would they really sell me to that **odious** old man? I cannot think so. I will **contrive** something. Luckily I am experienced at outwitting suitors.*

odious: repulsive, extremely unpleasant

contrive: think up or devise a plan

Given what you've learned about the time period and Catherine's character, to what degree do you think her plan to escape this "marriage trap" is realistic?

Notes

Name: _____   Date: _____

Exit Ticket

1. What major news does Catherine receive during Lent?

_____

_____

_____

_____

2. Why is this news important? How does Catherine respond?

_____

_____

_____

_____

Homework

Nightly Reading Directions: Read pp. 100–103 of *Catherine, Called Birdy* (24th Day of March through the 31st Day of March).

1. What story does William Steward tell by the fire? How does Catherine respond?

    _____

    _____

    _____

    _____

2. How are the marriage arrangements of Thomas the Baker and Meg from the dairy different from what Catherine experiences? Why?

    _____

    _____

    _____

    _____

3. Why does Catherine feel "confounded" on p. 103?

    _____

    _____

    _____

    _____

Note

1. Martha Daas, "The Salvation Diet," Medievalists.net. Accessed February 28, 2023. https://www.medievalists.net/2014/05/salvation-diet/.

Appendix B:
Full Sample Lesson, Ninth Grade

Name: _____   Date: _____

A Raisin in the Sun (pp. 54–60) "Fighting hard to suppress a scream"

Lesson Objective: Examine how Hansberry intensifies conflict and raises the stakes in Scene Two.

Do Now

Directions: In this conversation from p. 44, Mama and Ruth discuss how to use Big Walter's insurance money. Reread the conversation and answer the questions that follow.

RUTH:	Well—what are you going to do with it then?
MAMA:	I ain't rightly decided. *(Thinking. She speaks now with emphasis.)* Some of it got to be put away for Beneatha and her schoolin'— and ain't nothing going to touch that part of it. Nothing. *(She waits several seconds, trying to make up her mind about something, and looks at RUTH a little **tentatively** before going on.)* Been thinking that we maybe could **meet the notes** on a little old two-story some- where, with a yard where Travis could play in the summertime, if we use part of the insurance for a **down payment** and everybody

(continued)

> kind of pitch in. I could maybe take on a little day work again, few days a week—
>
> RUTH: *(Studying her mother-in-law **furtively** and concentrating on her ironing, anxious to encourage without seeming to)* Well, Lord knows, we've put enough rent into this here rat trap to pay for four houses by now . . .
>
> MAMA: *(Looking up at the words "rat trap" and then looking around and leaning back and sighing—in a suddenly reflective mood—)* "Rat trap"—yes, that's all it is.
>
> **tentatively:** hesitantly, with uncertainty
> **meet the notes:** make payments
> **down payment:** initial, partial payment for an expensive purchase like a home
> **furtively:** in a quiet or secretive way, without being noticed

1. How does Mama want to use the insurance money? Why might she share this idea with Ruth "tentatively"?

Notes

---

2. Reread Ruth's stage directions. What does Ruth think of Mama's plan for the money? Why might she be "anxious to encourage without seeming to"?

Notes

Vocabulary: Bastion, Suppress				
Word	Definition	Related Parts of Speech	Situations	Image
bastion *noun*	1. a place of defense or protection; a stronghold 2. something that preserves or defends a threatened quality or condition	bastioned *adjective*	• Because so many people live in my house, the attic can feel like the only **bastion** of solitude.	
suppress *verb*	1. to put down or subdue with authority or force 2. to hold back or repress	suppression *noun* suppressive *adjective*	• He struggled to **suppress** his feelings of jealousy when he saw his friend's brand-new cellphone.	

Use a form of the vocabulary word as you respond to each question.

1. Use the word **bastion** to describe what the kids are doing in the picture of the snowball fight.

2. Describe a situation when you might need to **suppress** a smile. Why might this be hard to do?

3. Why might an **oppressive** government try to **suppress** newspapers and magazines that criticize their decisions or voice opposition?

4. The word **bastion** is usually used in the phrase "a **bastion** of _____." Why might a school's art room be described as a **bastion** of creativity?

_____

_____

_____

Pages 54–57

1. **Turn and Task:** Plays are divided into acts and scenes to separate the action into sections. One scene is separated from the next by the lowering of a curtain, a black-out, or a brief emptying of the stage. Playwrights begin a new scene with stage directions that describe what's happening as the curtain opens.

    With your partner, read the stage directions describing Scene Two (p. 54) and respond to the following questions.

Where does this scene take place?	
What happened at the end of Scene One (p. 53)? How much time has passed?	
Which characters are onstage? What are they doing?	
Which characters are offstage?	

Annotation Task: As we read pp. 54–55, note any entrances, exits, or interruptions (e.g., sudden noises).

2. Reread these lines from p. 55:

MAMA:	Look out there, girl, before you be spilling some of that stuff on that child!
TRAVIS:	*(Safely behind the bastion of MAMA)* That's right—look out, now! *(He exits.)*
BENEATHA:	*(Drily)* I can't imagine that it would hurt him—it has never hurt the roaches.
MAMA:	Well, little boys' **hides** ain't as tough as Southside roaches. You better get over there behind the bureau. I seen one marching out of there like **Napoleon** yesterday.
BENEATHA:	There's really only one way to get rid of them, Mama—

(continued)

```
MAMA:        How?

BENEATHA:    Set fire to this building!

                              hides: skins (typically animal skins)
                Napoleon: French military leader who conquered much of Europe
                                                              in the 1800s
```

Cockroach infestations are notoriously difficult to get rid of because the insects hide in many areas, breed quickly, and may develop resistance to insecticides (poisons used to kill insects).

Turn and Talk: Why might Beneatha say the "only way to get rid of [the cockroaches]" is to "set fire to the building"? Use the word **futile** in your conversation.

Annotation Task: As we read pp. 55–57, note any entrances, exits, or interruptions (e.g., sudden noises).

3. On pp. 56–57, Mama and Beneatha share contrasting perspectives on the African continent. Use the following terms and explanations to support your understanding of their conversation.

colonization	The process of assuming control of someone else's territory and applying one's own systems of law, government, and religion. Many African nations were **colonized** by the British and the French and had to later fight to regain independence.
Nigeria	West African nation **colonized** and ruled by the British from 1851 to 1960
Liberia	West African nation **colonized** in 1822 as part of an effort to send formerly enslaved African Americans back to Africa (an alternative to emancipation in the United States)
Tarzan	Famous fictional character raised by apes in the African jungle.
heathen	A derogatory term used to describe someone who does not belong to a particular religion (in this case, Christianity). **Missionaries** are people who travel to new places to spread their religion by converting others.

Why do Mama and Beneatha start discussing Africa? What differences do you notice in their perspectives?

```
                              Notes




```

Dramatic Plot Structure

Dramatic structure refers to the framework playwrights typically follow when writing the plot of a story. Conflict drives the story forward: a character wants something, and this goal motivates the character and affects their choices. However, something or someone prevents them from getting what they want. The action in a plot often comes from the character's efforts to overcome this obstacle.

Additionally, there will be a consequence if the character fails to get what they want. These consequences create the story's stakes, or what is at risk if the character doesn't achieve their aim. The higher the stakes, the more the characters have to lose. Without stakes, an audience might not become invested in the characters and their conflict.

♂ 4.   a. Use these terms to complete the sentence defining conflict:

   obstacles   conflict   stakes   motivation

_____ is created when a character has a _____ (something they want or need), but there are _____ in their way. The _____ of the conflict refer to what is at risk if the character fails.

b. **Turn and Talk:** What is the central conflict in *A Raisin in the Sun* so far?

Notes

Annotation Task: As we read pp. 57–60, annotate any lines that raise the **stakes** or increase the emotional intensity of the scene.

5. Reread this conversation with Mama, Ruth, and Beneatha on p. 58.

---

*(Ruth comes in **forlornly** and pulls off her coat with **dejection**. They both turn to look at her.)*

RUTH: *(**Dispiritedly**)* Well, I guess from all the happy faces—everybody knows.

BENEATHA: You pregnant?

MAMA: Lord have mercy, I sure hope it's a little old girl. Travis ought to have a sister.

                        (BENEATHA and RUTH give her a hopeless look for this grandmotherly enthusiasm.)

[. . .]

BENEATHA: Did you plan it, Ruth?

RUTH: Mind your own business.

BENEATHA: It is my business—where is he going to live, on the *roof*? *(There is silence following the remark as the three women react to the sense of it.)* Gee—I didn't mean that, Ruth, honest. Gee, I don't feel like that at all. I—I think it is wonderful.

RUTH: *(**Dully**)* Wonderful.

> **forlornly:** in a miserable or hopeless way
> **dejection:** low spirits
> **dispiritedly:** in a discouraged or disheartened way
> **dully:** without interest or excitement

a. How is Mama's response to Ruth's pregnancy different from Ruth's and Beneatha's?

Notes

---

b. Reread Beneatha's final line in this excerpt.

It is my business—where is he going to live, on the *roof*? (*There is silence following the remark as the three women react to the sense of it.*) Gee—I didn't mean that, Ruth, honest. Gee, I don't feel like that at all. I—I think it is wonderful.

Why is there "silence following the remark"? How might Beneatha's tone change after the silence?

_____

_____

_____

_____

c. **Turn and Talk:** How does Ruth's pregnancy raise the **stakes** of the **conflict**?

6. Reread these moments from pp. 58–59.

BENEATHA: [. . .] Oh Lord, they're chasing a rat!
           (*Ruth covers her face with hands and turns away.*)

MAMA: (*Angrily*) Tell that youngun to get himself up here, at once!

BENEATHA: TRAVIS . . . YOU COME UPSTAIRS . . . AT ONCE!

RUTH: (*Her face twisted*) Chasing a rat . . .

TRAVIS: *(Excited and full of narrative, coming directly to his mother)* Mama, you should of seen the rat . . . Big as a cat, honest! *(He shows an exaggerated size with his hands.)* Gaaleee, that rat was really cuttin' and Bubber caught him with his heel and the janitor, Mr. Barnett, got him with a stick—and then they got him in a corner and—BAM! BAM! BAM!—and he was still jumping around and bleeding like everything too—there's rat blood all over the street—

(RUTH reaches out suddenly and grabs her son without even looking at him and clamps her hand over his mouth and holds him to her. MAMA crosses to them rapidly and takes the boy from her.)

a. **Turn and Task:** Annotate Ruth's stage directions in the excerpts. What is she reacting to? What emotions does she seem to be feeling?

Notes

---

b. On p. 59, after these interactions, Ruth "has her fists clenched on her thighs and is fighting hard to **suppress** a scream that seems to be rising in her." Why might Ruth feel like screaming in this moment? Try to think of more than one reason.

_____

_____

_____

_____

_____

_____

_____

c. **Challenge:** How might a director emphasize the contrast between Travis and Ruth in this moment?

Cycle 3

Dramatic Plot Structure (cont'd)

The elements of dramatic plot structure are often represented with a pyramid. The beginning of a story usually features two parts:

- **Exposition.** Introduces key elements of the story (e.g., setting, characters, and relationships). The exposition may also present an inciting incident or exciting force that disrupts the status quo or usual state of affairs of the story and begins the conflict.

- **Rising action.** The majority of the plot. During the rising action, tension increases, and the stakes are raised, intensifying the conflict as the play builds toward the climax. There are often complications, which means the problem the character tries to solve becomes more complex.

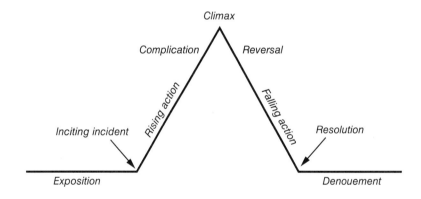

---

7. **Turn and Talk:** Which of the following would you describe as the major inciting incident in *A Raisin in the Sun*? Why?

- Moving into the kitchenette apartment

- The promise of Mr. Younger's insurance check

- Ruth's faint at the end of Scene One

- The ringing of the alarm clock at the beginning of Act One

8. How do you know the beginning of Scene Two is part of the **rising action** of the play?

Notes

Name: _____   Date: _____

Exit Ticket

1. Explain the purpose of pp. 54–60 (the beginning of Scene Two) in the structure of the play. Include at least two of the following terms in your response:

   conflict   stakes   complication   rising action   dramatic structure

   _____

   _____

   _____

   _____

   _____

2. On p. 44, Ruth describes the apartment as a "rat trap." What does she mean by this? Why is the state of the apartment relevant to Ruth in this scene?

   _____

   _____

   _____

   _____

   _____

Name: _____   Date: _____

Homework

Directions: Respond to the following questions using pp. 54–60 of *A Raisin in the Sun*.

1. On p. 58, Beneatha goes to the window when she hears "a sudden commotion from the street." Describe what she sees from the window. Begin with the phrase, "When Beneatha opens the window" and use the word **raucous** in your sentence.

_____

_____

_____

_____

_____

2. Write a sentence that explains why the Youngers' apartment could not **accommodate** a new baby. Include at least two of the following words in your response:

      accommodate   **permeate**   **futile**   **suppress**   **bastion**

_____

_____

_____

_____

_____

3. Travis teases Beneatha from "safely behind the **bastion** of Mama" (p. 55). What does this mean? What might the actor do on stage at this moment?

_____

_____

_____

_____

_____

4. Recall the way characters speak about Ruth before she enters (pp. 54–56).

> TRAVIS: [. . .] Where did Mama go this morning?
>
> MAMA: *(Looking at BENEATHA)* She had to go on a little errand. *(The phone rings. BENEATHA runs to answer it and reaches it before WALTER, who has entered from the bedroom.)*
>
> BENEATHA: Brother, where did Ruth go?
>
> WALTER: *(As he exits)* How should I know!
>
> BENEATHA: [. . .] Mama, where did Ruth go?
>
> MAMA: *(Looking at her with meaning)* To the doctor, I think.
>
> BENEATHA: The doctor? What's the matter? *(They exchange glances.)* You don't think—
>
> MAMA: *(With her sense of drama)* Now I ain't saying what I think. But I ain't never been wrong 'bout a woman neither.
> *(The phone rings.)*

a. How do the phone calls in these interactions impact the **tension** and **conflict**?

_____

_____

_____

_____

_____

b. Recall that Ruth was the only character who never left the stage in Scene One. How does her absence increase the **tension** in Scene Two?

_____

_____

_____

_____

_____

_____

Appendix C:
Decoding Tips

Given the bedrock importance of decoding, teachers should strive to correct decoding errors whenever it's viable to do so, no matter what subject or grade level they teach. Making your corrections as quickly and efficiently as possible is arguably the single most important factor in your success overall. Except in cases where your lesson objective focuses on decoding skills (which is never the case for nonreading teachers), *you should strive for the lowest possible transaction cost in making corrections.* Consider these two corrections of a student's decoding error when reading the word *inspection*:

- Teacher 1: "You said in-SPEAK-tion. Can you go back to the beginning of the sentence and read that word again?"

- Teacher 2: "In-*SPEAK*-tion?"

The difference between these corrections may seem trivial but is in fact huge. The time it takes to say the first phrase—the transaction cost—is at least *five times* greater than the transaction cost of the second. Every extra word the first teacher says takes time and disrupts the flow of student concentration on the narrative. Thus, every extra word potentially disrupts comprehension. If you used the second phrase to correct, you could make three or four interventions in the time you would spend on just one with the first phrase.

Like the second teacher, strive to make a habit of using the simplest and quickest intervention when correcting decoding errors. If you are consistent in the manner that you do so, your students, too, will get in the habit of self-correcting quickly and efficiently. This requires rigorous economy of language and a systematic approach to fixing decoding errors without having to explicitly double down on phonics instruction across grade levels. The following tools help consistently support students in effectively decoding what they read while maximizing road miles and maintaining comprehension.

It's important to note that we can only use the tools described here in conjunction with what we know about our students' mastery of sound letter correspondence for words they'll encounter in a given text. For example, "In-SPEAK-tion?" only works if I'm confident that the student knows that the letter *e* can also correspond to the sound /e/ and will take my prompt as a cue to flex the vowel.

Before asking students to read a text orally, they must have sufficient sound letter correspondence to decode most of the words in the text, even if that decoding is effortful. For students that are still missing/working on encoding enough sound letter correspondences to become independent decoders, their time is better spent listening to teacher read aloud and practicing their missing letter-sound correspondences.

MARK THE SPOT

Reread the three or four words immediately prior to the word that the student was unable to decode, inflecting your voice (usually by extending the last syllable or two of the last word) to show that the student should pick up there. For example: student reads, "He quickly ran *through* the door"; teacher corrects: "He quickly ran?" This correction provides a minimal prompt and helps the student learn to self-correct by briefly highlighting the mistake she has made.

PUNCH THE ERROR

Repeat the word a student misread back to him, replicating and putting emphasis on the part where the error occurred (for example: "Is that word in-SPEAK-tion??" "CARE-pet??" "You said 'cat'—try again"; student: "Catch"). Like Mark the Spot, Punch the Error also encourages students to self-correct. A subtle difference is the use of inflection on the exact error, more directly calling attention to what a student needs to fix.

Of all the decoding corrections described here, Punch the Error and Mark the Spot usually carry the smallest transaction cost, assuming that students know how to self-correct when you have called their attention to an error.

NAME THE SOUND OR THE RULE

Naming the sound a letter corresponds to is one direct way to correct a decoding error. When naming the sound, you might identify the sound of a vowel as long or short and ask students to apply it. (For example: "[That's a] long *a*"; "Long vowels say their name"; "Read that again: long *a*"; "That has a bossy *e*.") Or you might identify the sound of a consonant, especially whether a *c, g,* or *s* is hard or soft, and ask students to apply it. (For example: "[That's a] soft *c*"; "Hard *c*: /c/ or soft *c*: /s/.") You could also spell a pattern of letters and then say the sound they make (For example: "T-C-H: /tch/. '[Try it again.]") If there's a clear and identifiable rule, remind students of it and ask them to apply it. (For example: "*e* at the end means this is a long vowel.")

SPEED THE EXCEPTIONS

Decoding rules always have exceptions. When a word does not conform to standard rules, identify the correct pronunciation quickly and directly. (For example: "That word is written 'bury' but pronounced 'berry.'"; "That word is *through*.") If a student should know a word's distinctive pronunciation (that is, it is a sight word or has recently been discussed), quickly identify it as an exception. (For example: "That's one of our sight words"; "That word doesn't follow the rules, but we studied it yesterday"; "We'd expect the *e* to make that say 'g-IVE' [as in *hive*], but this word is an exception.") By calling attention to the fact that the word is an exception to a rule, you make students aware of the words that don't conform to general rules. Ideally, students are then more likely to remember these exceptions (or at least that they exist) when they encounter them independently.

CHUNK IT

It can also be quite useful to ask students to chunk difficult words by recognizing familiar patterns and words within words. For example, if a student struggles to read the word *hopeless,* you might say: "Do you see a part of that you already know?" or "The first four letters are a word you know" or "Cover the *-less* and read what you have." When asking students to chunk a word, it can help to affirm and reiterate what the student got right, focusing him on the problem "chunk." (For example, "You got *hope,* but the second part isn't *-ing*.")

USE POSITIVE FEEDBACK

For developing readers especially, it's also important to use positive feedback—quick and simple positive reinforcement when students read a word correctly. This not only encourages students but also lets them know explicitly that they got it right. Because correction of mispronunciation and misreading may not be consistent for them, struggling readers may not know when they've read a word accurately. As students continue reading, say "Yup," "Perfect," "You got it," "Nice," and so on. It can also increase efficiency by reducing the amount of time students spend pausing and wondering whether they've gotten a tough word correct. Obviously, you want this method to speed, not slow, your reading. You can minimize transaction costs by making your feedback phrases both quick and consistent. Too much variation can draw too much attention to your words.

Appendix D:
Reading Reconsidered Curriculum: *The Giver* Fluency Practice: Sample Materials

Name _____

Date _____

What is fluency?

Reading fluently means reading words accurately, at a speed that matches normal conversation, and with expression in order to understand the text. Fluent readers pay attention to the following:

- **Punctuation.** Which punctuation marks appear in the sentence? What clues does punctuation give you about when you should pause or how you should convey emotion?

- **Important words.** Are there any words that require special emphasis or give clues about the emotion of a sentence?

- **Dialogue.** How does the dialogue change what kind of expression you use? How is the person who is speaking feeling? What might they sound like?

- **The tone of the passage.** Are you capturing the intended meaning behind what you are reading? Are you capturing the voice of the narrator in your reading?

Directions for students:

1. Write your personal reading goal at the top of the page.

2. Listen to the teacher read aloud the set of sentences. Pay attention to when the teacher's voice pauses or changes.

3. Reread the set of sentences with your peers.

4. Now reread the set of sentences with your partner.

    a. Partner 1 (reader) reads the first sentence.

    b. Partner 2 (listener) listens while following along with a ruler.

    c. Let the reader try to decode the words. If they are stuck, the listener can help after the reader has given it a try.

    d. If neither student can read the word, jot it in your "Words to Practice" box.

5. Switch roles for the next sentence and continue alternating through the set of sentences.

6. Reread the set following these directions three to four times.

7. Listen for your teacher's directions to see which questions you will be answering on the back of your sheet.

Name: _____

My Goal: _____

_____

The Giver

Set 1: Lesson 2   Total Words: 210
Following are some sentences that describe rituals and traditions.

1. A ritual is an activity or ceremony that is performed the same way every time.

2. Rituals are part of every society and might be as elaborate as a graduation ceremony or as simple as shaking hands to say hello.

3. A ritual can refer to any sequence of activities that carries importance and follows a consistent set of rules.

4. Usually, rituals are connected to the traditions of a particular community, especially a religious community.

5. One common type of ritual is a rite of passage, which marks a person's transition from one phase of life to another.

6. In Judaism, for example, boys and girls celebrate a *bar* or *bat mitzvah* at thirteen years old to signal that they have transitioned from childhood to adulthood.

7. Many religions have specific marriage rituals to mark the shift from singlehood to coupledom.

8. Households can also have their own rituals, such as holiday celebrations or mealtime traditions.

9. Rituals often depend on individuals performing specific roles within the ceremony, and these roles can serve to create or reinforce power dynamics within social organizations.

10. By encouraging participants to engage repeatedly in the same ritual, people in power can normalize their authority and define the social order of a community.

Name: _____   Date: _____

Reading Comprehension Questions

Set 1: Lesson 2
Following are some questions about the sentences you just read about rituals.

1. What is a ritual?

2. Give at least two examples of rituals.

3. What is a rite of passage ritual?

4. What life transitions might be marked with rituals?

5. Name one ritual in Judaism and describe it.

6. What is the purpose of a ritual?

Name: _____

My Goal: _____

_____

The Giver

Set 2: Lesson 3   Total Words: 297

Following is a passage from *The Giver* where Jonas and his family reminisce about the Ceremony of the Ones, and when Jonas's father confesses to breaking a rule.

The Ceremony for the Ones was always noisy and fun. Each December, all the new children born in the previous year turned One. One at a time—there were always fifty in each year's group, if none had been released—they had been brought to the stage by the Nurturers who had cared for them since birth. Some were already walking, wobbly on their unsteady legs; others were no more than a few days old, wrapped in blankets, held by their Nurturers.

"I enjoy the Naming," Jonas said.

His mother agreed, smiling. "The year we got Lily, we knew, of course, that we'd receive our female, because we'd made our application and been approved. But I'd been wondering and wondering what her name would be."

"I could have sneaked a look at the list prior to the ceremony," Father confided. "The committee always makes the list in advance, and it's right there in the office at the Nurturing Center."

"As a matter of fact," he went on, "I feel a little guilty about this. But I *did* go in this afternoon and looked to see if this year's Naming list had been made yet. It was right there in the office, and I looked up number Thirty-six—that's the little guy I've been concerned about—because it occurred to me that it might enhance his nurturing if I could call him by a name. Just privately, of course, when no one else is around."

"Did you find it?" Jonas asked. He was fascinated. It didn't seem a terribly important rule, but the fact that his father had broken a rule at all awed him. He glanced at his mother, the one responsible for adherence to the rules, and was relieved that she was smiling.

Name: _____   Date: _____

Reading Comprehension Questions

1. What is the Ceremony of the Ones?

2. What is a Nurturer?

3. How did Jonas's mother know that she was going to be getting a girl at the Ceremony of the Ones?

4. What rule did Jonas's father break? Why?

5. How did they refer to the children before they had names?

6. Why was Jonas worried about his mother's reaction when his father confessed to breaking a rule?

Appendix E:
Materials for Knowledge Building:
Embedded Texts

Example 1: *Stellaluna* by Janell Cannon

All About Bats

Bats are mammals. Mammals are warm-blooded animals that have fur or hair on their bodies, and female mammals feed their babies milk from their bodies. Bats are the only mammals that can fly.

Most bats live in caves and trees. They are nocturnal, which means they sleep during the day and are active at night. Bats sleep hanging upside down.

Bats are helpers. Most bats eat insects, which helps keep the bugs away from farmers' crops. Some bats eat fruit, and they scatter the seeds so that plants can grow in many different places.

1. Underline one fact that connects to something from *Stellaluna*.

2. **Turn and Talk:** Based on what you learned from the article, why might the birds think Stellaluna is unusual?

Example 2: *Where the Mountain Meets the Moon* by Grace Lin

Annotation Task: While we read pp. 1-2, underline details that describe Fruitless Mountain and the village near it.

1. **Turn and Talk:** Share your annotations with a partner. What details about the setting seem most important?

Notes

Rice grows in flooded fields called paddies. This type of farming originated thousands of years ago in southern China and continues today in many parts of the world. Paddy fields take a lot of hard work to create and maintain.

Example 3: *Number the Stars* by Lois Lowry

Mama, Annemarie, Ellen, and Kirsti travel from **Copenhagen** along the coast of Denmark to **Gilleleje**, the place Uncle Henrik and Mama grew up (see map, left)

Klambenborg is a nature preserve known for more than 2,000 deer that roam freely in the park.

Kronborg Castle is a famous castle in Northern Denmark

Annotation Task: As you read, annotate details that help answer the following questions:

- Who does the family encounter on the train?
- What worries Annemarie?

Example 4: *Bud, Not Buddy* by Christopher Paul Curtis

Foster Care during the Great Depression

Foster care refers to a **temporary** living situation for children whose parents are not able to take care of them. Caseworkers are responsible for finding foster placements for children who need care; in a foster placement, a child goes to live with a family who is often paid to take them in temporarily. Children without foster placements may live in orphanages or children's homes. During the Great Depression, there was a **drastic** increase in the number of children in orphanages and foster care because many families could no longer afford to provide for their children.

temporary: not permanent, lasting for a limited period of time
drastic: extreme and sudden

1. **Turn and Talk**: In your own words, explain to your partner what foster care means.

Annotation Task: As we begin the novel, annotate any details about Bud's experiences with foster care.

Example 5: *Wonder* by R. J. Palacio

Annotation Task: As you read, underline changes that occur for a person during their middle school years.

Middle School Changes

During middle school, children's brains change dramatically. Neuroscientist Dr. Jay Gieed explains, "In many ways, it's the most **tumultuous** time of brain development since coming out of the womb." An article from PBS notes:

> Though the brain's physical structures are fully developed by age 6, the connections among them take longer to form. Early adolescence is when much of this wiring takes place. The middle school years are also what scientists call a "sensitive period" for social and emotional learning, when the brain is **primed** to learn from social **cues**.

During early adolescence (typically defined as ages 10-14), young people develop greater empathy, maturity, and awareness of those around them. These are the years when the transition from childhood to adulthood begins. New emotional and social challenges arise, and middle school students may feel powerful pressure to **conform** to the values and beliefs of others. According to the Association for Middle Level Education, "Many adolescents experience heightened levels of **self-consciousness**, particularly about their physical appearance and the ways they differ from peers."

In fact, the transition from elementary school to middle school can be one of the most stressful events in a young person's life. Bullying often hits a peak in middle school. Amy Bellmore, a researcher on peer relationships, explains, "Early adolescence [...] is the point at which children [...] value being popular, which means being well-known, well-liked, or both." As young people try to figure out who they are and how they fit in, they may be more influenced by their peers and more afraid of standing out or being different.

tumultuous: full of change, disruption, or uncertainty
primed: prepared; made ready
cues: signals or signs
conform: to be like or agree with
self-consciousness: feelings of nervousness or embarrassment caused by heightened awareness of oneself

2. August starts school in fifth grade. At Beecher Prep, this is the first year of middle school. According to the article, why might this be an especially difficult time to start school?

_____

_____

_____

_____

_____

Challenge: To what extent do you agree with the claims in this article? Does it align with your experience? What else would you want researchers to understand about early adolescence?

Example 6: *The Giver* by Lois Lowry

Annotation Task: While we read, underline details that explain the purpose of rituals.

Ritual

A ritual is an activity or ceremony that is performed the same way every time. Rituals are part of every society and might be as elaborate as a graduation ceremony or as simple as shaking hands to say hello. A ritual can refer to any sequence of activities that carries importance and follows a consistent set of rules.

A citizen performs the ritual of bowing to a king.

Usually, rituals are connected to the traditions of a particular community, especially a religious community. One common type of ritual is a **rite of passage**, which marks a person's transition from one phase of life to another. In Judaism, for example, boys and girls celebrate a *bar* or *bat mitzvah* at 13 years old to signal that they have transitioned from childhood to adulthood. Many religions have specific marriage rituals to mark the shift from singlehood to coupledom. Households can also have their own rituals, such as holiday celebrations or mealtime traditions.

Rituals often depend upon individuals performing specific roles within the ceremony, and these roles can serve to create or reinforce power dynamics within social organizations. By encouraging participants to engage repeatedly in the same ritual, people in power can normalize their authority and define the social order of a community.

---

1. **Turn and Talk:** What is one **ritual** in which you participate?

2. Why might someone in power want people in their community to engage in **rituals**?

_____

_____

_____

_____

Annotation Task: While we read, underline details that help you understand Jonas's family **ritual**.

Example 7: *Bomb* by Steve Sheinkin

Engaging Readers, Part 1

Bomb is a book of narrative nonfiction. Narrative nonfiction is a genre of writing that presents true facts that inform a reader, like a nonfiction text does, but does so in a way that entertains a reader, as a story or narrative would.

Therefore, a narrative nonfiction author has two jobs. First, they do a lot of research, to make sure that they accurately convey what really happened. Then, they link their facts together in a story that excites and engages their readers.

1. **Turn and Talk:** Which would you find more exciting, researching facts or turning facts into a story? Why?

Engaging Readers, Part 2

In an interview with the International Literacy Association, Steve Sheinkin was asked how he brings "life and excitement" to the historical events he writes about. Sheinkin explains:

> Really, history is just stories about people and dramatic events, so there's nothing **inherently** boring about it. The problem is, if all kids know about <u>history comes</u> from textbooks, they think history is boring. <u>So</u> my job is to bust through the resistance by telling exciting and entertaining stories.
>
> I try to take all the sources I find and craft the material into scenes, just like you'd do if you were making a movie. Hopefully, readers will have so much fun reading the book, they'll forget they're supposed to be learning. That's what I'm going for with Bomb.

As Sheinkin reminds us, sometimes excitement comes from what an author writes about: the content of the story. In *Bomb*, for example, Sheinkin shares stories about spies and military missions, which, by their nature, are generally exciting to read about.

But authors can also keep their readers engaged in their stories by using different writing choices: as Sheinkin says, "craft[ing] the material." For example, Sheinkin increases the drama of *Bomb* by emphasizing the feelings and emotions of the historical figures he is writing about, so they come to life for us and seem more like characters in a story or novel. He also adds dialogue, so we feel like we are standing alongside them as they make history. In addition, Sheinkin often builds suspense, that feeling of anticipation as we wonder about what will happen next, by not giving us all the information about a topic. Instead, Sheinkin stops telling one part of his story, like the scientists' discovery of a nuclear chain reaction, and jumps into another part, such as the mission to Vemork. Sheinkin wants to keep readers turning the page to find out what happens next!

inherently: naturally, as part of its make-up

2. **Turn and Talk:** Share your annotations with a partner. What are some ways Sheinkin engages readers? Why does Sheinkin do this?

Example 8: "Justice" by Langston Hughes

> ### Justice Is Blind
>
> **Lady Justice** is the personification of the ideals of justice in legal or judicial systems. Based on the goddess Justitia (Roman) or Themis (Greek), Lady Justice is usually depicted holding a sword, which represents swift and final justice, and scales, which symbolize the idea that evidence should be carefully balanced and weighed.
>
> Lady Justice almost always appears with her eyes blindfolded. The blindfold represents impartiality, the idea that justice should be applied without regard to wealth, power, race, gender, or other status. The phrase "justice is blind" is commonly used to evoke the idea that justice shouldn't "see" things like class, wealth, or social status; it should only consider the truth of a person's actions and character.

1. Based on this article, is Lady Justice's blindness meant to be a positive or negative thing? Explain your thinking.

2. Read this poem on your own, then answer the question that follows.

Justice
by Langston Hughes

That Justice is a blind goddess
Is a thing to which we black are wise:
Her bandage hides two festering[1] sores
That once perhaps were eyes.

[1]**festering:** oozing and producing pus

What are your initial thoughts on Hughes's opinion of justice? Jot some ideas here.

Langston Hughes and "Justice"

Langston Hughes was a writer and poet who was a central figure of the **Harlem Renaissance**, a movement of black literary, intellectual, and artistic work in the United States during the 1920s. His poem "Justice" was originally published in 1932, almost 100 years after Douglass wrote his *Narrative*, in response to the case of the **Scottsboro Boys**, a group of nine black teenagers who were falsely accused and convicted of committing crimes against two white women. The case was controversial at the time and today is considered a stark example of a failure of the American justice system.

3. **Turn and Talk:** In traditional imagery, Lady Justice wears a blindfold to cover her eyes. How does Hughes manipulate this image in his poem? What might he be trying to suggest?

Example 9: *Romeo and Juliet* by William Shakespeare

2. Reread Sampson's line (1.1.12-13):

   A dog of that house shall move me to stand. I will take the wall of any man or maid of Montague's.

a. Who does "that house" refer to? _____

b. Read the line note for "I will take the wall of any man or maid of Montague's" and then paraphrase what Sampson is saying:

   _____

   _____

London Streets

London streets were filthy. In Shakespeare's times, there was no plumbing, so people in homes and shops just dumped anything that they did not want in their homes out into the streets: rotten food, human waste, animal blood from butcher shops. Then, because there were no drains in the streets, that garbage sat there, growing more disgusting day after day.

Note also that the second story was built out over the first story. If someone were to throw garbage out of their window, a person would be protected if they were walking closer to the wall.

Elizabethan style architecture

Example 10: *Of Mice and Men* by John Steinbeck

 Annotation Task: The following article explains two concepts that will help us deepen our analysis of *Of Mice and Men*. As you read, annotate details that help you answer the following questions:

- What does "survival of the fittest" mean?
- What is social Darwinism?

Survival of the Fittest and Social Darwinism

Charles Darwin (1809-1882) was an English biologist and naturalist, most famous for his contributions to evolutionary biology. The term "survival of the fittest" is a biological theory Darwin proposed in his book *Origin of the Species*, published in 1869. In this book, Darwin explained how evolution occurs: he argued that organisms which are best suited to their environment are the ones that survive and reproduce, passing on the physical features that helped them survive to their offspring. In contrast, organisms with traits worse suited to the environment die without reproducing, so those features are eliminated from the population. Because those characteristics are preserved over generations, they ensure continued survival of the species. This process of a species' continued existence became known as survival of the fittest.

Survival of the Fittest

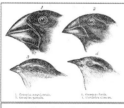

Darwin's finches

For example, Darwin studied finches (a type of bird) living on different islands. Although all the finches were similar, they were not identical. On one island, the finches had narrow, skinny beaks that helped them eat insects. On the other island, the finches had bigger, stronger beaks to help them eat seeds. Darwin suspected that on each island, over many generations, the finches adapted traits (in this case, beak size) and passed the traits on to future generations to better help them survive the conditions found on their particular island (one with more seeds available, one with more insects available).

Social Darwinism

Survival of the fittest explains how biological diversity in a species evolves over time; Darwin never intended that his argument would apply to humans. Other people, though, soon began to **appropriate** Darwin's ideas and to apply them to people, justifying certain economic, political, or social views. Applying survival of the fittest to situations outside biological evolution became known as "Social Darwinism."

Example 11: *Animal Farm* by George Orwell

Fables

A **fable** is a story told through nonhuman (frequently animal) characters that provides a moral lesson at the end. Fables appear frequently in children's literature, but a number of novels and poems intended for older readers also use this form as well.

Consider the following fable.

"The Lion and the Mouse" by Aesop

A Lion lay asleep in the forest, his great head resting on his paws. A timid little Mouse came upon him unexpectedly, and in her fright and haste to get away, ran across the Lion's nose. Roused from his nap, the Lion laid his huge paw angrily on the tiny creature to kill her.

"Spare me!" begged the poor Mouse. "Please let me go and someday I will surely repay you."

The Lion was much amused to think that a Mouse could ever help him. But he was generous and finally let the Mouse go.

Some days later, while stalking his prey in the forest, the Lion was caught in the toils of a hunter's net. Unable to free himself, he filled the forest with his angry roaring. The Mouse knew the voice and quickly found the Lion struggling in the net. Running to one of the great ropes that bound him, she gnawed it until it parted, and soon the Lion was free.

"You laughed when I said I would repay you," said the Mouse. "Now you see that even a Mouse can help a Lion."

Through its animal characters, this famous fable teaches its readers about the importance of acts of kindness as well as the idea that those who are small (and perhaps weak) can be a help to those who are big (and perhaps strong).

Fables rely on **anthropomorphism,** a device where animals or objects are given human traits, ambitions, emotions, and behaviors. This differs from personification. Anthropomorphism literally means "to make or turn human," so the nonhuman characters exhibit a sustained array of human capacities, such as the ability to speak and reason. By contrast, personification is less sustained; it may be as simple as using a human verb or adjective to describe something nonhuman, as in the sentence, "*The flowers danced in the gentle breeze."*

1. **Turn and Talk:** *Animal Farm* can be classified as a **fable**. Name two features you can expect from this text based on its **fable** classification. Underline two examples of **anthropomorphism** you encounter on pages 3–4.

Example 12: *The Curious Incident of the Dog in the Night-Time* by Mark Haddon

The Theory of Mind and the Smarties Test

"Theory of Mind" refers to a person's ability to think about mental states—their own and those of other people—and to realize that other's people's minds are unique and different from their own. In order to interact well with other people, we need to realize that every person has different beliefs, thoughts, and ideas. This helps us form empathy with others—knowing that a friend feels pain or anger or happiness, even if we are not feeling that same pain, anger, or happiness, allows us to react appropriately: to comfort them, or to understand why they are snapping at us, or to share in their laughter. In most children, theory of mind develops around age four, and is crucially important to developing social **cognition**, or the ability to get along with others and to understand their perspectives. Research has shown that a well-developed theory of mind can help children to put themselves in other people's shoes, and therefore communicate better and resolve conflicts more easily.

The Smarties test is an important test for the theory of mind. In the Smarties test, a tester presents a child with a box of Smarties and asks what is inside. The child typically responds "Smarties." But the tester has replaced the Smarties with something different—buttons or a pencil—and shows the child what is actually inside. The tester then says, "What if we show your mom (or your brother, or your friend—any person who is not present) this box of Smarties. What will she say is inside?" The obvious response remains "Smarties." Since Mom is not here, she, too, will assume a box of Smarties holds Smarties, not buttons or pencils. However, if the child believes that Mom will say "buttons" or "a pencil," then the child does not have a developed theory of mind—the child does not recognize that other people's minds are separate from their own.

1. What is theory of mind? Why is it important?

_____

_____

_____

_____

2. On p. 116, Christopher describes his experience with the Smarties test.

a. After testing Christopher, what does Julie tell Mother and Father?

_____

_____

b. What is Christopher's response?

_____

_____

_____

c. What evidence do we have that Christopher is wrong, and Julie is right? How does this response give us insight into Christopher's character?

_____

_____

_____

d. Why might Haddon have included a reference to Christopher's experience with the Smarties test at this point in the novel?

_____

_____

_____

Additional Insights:

_____

_____

Index

Nation, Kate, 19

National Assessment of Educational Progress
(NAEP), xxi, 8, 9

National Cancer Institute, 100

National Center for Education Statistics, 9

National Council of Teachers of English, 24,
53, 251, 283

"The Necklace" (Maupassant), 244

Network effects, 279–280, 295

Networks, of connected knowledge, 138–140

Neuman, Sarah, 155

Neuroplasticity, 5–6, 55

Night (Wiesel), 120–121, 173

1984 (Orwell), 279–280, 295, 297

Nintendo effect, 38

Nondirective annotation, 73

Nonfiction texts. *See also* Embedded Nonfiction
expressive reading of, 103
skills- vs. knowledge-based approach to
reading, 145–146

Nonlinear texts, 323–324

North Star Academy, 259

North Star Vailsburg Middle School, 177

Norton, Mary, 271–272

Notes:
in attentional privileged
environments, 336–337
before discussions, 225, 228
on discussions, 265, 266
handwritten, 72, 75
journals of, 75
on screens, 71–72, 75

Number the Stars (Lowry):
annotation during Teacher Read
Aloud, 107–108
Embellishments for, 167–168
Explicit Vocabulary Instruction for,
194–198
FASE Reading of, 69, 112–113
and other books on World War II, 297
practicing challenging words for AIR with, 128
sample Embedded Nonfiction, 405
social reading on, 59

student enjoyment of lesson, 39–41
timely Embedded Nonfiction for, 157–158

Nuthall, Graham, 175

O

Oatley, Keith, 287, 288

Objectives:
book-driven, 76–79
skills-driven, 76–77, 79

Observations:
of Accountable Independent Reading, 130–133
of partner reading, 118

"An Occurrence at Owl Creek Bridge"
(Bierce), 152–153

O'Dell, Scott, 64–65, 210

Of Mice and Men (Steinbeck), 240, 413

Open-ended learning, xxxivn.9

O'Reilly, T., 8

Origin of Species (Darwin), 323

Orthographic mapping, xxxivn.16, 92–95, 196

Orwell, George, 146, 151, 160–162, 278–280,
295, 297, 301, 414–415

Oulette, Gene, 20

Our Lady Queen of Angels, 232

The Outsiders (Hinton), 31, 107, 170–172

Overlapping Questions, 160, 162, 163,
167–168

Oversimplification, in definitions, 200

Overt retrieval, 176–178

P

Packets, student, *see* Student-facing handouts
and packets

Paige, David, 8–10, 42n.21, 131

Palacio, R.J., 103, 158–160, 176, 203, 204,
233–234, 281, 407

Parish, Juliane, 121–122

Partner reading (paired reading), 89, 118

Part of speech, vocabulary word's, 195, 200, 203

Passage-based reading instruction, 26, 145,
283, 284, 321

Past, books for connection to, 281–282

Pastore, Patrick, 94, 152–155